THE GREEN BOOK

New Directions for Liberals in Government

THE GREEN BOOK
New Directions for Liberals in Government

Edited by

DUNCAN BRACK

PAUL BURALL

NEIL STOCKLEY

MIKE TUFFREY

Biteback Publishing

First published in Great Britain in 2013 by
Biteback Publishing Ltd
Westminster Tower
3 Albert Embankment
London SE1 7SP

ISBN 978-1-84954-409-2

10 9 8 7 6 5 4 3 2 1

A CIP catalogue record for this book is available from the British
Library.

Designed and typeset in Minion by Duncan Brack.
Printed and bound in Great Britain by
CPI Group (UK) Ltd, Croydon CR0 4YY.

Contents

Foreword

Nick Clegg MP

As a philosophy, liberalism needs constantly to re-examine itself: its assumptions, its values and their application in changing circumstances. This is even more true today, given that we are implementing many of our policies in government. This process of intellectual debate and renewal is one of the most important characteristics of the Liberal Democrats, and one which I am determined to encourage.

It therefore gives me great pleasure to contribute this Foreword to *The Green Book*. This publication follows *The Orange Book* of 2004 and *Reinventing the State* of 2007 in mapping out a vision of what liberalism means in practice and what path the Liberal Democrats should follow.

The Green Book concentrates on environmental policy – rightly, given its ever more crucial importance to economic recovery and prosperity and to our citizens' well-being and quality of life in both the short and the long term. It is a central component of the stronger economy and the fairer society that Liberal Democrats are striving to build.

I am proud to be the leader of a party which has championed the green cause for decades, and continues to do so in government. *The Green Book* is a welcome and provocative challenge to our thinking, and a valuable source of ideas for the future. I hope liberals everywhere will read *The Green Book* and respond to its arguments.

Rt Hon Nick Clegg MP, Leader of the Liberal Democrats and
Deputy Prime Minister
February 2013

Acknowledgements

This book has been in gestation for quite some time, and we acknowledge those who helped in planning in the early stages, including Joel Kenrick and Lisa Poole.

The Joseph Rowntree Reform Trust Ltd made the publication of the book possible, through a generous grant to cover publication costs. Our thanks also go to all those involved in the production of the book, including Lewis Carpenter and Iain Dale at Biteback Publishing, who have been more than patient with challenging deadlines. Jane Vaus, Steve Malone and Ben Wood provided invaluable assistance with promotion.

Most of all, though, our sincere thanks go to all the chapter authors, without whom the book would not have been possible. It should be noted that while most are Liberal Democrat party members, some are not; several provide advice also to members of other parties. All contributors have written independently, and do not necessarily endorse every proposal contained in the book.

We hope that what they have written will inspire a wide-ranging debate, both inside and outside the Liberal Democrats.

Duncan Brack, Paul Burall, Neil Stockley and Mike Tuffrey
February 2013

Contributors

Louise Bloom is Cabinet Member for Environment and Sustainability at Eastleigh Borough Council in Hampshire – which, under her leadership, won Beacon Council status in 2008–09 for tackling climate change. She was a Greater London Assembly Member, 2000–02, and worked on the first London-wide waste strategy. Louise has been an environmental campaigner since the early 1980s, long before it became popular or fashionable (she says)!

David Boyle is a former Liberal Democrat parliamentary candidate, and was a member of the party's Federal Policy Committee 1998 to 2012. He is a fellow of the New Economics Foundation and the author of *The Human Element: Ten new rules to kickstart our failing organisations* (Earthscan, 2011).

Duncan Brack is an independent policy analyst and adviser, and an Associate of Chatham House and Green Alliance. From 2010 to 2012 he was a special adviser to the Secretary of State for Energy and Climate Change, Chris Huhne. He is also Vice Chair of the Liberal Democrats' Federal Policy Committee and its manifesto writing group. In 2007, with Richard Grayson and David Howarth, he edited *Reinventing the State: Social Liberalism for the 21st Century.*

Steve Bradley is Chair of the Green Liberal Democrats and a councillor in the London Borough of Lambeth. He is involved with a variety of environmental organisations, including the Transition Towns movement, and is a passionate advocate of the concept of community ownership. Steve has a Masters Degree in Urban Regeneration, with a particular focus upon sustainable communities, and he also writes on sport, politics, history and the environment for a variety of publications.

Paul Burall is a freelance writer specialising in environmental issues. A former County and District Councillor, Paul has served as Vice Chair and a

Policy Council member of the Town and Country Planning Association and a Board member of the East of England Development Agency.

Tom Burke is the Founding Director of E3G and Environmental Policy Adviser to Rio Tinto. He is a former Director of Friends of the Earth and the Green Alliance and was a special adviser to three Secretaries of State for the Environment. He is also a Visiting Professor at both Imperial and University Colleges, London.

Ben Earl worked on Liberal Democrat environmental policy in Parliament, and is now part of the CSR team at B&Q plc; working with staff, suppliers and government, he is helping to bring about a step-change in influencing consumers on green issues. He is a board member of Future Solent, promoting a low-carbon economy and sits on the CCG of South East Water, overseeing the new price review process. He writes here in a personal capacity.

Dr Robert Falkner is a Reader in International Relations at the London School of Economics and Political Science. He is an associate of the Grantham Research Institute on Climate Change and the Environment at LSE and of the Energy, Environment and Development Programme at Chatham House. He has published widely on global environmental politics, including *Business Power and Conflict in International Environmental Politics* (2008) and *Handbook of Global Climate and Environment Policy* (2013).

Fiona Hall has been the Liberal Democrat MEP for the North East of England since 2004 and is the leader of the Liberal Democrats in the European Parliament. As a member of the Industry, Research and Energy Committee, she has been the lead negotiator for the Alliance of Liberals and Democrats for Europe (ALDE) on legislation concerning renewable energy and energy efficiency.

Dr Mark Hinnells has worked in energy policy since 1992, as an academic at the University of Oxford Environmental Change Institute, policy adviser to Defra and as project manager at the Energy Saving Trust. He is now Solutions Director of Susenco (the sustainable energy company). Over most of his career he has been closely involved with the development of Liberal Democrat thinking, and has serving on a range of policy working groups, as chair of the Green Liberal Democrats and on the party's Federal Policy Committee.

David Howarth is Director of the M.Phil. in Public Policy and Reader in Law at the University of Cambridge, where he is also a Fellow of Clare College. He was previously MP for Cambridge, during which time he served as the Liberal Democrats' Shadow Energy Minister and Shadow Justice Secretary.

Chris Huhne was MP for Eastleigh from 2005 to 2013 and was Secretary of State for Energy and Climate Change from 2010 to 2012.

Julian Huppert is the Member of Parliament for Cambridge. Before being elected to Parliament in 2010, Julian was a research scientist and a Cambridgeshire County Councillor. He had also set up a small biotech company, which won a DTI SMART award. Since entering Parliament, he has focused on science policy, green growth, transport, civil liberties and home affairs.

Dr Susan Juned is a director of Greenwatt Technology (www.greenwatt.co.uk). In 2010 she was named a West Midlands Green Leader by Sustainability West Midlands. Her recent work has included dissemination advice for university research groups, resource management studies and low-carbon / renewable energy consultancy. She is Chair of Directors of the energy efficiency advice charity, Act on Energy, and helped to found the former BREW Centre for Local Authorities while working for NISP as their liaison officer.

Tim Leunig is an international-prize-winning academic economist who has advised the UK government and OECD on transport issues. He is currently on leave from the LSE to work for the Department for Education. This chapter was written when he was chief economist at CentreForum think tank and should not be seen as reflecting government policy.

Kate Parminter is the Defra spokesperson for the Liberal Democrats in the House of Lords, a trustee of IPPR, and a former Chief Executive of CPRE.

Stephen Potter is Professor of Transport Strategy in the Design Group at the Open University. His research includes work on the diffusion of cleaner vehicle technologies, low-carbon transport systems and more sustainable travel behaviour. He has also worked on research on factors influencing the adoption and use of domestic low-carbon products and systems and on the LCNF *Project Falcon*, exploring how to achieve effective user engagement in

Smart Grid design and development. He has previously been a member of the Liberal Democrat Working Group on Transport Policy.

Dr Patrick Sheehan is a founding partner of Environmental Technologies Fund. He has worked in venture capital since 1985, was instrumental in founding 3i's venture capital practice and was founding MD of its Silicon Valley business. Patrick has been Chair of the European Venture Capital Association's Venture Capital Committee, and served on its Board and Executive Committee. He currently chairs its Environmental Task Force.

Shas Sheehan was the Liberal Democrat Parliamentary Candidate for Wimbledon in the 2010 general election, and a GLA candidate in 2012. She is a former councillor and Assistant Cabinet Member for Energy and Climate Change for the London Borough of Richmond-upon-Thames.

Neil Stockley is a director of a communications consultancy and a former Policy Director for the Liberal Democrats. He has been involved for some years in developing energy and climate change policy for the party and chaired the working group that produced *Zero-Carbon Britain* (2007). He also writes a blog about political narratives.

Mike Tuffrey has combined his public service career with working in business to help large companies adopt strategies for sustainable growth. After qualifying as a chartered accountant with KPMG, he was director of a national charity before founding Corporate Citizenship, a management consultancy on responsible and sustainable business. In public life, he served as an inner city councillor and leader for twelve years, before spending the last decade elected to the London Assembly, where he was a member of the London Sustainable Development Commission.

Christian Vassie is editor of the Green Liberal Democrats' *Challenge* magazine. He produces environmental films on the energy transition in cities across Europe for Energy Cities and the Covenant of Mayors. For eight years he was a city councillor in York, including two years on the ruling executive and seven years as the city's Energy Champion. As well as directing films, Christian is a film and television composer, author, and designer, and has run his own production company for twenty-five years.

Myles Wickstead CBE is Visiting Professor of International Relations at the Open University and a special adviser to the House of Commons International Development Select Committee. He has a long history in international development and diplomacy, and represented the UK on the Board of the World Bank 1997–2000; was British Ambassador to Ethiopia, 2000–04; and Head of Secretariat to the Commission for Africa 2004–05.

Christopher J. Wigley has been a fixed income portfolio manager for more than twenty-five years, most recently at Epworth Investment Management. He is also a specialist in Sustainable Investment. In 2005, Chris stood as the Liberal Democrat Parliamentary Candidate for Wealden.

Stephen Williams was elected as Member of Parliament for Bristol West in 2005. He was appointed the chairman of the Liberal Democrat backbench committee for Treasury matters in 2010. He qualified as a Chartered Tax Adviser and, before becoming an MP, he worked for several large firms, including PricewaterhouseCoopers and Grant Thornton.

Simon Wright was elected as the Member of Parliament for Norwich South in 2010. Soon after the election, he was appointed as the Liberal Democrat member of the House of Commons Environmental Audit Committee. A former teacher, Simon is currently the Parliamentary Private Secretary (PPS) to the Minister of State for Schools, David Laws.

Dimitri Zenghelis is a Senior Visiting Fellow at the Grantham Research Institute at the LSE and an Associate Fellow at Chatham House. He was recently Senior Economic Adviser to Cisco's long-term innovation group. Previously, he headed the Stern Review Team at the Office of Climate Change, London, and was one of the authors of the Stern Review on the Economics of Climate Change, commissioned by the then Chancellor Gordon Brown. Before working on climate change, Dimitri was Head of Economic Forecasting at HM Treasury.

Chapter 1

New Directions:
Introduction to *The Green Book*

Duncan Brack, Paul Burall, Neil Stockley and Mike Tuffrey

This book presents the case for the Liberal Democrats to adopt a fundamentally different approach to economic and social policy – now, in government, for the coming general election, and beyond. We believe that the party must put centre stage the need to preserve the natural world on which our society and economy depends for its health, well-being and prosperity. We argue this for three reasons.

First, because low-carbon and environmental investment offers the UK a chance to create new jobs and prosperity – a route out of recession and towards a modern and competitive economy. Green technology, infrastructure and services companies now account for almost 10 per cent of UK GDP and employ almost a million people. Even throughout the depths of the recession, they have grown between 4 and 5 per cent every year. Britain's real strengths in technologies such as offshore wind and marine renewables, and in green finance, mean that the country is well placed to compete in new international markets; these sectors are expanding much faster than the sluggish global average. No other sectors are as well placed to give the economy the boost it needs in the short term and the competitive strength it needs in the long term.

Second, because environmental challenges, particularly those of climate change and finite limits on natural resources, are more serious and more urgent than most people think. There is no real chance that the world's nations will succeed in limiting temperature rise above pre-industrial levels to the 2°C that scientists say marks the boundary between dangerous and very dangerous climate change. Britain's economy and society will have to adapt, in quite radical ways; if we start now the process will be more gradual, less costly and less disruptive. To believe that the transition to a low-carbon, resource-efficient economy can be put off until the country's economic performance is stronger is not just short-sighted, it is counterproductive: all this does is store up more costs for the future and delay the recovery by ignoring a powerful instrument for economic revival.

Third, because green policies are a recognised strength of the party and, especially after a period in coalition, offer a clear distinguishing issue between Liberal Democrats and Conservatives. At the next election the party will face the challenge of showing what difference it has made to government – never an easy task, as junior coalition partners elsewhere have found. But high-profile disagreements between Liberal Democrat and Conservative ministers over a wide range of environmental issues leave little doubt about the coalition partners' differences.

Liberal Democrats need a more radical approach to environmental policy, one that maintains our political strength as the greenest of the three main parties and provides us with distinctive policies and messages for building long-term economic prosperity. We need to stop treating 'the environment' as a separate issue and to stop focusing our green thinking only on energy or conservation policies, vital as they are. We need to consider economic, environmental and social policies as an integrated whole.

Our alternative vision: Green Liberalism

Most people realise that the last Labour government made serious mistakes in managing the economy; they want to support a party that spells out what it will take to get the economy on the right track in a way that is fair to all.

We believe that short-term fixes, such as blanket deregulation or ever more austerity, fail to face the reality of a global economy that has turned decisively to Britain's disadvantage. Rising energy costs, increased raw material prices, growing competition, even fears over food security, all point to a more serious economic challenge than has yet been recognised.

We believe that there is an alternative, based on Green Liberalism. The policy ideas set out by the contributors to *The Green Book* aim to foster private investment in low-carbon infrastructure, use regulation and taxation to empower businesses, consumers and communities to behave sustainably, value natural resources, recognise that pollution damages human health, promote new business models which minimise energy and resource use, are open and constructive to international alliances, especially through the EU, and adapt to the reality of climate change while continuing to mitigate its worst effects. In short, they present an agenda for a government that puts the long-term interests of citizens at its heart.

Aren't the Liberal Democrats green enough already?

As Chapter 5 shows, the Liberal Democrats have a good record on the environmental agenda, in the party's policy stance from the 1970s and in its performance running local councils and participating in coalition governments in Scotland, Wales and the UK.

As successive NGO assessments have shown, the party's election manifestos have done a better job than those of their Conservative and Labour opponents in including environmental policies and in starting to integrate them across all policy areas. However, environmental aims have not really been built into core economic policy commitments aimed at sustainable growth; nor has the party recognised the extent to which environmental factors contribute to social inequality. At election times, green policies have not been promoted strongly nor the links explained adequately. Liberal Democrats have sometimes been complacent about the radicalism of their environmental stance and their image as the greenest of the three main parties.

More importantly, the party has suffered from problems of association, through the coalition, with an increasingly anti-green Conservative Party. The last two-and-a-half years has demonstrated just how shallow is the Tories' belief in their own environmental policy stance. If the Prime Minister believed his own commitment to lead 'the greenest government ever', he would have reined in the ever more shrill assaults his Chancellor has mounted on environmental regulation in general and on renewable energy in particular; he would not have appointed as Secretary of State for Environment, Food and Rural Affairs a known climate-sceptic, or as Energy Minister a known opponent of onshore wind farms. Those few Conservatives who do actually believe their pre-election 'vote blue, go green' mantra are increasingly the prisoner of their party's anti-wind power, anti-renewables, anti-green right-wing majority.

Against this background, the achievements of Liberal Democrat ministers in coalition have been impressive. The Green Investment Bank has been established, levels of support for renewable energy have been maintained (and in some cases increased), the railways have seen greater levels of investment than at any time since the Victorian era, future finance for renewables (to accompany electricity market reform) has been agreed, and highly ambitious climate targets for the mid-2020s have been set through the fourth carbon budget – mostly in the teeth of mounting Conservative opposition. Liberal Democrat ministers have worked through the EU and the UN to argue the case for global action on climate change and to level the playing field for Britain's new green industries.

Having said that, the party's record has in some cases been disappointing. The Department for Business, Innovation and Skills, for example, has not always championed the growing low-carbon and environmental industries, for instance arguing against the initial proposal for the fourth carbon budget and failing to implement the coalition commitment to 'green' the Export Credits Guarantee Department. Nevertheless, despite the inevitable compromises of coalition, we have no doubt that, without Liberal Democrat influence, a Conservative administration would have been far less green than the coalition government is proving to be.

Facing the challenges

We do not underestimate the task facing the Liberal Democrats – and liberals in other parties – in pursuing the ambitious agenda the contributors to *The Green Book* set out. The scale of the challenge is both serious and urgent.

The centre of gravity in the world economy is moving decisively to the fast-growing and populous emerging economies such as Brazil, India and China. Their demand for energy and raw materials is rising sharply, putting upward pressure on prices despite the recession affecting the older industrialised world. Analysis by McKinsey shows that commodity prices have increased by 147 per cent in real terms over the past ten years.[1] The UK has already felt the effects in terms of higher energy costs and increased food prices, reducing its citizens' standard of living and its businesses' ability to compete in world markets. Severe weather incidents are interrupting the now very extended supply chains that the UK economy depends on; global warming will only exacerbate the risks and vulnerabilities. Talk of a 'lost decade' for the UK economy, induced by the financial crash and subsequent fiscal austerity, ignores the fundamental reality that trends in the global economy are moving decisively away from Britain. We must make our own futures; no one owes us a living.

At home, the urgent need for major new investment in energy infrastructure, to replace ageing power stations and to 'keep the lights on', offers a great opportunity. New generation capacity must be low-carbon and renewable if we are to guarantee energy security and independence and to meet emissions targets. At the same time, public finance is constrained, and the way in which current support for renewables and energy efficiency is raised – mainly through levies on electricity bills, a legacy of the last Labour government – means that it is easy for the right-wing press and Conservatives to equate going green with high energy costs.

Although, as Chapter 12 shows, there is currently a surplus of private-sector savings, investment in new resource-efficient technologies is often perceived to be high risk, and private investors tend to be cautious. In the Green Investment Bank the government has created the perfect opportunity to de-risk leading-edge investments and unlock billions of pounds of private capital, but risks failing to realise the benefits through its excessively cautious approach to investment and a refusal, imposed by a rigidly orthodox and intellectually bankrupt Treasury, to signal when the Bank will be given borrowing powers – as one observer put it, 'a bit like driving with the handbrake on'.

As several chapters in this book demonstrate, the potential to increase energy efficiency standards provides an enormous untapped opportunity. Demand-side management measures are essential, yet the current Energy Bill looks like falling short of what is needed. The Green Deal is a good start but its take-up seems likely to be slow. The notoriously poor state of British housing constrains the use of taxation to encourage reductions in energy use, as those in fuel poverty are in no position to respond to energy price signals; what they need is not the fuel subsidies demanded by some but help with upgrading the energy performance of their homes to reduce their need for energy.

Indeed, as the environmental challenge grows, it is those on low incomes and vulnerable citizens such as children and senior citizens who will be most affected. Air pollution, for example, disproportionately damages the health of those living in inner urban areas or next to main roads, where housing tends to be cheaper. Conversely, access to open space in cities increases health and well-being. The incidence of death during heat waves rises among older people.

Contributing to all these challenges is a central government structure that is not well suited to delivering the necessary policies – even where the political will exists at the centre. No administration has yet succeeded in mainstreaming sustainable development – or even just 'environmental' – objectives across government, and in this respect the coalition is faring no better than its predecessors.

The Liberal Democrat opportunity

These are daunting challenges; but we believe that the Liberal Democrats are uniquely placed to meet them. As Chapter 6 shows, liberalism is an intrinsically green political philosophy; the green approach comes more naturally to us than it does to either the Conservatives or Labour. Free from vested interests, we have been more open to new thinking and more prone to think for the long term. With a philosophy based on liberty, rather than the defence of sectoral interests, we are pragmatic about using government intervention – regulation, taxation or behavioural 'nudges' – in whatever combination works best to deliver these objectives. By putting individual consumers and citizens at the heart of Green Liberalism, we believe that rules, incentives and the simple power of good-neighbour community instincts can achieve remarkable changes in behaviour – as, for example, the dramatic reduction in smoking has shown. Instinctively internationalist, we have been enthusiastic about pursuing European and global solutions to international environmental problems. Traditionally decentralist, we understand the value, and the necessity, of community and local authority action.

And there are many reasons to be optimistic about the future. As we argued at the beginning of this chapter, the green economy is expanding across the globe; in 2010, for the first time, worldwide investment in renewable energy exceeded that in fossil fuels. Britain is well placed to compete in these new and expanding markets. We lead the world in installed offshore wind power, for example, and have a strong scientific and industrial research base in wave and tidal power and carbon capture and storage. CBI data shows that the UK's share of the £3.3-trillion global green market grew by 2.3 per cent in real terms in 2010–11, reaching £122 billion. Green businesses accounted for over a third of all UK growth in 2011–12.[2]

As several chapters in this book demonstrate, energy efficiency offers huge untapped potential: if we realised the opportunities available, business and household energy bills would fall, the need for new power stations would diminish, and emissions targets would be easier to meet – and all more cost-effectively than through any other low-carbon strategy. Digital technology and creative innovation in business can significantly reduce energy and natural resource consumption – and help consumers lower their own carbon footprints.

We understand the value of regulation and taxation in creating new markets. To choose one example, the controls imposed under the 1987 Montreal Protocol on ozone-depleting substances unleashed a wave of industrial innovation, as businesses raced to compete in the new markets for alternative substances and technologies, allowing the Protocol to achieve total phase-out of chlorofluorocarbons faster and cheaper than anyone had initially anticipated. The same is happening again in, for example, solar power, where PV panel prices fell by 58 per cent between 2008 and 2011, with further reductions predicted.[3]

Industries and companies everywhere are realising that rising natural resource prices need not simply be absorbed. The enormously wasteful nature of the twentieth-century industrial model, which grew on the back of cheap energy and raw materials, means there are almost limitless opportunities to cut costs by cutting waste, by operating more efficiently, and by adopting new business models. Ultimately this should lead to a circular-economy or closed-loop model which eliminates waste through superior design of products and systems, avoids toxic chemicals and uses renewable resources: 'cradle to cradle' rather than 'cradle to grave'. One report in 2012 estimated the potential savings to manufacturing industry across the EU of US$520 billion–630 billion per year, equal to 19–23 per cent of current total input costs.[4]

The UK is well placed to lead the international race to develop the new technologies needed. Our higher education and research sectors remain among the best in the world and, despite the depletion of our manufacturing industry, we still have world-leading firms in engineering, software, aerospace, automotive, electronics, food and drink and pharmaceutical industries. New industries are growing rapidly, in low-carbon energy, industrial biotechnology, nanotechnology, digital technology and advanced materials such as composites. With support from government, a stable regulatory environment and a strong home market, these industries could help rebalance the economy away from over-reliance on financial services and so sustain high-value-adding jobs when the UK's competitive advantage is being lost to emerging economies. This approach is more likely to underpin market confidence in the country's ability to support the national debt – and to create taxable growth to reduce the deficit – than to rely simply on promises of yet further austerity.

Britain's poor standard of housing and our failure to invest in renewing our urban areas – especially our great cities, where higher productivity, creativity and human interaction all enhance the potential for sustainable living – is both a major challenge and an opportunity. The Green Deal can open up the home insulation market, creating tens of thousands of new jobs spread round the country and stimulating innovation in technologies such as solid wall insulation, opening up further new jobs and export possibilities. Similarly investment in energy-efficient, lower-pollution transport – from long-distance rail to electric-vehicle infrastructure – can provide durable jobs, improved human health and an overall better quality of life.

This is the prize on offer.

New directions

The separate chapters in this book each make the case for change; they put forward proposals for the new directions that Liberal Democrats should promote in government and argue for at the next election. Chapter 3 provides a summary; here we draw together the arguments they build up collectively, in five main areas.

Modernising the economy and building long-term resilience

To secure Britain's future prosperity, we need a more robust economic model, less exposed to volatile and increasingly expensive imported raw materials and energy; a modern 'circular economy' based on zero waste and closed-loop production processes; and businesses that embrace the spur to innovation that government regulation and standard-setting can bring.

A modernised economy will play to the country's remaining industrial strengths, with investment to support the low-carbon and environmental goods and services sectors. Government should not be afraid to 'pick winners' – as canny investors have always done – and focus its support on those with the greatest potential for long-term return, such as offshore wind, with 'clean-tech' innovation leading export-focused growth. It should use a reformed Green Investment Bank, with the power to borrow, to unlock private investment and support venture capital; green bonds and green ISAs can provide additional funds. Through public procurement policy, it should use its considerable buying power in the market to boost green technologies and products.

The result will be a more resilient and innovative economy, capable of sustaining the living standards we rightly aspire to, in a world where others can also enjoy a fair share of the planet's finite resources.

Rebuilding infrastructure and regenerating communities

Unlike Norway and the Gulf states, which have used their natural resources to build up sovereign wealth funds and invest in their national infrastructure, British governments have neglected long-term investment, and funded current consumption out of borrowing. Liberal Democrats must win the argument for a new approach to economic prosperity, recognising that a warming planet threatens the economy and the country's productive capacity. The place to start is a dramatic improvement in energy efficiency and a renewal of energy infrastructure based on renewables, carbon capture and storage for gas and a significant increase in decentralised and community-based generation and new electricity interconnections with our European neighbours, including a North Sea grid.

Rebuilding infrastructure for sustainable living also includes a new commitment to land-use planning, so that our built environment shifts to the same low-energy, zero-waste, closed-loop approach as the wider economy. Far from causing a 'nimby' reaction, new developments that enhance quality of life can be encouraged through land value taxation, which captures windfall increases in land values for the benefit of the community. In moving to a zero-waste approach, an effective ban on landfill will spur new recovery and energy businesses, with the Green Investment Bank mitigating some of the private sector risk.

More powers for local government are essential, with new duties for councils to promote health and well-being and develop their local economies sustainably. Since economic development is best supported at regional level, local enterprise partnerships must grow into a more strategic role without recreating the wasteful bureaucracy of the worst of the old regional development agencies. 'Total place budgeting' should be used to ensure that public money from procurement contracts and welfare transfers stays in the locality. Central and local government should agree measures of success based on new sustainability indicators, with a requirement to report regularly and engage with citizens locally.

Putting citizens and consumers at the heart of Green Liberalism

Protecting the natural environment and building a resilient economy and a fairer society will not happen unless individuals as citizens, consumers and voters are enabled to commit to changes in their own lifestyles.

The Green Book's contributors propose many different ways in which to empower consumers. Many focus on demand reduction in energy and resource consumption. An improved Green Deal can reduce energy bills and combat fuel poverty. Digital interventions, such as smart meters and ultimately a smart grid, can also play a role; indeed, the potential for information technology, digital and web media to open up access to information, empower individuals and inspire them to change remains largely untapped.

Product and service labelling with embedded carbon and full lifetime use costs can help inform consumers; steadily increasing product standards, for example for energy efficiency, can improve performance and spur innovation. A levy on advertising (similar to the existing 0.1 per cent ASA financing mechanism) can create a fund that will harness the creative power of the media to encourage sustainable living.

Explaining environmental damage in terms of its impacts on human health can help unlock engagement, with the costs of environmental protection seen in terms of ill-health prevention. A strong signal of the change in direction should be provided by the government giving the same weight to the new well-being indicators as it currently does to GDP.

Combating market failure and taxing pollution

Liberals recognise the creative power of the market economy in deploying resources efficiently in response to price signals. But markets are not good at factoring in costs to public welfare, such as the consequences of damaging the natural environment. So Green Liberals reject the false choice between free markets and regulation. The contributors to this book argue that a sustainable market economy requires government intervention through setting standards, and providing fiscal signals to promote behaviour that protects the environment as well as extending producer liability.

This includes a new approach to regulation, sweeping away anti-green rules that damage the economy (a 'green tape challenge') while progressively tightening product and service energy efficiency standards, with an independent scrutiny agency charged with achieving sustainability outcomes, based on the Dutch model. It also includes extending the 'polluter pays' principle to establish legal liability for long-term health damage caused by products in their manufacture, use and end-of-life treatment, learning lessons from America.

On taxation, contributors argue for a gradual move to selective carbon taxes, with protection, for example for the fuel-poor or rural drivers, as a step towards a more realistic valuation of energy and natural resources. Green tax instruments can cut harmful emissions from cars, with road user pricing and a radical change to vehicle excise duty, and encourage maximum fuel efficiency from buses, trains and aeroplanes. Revenue raised from taxing pollution and wasteful activities can be used to reduce personal taxation and fund equitable outcomes, such as subsidies for insulation for fuel-poor households, helping to sustain public support.

Reforming national government and making the best use of international alliances

No government has successfully integrated environmental objectives across the Whitehall machine and overcome short-term siloed decision-making. *The Green Book*'s contributors argue that Green Liberalism requires four changes to the way in which Britain is governed.

First is the creation of a single government department to champion sustainable development. As well as providing coherent leadership, a large new department will help counterbalance the overweening influence of the Treasury.

The second change is to integrate likely long-term environmental costs into all major government decisions, including assessments of the impacts on health and social care costs, with scrutiny of decision-making inside and outside government.

The third change is a fundamental rebalancing of power and responsibility to local, regional and devolved government.

The final element is a positive and engaged approach to international relations, especially with Britain's European partners. Green Liberalism recognises the integrated nature of the global economy and the fact that environmental damage from pollution and greenhouse gas emissions is no respecter of national boundaries. More, not less, international cooperation is essential.

About this book

The Green Book does not pretend to cover every area of policy important to a new approach of Green Liberalism. Our focus primarily on the green economy, policies for reducing carbon emissions, local and community solutions and international politics reflect both topical priorities in public debate and the interests and enthusiasms of individual authors.

Our purpose is to stimulate debate, to demonstrate the compelling case for Green Liberalism and to persuade the party to take these issues more seriously. Whether or not you are a Liberal Democrat, we hope you will join the discussion by commenting on our website (**www.green-book.org.uk**), by participating in events we organise and by blogging, tweeting and retweeting your own and others' ideas. We hope to use the website to develop ideas for other areas of policy and to develop priorities for the party's election manifestos.

Given the scale of challenges facing our country and our planet, it would be easy to be pessimistic. But we remain optimists, inspired by the passion and commitment of colleagues in and around the party to build a prosperous, just and sustainable future for all. Please join the debate.

Notes

1   McKinsey & Co, *The Resource Revolution* (2011).
2   Confederation of British Industry, *The Colour of Growth: Maximising the Potential of Green Business* (2012).
3   Bloomberg New Energy Finance Solar Value Chain Index (17 June 2011).
4   Ellen MacArthur Foundation, *Towards the Circular Economy: Economic and Business Rationale for an Accelerated Transition* (January 2012).

Chapter 2

Green Story Time for the Liberal Democrats

Neil Stockley

Environmental policy has long been a key priority for the Liberal Democrats. Since 1992, every Liberal Democrat general election manifesto has featured prominent green themes. The party has made ground-breaking commitments, including tougher national targets for reducing pollution, a shift in taxation from income and employment to pollution and resource use, and setting Britain on a path to be 'zero carbon' by 2050. However, these policies have not persuaded large numbers of voters to support the party. Nor have they played a significant role in its electoral successes. Indeed, green policies have barely featured in its campaign strategies and messages at all.

There is no evidence to suggest that the party's environmental commitments, either individually or in total, have pushed voters away. In public opinion polls, green issues are the only policy area on which the party's rating as the best of the three main parties has consistently been in double figures since the mid-1990s; in fact the Liberal Democrats have often been rated as the leading party on the environment or climate change.[1] Some long-standing Liberal Democrat environmental policies enjoy overwhelming public support. In October 2012, a YouGov survey commissioned by *The Sunday Times* showed that 72 per cent of the public think the UK should be looking to use more solar power, while 55 per cent think it should be trying to use more wind power. In contrast, just 17 per cent of people want to see more coal or gas-fired power plants.

Even so, one of the positive attributes of the party's brand has not yielded the Liberal Democrats any obvious electoral benefits. This is no longer simply a question of a political asset not delivering its full electoral potential. Since entering government in 2010, Liberal Democrats have been forced onto the defensive over, for example, the extent to which climate change policies are responsible for rises in consumer energy bills and the construction of more onshore and offshore wind farms. The party needs to gain public support for its environmental commitments in different, more challenging circumstances, co-governing in the age of austerity. The political challenges are sure to become more pressing. As Chapter 3 shows, the environmental crisis is deepening and the news about the magnitude and impacts of climate changes becomes grimmer every year. The complex challenges will surely require more robust and ambitious policy responses, for which the party, and any government it may become part of in future, will need a clear electoral mandate.

The main reason the Liberal Democrats' green themes have not translated into votes is straightforward enough: the environment has not historically been a priority for most voters, including those in the party's target constituencies.[2] Even so, the party could gain more public support for its environmental policies by addressing a long-term fundamental weakness in its approach to communications and marketing. In successive policy papers, speeches and election manifestos, the Liberal Democrats have provided a substantial amount of analysis to support their environmental and climate change policies. However, as in most areas, they have not accompanied the analysis with a compelling narrative that makes their environmental policies more relevant and attractive to voters.

What is a political narrative?

First and foremost, a political narrative is a *story,* with a setting, characters (usually a hero and a villain) and, crucially, some kind of unanticipated event.[3] Drew Westen, Professor of Psychology at Emory University and author of *The Political Brain*, stresses that the story 'should be coherent, requiring few leaps of inference or imagination to make its plot line move forward or the intentions of the central actors clear'.[4]

The screenwriter Robert McKee emphasises the need for the events in the story to portray a drama, or conflict, in which a protagonist is faced with a problem, obstacle or antagonist that he or she must overcome. 'As a storyteller, you want to position the problems in the foreground and then show how you've overcome them. When you tell the story of your struggles against real antagonists, your audience sees you as an exciting, dynamic person.'[5] Not every story needs a challenge or quest, but some sort of solution or transformation, effected by identifiable, authentic characters is especially relevant to politics.

A narrative should provide listeners with an easily comprehended account of the past and enable them to make sense of the present. But it can also enable large groups of people to project in their own minds a vision of the future, by showing them how it could look and feel. In his seminal book,

Leading Minds, Howard Gardner studies several successful leaders in history from a range of fields. He concludes:

> A leader must have a central story or message. The story is more likely to be effective in a large and heterogeneous group if it can speak directly to the untutored mind – the mind that develops naturally in the early lives of children without the need for formal tutelage. Stories ought to address the sense of individual and group identity, the 'we' and the 'they' thought that sense may actually be expanded or restricted by the story. They should not only provide background, but should help group members to frame future options.[6]

Both Westen and Gardner are clear that a compelling political story must be moving and emotionally evocative. In politics, the emotions used will usually be hope, fear and the offer of a sense of reassurance; a successful 'policy' or 'vision' story will usually explain in human, personal terms how peoples' lives will be improved. This will almost always involve, but not be limited to, a strong appeal to listeners' desire for financial security and their longer-term personal aspirations.

Westen argues that narratives need central elements that are easily visualised or pictured to maximise their memorability and emotional impact.[7] For his part, Gardner stresses the need for narratives to invoke existing values, symbols and archetypes:

> Leaders benefit from the ability to build on stories that are already known – for example, those drawn from religion or history or those that have already been circulated within an institution – and to synthesise them in new ways, as Martin Luther King Jr was able to do.[8]

The narrative concept should not be a difficult one. As Westen reminds us:

> The stories our leaders tell us matter, probably almost as much as the stories our parents tell us as children, because they orient us to what is, what could be, and what should be; to the world views they hold and to the values they hold sacred. Our brains evolved to 'expect' stories with a particular structure, with protagonists and villains, a hill to be climbed or a battle to be fought. Our species existed for more than 100,000 years before the earliest signs of literacy, and another 5,000 years would pass before the majority of humans would know how to read and write.

> Stories were the primary way our ancestors transmitted knowledge and values. Today we seek movies, novels and 'news stories' that put the events of the day in a form that our brains evolved to find compelling and memorable. Children crave bedtime stories; the holy books of the three great monotheistic religions are written in parables; and as research in cognitive science has shown, lawyers whose closing arguments tell a story win jury trials against their legal adversaries who just lay out 'the facts of the case'.[9]

One of the most successful storytellers in recent British political history was Margaret Thatcher. She persuaded her electorate to accept a major programme of economic and social change. She provided the public with an accessible account of the country's economic decline after World War II, by arguing that it was due to declining respect for institutions and traditional values, runaway state expenditure and out-of-control trade unions. In promising to make Britain great again, Thatcher offered her compatriots a sense of hope. By exhorting the British people to be proud of their country, its achievements and potential, she appealed to their deepest held values. Her promises to make sure that individual effort, thrift and success were rewarded both framed her vision in terms of established values and, with the British Gas and British Telecom privatisations and council house sales, explained the financial benefits that people would gain.

Thatcher was very clear that the British people had enemies abroad: the Soviet Union (at least until Gorbachev came along), the Argentinian generals who invaded the Falkland Islands and, as her premiership progressed, the bureaucrats, socialists and integrationists supposedly rampant in the European Community. There were enemies at home too: the trade union leaders who had brought the country to its knees in the 1970s, the Tory 'wets', Arthur Scargill and the miners. In promising to reverse the decline and confront the various villains, she created a sense of conflict, of drama, becoming the hero of the story.

A comparable Liberal Democrat narrative, let alone one that deals with environmental issues, is much harder to identify. At times, in this area as much as any other, the party has sometimes come close to offering what Westen scathingly refers to as a 'rational-utility laundry list'.[10] We need, then, to consider what a compelling Liberal Democrat narrative on the environment might look like.

Green growth and the green economy

Too often, debates about narratives and other political marketing concepts get bogged down in questions of ideological definition ('what is modern liberal democracy?') or attempts to describe quickly overarching policy themes and frameworks ('constitutional reform'). The latter are not, in themselves, political narratives but when based on sound analysis they can provide crucial elements of the story – for instance, the basis of the account or explanation, or the vision that drives the party's (that is, the hero's) intentions and actions.

One of the Liberal Democrats' guiding principles is environmental sustainability – defined in the 1987 Brundtland Report as 'development that meets the needs of the present without compromising the ability of future generations to meet their own needs'. There is little argument, however, that paying costs and acknowledging limits cannot be the basis for a political message when the vast majority of voters desire greater economic growth and the material security and job opportunities that it yields. The 'politics of gain' must be more attractive than the 'politics of pain'.

In the mid 2000s, the Liberal Democrats identified climate change as one of their top policy priorities, and focused their efforts in environmental policy-making and communications accordingly. Efforts to frame policies and issues in terms of the deleterious impacts of climate change open up some vexing questions. The British public has accepted for some years that climate change is happening, that it is a result of human actions, and that more effective action is needed to counter it. Studies of public opinion consistently show that only a small minority outright reject the notion of human-made climate change.

But climate change is not a top concern for most people,[11] and there is no public consensus as to what the country should do about it, particularly when it comes to strategic policy measures.[12] There is some evidence that 'horror stories' about the disasters that could result from a changing climate (which, it must be said, Liberal Democrats have generally avoided telling in recent years) may overwhelm many people and cause them to disengage from the issue.[13]

The global financial crisis and world recession that began in 2007–08 has had a profound impact on public debate about the environment and climate change, shifting attention to more immediate concerns, like jobs, living standards and incomes. In January 2007, Ipsos MORI found that 19 per cent of voters saw the environment as a priority issue facing Britain. By the end of 2008, just 6 per cent held the same view, a figure that had declined to just 4 per cent by spring 2012. By contrast, the proportion seeing the economy as a priority issue went from 14 per cent in January 2007 to 66 per cent at the end of 2008 and remains, by some way, the public's top priority.[14]

It is against the backdrop of the global economic downturn that the case for 'green growth' has come to prominence in public debate.[15] This is discussed extensively elsewhere in this book; a convenient short description is provided by the OECD, which says that green growth is 'about fostering economic growth and development, while ensuring that natural assets continue to provide the resources and environmental services on which our well-being relies'.[16] Michael Jacobs is clear that green growth is 'a level of environmental protection which is not being met by current or "business as usual" patterns of growth. It is this in turn which gives the concept its political traction.'[17] Its sister concept, the 'green economy', is defined by UNEP as one that 'results in improved human well-being and social equity, while significantly reducing environmental risks and ecological scarcities'.[18] Both green growth and the green economy embrace the principle of growth being compatible with environmental protection.[19]

This fits well with Liberal Democrat thinking, aiming at both environmental sustainability and enhanced economic prosperity – the creation of wealth and a better standard of living. Green growth not only insists that the two are perfectly compatible but assumes that protecting the environment can be a positive driving force of higher economic output and rising living standards.

With robust policy frameworks, the twin concepts of green growth and the green economy marry sound policy with good politics. In the UK, green sectors have outperformed the wider economy since the economic downturn began and now account for almost a million jobs. The British share of the global low-carbon environmental goods and services market was estimated to be more than £122 billion in 2010–11 – the sixth largest in the world, and growing at around five per cent a year, generating a trade surplus of £5 billion. The UK is the largest single market for offshore wind in the world, and currently leads the world in marine energy devices and installation development, leaving it well placed to compete in an expanding global market.

Green growth and the green economy also enable Liberal Democrats to reframe their environmental policy agenda around the drive for resource efficiency, which will enable businesses to be less reliant on imported supplies of energy, less exposed to volatile prices and political risks; in other words, to give the UK greater energy security and a more resilient economy. They offer an opportunity to shift the political discourse about the environment and climate change away from the negative frames of burden-sharing, melting ice caps and endangered species and on to propositions that are more attractive and relevant to voters, such as job growth and how to build a more modern and dynamic economy. These are voters' main concerns, and the very areas where the Liberal Democrats have long struggled for clear definition, supported by a strong narrative.

The public may well be receptive to such a story. In November 2012, a YouGov survey found that 54 per cent of the public agreed 'we can save the planet and the economy both at the same time by investing in green technologies'. And, as Jacobs has argued, the huge expansion over the last two decades of environmental industry sectors means that there are now many influential businesses with a direct commercial interest in strengthening environmental policy. With a strong basis in mainstream economic thinking, the concepts of green growth and the green economy could provide the basis for a broad and powerful political coalition in support of the party's environmental commitments.[20]

Liberal Democrats and green growth

It is hardly surprising, then, that Liberal Democrats have started to use both 'green growth' and the 'green economy' as communications themes. But the party has advocated in succession two different versions of green growth. The 2010 election manifesto promised a 'green stimulus plan', comprising £3.1 billion of public spending that, the party promised, would 'create 100,000 jobs and be a first step towards our target for a zero-carbon Britain by 2050'.

Since they joined the coalition government with the Conservatives, the Liberal Democrats have pursued a green growth strategy based on correcting market and policy failures preventing natural resources being used efficiently and pollution made more expensive. This switch, from 'green Keynesianism' to a focus on addressing market failures, is very much in line with similar strategies that other developed economies are pursuing.[21] The main tools are the policies being pursued at the Department of Energy and Climate Change under Chris Huhne and Ed Davey, aimed at meeting the UK's legally binding targets to reduce greenhouse gas emissions. Vince Cable's Department for Business, Innovation and Skills has also played an important part.

Key policies include the Green Deal, which aims to overcome barriers to improving the energy efficiency of the UK's building stock, most notably the expense to households and businesses; electricity market reforms, intended to give energy companies stronger incentives to invest in low-carbon generation capacity and improved energy efficiency on the part of consumers; the Green Investment Bank, established to mobilise finance at scale from institutional investors, whose attitude to risk discourages them from investing in low-carbon infrastructure; measures to foster low-carbon innovation, which the market is sometimes slow to pursue; support and incentives for renewable electricity and heat technologies; and the development of an external carbon price across different sources of emissions, using market-based instruments.

Liberal Democrats have started to frame their green growth (and climate change mitigation) policies as ways to deliver new jobs, expand economic opportunities for UK plc, enhance energy independence, create greater economic security and price stability, and lower greenhouse gas emissions. Ed Davey has, for example, described the electricity market reforms as an essential element of 'the green growth opportunity' and claimed that they will 'support our economic recovery, resulting in thousands of new jobs in every nation and region of the UK' and 'enable us to keep the lights on and to keep bills affordable for consumers while leading to a significant decarbonisation of the power sector in order to meet our climate targets'.[22] Nick Clegg has delivered very similar messages.[23]

Towards a new economic and environmental narrative

We can see, then, the first steps towards a 'green growth' narrative, with a discussion of the benefits and how Liberal Democrat policies will bring them about. But the story should be deepened and used more widely. The hero is clearly the party itself – or, more likely, Nick Clegg and Ed Davey. The unanticipated event (for most) is the world economic downturn, and the problem or challenge is the continuous shocks that worsen the economic and environmental crisis. They should be framed in terms of the damage or harm they are doing, or will do, every day, to identifiable people, communities and businesses.

The stories around individual policies should be as simple and straightforward as possible, relying less on process and more on outcomes, particularly the creation of new jobs. In this respect, the Green Deal and the Green Investment Bank (once it has full borrowing powers) are easier to explain than electricity market reform.

The quest for a green economy can be based on existing stories and archetypes. Margaret Thatcher, like Winston Churchill before her, appealed to the British people's sense of themselves as a strong island nation, taking on external adversaries. Liberal Democrats can tell a similar story (without the military angle), by showing how 'going green' can make Britain more competitive, a winner in the global economic race, at the forefront of the global green economic revolution.

Another less familiar but still powerful archetype, used most effectively by Churchill during World War II, is of the strong community, united in a common purpose. Business must be a key protagonist in the green economy, developing new, efficient products, processes and services, building new opportunities in export markets and creating new jobs. The mantra 'we're all in this together' has lost its sheen, but 'we can all win' may yet prove to be an attractive proposition.

But it is consumers who must be at the heart of the green economy narrative, both as economic actors, creating the demand for new innovations and approaches, and as voters. Rising energy bills will be addressed by Ed Davey's tariff reforms and measures to increase retail market competition. His moves to promote collective purchasing of energy will also become a key part of the story as will, in the future, the decentralisation of electricity generation.

Consumers will have new opportunities to control their energy consumption, with the roll-out of smart meters. We should develop new policies, including improving product standards, to promote the take-up of smart appliances and technologies, as they become more cost-competitive. The Green Deal will enable people to insulate their homes at no upfront cost; in the second half of this decade, programmes could also be introduced to improve the energy efficiency of dwellings on a street-by-street or neighbourhood basis.

Consumers need more powerful incentives to use energy efficiently. The use of more transparent tariffs are an obvious start, but Liberal Democrats' medium-term objective should be the creation of a new market for energy savings, in which new and existing companies compete with each other to enable domestic, residential and industrial consumers to conserve electricity and reduce their power bills.

So, where's the drama; who are the antagonists? Like all major programmes of change, the move to a green economy will have its critics and opponents, usually the representatives of old, vested interests. Parts of the right-wing media are already running a counter-story, that the government's energy and climate change (that is, green growth) strategies will force up consumer power bills. And another familiar set of antagonists is also apparent: the 'brown wing' of the Conservative Party, represented most obviously by the Chancellor, George Osborne, who has framed environmental regulation and policies to promote renewable energy as an economic cost and championed a significant role for unabated gas in the UK's future energy mix, regardless of the implications for legally binding targets to reduce greenhouse gas emissions.

Osborne and his colleagues have a narrative of their own: just as policies to promote renewable energy impose high costs on consumers and businesses, so gas prices will fall, and the UK economy and consumers would benefit from lower energy bills.

Liberal Democrats will have to confront these claims head on. The Committee on Climate Change has estimated that with current policies, average dual-fuel bills will increase in real terms by £40 from 2011 to 2015, and will be around £100 higher in 2020, due to support for investment in low-carbon generation technologies, including the costs of the required investments in the electricity grid; the £100 figure in 2020 comprises £75 of direct support and £25 of support via increases in the carbon price. Achieving a largely decarbonised power sector by 2030 will require further increases in the average annual bill of around £25 per household through the 2020s, with probable reductions thereafter.[24]

The pro-consumer policies described above, such as the Green Deal and changes in energy companies' tariffs, will help to address the counter-stories. So will explaining the uncertainties and exposing the trade-offs involved in keeping the lights on and meeting the UK's statutory target to cut emissions by 80 per cent by 2050. The Department of Energy and Climate Change's modelling shows that a balanced electricity generation mix in 2050, with 33 GW of nuclear, 45 GW of renewables and 29 GW of fossil fuels with carbon capture and storage is marginally cheaper than 'doing nothing'. Moreover, the costs of renewable energy are being driven down.

These arguments are appeals to reason, but the public will finally be won over by which vision – which story – of the future they find more attractive and plausible. Liberal Democrats can ask whether people want a future in which the UK is more reliant on imported supplies of gas, the price of which is uncertain and volatile, and which the International Energy Agency foresees rising to 2030, as demand pressures outweigh supplies – or one in which the UK has a diverse range of secure energy supplies? A future in which we allow green investment to go to countries like China, Korea or Germany, with Britain left behind, in the economic slow lane – or one in which we are big winners from the global market for environmental goods and services, already worth around £3 trillion and growing to more than £4 trillion by 2015? One in which we isolate ourselves from the EU, one of the world's strongest economic blocs – or one in which we use the institutions at our disposal and take the lead in arguing for a greener world economy?

The Liberal Democrat narrative should have a moral dimension too. While economic considerations, both for the country and individuals, can make the green growth story especially powerful, there is considerable evidence that most people adhere to a range of values, including pro-environmental and altruistic beliefs and behaviours. For some, such internal standards are stronger than material values; the environmental narrative should speak to those too.[25] Drew Westen is clear that 'a clear moral' is one defining feature of a compelling political story.[26] The Liberal Democrats' story can be about doing the right thing by other people, looking after our environmental infrastructure, or saving the planet for future generations to enjoy. Another important moral dimension is about ensuring that people on low incomes, suffering from fuel poverty, are better off.

Similarly, the party's narrative cannot be based solely on 'economic' benefits or financial gains to consumers from one policy or set of policies. The green growth strategy is tied closely to the UK's efforts to reduce greenhouse gas emissions, and will entail a whole sequence of policy initiatives aimed at delivering major change in energy and transport systems, across the domestic, commercial, industrial and public sectors and requiring major changes in business, personal and consumer behaviour. The available scientific evidence suggests that the changes needed will become more substantial and demanding. Any environmental narrative will need to enable the public to link the programmes and initiatives together as part of a bigger, longer-term story. Over time, this will surely require new efforts to engage the public on the issue of climate change and its impacts.

Conclusion

Environment policy is one of the positive attributes of the Liberal Democrats' brand, and a cause dear to many members' hearts, but it has not yielded the party any obvious electoral benefits. This needs to be addressed if the party is to make the best of one of its major political assets, and win public support for measures that it is taking forward in government now, or that it may have the opportunity to implement in future.

Green policies are not a priority for most voters who, now more than ever, are much more concerned with the economy and jobs. Liberal Democrats can make their environmental commitments more relevant to voters, and find new definition in the economic debate, by developing a new narrative – a political story – based on green growth and the green economy. The policies that the party is pursuing in government (particularly at DECC) leave it well positioned to further develop such a narrative. But it will need to deploy all the elements of a compelling narrative and keep the benefits to consumers at the heart of the story. Given that the policies are rooted in measures to mitigate climate change, the green growth narrative is vulnerable to counter-stories based on the costs to consumers. These claims can be countered, but the green growth narrative will need to have a moral dimension and to engage with the difficult issues around climate change.

If it is to ultimately prevail, however, the Liberal Democrats' new narrative must give people an easily visualised picture of what the 'new' (not necessarily 'green') economy will look like, showing what kinds of new opportunities there will be to work and to prosper, how businesses will be healthier, how consumers will be better off financially and gain more power in the market place and above all, how peoples' lives will be better.

Notes

1   See Ipsos MORI, 'Best party on key issues: environment' at http://www. ipsos-mori.com/researchpublications/researcharchive/; and Populus Limited, conference poll, September 2006, September 2007, September 2008, September 2009, at populus.co.uk/Poll.

2   http://www.ipsos-mori.com/researchspecialisms/socialresearch/specareas/politics/trends.aspx

3   See Drew Westen, *The Political Brain: The Role of Emotion in Deciding the Fate of the Nation* (Public Affairs, 2007), pp. 146–51.

4   Westen, *The Political Brain*, p. 147.

5   Bronwyn Fryer, "Storytelling that Moves People: A Conversation with Storytelling Coach Robert McKee", *Harvard Business Review* (June 2003), p. 7.

6   Howard Gardner, *Leading Minds: An Anatomy of Leadership* (Harper Collins, 1997), p. 290.

7   Westen *The Political Brain*, p. 147.

8   Gardner, *Leading Minds*, p. 291.

9   Drew Westen, 'What Happened to Obama?' *New York Times*, 7 August 2011.

10 Westen, *The Political Brain*, p. 149.

11 See A. Spence et al., *Public Perceptions of Climate Change and Energy Futures in Britain: Summary Findings of a Survey Conducted in January–March 2010* (Cardiff School of Psychology, 2010); W. Poortinga et al., 'Uncertain climate: an investigation into public scepticism about anthropogenic climate change', *Global Environmental Change: Human and Policy Dimensions* (2011); and Lorraine Whitmarsh, 'Scepticism and uncertainty about climate change: dimensions, determinants and change over time', *Global Environmental Change: Human and Policy Dimensions* (2011).

12 Matthew Lockwood and Andrew Pendleton, *Engagement and Political Space for Policies on Climate Change* (IPPR, 2008).

13 See M. Feinberg and R. Willer, 'Apocalypse soon? Dire messages reduce belief in global warming by contradicting just-world beliefs', *Psychological Science* (January 2011).

14 See http://www.ipsos-mori.com/researchspecialisms/socialresearch/specareas/
    politics/trends.aspx

15 Michael Jacobs, *Green Growth: Economic Theory and Political Discourse*
    (Grantham Research Institute on Climate Change and the Environment, October
    2012) provides an invaluable survey of the issues and arguments.

16 OECD, *Towards Green Growth* (2011), p. 18.

17 Jacobs, *Green Growth*, p. 5.

18 UNEP, *Towards a Green Economy: Pathways to Sustainable Development and
    Poverty Eradication* (2011), p. 16.

19 Jacobs, *Green Growth*, p. 5.

20 Ibid., p. 18.

21 Ibid., pp. 12–13.

22 Rt Hon Ed Davey MP, Speech at Liberal Democrat conference, 23 September 2012.

23 Rt Hon Nick Clegg MP, Speech on Green Growth, 11 April 2012.

24 Committee on Climate Change, *Energy prices and bills – impact of meeting carbon
    budgets* (2012).

25 Adam Corner, a research associate at Cardiff University, has written extensively
    on this. See www.guardian.co.uk/profile/adam-corner and www.talkingclimate.
    org

26 Westen, *The Political Brain*, p. 147.

Chapter 3

Policy Proposals: Chapter Summaries

The authors of Chapters 7–31 put forward a series of specific policy proposals for government and for the Liberal Democrats. These are summarised here.

Ch 7: Setting Standards: Environmental Regulation as if Human Health Mattered (Mike Tuffrey)

Too often regulation is seen as a burden but – done right – it can be a spur to innovation and enterprise, creating a level playing field where companies and individuals invest for long-term prosperity without being undercut by competitors and freeloaders. The evidence is now clear that more regulation is needed to prevent growing environmental damage.

This chapter draws from experience of successful regulation to show how intervention can be done well. It proposes a new approach based on setting the required standards, with more flexibility about the means of achieving them and with independent scrutiny and citizen involvement. A 'bonfire of regulations' that hinder environmental action is also called for.

Liberals in government will need to be more interventionist than their forebears, using regulations and pricing mechanisms to account for the cost to future generations of environmental damage. And if environmental damage is more clearly understood in terms of its impact on human health, voters will embrace measures to protect the environment and enhance the quality of life today. They will reward a party that seeks to do the right thing for the future – economically realistic, socially fair and environmentally prudent.

Ch 8: Green Taxes (Stephen Williams MP)

Carbon emissions can be cut through educating businesses and consumers about the environmental impact of their actions. This chapter proposes achieving this by introducing a carbon tax and road user pricing –

- A transparent and consistent tax on carbon emissions would price in the environmental impact of individuals and businesses' actions and simplify the current plethora of charges on electricity prices.
- The tax would be levied at the point of combustion, in the case of electricity generation and large industrial users; and the point of processing

and distribution, in the case of natural gas and other products which are consumed directly by individuals and businesses.
- The government would use the revenue from the tax to target support at the poorest households to cushion them from the effects of higher energy prices resulting from the tax.
- Road user pricing should replace road fuel duty and vehicle excise duty, with some of the revenue used to reduce the impact on rural drivers.

This is a Liberal approach to environmental taxation, giving individuals and others the freedom and information to change their own behaviour.

Ch 9: Can Behaviour Change Make a Difference? (Paul Burall)
- Behavioural change campaigns work best when linked to key moments in people's lives.
- Campaigns must be geared to the specific audience.
- Incentives must be consistent and maintained over the long term; those comprising a variety of methods are more successful.
- Technology will only deliver its full benefits if people find it easy to use; a standard for user-friendliness and better user information is needed.
- Local authorities should make recycling regimes consistent.
- A small levy on advertising to fund sustainability messages.
- Pronouncements by politicians and government officials are not generally trusted; people respond better to peer pressure.
- Government should give the same prominence to the well-being index as to the quarterly GDP figures.

Ch 10: Embedding Sustainability in Government (Simon Wright MP)
The coalition government has not yet succeeded in embedding sustainable development objectives across government. A combination of five key elements is needed:
- An agreed set of objectives across government: some have been articulated in key documents such as the Carbon Plan, but an overall strategy for sustainable development is overdue.
- One or more departments giving a strong policy lead: a new, larger and high-status department with the Deputy Prime Minister as Secretary of State, together with a sustainable development Cabinet Committee.
- An internal institutional set-up to monitor all departments' adherence to agreed policies, and question any department's decisions which impact negatively on agreed policies and objectives: a new Panel for Sustainability across government.

- An external scrutiny body: the Environmental Audit Committee and National Audit Office working together.
- Strong, consistent and obvious support from the Prime Minister and/or other senior government figures – largely lacking in the coalition government, apart from the Deputy Prime Minister.

Government can also lead by example by greening its own operations and procurement policies – both areas in which the coalition has a better record.

Ch 11: Green Growth (Chris Huhne)

The idea that growing and greening our economy are at odds is a classic false choice. In reality, as we invest to decarbonise our economy, we also grow it. Green investments – whether in resource efficiency or substitution for polluting processes – create jobs, raise incomes, and prop up demand. They produce green growth. In the future it won't just be that we *can* have green growth; it will probably be that we can *only* have green growth.

The main reason behind this is that resource costs are rising rapidly, even in a period of global recession; energy, transport and materials costs are all up. The failure to green our economy, to cut fossil-fuel dependency and buffer the impact of price shocks, has become painfully clear: we are paying in lost jobs, lost income, and lost growth.

A greener economy would enjoy lower resource costs and higher resilience to shocks. It is how we raise standards of living without creating systemic risk, and how we tease out growth in an age of scarcity. The new markets in fuel-efficiency, renewable energy and resource-productivity are what will increase business margins, boost sales, and create jobs. Many of the key policy instruments have largely been laid out: the Climate Change Act, vehicle emissions standards, subsidies for electric vehicles, the Green Deal, electricity market reform. But the government is sending out mixed messages, which is undermining investor confidence. Ministers need to show a united front.

Ch 12: Driving Growth through Green Innovation (Dimitri Zenghelis)

Market opportunities are opening up in fast-growing green sectors, but a lack of investor confidence has meant that desired saving has vastly exceeded desired investment, yielding record private financial surpluses and a collapse in long-run risk-free market interest rates. The associated lack of spending has meant that the UK economy has barely grown for half a decade.

Spare resources in the economy as a whole mean that currently, additional investment would not crowd out alternative investment or displace jobs.

Mixed or muddled policy signals always deter investors and raise project costs, but the potential to put off nervous investors is particularly acute in uncertain economic conditions. The flip side is that with so much nervous saving looking for a return, a green policy framework that is credible, long-term and ambitious could galvanise substantial private investment.

There is no shortage of private money, only a shortage of perceived opportunities. By alleviating policy risk, clear and coordinated long-term policy would allow investors to make productive use of record private savings. There is therefore a unique opportunity to capture business's imagination and help restore growth, investment and employment. An ambitious green investment programme would leave a lasting infrastructural legacy and improve the sustainability of public debt. The opportunity should not be missed.

Ch 13: Building a Green Economy in the UK: Supporting Innovation and Jobs (Patrick and Shas Sheehan)

Environmental challenges are beginning to create huge pressure for change, not just in energy generation, but across many industries. These pressures will create a new industrial revolution, which will be enabled by deploying new resource- and energy-efficient technologies (REETs).

Britain is already creating REETs, but far more needs to be done to ensure that the UK emerges as a winner from what is now a global race for new technologies. Government needs to play a far larger role in articulating a long term stable strategy for REET and in incentivising investors to take risk on emerging REETS. In short, the government needs to shape up to address the opportunity REETS present.

Ch 14: Green and Growing – the Importance of Cleantech (Julian Huppert MP)

The trillion-pound high-tech green industry is crucial to economic growth and environmental sustainability. The UK already excels in 'cleantech' but, through proper regulation and new government policies, we have the chance to capitalise on growing markets and become global leaders.

The government needs to provide incentives for research and development, as well as the scaling up of emerging 'cleantech' companies; the chapter outlines a number of ways in which this can be achieved, from business incubators to EU-wide reforms. With these policies in place, researchers and small businesses in Britain will have the opportunity to tackle climate change and create sustainable growth.

Ch 15: Revitalising the Green Investment Bank (Christopher J. Wigley)

The transition to a low-carbon economy in the UK will require hundreds of billions of pounds of investment capital.

The Green Investment Bank has made some positive first steps in this task, but could do more. An agency / asset-backed security model has the potential to raise the necessary finance, and would also help to provide credit to companies, stimulate green growth for the UK and provide more jobs. The public could play a key role in providing funds for the green economy through green ISAs and green bonds.

It would also be worth considering bringing the National Infrastructure Plan under the wing of the Green Investment Bank.

Ch 16: Empowering a Shift to a More Circular Economy (Ben Earl)

The limitations of our current extract–consume–dispose linear economic system are examined in this chapter. How can we massively cut environmental impacts in a finite world, while providing sustainable economic growth to lead us out of recession?

This chapter proposes a shift in system thinking, accepting the notion of the 'circular economy' allowing maximum resource productivity alongside built-in waste reduction, and changing the nature of our relationship with products and services, making more use of product rental and collaborative consumption models. Taxation and regulation should be employed to encourage reuse and minimise waste and resource use. Accelerating the transition will need leadership and communication within the business sector and with consumers.

Ch 17: A World Without Waste – Achieving a More Resource-Efficient Country (Susan Juned)

Demand for resources is increasing globally. We can only achieve a competitive economy that also addresses climate change and lowers environmental impacts by improving the efficiency of resource use, including:

- Developing a national resource management strategy incorporating closed-loop economic models, with the aim of achieving a zero-waste economy.
- Introducing strategic planning to raise the profile of resource management issues and to focus on the skills, investment, data gathering, research and policy development required.
- Setting the goal of reducing household and business residual waste by 50 per cent, and introducing a complete ban of biodegradable waste to landfill.

- Preparing the business sector to address energy efficiency and low-carbon replacements, investing in resource infrastructure and ensuring that energy generation capacity (including renewables) continues to be developed.
- Encouraging local authority partnerships across administrative boundaries to plan for large facilities, attract significant investment in waste infrastructure and support the development of small-scale community-owned and operated facilities.
- Develop further information and research on ways to save, store and recycle water and support an increase in responsible metering to help people and companies measure and manage their water usage.

Ch 18: The Choice – Energy Policy in a Changing Climate (Tom Burke)

The world will be fundamentally transformed, whether climate policy succeeds or fails; the choice is whether events or people drive the change. A hotter world will cost us civil liberties, human rights and the rule of law.

Seven policy imperatives will get us to a low-carbon energy system:

- Recognise the political importance of separating bills from prices. The government can do very little to change global fossil fuel prices, but much to ensure that those global prices do not translate inexorably into rising bills for home-owners and businesses.
- Get serious about energy efficiency – by a long way, the largest, fastest and cheapest source of carbon reductions.
- Halt the Treasury's theft of green taxes for disguised revenue-raising; revenues from the carbon price floor should be recycled directly into financing the low-carbon transition.
- Stimulate much wider participation in community energy projects.
- Stop dithering about renewables: provide a stable energy policy to keep investment flowing.
- Move forward urgently on carbon capture and storage, to enable the use of gas without damaging climate security.
- Work with our partners in the EU to build an integrated electricity grid and gas supply networks to increase energy security and accelerate further the falling costs of renewables.

Ch 19: Only Connect (Fiona Hall MEP)

For too long, energy policy in the UK has been blinkered and inward-looking. Successive governments have failed to assess or exploit the potential for controlling energy demand and have treated UK security of supply as an issue to be solved on national soil by means of an expensive basket of options – despite the development of a European energy market. The UK government should:

- Make energy efficiency and energy demand management its first and top priority, on economic grounds.
- Reassess how much electricity capacity will be needed to 2050, taking account of demand-side savings.
- Abandon the 'basket' approach to energy supply.
- Encourage a favourable investment climate for renewables, acknowledging that this primarily means wind. Electricity market reform must not act as a covert subsidy for nuclear power.
- Support the introduction of EU 2030 targets for renewables and energy efficiency.
- Integrate the UK fully into the European internal energy market by optimising interconnection to other countries.
- Work closely with Norway to exploit the additional balancing capacity of hydropower, including pumped storage.

Ch 20: A Liberal and Democratic Energy Market (Mark Hinnells)

The chapter argues that if climate change targets are to be met, the business landscape in which energy is supplied and used needs to change fundamentally, to become much more liberal and democratic, and with a change in the balance of power from utilities to consumers.

Three major new business models are explored, which government needs to open the market to: embedded generation, energy services, and community financing. Policy implications focus around energy use in buildings, finance, innovation, encompassing both technical and service models, and energy market regulation. A potential outcome could include more than half of households and businesses generating their own renewable electricity or heat within a decade.

Ch 21: A Green Deal for Transport (Stephen Potter)

Transport is an important area that needs to be at the heart of government policy-making. However, policy responses to transport's environmental impacts have tended to be add-ons to fundamentally unsustainable systems rather than attempts to seek a systemic solution.

There are opportunities emerging radically to reduce transport's environmental impacts; the key to transport sustainability may lie in finding alliances with social and economic trends towards the information society, leading to the reinvention of how access is achieved. Transport policy needs to engage with different players; not so much with the civil engineering and automotive industries, but with business development, IT services, marketing and education.

A new business model for sustainable transport needs a new policy model as well. Our institutional, regulatory and assessment structures, built around the existing models of transport provision make it difficult, if not impossible, for new design configurations to emerge.

Ch 22: Reducing Emissions from Transport: The Role of Taxation (Tim Leunig)

This chapter shows how we can use green taxation to cut emissions from cars, buses, trains and planes. Sensible changes can deliver meaningful environmental improvements quickly, and without big costs to consumers. For cars, replacing annual vehicle excise duty for all new cars with an upfront first registration fee equal on average to fifteen times the current vehicle excise duty would create a bigger incentive to buy a greener car – and an incentive for firms to produce greener cars. We should subsidise bus mileage or passenger mileage, not fuel use. Trains should be taxed on fuel, and subsidised in other ways, as appropriate. And taxing planes, not passengers, gives airlines an incentive to use planes efficiently.

Ch 23: Going Green Has To Be Fair (Chris Huhne)

Green efforts that hit poorer families and create real social injustices will not be seen as fair or legitimate, and they will gradually erode the coalition in favour of change. The environmental agenda must complement the social agenda, for example through:

- Taking care to delay excessive reliance on prices or quotas – carbon taxes or carbon budgets – until key differences in energy use due to poorly insulated buildings are evened out.
- Ensuring that green taxes are only introduced with accompanying offsetting tax cuts or other measures.
- Increase the Energy Company Obligation to complement the Green Deal's 'pay as you save' mechanism for low-income households and 'hard-to-treat' homes.
- Boost the Green Deal by making it an opt-out rather than opt-in measure at the point of sale and give the added incentive of lower stamp duty for participants.
- Protect people from side-effects of climate policies, for example with special transport help for the rural poor.

- Reform the Winter Fuel Allowance to focus help on low-income high-fuel-cost households.

Ch 24: Planning for Sustainability and Green Growth (Paul Burall and Kate Parminter)

Planning should be about meeting current needs without compromising the future: ensuring people's quality of life in the long term, securing sustainable economic prosperity, and safeguarding the sustainability of the environment. This chapter argues that government should:

- Review the impact of the National Planning Policy Framework in 2014; introduce a community right of appeal on planning decisions; and commission research to set guidance on using environmental limits as the prime basis for local planning policies.
- Encourage cities and towns to adopt food policies; and give local authorities a positive duty to protect local biodiversity.
- Challenge the near-monopoly of development land in many areas by requiring the registration of all land and options, reserving a fifth of all public residential development land for self-build, and allocating land for self-build in local plans; and use community land auctions to drive down market land prices.
- Use the Green Investment Bank to provide low-cost, long-term loans to boost the sustainability of major housing developments.
- Introduce mandatory financial incentives, paid by the developer, for individuals and communities affected by new wind farms.
- Introduce land value taxation to capture the increase in land values created by development; and equalise VAT on new build, renovations and repairs.

Ch 25: How to Save Our Cities from Economic Collapse (David Boyle)

The rising cost of energy and other resources will force cities to change, and focus attention on local production. This chapter proposes a ten-step programme:

- Plug the leaks that are draining local money away: setting up sustainable businesses and social enterprises to use local resources.
- Encourage local diversity and distinctiveness: places that feel authentic attract money and people.
- Bust local monopolies, such as supermarkets, to let enterprise flourish.
- Provide enterprise coaching, support and advice in every neighbourhood to help create new locally-owned businesses.

- Build an effective new local lending infrastructure: local banks for new sustainable businesses.
- Invest in local energy and local food, two areas where local economies can replace scarce imports.
- Use waste products as raw material for new enterprises.
- Use public sector spending to maximise local money flows: use local procurement to encourage local business, and green business in particular.
- Experiment with new kinds of money to provide credit.
- Experiment with new ways of creating national currency that can provide a stream of quantitative easing, created by the central bank, to provide the capital for new local energy infrastructure.

Ch 26: Power to the People? The Case for Community-Owned Renewable Energy (Steve Bradley)

With the UK approaching a crisis in its ageing electricity infrastructure, how can Liberal Democrats in government ensure that the decisions they take on this issue are not just environmentally sound, but also deliver the fundamental principles and benefits of liberalism for all? This chapter makes the case for:

- The creation of a preferential legal status for community-owned renewable energy infrastructure, to recognise its primary social function.
- Funding and legal support to be made available to kick-start community energy projects with a credible business case.
- An open-ended Feed-in-Tariff to accelerate growth in UK renewables.
- Greater price and service competition to be introduced into the UK's energy market by enabling community micro-generators to sell their power on to their own residents or to new market entrants.
- Government to use its financial, legal and scrutiny levers to encourage local authorities to play a leading role in the creation of district heating infrastructure.

Ch 27: Councils, Cities and Energy Transition (Christian Vassie)

Who should be in control if we are to create a low-carbon future – companies answerable to shareholders and profit, or bodies answerable to the common good? Government must learn from the federal nations of Europe and apply the principles of localism to decentralise the energy economy by giving local authorities responsibility for:

- Understanding and managing their territories' energy supply, energy resources and flows.
- Ending fuel poverty in their territory.

- Creating a territorial bio-waste management plan.
- Integrating future energy prices and the 'polluter pays' principle into their budget calculations and investment and development decisions.
- Developing smarter communication on energy to engage the public.
- Controlling public transport provision.
- Integrating a low-carbon future into urban planning.

Ch 28: Community Policies for a Low-Carbon Future (Louise Bloom)

Tackling climate change and building a low-carbon future can best be achieved at a local rather than a national level, by:

- Community-based locally funded sustainable energy projects.
- Local councils providing leadership, support and funding.
- Sharing best practice and expertise.
- Partnership working across councils, communities and businesses.
- Using the Green Deal to provide investment and create jobs.
- Truly sustainable town planning, taking the long view on how communities best develop.
- Recognising that while national government may need to legislate to achieve a low-carbon future, it is local communities and politicians who are best placed to lead on and implement the policies.

Ch 29: Adapting to Climate Change (Paul Burall)

Planning to adapt to climate change is now critical; the longer we put off the necessary action and investment, the greater the risks to human welfare and the higher the long-term cost to the economy. Action is needed on:

- Food security: improve the efficiency of water use by agriculture; reduce the loss and degradation of soils; maintain global genetic resources and breed new heat and drought-resistant crop varieties; fund research into new methods of food production.
- Built environment: ensure sufficient green space and tree planting in urban areas to counter the heat island effect; review building standards to minimise the need for air conditioning and respond to the increased risk of severe storms and droughts; set targets and policies to improve water efficiency and expand the water storage infrastructure; protect people and infrastructure from the increased risk of flooding, including avoiding development in at-risk areas; ensure that the transport infrastructure is upgraded to cope with higher temperatures and severe storms.
- Biodiversity: make local authorities responsible for developing and implementing natural adaptation plans for species at risk from climate change.

- Research: fund research to enable adaptation measures to be developed where the science is not properly understood.

Ch 30: The Crisis of Environmental Multilateralism: A Liberal Response (Robert Falkner)

Environmental multilateralism is in a state of crisis. Creating new and implementing existing international agreements is proving increasingly difficult, while global warming and biodiversity loss continue unhindered.

Liberals need to renew the case for environmental internationalism. Global leadership needs to be rooted in domestic action, and Britain should continue to be a driving force behind ambitious environmental policy in Europe and internationally.

The processes and institutions of environmental multilateralism need to be reformed. Established UN-based negotiations need to be augmented with new forms of mini-lateral and partial agreements that serve as stepping stones towards broader international solutions. Institutional reform is needed to strengthen existing UN bodies.

A broader range of actors needs to be engaged in global environmental policy. Private initiatives cannot replace multilateral policies but can be encouraged and directed to play an enhanced role where inter-governmental solutions fail.

Ch 31: Green Policies for Global Economic Justice (Myles Wickstead)

Global economic, social and environmental issues cannot continue to be addressed in isolation. The next three years provide an opportunity to bring together growth, equity and sustainability in an integrated way as discussions on the Sustainable Development Goals and a successor to the Millennium Development Goals gather momentum. This chapter identifies a number of areas in which UK leadership could make a significant difference, and concludes that issues of economic development, poverty and social inclusion must be addressed along with those about the survival of the planet if progress is to be achieved.

Chapter 4

The Threats We Face

Paul Burall

When Chancellor of the Exchequer George Osborne told the 2011 Conservative Party conference that 'We're not going to save the planet by putting our country out of business', and announced an attack on measures aimed at protecting the environment, he was merely echoing the views of many right-wing politicians around the world. But he should have looked back at his hero Margaret Thatcher who, as a scientist, recognised the very real threat of climate change, warning in a speech in 1990 that: 'The danger of global warming is as yet unseen, but real enough for us to make changes and sacrifices, so that we do not live at the expense of future generations'.[1]

The effects of global warming are now being seen clearly. There is overwhelming evidence that, unconstrained, humankind's impact on the planet threatens our very future. Without urgent action, we face not just environmental disaster but economic catastrophe.

And it is not just climate change that we need to worry about. We are using resources at an unsustainable rate, creating health risks that threaten our well-being, destroying our ability to produce the food needed to feed the burgeoning global population, and are well on the way to a massive extinction of biodiversity.

Of course, climate change is the threat which receives the most attention, not least because its potential impacts are so extensive and serious. A 2007 study by the Organisation for Economic Co-operation and Development (OECD) found that cities including New York, Tokyo, Amsterdam and Shanghai will be exposed to the risk of severe flooding due to climate change; by 2070 the value of economic assets at risk of loss in those cities could be as much as US$3,000 billion.[2] Many other heavily populated areas of the world will also be at risk from shoreline erosion, coastal flooding and agricultural disruption, leading to widespread socially disruptive migration that might, according to the UN, affect as many as 200 million people, again causing huge economic disruption.

And climate change means just that. The *Climate Change Risk Assessment* (CCRA) published in 2012 by the UK Department for Environment, Food and Rural Affairs (Defra) illustrates some of the consequences for the UK that are almost inevitable even if greenhouse gas emissions are stabilised to constrain the average temperature rise to 2°C from the pre-industrial era.[3] For example, by 2050, the number of days a year when the temperature exceeds 26°C in London will increase from the current 27 to more than 120 and the number of people affected by water deficits will double to almost 60 million. By the end of the century the area of high-quality agricultural land subject to flooding at least once every three years will increase from 30,000 hectares to 130,000 hectares.

Globally, the consequences will be even worse: in 2007, the Intergovernmental Panel on Climate Change (IPCC) concluded that: 'Evidence is growing that climate change already contributes to the global burden of disease and premature deaths'.[4] Particular impacts include:

- *Extreme weather events*: the European heat wave in 2003 led to more than 20,000 excess deaths in two weeks; extensive flooding across the globe has already resulted in increases in the incidence of infectious diseases, respiratory symptoms and mental health problems; and droughts and floods are having a devastating effect on already scarce food supplies.
- *Infectious diseases*: rising temperatures will allow the wider spread of vector-borne diseases, particularly malaria and dengue; the incidence of rodent and water-borne diseases are likely to increase; and the range of animal diseases such as bluetongue will extend.
- *Respiratory disease and immune disorders*: increasing levels of ozone at ground level could lead to a wide range of adverse respiratory conditions; changing levels of allergenic pollen are likely to increase the incidence and intensity of allergic rhinitis.
- *Increasing exposure to UV radiation*: climate change could slow the recovery of the ozone layer and increase exposure to UV radiation, increasing the risks of skin cancer and the incidence of cataracts.

In 2010, the World Health Organisation reported that global warming was already causing 140,000 excess deaths annually.[5] In 2012, the US Natural Resources Defense Council and the US Geological Survey forecast that, if climate change emissions continue to rise unabated, extreme heat events could kill 150,000 Americans by the end of the century.[6]

Rising temperatures may not be the only problem. In 2012, the summer sea ice in the Arctic Ocean shrank to the lowest area ever recorded and is expected to disappear completely within the next thirty years (much earlier than predictions made just a few years ago). Not only will this speed up global warming because sunshine will no longer be reflected back by the white ice but the lack of cold freshwater sinking to the bottom of the ocean to feed the 'Great Ocean Conveyor' may disrupt the Gulf Stream that drives warm water north from the equator. This could see Europe's average temperature dropping by as much as 10°C and a lesser drop in parts of eastern North America, reaching temperatures experienced in the last Ice Age.

Things will get even worse if the IPCC's stated need to avoid catastrophic impacts – to stabilise greenhouse gas levels in the atmosphere at 450 parts per million – is not achieved. This may lead to spiralling global warming, with temperatures rising by 6°C or higher, eventually resulting in the melting of the Greenland and Antarctic ice caps and sea level rise of many metres, inundating huge areas around the world, including London and much of the East of England.

So will climate change be constrained within the IPCC's limits? The outlook is bleak: one study published in advance of the 2012 Doha climate change conference found that sea levels are rising 60 per cent faster than the IPCC forecast.[7] Another 2012 report, this time from the International Energy Agency, concluded that there was no stabilisation of greenhouse gas emissions in sight and that, without action, energy use in 2050 would be twice that of 2009, leading to a long-term temperature rise of 6°C.[8]

Tim Jackson, Professor of Sustainable Development at the University of Surrey, highlights the extent of the challenge, pointing out that the IPCC's target requires annual global CO_2 emissions not to exceed 5 billion tonnes by 2050.[9] Even without any economic growth, that works out at an average carbon footprint of less than 0.6 tonnes per person – lower than in India today, and a fivefold reduction at current levels of global GDP. But add in continuing GDP growth, and emissions for every unit of output will have to fall to one-eleventh of the current level to meet the IPCC's target.

The *PwC Low Carbon Economy Index*, published by Pricewaterhouse–Coopers at the end of 2012, underlines the gloom, pointing out that even doubling our current annual rates of decarbonisation globally every year to 2050 would still lead to 6°C warming, making ambitions to hit the 2° limit appear highly unrealistic.[10] PwC's director of sustainability and climate change, Jonathan Grant, pointed out the economic risks: 'The risk to business is that it faces more unpredictable and extreme weather, and disruptions to market and supply chains ... More radical and disruptive policy reactions in the medium term could lead to high carbon assets being stranded.'

The picture is no better for the future of the planet's resources. Before it was abolished, the Commission on Sustainable Development published a think-piece by David Woodward, a former economic policy adviser in

Whitehall, who wrote: 'The question, therefore, is not whether we will run out of mineral reserves if we do not reduce our consumption, but, rather, when?'.[11] This conclusion was supported by a study by Pavan Sukhdev, Head of Global Markets at Deutsche Bank India, that found that there was not enough metal in the ground to manufacture the laptops, televisions and vehicles needed to meet the expected future demand from the emerging economies in the East.[12]

Some much-vaunted new technologies rely on rare metals; for example, if global car production switched to fuel cells there will be a requirement for around 1,500 tonnes of platinum a year, six times current production and exhausting all supplies within seventy years. Other metals that play a critical role in the world economy and that are forecast to run out within fifty years if current levels of consumption continue include bauxite (from which aluminium is extracted), nickel, tin, tungsten and zinc.

Optimists argue that past experience shows that technological progress and human ingenuity always overcome such problems by finding new resources, increasing the efficiency of use or switching to alternatives. But in a 2011 report the United Nations Environment Programme (UNEP) disagreed, pointing out that: 'Global consumption of natural resources could almost triple to 140 billion tonnes a year by 2050 unless nations take drastic steps … The world cannot sustain the tearaway rate of use of minerals, ores and fossil and plant fuels'.[13] With the world population expected to reach 9.3 billion by 2050 and developing nations becoming more prosperous, the report warned that: 'the prospect of much higher resource consumption levels is far beyond what is likely to be sustainable', and pointed out that the world is already running out of cheap and quality sources of some essential materials such as oil, copper and gold.

Worryingly, such conclusions are nothing new; governments have simply ignored the warnings. As long ago as 1987 the Brundtland Report, *Our Common Future*, alerted the world to the urgency of making progress toward economic development that could be sustained without depleting natural resources or harming the environment.[14] Resource consumption and environmental damage have since accelerated.

And before that, in 1972, there was the seminal *Limits to Growth* report, published by the Club of Rome, that claimed that exponential growth would eventually lead to economic and environmental collapse.[15] Most economists rubbished the book and its recommendations have been ignored by governments. But in 2008 Graham Turner of the Commonwealth Scientific and Industrial Research Organisation in Australia compared the book's predictions with data from the intervening years and found that changes in industrial production, food production and pollution were all in line with those forecast.[16] If correct, the world is on a path leading inexorably to decreasing resource availability and escalating costs of resource extraction that will trigger a slowdown of industry and eventual global economic collapse some time after 2020.

The Dalai Lama may have got it right in 2002 when, in his *Little Book of Inner Peace*, he wrote that there are: 'Almost imperceptible changes – I am thinking of the exhaustion of our natural resources, and especially of soil erosion – and these are perhaps more dangerous [than the nuclear threat] because once we begin to feel their repercussions it will be too late'.

The Dalai Lama was certainly right to highlight soil erosion: a recent UNEP-funded report estimated that around 15 per cent of the Earth's ice-free land surface is afflicted by land degradation, threatening our ability to feed the world's rising population.[17] And according to John Reganold, a soils scientist at Washington State University, a further 1 per cent of the world's soil is lost every year, mostly due to agriculture.[18]

The food challenge was picked up in a major United Nations report early in 2012 that warned that time is running out to ensure there is enough food, water and fuel to meet the needs of the world's rapidly growing population: 'Within the next twenty years the world's population will need 50 per cent more food and vast new reserves of energy and water: failure to secure resources will condemn up to 3 billion people to poverty.'[19] Climate change may improve agricultural productivity in some areas but is likely overall to cause a reduction in output.

In a portent of what may come, drought in the major food-producing areas of the United States and Russia in 2012 led to significant price rises, and the UN Food & Agriculture Organisation (FAO) is forecasting a significant reduction in world grain inventories in 2013, despite a reduction in demand due to higher prices. In the longer term, the FAO warned that the 'slow-onset' impacts of climate change are 'expected to bring deeper changes that challenge the ecosystem services needed for agriculture, with potentially disastrous impacts on food security during the period from 2050 to 2100'.[20]

Water – both too much and too little – is already a critical issue in many parts of the world. Already 780 million people lack access to safe drinking water, according to the United Nations. And the OECD has warned that, by 2030, 47 per cent of the world's population will be living in areas of high water stress.[21] So it is little wonder that a 2012 report from the office of the US Director of National Intelligence predicted that the risk of conflict will grow as water demand is set to outstrip sustainable current supplies by 40 per cent by 2030.[22] 'These threats are real and they do raise serious national security concerns,' commented US Secretary of State Hillary Clinton.

Climate change will bring increased rates of evaporation from the soil, from vegetation, and from areas of open water. Droughts will not be the only result, for what evaporates must come down, bringing a severe risk of flooding to areas where such events are currently rare, including the United Kingdom. Defra's 2012 *Climate Change Risk Assessment* estimated that, if no further plans are made to adapt to changing flood risks, the effects of climate change and population growth will, by 2080, bring the annual cost of damage to buildings and property to between £2.1bn and £12bn, compared to current costs of £1.2bn.

The CCRA also forecast that, without action to improve water resources, there could be major supply shortages by the 2050s in parts of the north, south and east of England. Solving this by piping water from the North and West to the South and East would not only be extremely expensive but might simply exacerbate climate change by adding significantly to carbon emissions; in California, where water already has to be pumped over similar distances, almost 20 per cent of all the state's electricity and a third of all non-electricity natural gas use is needed to pump water. As a report produced by the United Nations Global Compact and the Pacific Institute in 2009 pointed out: 'The risks of managing water and energy/climate change in isolation of one another are woefully underappreciated by policy-makers'.[23]

Pollution is also a threat. Virtually every region of the globe now has traces of industrialised toxins. The amount of hazardous wastes in the United States increased over 250 times in the latter half of the twentieth century. Various types of radioactive wastes will remain toxic for thousands of years. Estimates suggest that, globally, up to 30 million people have been killed by air pollution since 1980. A study by the US National Institutes of Health suggested that between 80 and 90 per cent of all cancers may be due to pollution of one kind or another.[24] There are now some 150,000 synthetic compounds in commercial use around the world: very few have been examined for their potentially harmful effects on living things. It is known that many of these chemicals are carcinogenic, endocrine-inhibiting, bioaccumulative, toxic heavy metals or volatile organic compounds. And more are being introduced every year.

Another threat that has been ignored by almost every government globally is the loss of biodiversity. The Millennium Ecosystem Assessment, published by the United Nations in 2003, warned that: 'Human activities have taken the planet to the edge of a massive wave of species extinctions, further threatening our own well-being,' putting the threat on a par with global warming.[25] A research paper published in Nature in 2012 pointed out that the loss of biodiversity reduces the ability of ecosystems to protect humans and crops from pests and diseases and decreases the ability of nature to regulate the global climate; that genetic variation within crops makes them better able to resist disease; and that extinction rates are now 1,000 times higher than occurs naturally.[26] 'There is a strong likelihood that there will be another mass extinction in the foreseeable future,' concluded the paper.

Much of the damage to biodiversity is being caused directly by human activity, mainly by the destruction of habitats. But changes in the environment caused by climate change are also an important factor: another paper in Nature suggested that climate change alone could force between 15 and 37 per cent of species into extinction by 2050.[27]

The final risk may be the most worrying of all. It is the George Osborne risk – the failure of those who could make a difference to understand what the results for the world are likely to be if they continue to fail to act to tackle these extreme challenges. Some politicians are in total denial – US President George Bush was renowned for censoring government scientists from warning about the dangers of climate change. In 2012 the North Carolina Senate passed a bill banning coastal managers from predicting that sea level rises would accelerate.

But even governments that recognise the risk have failed to take significant action. The excuses are legion, ranging from prioritising economic growth to arguing that action by any one country is insignificant and will have little impact. Internationally, the repeated failure of the UN climate change conferences to agree an effective global framework demonstrates a lack of willingness and a lack of urgency to take action that will make any difference.

There is little doubt that many of the threats highlighted in this chapter can be resolved if we act urgently and effectively. And the potential harm of others can be substantially mitigated if we follow the kinds of policy outlined elsewhere in this book.

And, of course, there is a positive story: taking a proactive approach to tackling these threats will also create jobs, reduce the cost of living for many, especially the poorest in society, and improve the quality of life for everyone.

But time is running out...

Notes

1   Margaret Thatcher in a speech at the second World Climate Conference, 1990.
2   OECD, *Ranking of the World's Cities Most Exposed to Coastal Flooding Today and in the Future* (2007).
3   Defra, *Climate Change Risk Assessment* (2012).
4   IPCC, *Health Impacts of Climate Change* (2007).
5   Jacob Kumaresan and Nalini Sathiakumar, *Climate Change and its Potential Impact on Health* (WHO, 2010).
6   Peter Altman, *Killer Summer Heat* (Natural Resources Defense Council, 2012).
7   Potsdam Institute for Climate Impact Research, Tempo Analytics and Laboratoire d'Etudes en Géophysique et Océanographie Spatiales, published in *Environmental Research Letters*, 28 November 2012.
8   International Energy Agency, *Tracking Clean Energy Progress* (2012).
9   Tim Jackson, 'Why politicians dare not limit economic growth', *New Scientist*, 15 October 2008.
10 PwC, *PwC Low Carbon Economy Index* (2012).
11 David Woodward, *The Commodities Boom: Just Another Cycle, or Entering an Era of Scarcity?* (Sustainable Development Commission, 2008).
12 Reported in *greenfutures*, February 2009.
13 UNEP, *Decoupling Natural Resource Use and Environmental Impacts from Economic Growth* (2011).
14 United Nations, *Our Common Future* (1987).
15 Club of Rome, *Limits to Growth* (1972).
16 Graham Turner, *A Comparison of the Limits to Growth with Thirty Years of Reality* (Commonwealth Scientific and Industrial Research Organisation, Australia, 2008).
17 UNEP & GRID-Arendal, *Global Environment Outlook 3* (2012).
18 'How farmers are saving the soil by parking their plows', *Scientific American*, June 2008.
19 United Nations, *Resilient People, Resilient Planet* (2012).
20 See http://www.fao.org/news/story/en/item/54337/icode/.
21 OECD, *Environmental Outlook 2012* (2012).
22 Annual Threat Assessment presented to the United States Senate by the Defense Intelligence Agency, February 16, 2012.
23 United Nations Global Compact & Pacific Institute, *Climate Change and the Global Water Crisis: What Businesses Need to Know and Do* (2009).
24 See http://www.sustainablescale.org/ConceptualFramework/CausesofScaleProblems/ExcessThroughput.aspx
25 United Nations, *Millennium Ecosystem Assessment* (2003).
26 Chris D. Thomas et al., 'Extinction risk from climate change', *Nature*, January 2004.
27 'Feeling the heat', *Nature*, January 2004.

Chapter 5

The Liberal Record

Duncan Brack[1]

A s David Howarth argues in Chapter 6, liberalism is not only compatible with environmentalism – it *requires* an environmental approach. And indeed, in the UK the Liberal Party, and then the Liberal Democrats, have consistently shown themselves to be the greenest of the three major political parties.

Policy stances

The Liberal 'Yellow Book', *Britain's Industrial Future* (1928), is best remembered for its advocacy of a proto-Keynesian approach to unemployment and the economy, but it also contained a strong defence of the countryside, advocating, for example, the establishment of National Parks. Later in the century the Liberal Party was the first of the major parties to recognise the upsurge of environmental concern, holding a landmark conference on pollution in 1970 and publishing a comprehensive *Report on the Environment* in 1972 (the year in which 'People', later the Ecology Party and now the Green Party, was founded). The party called for a reduction in pollution and greater protection for endangered wildlife; it opposed the expansion of nuclear power, at least until the problems of waste disposal could be dealt with, and called for more energy conservation measures and the development of renewable sources of power. In 1979 the Liberal assembly adopted a resolution declaring that 'economic growth, as measured by GDP, is neither desirable nor achievable'. It was not until the late 1980s that the environmental critique of orthodox economic growth models was to become more widely accepted; in 1979 the Liberals were considerably ahead of their time.

Liberal support for environmental causes, and in particular the party's opposition to nuclear power, was a source of some tension with their SDP partners in the Alliance of the 1980s. The creation of the merged party, the Liberal Democrats, in 1988, together with the election of Paddy Ashdown as its first leader, led to the party adopting a more consistently green approach. This fitted well with the growing concern over the environment exemplified by the 1992 'Earth Summit' in Rio, and the gradual under-standing that environmental degradation was an inevitable consequence of the way in which Western economies were structured, culminating in the concept of environmentally sustainable development. The party called for much stricter national targets for reducing pollution, and argued for a shift in taxation from income and employment to pollution and resource use. It also argued for some environmental constraints on free trade, recognising the impact that trade liberalisation could have on magnifying the effects of unsustainable patterns of production and consumption. The 2001 and 2005 election manifestos saw green policy points picked out in every major policy area. Since 1992 the party's manifestos have been rated (by environmental NGOs) just behind those of the Green Party, and well ahead of those of the Conservative and Labour parties, and opinion polls have regularly shown that the public viewed the party as the best of the three main parties on environmental issues (a rating it achieved in no other policy area).

Why should the Liberal Party and Liberal Democrats have adopted green policies so enthusiastically? The party's basic philosophy provides the underpinnings, but it was not inevitable that this would result in such a con-sistently green approach; some European liberal parties have not followed the green route (which in turn has provided political space for the growth of explicitly green parties, most notably in Germany). The Liberals' and Liberal Democrats' consistently social-liberal stance, comfortable with the prin-ciple of state intervention where necessary, has made the adoption of green policies easier. Just as important has been the party's freedom from vested interests; it has not been held back by producer interests, whether in business or organised labour, and has always prided itself on its openness to new ideas and new ways of thinking and its willingness to think long-term. In addi-tion, party activists and, to a lesser extent the party's voters, have been drawn disproportionately from the educated middle classes, the group most likely to care about environmental issues. And finally, environmental policy has always offered a way to distinguish the party from its two main competitors, always a main goal of Liberal Democrat leaders (as Paddy Ashdown once said, 'I'd sell my grandmother for a bit of definition').

It should be noted that the adoption of green policies by the party was not a smooth process and did not always go unchallenged. Proposals for higher taxation on transport fuel have always caused some tensions with MPs from rural constituencies. And the party's localist and green approaches have sometimes clashed; local Liberal Democrats have generally, for example, opposed schemes for urban congestion charging, despite the fact that support for the principle has consistently featured in the party's national policy platform. Successive party leaders, however, and in particular Paddy Ashdown, have given a consistent lead for the adoption of the green approach.

Local government

Liberal Democrats may only have entered UK government in 2010, but the party has been running local authorities for decades, and in many cases Lib Dem councillors have put effective green policies into place at a local level. This section provides some examples.

In housing, Lib Dem local authorities have implemented initiatives to improve energy efficiency and install solar panels. Wrexham Borough Council has delivered Europe's biggest social housing solar PV scheme, with 30,000 locally made panels installed on 3,000 council houses. In Portsmouth between 2008 and 2012, over 500 private householders were taken out of fuel poverty thanks to a council loans-to-homeowners scheme. Birmingham City Council, when run by a Lib Dem–Conservative coalition, was the first in the UK to declare its intention to implement the government's Green Deal programme; the council set up the Birmingham Energy Savers project, planning to roll out energy efficiency measures to 15,000 homes, at a cost of £100 million. In Cambridge, a heatseeker van equipped with thermal imaging cameras has toured the city to identify and offer help for homes that would benefit from improved insulation. The London Borough of Sutton was one of the five pilot areas for the Green Deal, and the council is running a second energy-cutting project in Hackbridge, which aims to become the UK's first sustainable suburb. Sutton also supported the Beddington Zero Energy Development (BedZED), which in 2010 was voted, by green building experts, one of the five most globally important green buildings constructed since 1980.

Ask the average person what services their local council provides, and 'collecting the rubbish' always features. Using this essential service to spread a green message, as well as reducing waste sent to landfill, has been a focus of many Lib Dem local authorities. Watford Borough Council, for example, achieved an improvement in recycling rates from 11 per cent in 2002 to 42 per cent in 2012, through education campaigns and support for events such as Recycle Now week. Stockport has increased recycling rates to more than 60 per cent, bringing an annual financial saving (from avoided landfill tax and other rebates) of £5.2 million.

County and unitary councils are responsible for local transport policy. Portsmouth has become known nationally for its pioneering 20mph scheme across residential roads in the city centre, helping persuade other councils to follow suit. The introduction of a 20mph zone in Bristol reduced numbers of accidents by two-thirds. Bristol has also seen a sharp increase in cycle use, and in 2010 was named the best city in the UK for cyclists. In Watford councillors focused on reducing car use, appointing the company TravelSmart to go door to door, informing residents on alternatives; the impact was a 12 per cent reduction in car use between 2005 and 2009.

Liberal Democrat councils have aimed for significant reductions in carbon emissions from their own buildings and operations. In Eastleigh, climate change strategy has been embedded in every department, with each service area having to contribute. Many councils, including Portsmouth, Eastleigh, Bristol and South Somerset, have improved the energy efficiency of their own buildings and used them to install micro-generation equipment; Bristol, for example, has invested £16 million in solar panel installation, wind turbines and biomass boilers. Chesterfield installed a geothermal heating system, utilising heat from 100 metres underground, in an office and workshop building; and also built Staveley Healthy Living Centre, in an area of high deprivation, which features high insulation standards, solar water heating, a combined heat and power unit, waste heat recycling, grey water recycling and a computer-controlled building energy management system.

Councils can also play a key role in encouraging residents, local businesses and public sector organisations to reduce carbon emissions. Cambridge has worked in partnership with the university to look at setting up a district heating scheme for university and faculty buildings, with funding from the EU. Under Liberal Democrat leadership, Southwark set up the 200 Club, involving the largest businesses in the borough to share best practice on reducing carbon emissions; early members included Ernst & Young, PriceWaterhouseCoopers and Tesco. Portsmouth incorporated carbon reduction measures in its Local Plan and Regeneration Strategy, and supports the Portsmouth Network of the Sustainable Business Partnership, which works with small- and medium-sized enterprises to help them become more sustainable. Birmingham established 'Be Birmingham', a partnership organisation involving the public, private, voluntary and community sectors signing up to a shared vision for the city, including carbon reduction. Perhaps the most innovative part of the project was the creation of a Sustainable Procurement Contract, which commits the organisations involved to consider a raft of social and environmental factors when procuring goods and services.[2]

Bristol City Council worked with local businesses on an award-winning Hydrogen Ferry scheme (opposed by Labour and Conservative councillors), helping to quantify the reductions in carbon emissions hydrogen power can bring. The city has also received a £2.5m grant from the European Investment Bank to meet most of the costs of developing an energy services company and investment programme; the city-wide company will drive projects forward worth up to £140m, and help create at least 1,000 jobs, as well as increasing energy efficiency across the city and reducing energy bills for local residents.

Newcastle offers a good example of how initiatives like these can be combined in an overall ambitious programme. During the period in which the city was run by the Liberal Democrats, it was declared the UK's 'most sustainable city' by the environmental think-tank Forum for the Future in 2009 and 2010, the only city to have won the award twice. Achievements included increasing the recycling rate to 46 per cent, placing solar panels on council houses, installing energy efficiency measures in 36,000 homes, creating thirty-two electric vehicle charging points across the city, establishing a freight consolidation centre to switch freight from lorries to low-carbon vehicles for delivery into the city centre and a highly innovative carbon route mapping project (in collaboration with Newcastle University) to map carbon emissions down to individual buildings.

These and many other examples illustrate the importance that Liberal Democrat councillors across the country place in tackling environmental issues. A passion for the environment is not something that is imposed from the top in the party; it is a cause that Liberal Democrat councillors and activists have been pursuing for many years.

The financial climate for local authorities is proving ever more challenging, with large cuts in government grants and political pressure to keep Council Tax down. The financial benefits of early investment in energy efficiency and renewables, as well as in avoiding landfill tax by increased recycling, are now more keenly felt than ever – and Liberal Democrats in local government up and down the country have led the way.

Scotland

The first elections to the new Scottish Parliament took place in 1999. No party won an overall majority, and the Liberal Democrats formed a coalition government with Labour. The Scottish Liberal Democrat leaders Jim Wallace (until 2005) and Nicol Stephen (from 2005) served as Deputy First Ministers; Ross Finnie joined them in the Cabinet throughout the period, as Minister for Rural Affairs 1999–2003 and for Environment and Rural Development

2003–07. From 2003 the party had a third Cabinet post as Minister for Transport, held by Nicol Stephen 2003–05, and Tavish Scott 2005–07.

The party gained recognition for the inclusion of all the environmental commitments in the Scottish Liberal Democrat 1999 manifesto in the coalition agreement for 1999–2003, namely to: promote renewable energy; insulate lower-income families' homes; open new rail links, encourage freight on rail, and support concessionary fare schemes; promote safe cycling routes; enable road user charging to be introduced; establish national parks; promote sustainable agriculture, forestry and fisheries; improve water quality and reduce pollution; set targets to increase recycling; and introduce strategic environmental assessment.

The party's support for sustainability in Scotland was even more widely recognised during the second term of the Parliament, with, once again, all the commitments made by the Scottish Liberal Democrats in the 2003 election adopted, including using measures of quality of life and environmental degradation alongside GDP; the adoption of proper measures on climate change progress; strategic environmental assessment across government; a requirement for public bodies to reduce energy, water and private transport use; procurement policy to promote sustainable development, including, specifically, recycled products; setting high environmental standards for the rebuilding of the school estate; more environmental studies at school; continued support for sustainable agriculture and fisheries, and nature conservation; continued support for renewable energy; expansion of community heating schemes; higher targets for recycling domestic waste; further improvements to public transport and rail freight; and establishing access to environmental justice.

To emphasise the significance the Scottish Liberal Democrats made in moving Scotland towards improved sustainable development, the document *Choosing Our Future: Scotland's Sustainable Development Strategy* was published in December 2005. In addition, *Changing Our Ways: Scotland's Climate Change Programme* calculated for the first time Scotland's contribution to the Kyoto Protocol's target for emissions reductions, and with the insistence of the Scottish Liberal Democrats, that target was increased dramatically beyond Scotland's population share.

When the coalition government came into office in 1999, electricity generation from all renewable sources amounted to some 11 per cent. *Securing a Renewable Future: Scotland's Renewable Energy*, launched by the Liberal Democrats, set the target at 40 per cent by 2020, double the UK rate of 20 per cent. That formed the basis of the first climate change legislation, adopted in Scotland in 2009. The government funded the 'warm deal programme' which led to 209,000 homes of those on lower incomes being insulated by 2006, saving some 39,000 tonnes of carbon dioxide. The proportion of the Scottish government's transport budget devoted to public transport rose significantly during the period in which Liberal Democrats held the transport portfolio, from 38 per cent to 53 per cent; this has now fallen, with the biggest drop in support for rail services in Scotland.

The *National Waste Plan* in 2003 set a target for recycling and composting of 55 per cent by 2020 (Scotland's recycling rate for municipal waste was 6 per cent in 2002), and the government created a £500 million strategic waste fund. The recycling rate increased to 26 per cent by 2007 and had reached 38 per cent by early 2012.

Liberal Democrats in government in Scotland brought in new approaches to climate change, renewable energy generation, waste management and public transport. All saw budget priorities shifted towards them and in each area major progress was made in the first two terms of devolution.

Wales

In Wales, after a period of minority government the Labour Party chose coalition with the Liberal Democrats in October 2000; it lasted until the second election for the Welsh Assembly, in 2003. The Welsh Liberal Democrat leader Mike German served as Deputy First Minister and Minister first for Economic Development and later for Rural Affairs; there was also one other Liberal Democrat Cabinet member. As in Scotland, the Liberal Democrats were able to implement a significant number of policies; indeed, they claimed that 80 per cent of the policies in their manifesto would be introduced.

The party afforded a high priority to green issues. Achievements included reopening the Cardiff to Ebbw Vale railway line and increasing investment in bus subsidy schemes, particularly in rural areas. Planning regulations were developed to create green spaces around urban centres across Wales, to encourage the development of brownfield sites and to introduce a strong presumption in planning regulations against out-of-town shopping centres. A strategic spatial plan was developed for the whole of Wales. A waste strategy was introduced to promote the minimisation of packaging, re-use and recycling, and to reduce incineration and landfill. An air quality strategy was also introduced, with strengthened powers for the Environment Agency and with higher standards. Within the framework of the Assembly's Sustainable Development Strategy, a 'green audit' of the Assembly's policies and spending commitments, including quality-of-life indicators, was brought in.

Coalition government

In 2010 Liberal Democrats finally returned to UK government after an absence of sixty-five years. In recognition of the importance the party has placed on environmental issues, one of its five Cabinet ministers was the Secretary of State for Energy and Climate Change – Chris Huhne from May 2010 to February 2012, and Ed Davey from February 2012. An informal group of Lib Dem green ministers started to operate, including junior ministers in other departments, most notably, Norman Baker in Transport and Andrew Stunell in Communities and Local Government.

As Chapter 1 made clear, Liberal Democrat ministers in the coalition have faced an uphill struggle in putting into practice green policies, including some of the commitments agreed between the coalition partners in 2010; the last two and a half years has revealed just how weak is the Conservative Party's commitment to the green agenda (with a few notable exceptions), even to those policies on which it fought the 2010 election. Nevertheless, green policy achievements have been real, particularly in those policy areas for which the Department of Energy and Climate Change (DECC) holds the lead, but not only there – recognising that environmental issues are fundamental to the whole economy, and not just optional add-ons, Liberal Democrats have fought to establish elements of the framework needed to achieve a low-carbon green economy and a government which takes sustainable development seriously.

In this respect one of the most notable achievements was reaching agreement on the fourth carbon budget, the total of greenhouse gas emissions allowed from the UK for the period 2023–27. If achieved, this will represent a step change for the economy, with a reduction of an average 50 per cent of emissions from 1990. (George Osborne, however, insisted on a review of the target in 2014, and if he stays true to form will argue for a reduction.) The government Carbon Plan was published in December 2011, explaining how the fourth carbon budget target would be met.[3]

UK climate policy of course operates within EU and global frameworks, and Liberal Democrat ministers, with their underlying belief in internationalism, have argued for more ambitious targets and measures at both levels. Chris Huhne and Ed Davey played key roles in keeping the UN climate conferences in 2010, 2011 and 2012 on track, operating through the EU delegation. The government's commitment to provide £2.9 billion for international climate spending over the spending review period of 2011–15 is more generous than that of many developed countries.

Domestic energy policy is facing a wholescale shake-up, as dealt with in detail in Chapters 18, 19 and 20. The draft Electricity Market Reform Bill published in November 2012 is designed to establish clear incentives for low-carbon generation at least cost to the taxpayer and consumer. Key components include support for low-carbon generation through contracts for difference (low-carbon generators will be paid the difference between their supply price and the market price for electricity), capacity mechanisms to ensure security of supply at periods of peak demand, and an emissions performance standard to set upper limits on emissions from coal and gas stations. The Liberal Democrat intention to include a decarbonisation target for the power sector in the Bill was resisted by the Conservatives, but the inclusion of the requirement to set one in 2016 was a notable success, as was agreement on the future level of the levy control framework, through which low-carbon generation will be subsidised.

Until the new arrangements come into force, the existing support system for renewable electricity is being maintained, and support levels were confirmed – after a struggle with the Treasury – in July 2012. Renewable energy is also being supported through the Renewable Heat Incentive, direct payments to business and householders installing renewable heat technologies such as solar thermal and heat pumps. The previous Labour administration's feed-in tariff scheme for microgeneration, mainly solar PV, was not designed to take account of the unexpectedly rapid fall in the capital costs of the solar panels, and in late 2011 the government was forced to make a drastic reduction in levels of support. Although this was justifiable in terms of cost-effective spending – and the final shape of the scheme, which incorporates gradual reductions in the tariff alongside falling costs, has been generally welcomed – the abrupt change did nothing to boost investor confidence; with the benefit of hindsight the government should have acted sooner.

Alongside policies to boost low-carbon generation, the other main plank of the government's energy strategy is to reduce energy use. Through the 2011 Energy Act, the government introduced the Green Deal energy efficiency programme, aimed to catalyse a major programme of retrofitting buildings to improve energy efficiency, paid for through reductions in energy bills, with no up-front costs to householders or businesses. Extra support will be available to low-income households and those living in hard-to-treat homes (such as those with solid rather than cavity walls). The programme is also expected to help generate significant employment opportunities, though it is proving slower than anticipated to get off the ground.

Liberal Democrat ministers outside DECC have also achieved notable green policy successes. This includes the establishment of the Green Investment Bank by Vince Cable's Department for Business, Innovation and Skills. Formally launched in October 2012, the Bank is designed to mobilise significant new sources of private investment into low-carbon infrastructure and technologies; this is particularly important for power generation, where an estimated £120 billion of investment is needed to replace ageing power stations by 2020. The Bank's initial capitalisation of £3 billion can only go so far in addressing this, and Treasury restrictions on its ability to borrow will limit it further (see Chapters 12 and 15).

Achievements in transport policy include a major programme of investment for rail upgrades and expansions, encouragement for cycling and walking, and subsidies for the use of low-carbon cars, including a £5,000 grant for anyone buying an electric car, and a national recharging network. The Local Sustainable Transport Fund, established in 2011 by Norman Baker, will support local transport authorities outside London in developing measures that support economic growth and reduce carbon emissions in their communities, as well as delivering cleaner environments, improved safety and increased levels of physical activity.

The difference Liberal Democrat ministers have made to the coalition is substantial; if the coalition succeeds in realising David Cameron's aim of making the government 'the greenest ever', it will be due to Liberal Democrats, not to his own party colleagues. The difference in approach can be most easily seen in the analyses of green policy achievements (against the coalition commitments) carried out by NGOs in the autumn of 2011.[4] In the fourteen policy areas in which DECC had the lead, the NGOs awarded it four green lights (good progress), seven amber (moderate progress) and one red (poor progress). In contrast, the Treasury received no green, one amber and three red. Defra, a department with (until September 2012) no Liberal Democrat ministers, received two green, six amber and four red.

As the *Business Green* editor James Murray commented in September 2012, after the Liberal Democrat conference:

… over the past week the Liberal Democrats have taken a series of steps that should prove of invaluable long-term benefit to the British economy. There has been little fanfare and scant media attention, but the junior coalition party has used its annual shindig in Brighton to revive one of its more attractive qualities: its unwavering support for the green economy and, more importantly, the desire to fight for it … The Lib Dems have been battered and bruised by their time in government … But if they can just deliver the essential energy market reforms that have eluded previous governments while holding the line against the regressive forces of the 'pollutocracy', then the country as a whole, and the green economy in particular, will owe them a considerable debt of gratitude.[5]

Notes

1   The author is very grateful for earlier draft chapters by, and input from, Rob Banks, Mike German, Martin Horwood MP, Jeremy Purvis and Sarah Whitebread.
2   See: http://www.bebirmingham.org.uk/documents/Compact_Doc_Complete_1. pdf?phpMyAdmin=b5998cc58dff68a4b03a480ef59038da Section 5.7
3   *The Carbon Plan: Delivering our low-carbon future* (HM Government, December 2011).
4   Christian Aid, Greenpeace, Green Alliance, RSPB and WWF, *Climate Check: An Analysis of the Government's delivery of its low-carbon commitments* (September 2011); Wildlife and Countryside Link, *Nature Check: An Analysis of the Government's natural environment commitments* (October 2011).
5   James Murray, 'In praise of the Lib Dems', *Business Green* 26 September 2012; http://www.businessgreen.com/bg/james-blog/2208374/in-praise-of-the-lib-dems

Chapter 6

Liberalism, Environmentalism and Green Politics

David Howarth

Conventional political theory tends to see liberalism as inherently inimical to green politics. Liberalism, on a view often taken for granted at least on the left, is taken to prioritise the satisfaction of individual human desires over all else, which not only means giving individuals priority over collectivities such as classes, nations and states, but also giving them priority over the natural environment. On this conventional view, green politics is holistic, seeing humans as part of nature, whereas liberal politics is particularistic, treating humans as fundamentally separate, not only from one another, but also from the natural world.

The conventional view, however, is plainly wrong. In the English-speaking world (with the possible exception of Australia), political parties that identify themselves as 'liberal' are more likely than parties of the right or left to promote policies aimed at environmental protection, and far more likely to promote radical action on problems such as climate change.

Parties of the right, such as the British Conservative Party, have long been close to economic interests that feel threatened by environmental politics, a position that reasserts itself as soon as environmental policies start to bite. Leftist parties, especially those close to the trade unions such as the British Labour Party, are often also captured by producer lobbies connected to polluting industries. Liberal parties tend to be free of such interests and have thus been able to move easily in the direction of environmentalism. Admittedly, one finds a much lower level of commitment to environmentalism in some of the more business-oriented liberal parties – the German FDP, for example, or the Dutch VVD – but social liberal parties display a clear preference for green policies.

Part of the reason for the failure of conventional political theory to explain the reality of liberal politics' engagement with environmentalism is an attempt, often an ideologically motivated attempt, to equate mainstream liberalism with the academic left's favourite bogeyman, 'neoliberalism' – that combination of market fundamentalism and prison-building promoted by political leaders as 'liberal' as Augusto Pinochet and George W. Bush. The insinuation is that all liberals, whatever they might say, prioritise individual material well-being over all else, recognise no collective responsibilities and promote competition as a good in itself regardless of its consequences. The accusation only has to be stated explicitly for its absurdity to become clear. In Britain, to drive the point home, it was not liberals who embodied 'neoliberalism', but Margaret Thatcher and Tony Blair (the former through conviction, the latter through his usual mixture of random following of fashion and fear of the media) – although, to confuse the position even further, both those prime ministers combined neoliberal views with more commitment to the environment than was usual in their own parties.

Another part of the explanation of the conventional view, however, is a broader failure by liberals to explain to non-liberals why the purposes liberalism pursues include protection of the environment. Liberals have developed explanations of how their core beliefs are compatible with environmentalism, but they have not gone on to explain how anti-environmental stances are *incompatible* with liberalism.

Liberalism compatible with environmental protection

The compatibility of liberalism and environmental protection is easy to show. Because liberalism, unlike libertarianism, treats the delimitation of property rights as a potential instrument of public policy and not as a sacrosanct pre-political totem, it can easily incorporate, for example, the environmentalist principle, suggested by Marcel Wissenburg, that resources should not be destroyed without adequate replacement.[1] Environmental harm also often involves physical injury to individual people and thus frequently counts as 'assignable' harm for the purposes of John Stuart Mill's harm principle, which permits (but does not require) state action to prevent such harm.[2]

Libertarianism not compatible with environmental protection

One might add that libertarianism does have difficulties explaining how it might be compatible with environmentalism. Libertarians need to explain how environmental issues can be resolved solely by the delimitation of property rights. That might be possible where the problems are quite small – where one person is polluting the property of another and the dispute can be resolved by declaring one side or the other to have the superior right. But where the proportion of human activity causing environmental damage is very high, and the size of the potential damage very great, as in the effects of climate change, the property rights approach collapses. It is difficult to maintain that the state is merely protecting existing rights if it intervenes to tell a very high proportion of the population that they may not use their property as they want. But not to do so would risk destruction on such a vast scale that the state would be failing to protect property in a different way.

No wonder libertarians often resolve this contradiction by asserting that the climate change problem does not exist, and by treating environmentalism as nothing more than the latest excuse of statists to regulate and interfere. Of course, they might not be wrong about that last point – the motivation of some 'Red-Greens' does seem to include the desire to justify greater state control of economic life in an era in which socialist arguments based on efficiency have been discredited. But libertarians are wrong to think that the only justifications for environmental regulation are socialistic.

Beyond liberal compatibility with environmentalism

The question is, therefore: how can liberals maintain that environmentalism is not just compatible with liberalism but *required* by it? On the face of it, that is a difficult task. Liberals have a whole armoury of principles to help them decide whether the state is permitted to act – Mill's harm principle not least among them – but it has very few principles that help them to decide whether the state has a duty to act.

The European Court of Human Rights has developed the idea that states have positive duties to protect the rights of citizens, including several in the environmental field, such as duties to provide information about environmental hazards, but it has failed to provide any coherent theory of when and why such duties should arise. The clearest such positive obligation is the duty to take steps to protect the life of citizens, and one might argue that many environmental threats, up to and including climate change, do ultimately put life at risk. The problem with that argument, however, is how to keep it within reasonable bounds. Does any threat, no matter how small and distant, oblige the state to impose enormous burdens on the current population? No one, except perhaps for a Red-Green looking for new arguments for state intervention, thinks so. The obligation is therefore usually seen as one to take reasonable or proportionate measures, one which liberals might be content to endorse – but this merely postpones the question of what counts as reasonable or proportionate.

The central difficulty with the concept of reasonable or proportionate measures is what do we count as the gains and losses from intervention? Greens claim that the problem with liberalism is that it values personal freedom so highly that it can only use the satisfaction of individuals' subjective desires in deciding what is reasonable or proportionate. According to Greens, especially those of the deep Green variety, one has to count in the value of nature itself, regardless of human preferences, to arrive at a proper valuation of the environment. Moreover, Greens claim that the origins of ecological crisis lie in humans' untrammelled desires to consume, so that there is no long-term solution without acting to limit those desires – a course of action that liberals, committed to the idea of personal freedom, will be unable to endorse. From a deep Green perspective, liberalism cannot help but count as 'anthropocentric' – that is, it holds that nature has value only in so far as it has value for us as humans. Even the fact that liberals tend to speak not of 'nature' but of the 'environment', which is to say that which surrounds humans, confirms that orientation. Environmentalism, on this view, is not enough. One has to see humans ecologically, as part of nature, not separate from it.

There is something in this. Liberals *are* anthropocentric. Their first and last concern is with human freedom. But, contrary to what Greens claim, they are not committed to an unconsidered, subjective, market-based view of value. There might be a historical connection between liberalism and utilitarianism, but the intellectual connection is long broken. Liberalism, or at least modern social liberalism, is committed instead to promoting democratic processes of discussion through which groups of people can come to views not only about what they happen collectively to want at any one time (a process of merely adding up desires on the basis of one person, one vote, in parallel to the market's one monetary unit, one vote), but also, and crucially, through which they can discuss and decide about what they *ought* to want.

Indeed, one of the central points of having democratic institutions is that by discussing decisions on the basis of political equality, we can come to new, more comprehensive and more considered views of what we want. Those processes of discussion provide an opportunity for the inclusion of views of value that go beyond immediate desires. That opportunity does not extend to allowing the state to take a comprehensive view of what counts as good for individuals to want in their individual lives, but it does allow for views to be put forward about the value of, for example, ecosystem services that go further than the value that individuals would put on them before the discussion started.

Thus, when liberals make judgments about what counts as proportionate and reasonable intervention for the purposes of a positive duty to act, they take into account not just what level of environmental protection citizens happen to want at the time. They also take into account what can be persuasively argued for in the course of democratic debate.

Preventing a catastrophic conflict between environmental degradation and democracy

The challenge of liberals back to Greens is a fundamental one about democracy. What happens if democratic discussion of what we ought collectively to want fails to come up with the valuation of the environment, or nature, that Greens propose? Does the Green commitment to the objective value of nature and their objection to what people currently want imply a belief in the overthrow of democracy itself? If it does, then we have identified an important difference between the two views. If not, we have identified limits to Green rhetoric about the objective value of nature and the need for a revolution in what people want.

It is possible, however, to construct scenarios in which the only way to preserve humanity at all is to adopt totalitarian methods. There are scenarios about out-of-control climate change, for example, that have that characteristic. Surely, Greens might say, it would be worth a period of totalitarianism, even a long one, to maintain the possibility of human life itself. But Marcel Wissenburg is right that, faced with a choice between a global totalitarian eco-state and a 'global Manhattan' (an unsustainable liberal mega-city), liberals would always choose global Manhattan.[3] Greens then respond, what if the choice is between *imminent* environmental apocalypse and totalitarianism? Would not survival trump all else? But for liberals, that choice itself is an apocalypse. A society faced with the choice between life and what makes life worth living is already intolerable.

The lesson of such scenarios for liberals is that it is important to work constantly to ensure that we never face such a choice, which means working constantly for an 'eco-Manhattan'. That is, the need to protect the environment so that we do not end up with a choice between survival and totalitarianism is itself an argument that environmental protection is not only compatible with liberalism but required by it. Environmental degradation that threatens human welfare so much that only illiberal political measures can save humanity from serious harm or even destruction is itself a fundamental threat to the freedom liberalism seeks to protect and promote. Only by working to prevent environmental degradation can we prevent the development of a situation in which environmental degradation threatens freedom.

Capacity to develop a plan of life

Liberalism recognises the value of the environment in another way that goes beyond immediate desires. If one asks what the individuality liberalism values consists of, the answer is not the capacity of people to desire things but their capacity to plan their own lives in ways that make sense to them. The existence of an acceptable environment is a condition of that capacity. At its most extreme, a global environment incompatible with human life or seriously damaging to human health defeats all plans of life. Even if the effects are more local, so that in principle those affected can move away (examples might include urban air pollution or the regional effects of climate change), the degree of disruption both to those directly affected and to those affected by the consequent movements of population will often be so great that their choices, or their 'capabilities', to use Amartya Sen's term, will be severely curtailed.

Admittedly, the standard of environmental acceptability liberalism uses is a human standard – what permits us to function as humans – not a standard set from what we might imagine is the point of view of the universe. It follows that there will be differences of view and divergences of interest about what degree of environmental protection is necessary. But those differences and divergences give rise to political problems of precisely the kind liberalism has been grappling with at a theoretical level for the past half-century, at least since the publication of Rawls' *A Theory of Justice*. Debate continues around the right way to deal with them. In particular, disagreement continues about the best way to reconcile the interests of current and future generations. As economists discovered when some of them tried to define as purely technical the issue of whether the Stern Report was right to count future humans as having the same value as existing humans,[4] these issues are ethical and political, not algebraic. But these debates can be conceived of as debates within liberalism, not debates about liberalism.

Equality
A third set of arguments that connect liberalism with the environment concern equality. Some forms of equality are inherent in all forms of liberalism – for example, equality before the law and equality of rights of political participation. Some forms of liberalism, however, take the commitment to equality further. What I have elsewhere called 'minimalist social liberalism' concerns itself with how inequalities of income and wealth might adversely affect political equality, worrying about not only the effects of money on political campaigning and on control over the means of expression, but also about how inequalities in access to education and health might produce inequality in ability to affect politics over the longer term. 'Maximalist social liberalism', in contrast, worries about inequality more directly, starting from substantive ideals of equality, such as the principle that no one is entitled

without further justification to use more than an equal share of their society's resources.[5]

Although there is no obvious connection between the environment and the formal equalities promoted by all types of liberalism, the forms of equality promoted by social liberalism do imply concern for the environment. The connection is clearer in the case of maximalist social liberalism. It takes two forms. The first connection is that the resources of society over which we might have only an equal claim without further justification include the environment and the benefits it bestows. Admittedly, one needs a further principle, of the form that resources should not be destroyed without justification, to exclude perverse methods of reaching equality by making some people's lives worse, but that further principle is not in itself illiberal.

The second connection is more direct. Many kinds of environmental problem bear more heavily on the poor, so that solving them is inherently egalitarian. Slightly more subtly, improvements in equality can arise even where burdens are not so unequally shared. It is difficult to exclude people from environmental benefits. Some are close to universal, for example ecosystem services such as the potential to provide new medicines. Others, such as a stable climate, might have differential geographical effects, but their benefits within regions are not confined to specific individuals or strata of society. The effect is that, on the whole, improving the environment in these ways tends towards equality in itself. As environmental benefits of this kind grow as a proportion of the total resources of society, the proportion of those total resources taken up by a relatively equally distributed resource also grows, and thus overall equality grows too.

The connections between the environment and equality might seem to be relevant only to maximalist social liberals. Indeed, one might be able to observe empirically a correlation within liberal politics between maximalism and environmentalism, a correlation that arises not from a red-green desire for state control but directly from the correlations between equality and environmentalism. But there are also reasons for minimalist social liberals to worry about environmental degradation. For example, serious environmental problems interfere with health in ways that should engage minimalists' attention. Geographically specific environmental problems that tend to interfere with the ability of those there to take part in politics should strike minimalist social liberals as a significant threat to political equality, a point which applies most obviously to local conditions, but which also applies at a global level. The threat posed by climate change to the very existence of small island states, or states whose population is concentrated in low-lying river deltas, for example, is precisely the kind of environmental problem with serious political consequences about which minimalist social liberals should worry.

The difference between maximalists and minimalists comes down to the difference between being attracted to the equalising effects of environmental improvement and being repelled by the political effects of environmental degradation. The former is likely to produce a larger effect than the latter, and, arguably, neither is likely to be as important in impelling liberals towards environmentalism as the need to avoid a threat to democracy itself or the connection between the environment and the capability of individuals to choose their own plans of life, but their effects are at least in the same direction.

Modern liberal parties, as alliances between minimalist and maximalist social liberals, might contain within them some tensions about the relative importance of the environment, especially about the importance of positive environmental benefits, but they are united in treating environmentalism as inherent in their political outlook.

Liberal means and rethinking the importance of 'choice'

Greens are not wrong, however, when they point out that liberals are unwilling to use whatever means might be necessary to deal with environmental problems. That is because liberals are generally unwilling to use certain types of means in politics. When Hobhouse declared that freedom means being treated as a rational being,[6] he was underlining a fundamental liberal commitment not so much to rationality (he knew, as we do, that people are not in fact always, or even often, rational) but to an important aspect of the respect liberalism believes is due to all individuals. That is why liberalism rejects methods of manipulation and mind control. It is also why liberals favour choice – not, as sometimes believed, because liberals have swallowed the market fundamentalist dogma that choice always leads, by quasi-magical means, to universal improvements in quality, but because providing choice pays appropriate respect to individuals. The result has been that liberals display a bias towards policy instruments that seem to leave the population with choices – for example, consumption taxes, tradable permits and subsidies – and a bias against those that appear to give no choice – especially the criminal law.

One might question, however, whether these distinctions really work in the way liberals have thought. Tax and permit trading schemes themselves ultimately depend on criminal law penalties against tax evasion and against carrying on an activity without a permit. Indeed, proposals for trading schemes that apply to most of daily life – personal carbon allowances, for example – have the effect of bringing the criminal law into a high proportion of daily life via the need to enforce the scheme. Choice is technically still present, but the pressure of regulation on the mental life of individuals might be so great that a line has been crossed into oppression. Having one's own plan of life presupposes having the time to formulate such a plan, time that might not exist if daily life is overwhelmed by rules.

A parallel point is that schemes of regulation that provide for low levels of fines, although perhaps intended as coercive, might end up being treated as mere costs of production. That might be seen from a liberal point of view as a good thing, as bringing back an element of choice, but the wider effect on the rule of law (and especially on equality before the law, since the wealthier the defendant the more likely they are to treat the fine as a cost) might be considered potentially disastrous.

A further challenge is how liberals should think about policy instruments that have developed out of the insights of behavioural economics and applied psychology – for example, 'nudge' techniques. At first sight, such methods are highly manipulative. They take irrational aspects of how people think – their inability to calculate risks properly, their susceptibility to simple errors such as excessively favouring an option framed as the middle one, and their sheer laziness – and use them to change behaviour. Can they ever be justified?

The time might have come to reconsider what should count as liberal means. One way forward is to return to basic liberal concerns and ask: what are the conditions of people being able to formulate their own plans of life and to participate freely in politics? From that point of view, what matters is less what form of choice a policy instrument offers – to pay a price in the form of a tax, a fee or a criminal penalty – and more the extent to which it hinders individuals in the formulation of plans of life and in political participation. One consequence of such a move would be that the *effects* of policy interventions would matter more than their *form*. Direct environmental regulation might not be objectionable in itself as long as it avoids producing conditions that interfere in individuals' ability to formulate life plans. Regulation that prevents the use of gas-guzzlers, for example, does not by itself interfere with the choice of any plausible life-plan (except perhaps for bizarre ones that revel in the waste of resources) and might be preferable to tax or subsidy measures that might not work. On the other hand, where nominally 'choice'-based techniques do have such effects, such as intrusive personal carbon allowance schemes, they should be ruled out. 'Nudge' techniques similarly might be acceptable as long as they are carried out openly, so that they do not involve the use of arbitrary power and do not cut off political debate. Indeed, it might be a usable principle about 'nudge' techniques that they should not be deployed if using them openly means that they fail.

The net effect of such a rethink would not be that liberals would turn into 'any-means-necessary' Greens, but they might be able to contemplate a wider range of measures, especially regulatory measures, than they do now.

Conclusion

Liberalism is not just compatible with environmentalism. It *requires* environmentalism. It might not require a commitment to dissolving human interests into the swirling flows of the natural universe, as deep Greens demand. Indeed, it might even require the rejection of such a view.

Liberals are unashamedly anthropocentric because they worry above all about the capability of human beings to lead their own lives and to govern their own, human, communities. But that capability itself presupposes a liveable environment, without which liberalism itself would not be possible. Above all, in the long term, uncontrolled accelerating environmental degradation is a threat to democratic institutions, and so constitutes a threat to all that modern social liberals hold dear.

Notes

1   Marcel Wissenburg, *Green Liberalism: The Free and the Green Society* (UCL Press, 1998), p. 166.

2   See *On Liberty* (Collected Works, University of Toronto Press, 1977) p. 282, where Mill elaborates, 'But with regard to the merely contingent, or, as it may be called, constructive injury which a person causes to society, by conduct which neither violates any specific duty to the public, nor occasions perceptible hurt to any assignable individual except himself; the inconvenience is one which society can afford to bear, for the sake of the greater good of human freedom.'

3   See Wissenburg, *Green Liberalism*, and Robyn Eckersley, 'Environmental Pragmatism, Ecocentrism and Deliberative Democracy' in Ben Minteer and Bob Pepperman Taylor, *Democracy and the Claims of Nature: Critical Perspectives for a New Century* (Rowman & Littlefield, 2002), p. 54.

4   See Nicholas Stern, *Stern Review on The Economics of Climate Change* (HM Treasury, 2006), pp. 31–33, and, e.g., Terry Barker, 'The economics of avoiding dangerous climate change: An editorial essay on The Stern Review', *Climatic Change* (2008) vol. 89, pp. 184–87.

5　See David Howarth, 'What is Social Liberalism?' in Duncan Brack, Richard Grayson and David Howarth (eds), *Reinventing the State: Social Liberalism for the 21st Century* (Politico's, 2007), pp. 1–16. 'Minimalist' social liberals, in common with all social liberals, care about democracy and social justice (unlike classical 'economic' liberals with whom they are often confused by journalists), but they care about social justice only to the extent that lack of social justice interferes with democracy. 'Maximalist' social liberals accept arguments in favour of social justice and equality over and above those based on protecting democracy.

6　L. T. Hobhouse, *Liberalism and Other Writings* (James Meadowcroft ed.) (Cambridge University Press, 1994), p. 59.

Chapter 7

Setting Standards: Environmental Regulation as if Human Health Mattered

Mike Tuffrey

Environmental regulation as health protection

In recent years the mood across the political spectrum has been almost universally hostile to government regulation. Initiatives for greater intervention are routinely accused of adding to 'red tape'. Those presenting themselves as 'pro-business' insist that regulation is essentially a bad thing – holding companies back, adding costs, discouraging innovation and destroying initiative-taking.

Little mention is made of the very real benefits which regulation to protect the environment can bring, spurring innovation and enterprise, while also also protecting human health. Yet even a cursory look at recent history shows how regulation can prove effective.

Take our capital city. The earliest recorded effort to protect London's notoriously bad air quality dates back to 1306. It took the Great Smog of December 1952 to spur effective action: 12,000 people died in the immediate aftermath, with a further 8,000 in the following months. Government only acted when the Select Committee on Air Pollution recommended legislation, and backbench MPs sought to pass a private member's bill on domestic coal burning. The Clean Air Act 1956 gave local authorities the power to create 'smoke control areas'. Even today, failure to implement EU directives to clean up modern day pollution, largely caused by the internal combustion engine, means that Londoners suffer heightened health risks. An estimated 450,000 people in the European Union die prematurely each year as a direct result of exposure to air pollutants.[1]

Another example of environmental regulations to protect health is how lead was eliminated from petrol in the UK, with a leading role for an erstwhile Liberal Democrat hero. Lead's toxic properties have been known since Roman times, yet for more than sixty years a form of the metal, tetraethyl lead, was added to gasoline to increase its octane rating. Evidence mounted in

71

America of the damage done, especially to children's brains, and the US acted in the 1970s. It took a concerted campaign in the UK, run by Des Wilson in 1982, and two EU directives in the 1990s finally to achieve the goal, requiring all new cars to have catalytic converters and eventually phasing lead out completely. Since 1 January 2002 all petrol sold in the EU is unleaded. Academic studies are now attributing lower levels of violent crime among teenagers to lower levels of lead in the atmosphere when they were growing up.[2]

For those who argue that necessary international agreements are too hard to reach, there is the success of phasing out the production of ozone-depleting substances. As a result the annual 'ozone hole' over Antarctica is now beginning to close and the risk of damage from ultraviolet light – which can contribute to skin cancer and cataracts – is diminishing. The breakthrough came in 1985 when twenty nations signed the Vienna Convention for the Protection of the Ozone Layer. This established a framework for negotiating international regulations on ozone-depleting substances and was followed in 1987 by the signing of the Montreal Protocol, which ultimately ended the production of the main culprit, chlorofluorocarbons (CFCs) completely in the 1990s in the developed world and ten years later in developing countries.

Aside from these examples, the evidence that unrestricted environmental damage harms human health is incontrovertible. The World Health Organisation estimates that a quarter of the global disease burden can be directly attributed to environmental factors – one in four premature deaths and billions of people suffering ill health during their shortened lives.[3]

The global impact on human life from the consequences of climate change, such as increasingly severe weather incidents, changes in rainfall patterns and ultimately from rising sea levels, is now widely understood. Measures to mitigate the impact are slowly being devised around low-carbon energy generation, changes to transport, greater efficiency in product manufacture and use, and higher efficiency standards for buildings. These will have immediate health benefits.

Lower emissions of pollutants from reduced burning of fossil fuels saves lives, cuts asthma and improves children's life-long healthy development. Similarly, switching to more walking and cycling in urban areas has a direct positive effect on chronic illnesses such as cardio-vascular disease, diabetes, certain cancers and depression. Improving access to green spaces not only increases quality of life but enhances health and reduces NHS costs. One recent study of the cause of death of almost 400,000 people found that the health gap between rich and poor could be halved if the least well-off had access to parks and woodland.[4]

If the evidence that an improved environment can increase quality of life and human health is clear, what are the costs and benefits of interventions to achieve this? Who will benefit and who should pay?

The economics of regulation

Since the start of the industrial revolution, the problem of what economists call externalities has been acknowledged. This is where individual producers or consumers cause harm to wider society or the environment without paying the resulting costs. Taxes and regulations have been progressively increased, so that more externalities are included in the normal price of transactions.

Examples abound. Individual businesses gain from being able to recruit workers already educated in basic skills. The corporation tax they pay in part supports the public education system. Health and safety regulations require spending on protective measures. This saves individuals from harm, ensures that responsible employers are not undercut by unscrupulous competitors, and ultimately helps reduce expenditure in the National Health Service and on disability benefits.

Where the benefit to human individuals is clear, few today would argue about the principle. However regulation for environmental protection is more contested. Most accepted are those where the public health benefits are patent and immediate, and the environmental damage is visible and directly traceable to source. Examples include preventing factories from emitting noxious fumes or discharging pollutants directly into rivers or groundwater. The Environment Agency is charged with enforcing these rules, with prosecutions and fines for breaches. Even here, business benefits. Preventing water pollution protects businesses downstream of polluters or those who extract ground water. Necessary costs are spread fairly among all companies, preventing freeloaders.

Regulations affecting individual industries tend to be hotly contested by those affected, at least initially. After the ban on CFCs was proposed, the fluorochemicals industry rapidly saw a commercial opportunity, as safe alternatives could be profitable too, so started racing to compete. Development went far faster than expected and the Montreal Protocol was successively amended to bring the phase-out dates closer. American companies like DuPont led the way, with the extra incentive of threatened court action after the US government published studies estimating that an additional 40 million cases and 800,000 cancer deaths were likely if no action was taken.

Another example of innovation, much cited by former US Energy Secretary Steve Chu, is how improved federal energy efficiency standards for fridges were set, despite opposition from the industry, which warned that higher standards would increase costs. In fact while running costs definitely fell, with a fridge in 2010 costing a third less to run than one made in 1975, the real cost to the consumer of the initial purchase fell too, while the typical size grew. Overall savings achieved by the minimum standards are estimated at US$300 billion up to 2010.[5]

A current example affects the European tyre industry, worth some €30 billion a year. As from November 2012, manufacturers and importers of all tyres in the EU must provide product labels about three environmental and safety aspects: fuel consumption (related to the rolling resistance), wet grip for shorter braking distances in the rain and external noise generated. Distributors and retailers must make sure this is visible at the point of sale.

Although the benefits of higher graded tyres had long been known, the industry vigorously resisted the proposed rules, but has since embraced the opportunity to promote A-rated versions. These tyres can reduce fuel bills by up to 9 per cent, saving a typical passenger car around €200 a year. Across the EU, by 2020 this measure is expected to reduce carbon dioxide emissions equivalent to removing 500,000 to 1.3 million cars from roads.[6]

In both examples, it took a government standard and a labelling regulation to unleash innovation and spur action even among supposedly rational buyers who should have upgraded long ago based on the economics alone.

And yet from the earlier examples, it is also clear that governments and politicians rarely take action without considerable pressure. To make progress, the health damage must first be convincingly proved, and long-term costs and benefits demonstrated. Those with vested economic interests in the status quo must be attacked and embarrassed. Technological alternatives must be devised – and shown to be workable. The public and the media have to be mobilised. Then governments have the 'space' (politics being the art of the possible) to use regulatory and fiscal measures to encourage a transition; they can set standards, usually escalating; and ultimately they can impose restrictions to capture externalities and overcome market failure.

The economics of the natural environment

However, this approach relies on a good understanding of the cost on externalities. Where the environmental damage is long term or hard to attribute to an individual, devising an effective regulatory intervention becomes difficult. Thankfully our understanding of the extent of economic dependence on (and increasing damage done to) natural ecosystems is growing. This is now exposing a gap between what is needed for planetary survival and the accepted limits of the current system of environmental protection and regulation.

A simple example illustrates this. The recent decline of the UK's bee population is revealing that much of British agriculture is fundamentally dependent on natural pollination by bees. If farmers had to pay for this to be done artificially, the annual cost would be in the order of £1.8 billion, dramatically pushing up food prices and lowering the standard of living for many.[7] Yet there is no consensus on whether to charge the food industry for the costs of protective measures.

The full extent of the UK economy's dependence on the natural environment was assessed in 2011 by a major study of the national ecosystem. Its central conclusion was that we depend on ecosystems and the services they deliver to underpin our very existence, to produce our food and regulate water supplies and climate. Yet we consistently undervalue them in conventional economic analyses and decision-making.[8]

Increasingly studies such as the 2006 Stern Review, *The Economics of Climate Change*, are estimating the long-term cost of failing to take action on climate change. The true value of natural ecosystems such as tropical rainforests is becoming better understood although not yet captured in conventional accounting. For example, halving the rate of deforestation by 2030 would reduce global greenhouse gas emissions and avoid damages from climate change estimated at more than US$3.7 trillion in net present value terms.[9] Yet forests continue to be cut down for little more than the current cost of clearance.

Estimates by Trucost show that global environmental external costs caused by human activity – principally related to greenhouse gas emissions, over-use of water, pollution and unsustainable natural resource use – amounted to an estimated US$6.6 trillion in 2008. To put that in context, the top 3,000 public companies cause over US$2.15 trillion of the damage, equivalent to half of their conventionally reported company earnings.[10]

The politics of regulation

If economic analysis and environmental science are now coming into better alignment, will politicians accept the urgent and serious consequences for human health and quality of life of failing to act? Can we overcome entrenched ideological reluctance to intervene, not least among those in the Liberal Democrats who align themselves to 'small state' thinking?

Actually, a look back at recent history shows that all parties have proved remarkably inconsistent in their approach. Even at the high water mark of socialist intervention, Harold Wilson greeted his appointment in 1947 as President of the Board of Trade with the promise of a 'bonfire of controls'. The last Labour government – which created 4,300 new criminal offences in its thirteen years – nonetheless promoted 'light touch' regulation of the financial services sector, with results now widely seen as disastrous. It also persistently delayed implementation of EU directives on air quality.

The Liberal Democrats – heirs to the legacy of social liberals like Lloyd George and William Beveridge – fought the last election on a platform to 'reduce the burden of unnecessary red tape', promising to 'properly assess the cost and effectiveness of regulations before and after they are introduced, using "sunset clauses" to ensure the need for regulation is regularly reviewed, and working towards the principle of "one in, one out" for new rules'.[11]

Deregulation provided common ground with the Conservatives and the subsequent coalition agreement contained pledges to 'cut red tape' and to 'end the culture of tick-box regulation', with three separate commitments to reduce the number of quangos. The agreement's foreword even closed with a rallying cry to deliver 'a stronger society, a smaller state, and power and responsibility in the hands of every citizen'.[12]

A 'Red Tape Challenge' unit in the Cabinet Office now leads a cross-government effort to 'get rid of unnecessary red tape – freeing up business and society from the burden of excessive regulation'.[13] The desire to find alternatives to regulation is exemplified in the Department of Health's approach to the public health crisis caused by excessive eating, consumption of alcohol and lack of physical exercise. Businesses are invited to sign up to a Public Health Responsibility Deal and 'commit to taking action voluntarily to improve public health through their responsibilities as employers, as well as through their commercial actions and their community activities'.[14]

Yet consistent antipathy to regulation is not a hallmark of Conservatives either. Lord Heseltine, who promised a 'bonfire of red tape' in the early 1990s, today leads calls for an interventionist industrial strategy. In the nineteenth century it was Conservative antecedents who more often than not introduced the early factory legislation and extended municipal powers to protect public health.

Sadly, despite the political pendulum of attitudes to the so-called 'red tape' burden, surprisingly little work has been done to assess what sorts of regulatory interventions are most effective. A recent academic review for the Environment Agency found relatively little evidence of rigorous assessments of outcomes from different interventions. The report concluded that: 'even fewer studies have examined relative cost-effectiveness, a vital assessment if cost-effective choices are to be made.'[15]

Recommendations for liberals in government

What, then, are the priorities for Liberal Democrats in an incoming government? And what is the right approach to regulation? They group into three categories.

From regulation to standard-setting

This new approach to regulation should move away from seeking to regulate by imposing rules on processes and limiting actions towards setting standards with clear end goals and helping players achieve them through innovation with minimum coercion.

The growing potential of social media can be harnessed to empower ordinary citizens in monitoring performance. Far from requiring armies of inspectors, service breakdowns are now instantly pilloried on Twitter and similar platforms. Companies that offer dodgy deals have nowhere to hide. Regulators can do much more to monitor this and seek direct feedback from consumers.

The examples of effective interventions cited above offer clear pointers to how a new approach to standard-setting for the environment should work, based on assessments of health outcomes. The elements of the new approach are:

- A strong legal framework – so that freeloaders cannot undercut those adopting the right approach.
- Clear and simple goals – so that participants are focused on achieving objectives, not complying with 'small print' rules.
- Open and regular reporting of results, as close to real-time as possible, with direct consumer and citizen feedback using smartphone apps.
- Unambiguous enforcement – unlike the 'responsibility deals' approach cited earlier.
- Inbuilt but infrequent reviews – stability and continuity is necessary if business is to invest in research and development and production and new markets are to develop.

In adopting this approach, regulatory agencies should be able to offer advice and guidance and – focused on results – be prepare to allow third parties such as trade associations or professional advisers to implement and monitor the 'rules' once outcomes are set.

Aligned with this new approach, a Liberal Democrat government should learn from the Netherlands, where our sister parties VVD and D66 established the Dutch Advisory Board on Administrative Burdens, Actal. This independent external advisory body advises government and Parliament on how to achieve its goals while minimising the hindrance of regulation.[16] The result is to limit regulatory burdens for firms and citizens in areas like health care, education, safety and welfare while still meeting society's expectations.

An Actal equivalent for the UK should have the overarching goal of sustainable development written into its mandate. All new standard-setting interventions should be subject to its independent scrutiny. It should seek advice from pioneering companies who have moved from always lobbying for deregulation to advocating smart regulation that will reward their innovation and investment.

This new body should also drive a 'bonfire of regulations' that hinder sensible environmental action. At present approval is needed from five bodies before community energy generation is connected to the grid, while onerous hazardous waste rules can prevent recycling. Furthermore, competition rules are stopping sensible cooperation between manufacturers to introduce new products with less packaging waste. Meanwhile EU rules require VAT to be charged on refurbishment while new build is zero-rated. The right approach is to aim for sustainability and set standards to help achieve it.

The immediate priority – energy efficiency

More efficient use of energy – in products, services, transport, housing and the wider built environment – has huge potential to save consumers money while reducing pollution, enhancing health, increasing energy security, helping combat climate change and spurring moves towards a more sustainable economy.

According to DECC estimates, EU ecodesign regulations, which require consumer products such as boilers, tumble driers and computers to use less energy, could save £26 billion over the next twenty years. That's equivalent to cutting £158 a year off the average household energy bill by 2020. However the Green Alliance has warned that administrative delays and lower than expected consumer take-up jeopardises this goal.[17]

A recent study by McKinsey for the Energy Efficiency Deployment Office confirms the huge potential for energy saving if standards are set and adopted. The potential to reduce electricity demand is as high as 36 per cent of likely demand in 2030 – approximately 146 TWh of generation capacity

– through a range of measures such as better thermal insulation and automated light-control systems in public buildings.[18]

McKinsey identified eleven obstacles that could slow down implementation of necessary measures. They predict that once the market for energy-efficient goods develops, the cost of initial investment will fall and payback periods reduce. However, mandatory standards remain important to overcome an instance of market failure – the problem of 'agency' in real estate where most commercial buildings and much housing is occupied by tenants, with space being rented from landlords themselves who lack the market incentives to invest.

Reductions in energy demand will improve health outcomes as harmful emissions are cut. It is estimated that premature deaths from air pollution in Europe cost between 1.5 per cent and 4 per cent of GDP. The European Commission has estimated that health benefits worth between €3.4 billion and €7.9 billion annually from 2020 would accrue if carbon reduction targets were increased from 20 per cent to 25 per cent, and that is without including ill-health factors such as working days lost and hospital admissions for people with respiratory or cardiac diseases.[19]

That is why achieving progressively higher eco-efficiency standards (in parallel with measures discussed elsewhere to increase the price of carbon) – and winning the political argument for the health benefits – is the single most important manifesto commitment the Liberal Democrats should make.

Longer term and systemic changes

There is potential too across other areas of government to overcome the 'silo effect' of separate decision-making – where DECC sets energy policy and Defra protects the environment, while DoH picks up the tab for continuing ill-health. This should focus on establishing three mindsets across government:

- The need for a long-term perspective: improvements to health and reductions in health inequalities take time, certainly longer than one budget round and usually longer than a single election cycle.
- The scope for co-benefits: improvements to the environment can have extensive health benefits, both from the removal of harm, such as from pollution, and the fostering of benefit, such as through walking and well-being.
- The potential for 'virtuous circles of improvement': better environmental health has powerful social spin-offs, by reducing inequalities, and economic gains too, by saving costs and boosting productivity; this is likely

to reduce future environmental damage and so reinforce positive health trends and economic gains, and so on.

To embed these three mindsets across government decision-making requires structural and organisational changes, in four areas.

First, all major government decisions should be subject to a prior (and published) assessment of the long-term environmental costs, measured as additional or reduced spending on health and social care. Already proposals for legislation are routinely subject to a public assessment of their financial implications, costs and benefit analysis, additional burden on public bodies, impact on human rights and the like. Making explicit the health and environmental costs will help make the right longer-term decisions. It will also reveal whether the public exchequer should remain liable for the costs, or if regulation and market pricing mechanisms (tax and subsidy incentives, fines and credits) should bring these externality costs into current business and household decision-making.

Second, this approach will also reveal where the 'polluter pays' principle should be extended, so that legal liability for the long-term environmental health damage done by products in their consumption, disposal and waste packaging is clear. Case study evidence from America shows that potential liability is a powerful driver of prudent and precautionary innovation.

The initial focus of an enhanced 'polluter pays' policy should be on chemicals and foodstuffs, where the risks are currently greatest. This extended liability approach will also create opportunities for the UK's financial services sector to become more 'socially useful' – by developing new insurance instruments to protect business with lower risk, greater cost certainty and incentives to innovate.

Third, work already being done by the coalition government to change and broaden how we view success in society should be extended. Already under consideration are alternatives to GDP to measure advances in the prosperity and well-being of the country as a whole – incorporating, for example, measures of environmental quality, natural resource depletion and social factors such as standards of health or literacy. This is consistent with moves internationally for a new set of worldwide sustainable development goals, to succeed the Millennium Development Goals in 2015. This offers a conceptual and practical framework to integrate current fragmented approaches to climate change, environmental protection, child health, food and nutrition.

Fourth, local government needs to be given new duties and powers to promote environmental health. The role of the new health and well-being boards should be broadened. Their current stated aim is to improve integrated working between local health care, social care, public health and other public service practitioners. They also have responsibility for leading locally on reducing health inequalities. Yet they were established with little reference to environmental aspects, despite social, economic and environmental factors being such powerful determinants of health.

A joined-up approach locally will not work without a big extension in 'total place budgeting' – where the various streams of Whitehall-controlled funding into an area are pooled under local authority coordination. The current cautious focus on problem families needs to be radically extended. If not, the new powers of general competency and duty to promote sustainable development will prove stillborn.

As a quid pro quo for this freedom and flexibility in delivery, central government should set exacting outcome goals and agree the measures of success based on the new GDP+ indicators, with requirements to report regularly and engage with citizens locally.

Conclusion

The Liberal Democrat manifesto for the 2010 election aligned the party firmly with the deregulation agenda, proposing a 'one in, one out' approach. Five years of coalition government will have accomplished the task of removing genuinely unnecessary 'red tape' that is inhibiting growth and freedom. For the next election, Liberal Democrats need to make the case that the environmental challenges are so severe, and the increased costs, both economic and in terms of human well-being, are so great from delaying action, that a new approach is needed.

They need to advocate an objective, health-based approach to environmental regulation that focuses on achieving high standards and uses social media to empower citizens.

An independent external advisory agency must scrutinise new initiatives to ensure these achieve their goals, with input from pioneering responsible businesses.

The priority for new government standards is in energy efficiency for products, services, transport, housing and the wider built environment.

All government spending decisions must be subject to prior assessment of their long-term environmental impacts, calculated in terms of increased or reduced spending on human health.

Legal liability on the 'polluter pays' principle should be extended.

Local government needs to be given greater duties, with commensurate powers to tackle environment and health in a joined-up way.

To make this happen, Liberal Democrats will need to move on from the deregulatory and 'small state' rhetoric in the coalition agreement and embrace effective regulation based on standards that meet the scale of the challenges facing us all.

The prize – environmental regulation as if people and their health really mattered – is not just right, it will also prove politically popular.

Notes

1   See http://acm.eionet.europa.eu/reports/ ETCACC_TP_2009_1_European_PM2.5_HIA

2   H. W. Mielke and S. Zahran, *The Urban Rise and Fall of Air Lead (Pb) and the Latent Surge and Retreat of Societal Violence* (Department of Pharmacology, Tulane School of Medicine, New Orleans, 2012).

3   WHO, *Preventing Disease Through Healthy Environments* (2006).

4   Richard Mitchell and Frank Popper, *The Lancet*, 7 November 2008.

5   See http://energy.gov/articles/ proof-pudding-how-refrigerator-standards-have-saved-consumers-billions

6   See http://ec.europa.eu/energy/efficiency/tyres/labelling_en.htm

7   Tom D. Breeze, Stuart P.M. Roberts, Simon G. Potts, *The Decline of England's Bees: Policy Review and Recommendations* (University of Reading, 2012).

8   Defra, *National Ecosystem Assessment: Understanding nature's value to society* (2011).

9   TEEB, *Mainstreaming the Economics of Nature: A synthesis of the approach, conclusions and recommendations of TEEB* (2010).

10 PRI and UNEP FI, *Universal Ownership: Why Environmental Externalities Matter to Institutional Investors* (2010).

11 *Liberal Democrat Manifesto 2010*, p. 25.

12 HM Government, *The Coalition: our programme for government* (2010), p. 9.

13 See http://www.redtapechallenge.cabinetoffice.gov.uk/home/index/

14 See http://responsibilitydeal.dh.gov.uk/

15 Environment Agency, *Effectiveness of Regulation: Literature Review and Analysis Report* (2011).

16 See http://www.actal.nl/english/about-actal/

17 Green Alliance, *Cutting Britain's Energy Bill: Making the Most of Product Efficiency Standards* (2012).

18 McKinsey, *Capturing the Full Electricity Efficiency Potential of the UK* (2012).

19 Health and Environment Alliance, *Acting Now for Better Health, A 30 per cent reduction target for EU climate policy* (2010).

Chapter 8

Green Taxes

Stephen Williams MP[1]

The fact that we must act to combat carbon emissions is now part of the political mainstream. But consensus is far from complete as to the tools we should use to squeeze out carbon use from the British economy. A long-term liberal solution could be to give everyone the same carbon budget, which could be adjusted over time. But so many social, technological and philosophical issues flow from this proposal that it is unlikely to be adopted soon enough to make a difference. So we must resort to traditional methods to drive individuals and businesses to change. That means new taxes and market incentives.

Successive governments have already imposed taxes, levies, duties, escalators of duties and a variety of mechanisms, obligations and schemes. Some of the very simplest have achieved their aims remarkably quickly. A tax difference of just a few pence per litre moved millions of car owners from 4 star to unleaded petrol. The Welsh Government's 5p per bag levy introduced in October 2011 reduced plastic bag use by 90 per cent in the first few months of operation. Other tax rises have aroused huge unpopularity. The decision of the Major government to raise VAT on domestic energy bills handed the Liberal Democrats one of their greatest by-election victories in 1993, as the residents of Christchurch saw a tax hike masquerading as a green policy. The Blair government eventually reduced the rate to 5 per cent, but put in place a labyrinth of charges and controls on industry that have driven up the price of electricity and gas.

Liberal Democrats in government are working hard to put in place the schemes and incentives to produce supply-side reform. Electricity generated from renewable sources and nuclear power will form a greater proportion of our energy mix. Investment in high-speed trains and rail electrification will offer an attractive alternative to motorway travel. But supply-side reforms will soon be futile if demand continues to grow. For consumers and producers to reduce their demand there will have to be a very clear price signal – delivered (unlike previous taxes and levies) in a transparent manner. Liberal Democrats in government could send this signal by making a carbon tax the main tax on energy, and road user pricing the main tax on car and lorry movements.

Transition to a low-carbon economy is necessary to ensure future economic and social sustainability: the world needs to reduce the amount of energy required and spur behavioural changes which change demand. The costs and risks associated with a low-carbon transition are likely to be outweighed by the costs and risks of staying with conventional energy. A low-carbon transformation will avoid many wider costs associated with climate change and its damage, and reduce the UK's dependence on volatile and finite fossil fuels. It is also a chance to open up economic opportunities for British companies to expand into the global low-carbon market for energy, products and services, providing new employment opportunities.

The introduction of a carbon tax and road user pricing should not lead to an overall increase in the tax burden, in particular on the poor. The primary purpose of both taxes is to shift behaviour, not raise revenue for the government. Some of the revenue raised could be recycled within the scheme. Poorer households would be protected against the rise in energy bills, through a mix of cashable credits or grants to reduce energy consumption. Low-income motorists in rural areas would find it cheaper to use their car while a city-centre commuter would experience a rise in the cost of driving if they decided not to switch to public transport.

Why a carbon tax?

A revenue-neutral carbon tax would cover all carbon emissions with a consistent and rising carbon price. It would offer a fair and efficient means for the UK to reduce its carbon emissions and drive the transition to a low-carbon economy. A carbon tax allows all consumers, workers and businesses to make decisions on their purchases and investments based not only on their needs but the carbon costs, knowing the environmental impact of their actions.

Taxing carbon emissions provides an appropriately liberal way in which to identify a collective problem, determine solutions and then allow individuals, communities and businesses to address the issue as it works best for them. This contrasts with a Conservative 'market alone knows best' or a Labour 'the government alone knows best' approach. Liberal Democrats believe in shifting taxes away from things that we want to encourage, such as earnings from work, on to those things that we want to discourage, such as pollution. A rise in 'green taxes' such as a carbon tax complements the £10,000 income-tax-free allowance being introduced by Liberal Democrats in government. As the primary purpose of the emissions levy is to reduce emissions, not to raise revenue for increased public spending, the roll-out of a carbon tax should be revenue-neutral, with all proceeds returning to individuals, households and businesses for them to spend and invest as they feel appropriate.

A single charge reflecting wider environmental costs would influence millions of transactions daily with clear price signals for all to respond to. The advantage of these signals is that they allow everyone to make rational decisions, about both their own and others' actions, which unconsciously integrate across the economy through the best aspects of market mechanisms. From individuals deciding on whether to make a car journey to companies looking to invest in multi-billion pound schemes, each will recognise a consistent and rising cost of the carbon emissions associated with their actions. Individuals and businesses will be presented clearly with the details, impacts and consequences of their actions and make their individual decisions accordingly. They will balance these costs by either reducing their actions, shifting to other options or moving spending from elsewhere. With rising tax rates over time, carbon emissions will become ever more costly, increasing the incentive to reduce or eliminate them through increasingly ingenious and widespread measures.

International examples of a carbon tax

The UK would not be the first country to introduce a carbon tax. Sweden has one of the most extensive systems, raising SKr 26 billion (£2.5 billion: 1.5 per cent of total government revenue, or £270 per head) a year.[2] Denmark's carbon tax also works alongside a more general energy consumption tax; revenues raised reduce taxes and social security charges on labour as well as fund environmental efficiency measures. The Netherlands introduced a carbon tax in 1990, which is now largely integrated with a wider energy tax. It pays for tax breaks for green investments, reduced social security contributions and lump-sum transfers to households. Since May 2010, the Republic of Ireland has had a €15 per CO_2e tonne carbon tax on fuels not covered by the EU Emissions Trading System (ETS), raising €330 million a year (£280 million, 1 per cent of total government revenues, or £63 per head).[3] Average household energy prices are expected to rise by €2–3 per week depending on the fuel mix used (e.g. natural gas prices have gone up 6 per cent, but coal prices by 11 per cent). Receipts are used for energy-efficiency support for low-income households, as well as general government revenue.

In Canada, British Columbia introduced a comprehensive carbon tax in 2008, raising C$737 million in 2010–11 (£460 million, 1.9 per cent of total government revenue or £100 per head).[4] The tax rate rose from C$10 per tonne in 2008 by C$5 a year to C$30 (£19) by 2012. Tax receipts are used to provide roughly equivalent tax reductions for individuals (including tax credits for poorer households) and businesses. The Australian federal government is in the process of introducing a carbon tax.

Implementing the carbon tax

The carbon tax would be collected at the point of combustion for electricity generation and large industrial users, based on fuel mix, and at point of processing and distribution for natural gas and other products which are consumed directly by households and small businesses. In this approach, the carbon tax would already be included on energy and products in both wholesale and retail markets. This upstream carbon tax reduces both the number of entities who need to administer the tax and provides much stronger protection against revenue leakage through evasion or fraud. As tax will already be included in every kilowatt-hour of energy distributed, it ensures that the tax is borne by all those who ultimately consume energy. Producers should report the levy amount (even if this is averaged across production) to the final customer in bills, as is done with VAT. This transparency is essential in order to drive change through the energy chain.

Energy production from renewables and nuclear fuels would not be liable for carbon tax directly, as these are carbon-neutral *at the point of generation*. However, carbon taxation would be embedded in the cost of materials and fuels used in components, construction and maintenance. In particular, the nuclear industry's processing, decommissioning and disposal of spent fuels would pay carbon tax on their consumption of other fuels and materials. In order to recoup any advantage gained by the nuclear industry on its existing plants, Liberal Democrats have proposed a windfall tax on the sector. The proceeds could be used for the same purpose as the carbon tax or, as it may be a one-off tax, for a specific project; another possibility would be to allocate windfall tax proceeds to the Green Investment Bank's capital fund, giving a direct link from the fiscal effect of the carbon tax through to the building of Britain's renewable energy sector.

The current plethora of taxes and levies – the Climate Change Levy (CCL), the Carbon Reduction Commitment (CRC), the Carbon Price Floor, the Renewables Obligation, the Energy Company Obligation – bear much more heavily on electricity than on gas. A comprehensive carbon tax on emissions would cover all sources more fairly, and would support a shift towards widespread electrification by levelling the cost base of different energy types.

Gas will continue to have an important industrial and power generation role (where it can be used at maximum efficiency) as a low-carbon alternative to renewables. However, gas's domestic role is expected to diminish in favour of electric heating and cooking appliances over the coming decades. And the coalition government's flagship Green Deal programme now offers house-holds a real opportunity to invest in energy conservation, reducing their need for gas and electricity for heating.

In place of this confusing array of taxes and levies, businesses would have a single system, with the EU Emissions Trading System (ETS) and the carbon tax. Equal treatment of consumption enables tax collection further upstream in the production process, significantly reducing complexity and costs.

There would not be any additional levy on transport fuels as their car-bon content is already – at current rates – sufficiently taxed. However, there should be a legal link between the carbon tax and fuel duty or any new road pricing system (see below) to ensure that the charge is at least equal to the carbon price on the fuels' carbon content. Aviation fuel, which is currently tax-exempt under international conventions, may have to be excluded, though it is of course covered by the EU ETS. Exceptions to the tax might also have to be made for agriculture, where significant reform of the subsidy regime is needed and the monitoring costs for the breadth of carbon emis-sions could be prohibitively expensive.[5]

All UK carbon emissions will be covered be the regime, but as a green tax shift, all revenues will be distributed back to individuals and businesses. This will encourage a cross-economy demand shift towards low-carbon goods and resources while avoiding net additional taxation on the economy, supporting the coalition agreement's commitment to raise environmental taxation's share of UK total taxes and existing Liberal Democrat policy.[6]

Relative price changes will encourage a general demand shift from more carbon-intensive to less carbon-intensive consumption, both within and across industries. These demand shifts would increase the economies of scale and efficiencies of low-carbon goods, enabling them to be provided both more cost-effectively and more widely.

While initially set low, the carbon tax rate would climb steadily and pre-dictably over time. This would bolster the incentive for long-term investment and change but also provide an appropriate technological and implementa-tion window for more challenging and costly adjustments to be addressed. As the costs associated with carbon emissions rise over time, these costs would be more appropriately allocated through market mechanisms to the highest value use – reducing total carbon emissions, promoting economic competitiveness, and enabling the UK to meet its binding emissions commitments while providing international leadership.

A consistent tax

The current UK emissions taxation system has varying impacts, creating a non-level playing field for individuals, communities and businesses for decisions on their activities and investments. The current levels of Climate Change Levy, for instance, do not equate to individual fuels' carbon content. A proper carbon tax should set the tax on a carbon-content basis.

Consistency and confidence requires realistic future expectations and integration with complementary programmes. Alongside current pricing policy, the government would set publicly a carbon price trajectory required to achieve UK carbon budgets. Future price expectations would be clearly signalled, so businesses and individuals had the time and incentive to put in place the investments and changes required to reduce their carbon intensity. The carbon price floor to be introduced this year sets a real-terms trajectory from £16 per tonne in 2013 to £30 per tonne in 2020 and £70 in 2030, providing a good basis upon which to build an economy-wide tax. While not possible to lock in completely future governments, the current government could pass primary legislation to fix the procedures and emissions targets and, as far as practical, use independent bodies, such as the Committee on Climate Change, to recommend future price changes and the medium-term trajectory.

The carbon tax would work with the existing structures. Some would be amalgamated into the proposed tax regime. CCL and CRC receipts would be merged and extended to cover a wider range of emissions producers. Their individual rates would be superseded by a general carbon price. No new Climate Change Agreements (which enable energy-intensive businesses to lower their CCL charges in return for meeting agreed energy efficiency targets) would be entered into, and existing ones would be run down. CRC reporting schemes would be continued and would be expected to merge into mainstream corporate reporting requirements in the low-carbon transition.

Other tax-raising schemes, primarily fuel duty and the EU ETS, would need to align with the emissions tax structures to ensure complementarity. Coordinating policies ensures the emissions tax operates an effective carbon floor price, but companies and individuals do not face double taxation. In some instances, this may require adjustments to the proposed approaches, and, in others, reasonable adjustments in existing UK and EU schemes. For fuel duty, there would be the lock-in of the legal pricing link of a carbon-content floor rate; this could become particularly important if a future move towards road-user charging leads to fuel duty reductions.

UK users of the EU ETS would offset their UK carbon tax assessments using EU ETS allowances at the prevailing price. Any additional tax due after offsetting all their allowances would need to be paid. Policies that support the transition to more renewable power generation – such as Renewables Obligation and Feed-in Tariffs – and those that support energy efficiency – such as the Green Deal and Energy Company Obligation – would continue as important supports to update the energy generation system and energy efficiency of the built environment.

Impacts

At a rate of £25 per CO_2 tonne (where the 2011 Budget set the carbon price floor in 2016, including inflation[7]), the carbon tax would raise £6 billion annually, split equally between business and domestic consumers.[8] This would be ten times the current level of total CCL receipts. Average household energy expenditure should rise by £2.40 a week – less than a pint of beer – representing an increase of just 0.5 per cent in average household spending. This could lead to a 5 per cent reduction in domestic energy use, equal to 6.5 million CO_2e tonnes (1 per cent of UK emissions).[9]

The overall net economic impact would be small (less than 1 per cent of GDP[10]) in the short term – much less costly than cleaning up the financial system – and reduce emissions by 2 per cent in the first year alone, with much steeper reductions expected as businesses and individuals react to the new regime.[11] Given the need to build a more sustainable economy eventually, this is more akin to bringing investment forward rather than permanently lost output. As a society, we would have our low-carbon investments in place and paid for as soon as is practical. The longer-term positive economic impacts would be potentially vast and transformational if they enable the UK to make a smooth and early transition to a low-carbon economy.

The tax would encourage individuals to learn to reduce their environmental impact. In the longer term, individuals may need to consider choices related to their residence, transport choices and careers. However, by promoting an early transition before fossil fuel prices rise too high, people will be able to adjust more gradually, minimising costs and adjustment impacts. Some adjustments may come quite quickly as changes and investments which are already technically feasible become increasingly economically viable.

Communities will see more clearly where they can act collectively to enable their residents to operate in a more carbon-efficient manner. This may require investment in activities (e.g. education), direct facilities (e.g. renewable energy generation) and wider infrastructure (e.g. greater energy efficiency in community buildings). They must also consider how they will provide support to those who require additional assistance to make the low-carbon transition.

Protection from rising carbon tax rates would be put in place for households already in or tipped into fuel poverty. Government must continue to support those groups who may be particularly hit by price changes, such as pensioners and families with children, through the existing benefits system and programmes such as the Warm Homes Discount. Some carbon tax revenues could be used to focus support on the neediest groups. At the carbon tax rates suggested above, approximately £900 million would be needed to offer a 100 per cent offset of the tax for the poorest tenth (decile) of households, plus a 67 per cent offset for the ninth decile and a 33 per cent offset for the eighth decile. Financial cushioning for energy price increases would be fed into Universal Credit, but schemes such as the Green Deal should also be used to target help more directly on a wider range of vulnerable individuals, helping them to reduce their energy costs for good. This dual-track approach is essential so that low-income households are both given immediate support in response to higher energy bills and also the ability to invest in changing their homes' longer-term energy efficiency levels.

Businesses will need to work through changes that enable them to operate and compete in a low-carbon world. For some, this will require developing their central processes and investments to reduce their carbon intensity. Others will need to address their facilities, transport needs and other support activities. Those businesses not able to adjust will need to consider whether they will be able to pass costs on to their customers as part of relative price (and demand) changes.

When, in 2011, the carbon floor price was announced by the Chancellor, the subsequent debates on the Budget featured several MPs highlighting the cost to energy-intensive industries in their constituencies: steel works, chemicals and potteries were among those identified as needing transitional relief. It is certainly true that there is no point in the UK having an ambitious green taxation regime if one of the consequences is an offshoring of British firms and jobs to more lax regimes. The long-term goal must be an international agreement to ensure a common contribution from all carbon emitters, but in the mean time, limited and specific protection and support should continue to be implemented. This should include assistance to make adjustments in industrial process to reduce emissions and energy use, and also additional allowances and reliefs where companies are working towards reducing their carbon intensity but face significant competition from companies (for example in other countries) which are not bound by similar carbon prices and regulations. The UK government and industry need to agree clear goals as to what the final objectives for these industries should be and the expected timetable to accomplish them.

Moving from fuel duty to road user pricing

The coalition government has been resolute in setting out a carbon floor price. It has also acted decisively, and not without controversy, in limiting the costs of various clean energy incentives. It has legislated for the Green Deal, which should over time enable the retro-fitting of millions of homes with energy-reducing measures. But in the area of cars and road fuel tax the government has failed to give a lead, instead bowing to populist pressure from the tabloids and nervous backbenchers to hold down the cost of road fuel duty. The Chancellor has scrapped the previous government's fuel duty escalator, and deferred or cancelled each of the rises in fuel duty that had been planned since May 2010.

Road fuel duty is a major source of revenue for the Treasury. The Office for Budgetary Responsibility has estimated the 2012–13 yield to be £26 billion, making the duty the joint fifth largest source of revenue, roughly the same as Council Tax. It is fairly clear that in my lifetime the underlying price of petrol and diesel is going to follow an upward trajectory. A sustained attempt by any government to shield people from this inexorable rise by tweaking the duty will ultimately be fruitless. Efforts so far have been enormously expensive: the cancellation of the January 2013 rise cost £890 million in 2012–13 and will cost over £1.6 billion in a full year. Arguably such sums would have been better spent on reaching the Liberal Democrat goal of a £10,000 tax-free allowance sooner than intended in this Parliament, or softening the impact of various benefit changes.

Road fuel duty has effectively ceased to be a green tax, as the underlying price of petrol itself becomes more of an incentive for people to change behaviour. But for as long as it remains it will be a fairly blunt instrument, neither effective at a macro nor a micro level; it is unlikely to hold back or reduce the overall level of road usage. As a uniform national tax it is an indiscriminate cost to the motorist. There can be no distinction between either time or location of travel. The tax paid for a journey into central Bristol at 8.30am is no different for a journey into Brecon or Brechin at the same time. Fuel duty hits a Bristol commuter as much as a Mid Wales farmer or a rural

Scottish pensioner. It is a regressive tax, especially in rural areas where use of the car is often an essential means of travelling. It would clearly be impractical to have different rates of duty in various parts of the country. Fuel duty is an inflexible fiscal tool that ought to be replaced by a tax that is more responsive to geographical, economic and social factors.

Road user pricing is the most obvious alternative to road fuel duty. Road user pricing could be levied at different rates in cities and sparsely populated areas, to encourage a switch to public transport in urban Britain but recognising the lack of such alternatives in some parts of the country. It could also be set at different rates at certain points of the day in order to reduce congestion at peak times.

A move to road user pricing would clearly require significant capital investment by government in equipment to identify car movements. Satellite-based tracking is already familiar to everyone through the rapid take-up of 'sat-navs'. It would hardly be a major technological leap for a similar tracking system to be linked to a payment regime. The major barrier to road user pricing now is political will.

Road user pricing could also replace vehicle excise duty (VED). The current annual yield from car tax discs is approximately £5.9 billion. VED is more flexible than fuel duty, as it varies according to the fuel efficiency (and propensity to pollute) of a car's engine. It would surely be easy to abolish this tax too and incorporate it into road user pricing.

Conclusion

Humanity needs to rapidly and substantially reduce its global climate change emissions. The UK could choose to take a key leadership and exemplar role. Both a carbon tax and road user pricing would give fiscal clarity to individuals and businesses about the cost of deciding not to change their behaviour. An impact on household budgets and business expenditure is much more likely to drive change than exhortations from government and campaign groups.

The costs of an early low-carbon transition are likely to be significantly lower than a forced later switch, with continued reliance on fossil fuels. As the Green Fiscal Commission reported, it is the exposure to expensive and volatile fossil fuel prices that leads to the greatest economic cost in the low-carbon transition.[12] Earlier and planned transition not only reduces costs and risks but also enables UK firms and workers to seize emerging opportunities in global low-carbon generation and product markets.

There is a future to be won where Britain decarbonises its energy production and enjoys another industrial revolution, turning sustainable production into an economic winner. Homes will be more energy-efficient and people will drive their cars with more thought for the consequences. Regulation, publicity campaigns, peer pressure from friends and neighbours will all help to change behaviour. But much clearer and predictable green taxes are an essential step to a more sustainable future.

Notes

1   The author is grateful to Charles Tarvin for his research support during his secondment from PWC to the Liberal Democrat Policy Unit, and to his Parliamentary Researcher, Lara Greer.

2   Swedish Tax Agency, *Taxes in Sweden* (2010).

3   Republic of Ireland Ministry of Finance, *Budget 2010* (2010).

4   British Columbia Ministry of Finance 'What is a Carbon Tax?', www.fin.gov.bc.ca

5   Natural carbon emissions from agriculture, forestry and fisheries (such as from digestion and decomposition) should not be included in the tax regime due to the difficulties and costs of measuring and monitoring. However, agricultural, forestry and fishing producers would pay tax on the carbon emissions associated with the fuels, goods and services that they use in the activities – though they should continue to be able to use 'red diesel', which has a reduced fuel duty price but still prices the carbon content.

6   As set out in the September 2010 conference motion on green taxation.

7   Based on a £22 per CO_2 tonne price floor in 2009 prices (as per the Treasury and HMRC response on the carbon price floor consultation) and a 2 per cent annual inflation rate to 2016.

8   Liberal Democrat Policy Unit analysis, based on DECC and ONS data; the calculations incorporate first-round short-term demand changes and revenue recycling.

9   Liberal Democrat analysis based on demand changes.

10 Green Fiscal Commission and Committee on Climate Change.

11 Committee on Climate Change, *The Fourth Carbon Budget: Reducing emissions through the 2020s* (December 2010).

12 Green Fiscal Commission, *The Case for Green Fiscal Reform* (2009).

Chapter 9

Can Behaviour Change Make a Difference?

Paul Burall

Technology almost certainly provides the most direct route to reducing our use of energy and other resources. However, human behaviour can also be a significant factor, not least in making sure that technology is used in ways that achieve the best results.

But changing behaviour presents problems. For a start, for liberals, there is always a disinclination to force individuals to change their ways unless there is a substantial public benefit. Thus it is acceptable to ban smoking in public places to protect non-smokers, but there is considerable reluctance to apply such a ban to the home. Even more of a challenge is simply the sheer difficulty of achieving behavioural change: years of dire warnings of the harm caused by poor diet, illegal drugs and excess alcohol have made very little difference to the way people behave.

The coalition government recognised the challenge when, soon after being elected, it set up the Behavioural Insights Team – popularly known as the 'Nudge Unit' – with a remit to 'find innovative ways of encouraging, enabling and supporting people to make better choices for themselves'.[1] A year later, the House of Lords Science and Technology Sub-Committee's report on behaviour change welcomed the government's desire to take the science behind behaviour change seriously because: 'Societal problems, like the need to reduce obesity and reduce carbon emissions, aren't going away – and are even getting worse'.[2] But the report warned that the task was not easy and that using 'nudges' or any other single intervention in isolation was unlikely to work.

So what works and what doesn't?

In 2010, the American Psychological Association published a report bringing together research and practice that casts light on how behaviour can be changed. *The Interface Between Psychology and Global Climate Change* concluded that, despite warnings from scientists and environmental experts that limiting the effects of climate change means humans need to make some severe changes now, most people do not feel a sense of urgency.[3] The report cites numerous psychological barriers to explain this, including:

- *Mistrust*: most people don't believe the risk messages of scientists or government officials;
- *Uncertainty*: uncertainty over climate change reduces the frequency of 'green' behaviour;
- *Denial*: a substantial minority of people believe climate change is not occurring or that human activity has little or nothing to do with it;
- *Lack of control*: people believe that their own actions would be too small to make a difference, so choose to do nothing;
- *Habit*: ingrained behaviours are extremely resistant to permanent change; habit is the most important obstacle to pro-environment behaviour.

Taking this last point first, Professor Bas Verplanken, from the University of Bath, has suggested that there are key moments in life when it is much easier for people to change their habits – moments such as moving house, starting university, switching jobs, retiring from work, or becoming pregnant. At a seminar in Melbourne, Australia, in 2012 he analysed the effect of moving house on the choices people make about transport, and found that eco-conscious people who had moved recently commuted by car less often than like-minded people who had stayed put. And they did it without any outside prompting:

> Many of our everyday behaviours are habits that are undertaken without much thought or deliberation. But when the previously stable contexts of these behaviours change, our habits become vulnerable. The timing of a behaviour change intervention can therefore be just as important as its content. We have a greater chance of both breaking and developing habits at certain moments of change, so it's an ideal opportunity to try to encourage new water-saving, energy-saving and waste-reduction behaviours.[4]

So intervention at these life change points may be among the most fruitful actions that a government can take. Examples might include:

- *Retirement*: worries about the loss of income following retirement makes people more likely to respond to offers to cut expenditure on items such as energy, travel and food. So help with home insulation and PV installations, information about local public transport, and invitations to take on an allotment should all be focused on the period leading up to retirement.
- *Changing jobs*: offering personal travel planning advice to people when they start a new job may persuade them to adopt greener modes of transport before their habits become ingrained.

- *Moving house*: providing clear information about the annual energy running costs of houses on the market to influence purchasing decisions and
  targeting buyers to include energy-cost-cutting measures as part of the
  home improvements that often follow.

This last point illustrates a generic issue in persuading both individuals
and businesses to invest in energy-efficient buildings, appliances and other
equipment, as most decisions are based on the initial capital cost rather
than the lifetime cost of ownership. Some years ago, the British Airports
Authority looked at how it was specifying passenger lifts at Gatwick and
discovered, to its surprise, that the lifetime energy costs were many times
the initial purchase price; choosing a more energy-efficient lift that was not
the cheapest to buy could result in considerable lifetime savings. The same is
often true of buildings and appliances, and a new regulation to ensure that,
where appropriate, lifetime cost information is provided at the time of purchase could have significant benefits.

As for people's mistrust in many information sources, this can be overcome by ensuring that messages appeal to the specific audience at which
they are aimed. In 2009 the Joseph Rowntree Foundation published a useful report describing effective behavioural change case studies illustrating
how understanding what motivates the target audience is a key to success.[5]
One described a successful campaign in Florida which aimed to persuade
young people not to smoke. Research had shown that young people knew
the health risks but carried on regardless, partly because this meant going
against habits prescribed by adults: they used smoking to indicate rebellion
and 'coolness'. So the campaign aimed to convince young people that smoking, far from being a sign of rebellion, was conforming to what the tobacco
industry wanted. It exposed facts about the manipulative power of the industry – such as its expenditure of US$10 billion annually on advertising – and
used posters displaying fat businessmen dressed in bikinis, with the slogan:
'No wonder tobacco executives hide behind sexy models'.

Another successful campaign described in the JRF report promoted green
travel in Seattle. The city's InMotion campaign was based on research showing that residents were unimpressed by traditional messages about the cost
and congestion of private travel, but did care about improving their health
through increased cycling and walking. So 'improving our community
through healthier travel choices' was one of the key messages. Combined
with providing localised information about alternative transport modes and
other activities, the campaign resulted in a notable switch from cars to public
transport.

The source of information can also be a key to effectiveness. One fact that politicians and governments need to accept is that any exhortations from them are at best likely to be ineffective and at worst counter-productive, as this source is viewed with suspicion by much of the public. Using peer pressure is likely to be far more effective.

A study published by the Transport Research Laboratory in 2012, using both focus groups and an online survey, found respondents saying that they were more likely to be influenced by information that they received via personal networks (such as friends and family) than via formal networks (such as from the government, a commercial organisation or independent body or charity).[6] The study concluded that this made social networking sites a potentially valuable tool in getting messages across.

Social pressures can work in another way, as was shown by research at California State University which found that people cut their electricity usage if told that their neighbours used less than they did. In one trial, householders were told what the average electricity usage was in their area; those using more than the average cut their use. However, low users increased theirs, a problem that disappeared when the message to the low users carried a smiley face to encourage them to continue their good practice. In another experiment, the researchers provided information asking residents to take certain actions to save electricity. Some messages simply stressed energy conservation; some talked about protecting future generations; and others stressed financial savings. But it was the leaflets that asked residents to join their neighbours in saving energy that were the most effective.

Research also shows that political attitudes can affect how people react. A study into the energy use of more than 80,000 Californian households by the University of California showed liberal-leaning people cut their electricity use most in response to information about their neighbours' consumption while those declaring themselves as Republicans reduced their consumption by less than a quarter of the average; and Republicans who said they had no interest in environmental causes reacted by increasing their consumption.[7] However, evidence suggests that such prejudices can be overcome if the message comes from someone recognised to have the same political leanings as the target audience: so in the US Republicans are hardly likely to take notice of Democrats or those they perceive to be liberal but may listen to someone from their own party.

Research has also shown that scientific evidence is unlikely to convince sceptics of the reality of climate change. But research at the University of Queensland has found that informing climate change sceptics of the 'co-benefits' of action to reduce climate change encourages them to adopt green activities, whereas telling them that climate change may lead to millions of deaths has little effect.[8] Sceptics persuaded that action on climate change would make people more considerate or would promote technological development were more likely to express pro-environmental intentions than those told about the risks of climate inaction.

Of course, persuading people that green actions are desirable does not mean that they will change their behaviour: there is considerable evidence that there is no direct link between people's professed values and their actions. For example, in one study, all the forty participants who attended energy efficiency workshops claimed they now knew and cared more about energy conservation; but only one actually changed their behaviour. Another study found that 94 per cent of those questioned believed that individuals had a responsibility to pick up litter – but only 2 per cent picked up litter that was 'planted' by the researcher.

Achieving greater buy-in is one of the benefits of using social pressures, and this can be boosted by associating the message with an individual whom the audience respects. The state of Texas reduced visible roadside litter by 72 per cent using an ad campaign targeting macho men in pickup trucks who were unresponsive to a simple 'Please don't litter' message. Instead, the campaign used Texan celebrities such as stars from the TV cowboy series *Dallas* who were featured crushing littered beer cans with their fists and declaring 'Don't mess with Texas'.

Peer pressure can also enhance the effectiveness of such simple green messages as the ubiquitous plea for towels in hotels to be used for more than one day. Social psychologist Robert Cialdini found that the straight message resulted in an average of 40 per cent of hotel guests reusing their towels at least once during a stay, but that changing the message to say that the majority of people who stayed in the hotel reused their towels led to an increase to 66 per cent. Making the message even more specific by tying the majority reuse message to the individual room raised the average to 73 per cent.

The power of majority opinion to influence has been highlighted in research by Dr Chris Jones of the Department of Psychology at the University of Sheffield, who has pointed out that psychological theory shows that groups can exert power over the beliefs and attitudes of individuals if they are perceived to be in the majority, even if they are not.[9] In the context of wind turbines, Jones suggested that opponents tend to be more highly motivated and may therefore have a disproportionate influence on planning decisions even when the majority of local people support the proposal. He argued that the impression that opponents are in the majority can be reinforced by the news media: 'Conflict sells, and with the increasing perception of wind development as controversial per se, newspapers in communities earmarked for wind development have, in effect, a licence to print money.' Jones suggests that there is a need for a fundamental restructuring of wind-development strategy and that developers need to move from their current autocratic approach towards engaging the public. Communities need to be involved from the start in order to give confidence to local people who support such developments.

Governments have traditionally used financial incentives to encourage behavioural change but research suggests that these work notably better if combined with other means. For example, research into campaigns aimed at persuading people to improve the insulation of their homes has shown that using social marketing techniques and supporting the incentive with a quality insurance guarantee adds notably to their effectiveness.

People also respond better to incentives if the benefits are fairly immediate. So majoring on the benefits of restricting global warming that will not be felt for decades is not especially appealing. Research at Columbia University found that people react to decisions involving future environmental gains and losses in exactly the same way as they do when making financial decisions.[10] So schemes that give people an upfront cash payment for insulating their home work better than those promising long-term savings, even if the people receiving the cash end up paying a little more in the long run. The research also found that people are more worried about future losses than they are persuaded by future gains, so a warning that they would lose US$500 if they didn't follow a particular course of action was more effective than being told that they would be US$500 better off if they did take action.

But using financial incentives carries a risk. Research published in 2010 by the University of California found that, if altruistic motives for green actions were replaced by incentives, the original motivations could be undermined if the incentives could not be maintained for a long time.[11]

Even when behavioural change is achieved, the change may not last. A 2006 Defra-funded study found that, as a rule of thumb, a new type of behaviour formed over a three-month period or longer was likely to persist, but continued feedback was needed to help maintain the change and, in time, encourage other changes.[12] This was especially important for the use of technologies such as smart meters, as experience suggested that, without additional support such as information about their neighbour's energy use, the resulting new habits only lasted for a few weeks, after which people reverted to their old ways.

There is also considerable evidence that a comprehensive programme of different actions is far more likely to achieve long-lasting behavioural change than individual initiatives. An excellent example of this was the Sustainable Travel Towns initiative funded by the Department for Transport over a five-year period to 2009. This was aimed at assessing the effectiveness of an intensive programme in three towns, Peterborough, Darlington and Worcester. The programme comprised workplace and school travel plans; awareness programmes, such as personalised travel planning and public transport information; and the introduction of car clubs. The result was a reduction of 9 per cent in car trips under 50 km over the five years, with an estimated cost/benefit ratio of at least 4.5 from reduced congestion.

This success pales into insignificance when compared with the switch from private to public transport achieved in the German city of Freiburg where, between 1982 and 2007, cycle trips almost doubled to 27 per cent of all trips and the share of trips by public transport rose from 11 per cent to 18 per cent at a time when car use elsewhere was soaring. Among the factors accounting for this were a reduction in the cost of travelcards, and the addition of features such as transferability to friends and family and across public transport networks; increased route coverage and frequency of public transport services; and disincentives to car use in the form of extensive pedestrianisation, high parking charges, and traffic-calming measures.

Technology is providing ever better ways for people to save resources and energy. But these savings often rely on the user operating the technology in the optimum way, which means making systems easy to understand and control. Some years ago, Honeywell carried out a survey that showed that more than two-thirds of home-owners failed to benefit from the energy-saving potential of programmable central heating controllers because they found them too difficult to operate. The engineers who had designed the programmers had concentrated on finding the best technology to control the system; users, on the other hand, were not interested in engineering quality but simply wanted something that was easy to use.

Since then, the technology to control home energy use has become ever more complex. My house has two heating programmers, nine separately programmable thermostats and a programmable air change unit; the thermostats alone take ten minutes each to set up even after the instructions have been deciphered. So it is perhaps not surprising that at least one of my neighbours simply gave up and left everything on the whole time, opening windows when the house got too hot.

With complex technology extending rapidly and already including remote control of heating and appliances via either the Internet or mobile phone, as well as various switching devices to save standby energy, there is an urgent need for a standard to be established for ease of use to guide installers and consumers to systems that ordinary people can operate simply. House-builders should also be encouraged to provide a home instruction book with every new property to provide simple operating instructions for the installed appliances and systems; this would not duplicate the manufacturers' instruction manuals but merely pull out the essential information needed for setup and day-to-day operation.

Recycling is one of the most generally accepted routes to improving sustainability. However, once again, persuading people to recycle is inhibited by over-complex systems, in this case by local authorities having very different rules about what can be recycled and what cannot. Councils cannot even agree on standard colours for the bins for different materials, puzzling visitors and people moving from a different area. And some local authorities provide such a variety of bins that their residents can only be confused about what they are meant to put where; one recent survey found some twenty local authorities providing seven or more different containers into which householders were supposed to separate their rubbish; one, Newcastle-Under-Lyme, offered a choice of nine.

But perhaps the biggest obstacle to make people's behaviour more sustainable is advertising. While no liberal would argue that companies and organisations should be banned from advertising, there are two major areas of concern.

The first is where advertising leads directly to harm to the individual consumer. The House of Lords Science and Technology Sub-Committee report on behaviour change mentioned at the beginning of this chapter looked specifically at the way in which the marketing of food fails to guide consumers towards a healthy diet, and called for the government to take more action. The committee chair pointed out that: 'Businesses try to influence our behaviour all the time – supermarkets influence us though the location of, and promotions for, certain foods and all businesses use advertising and marketing to change our behaviour'.[13]

The second area for concern is simply the sheer weight of advertising that is primarily geared to persuading people to change their behaviour to buy more stuff, drive more miles in more expensive cars, or fly more often to long-distance destinations. In 2011, the British public was exposed to £16.1 billion of advertising spend. Maybe it is time to consider taking a tiny proportion of that to present counter-messages to try and persuade people to reconsider what is important in their life, which may not be what some advertising is telling them. A levy on advertising is nothing new: the industry already contributes 0.1 per cent of its turnover to fund the Advertising Standards Authority. It does not seem unreasonable to suggest taking at least another 0.1 per cent to fund sustainability messages to try to persuade consumers to question advertising claims; £16 million may not go far but it would be a start. As the President of Independent Practitioners in Advertising recently pointed out, 'Some brands engender trust in a way that governments often do not'. So a visibly independent organisation – perhaps comprising representatives of green groups, behavioural scientists, consumer watchdogs and so on – could be responsible for such campaigns.

What kind of messages might such a fund promote? For a start, it could point out that some products are grossly over-hyped. For example, the Dettol 'No Touch Hand Wash System' which dispenses soap without touching it is an extreme example of a fetish approach to home cleanliness that may actually damage health, as exposure to some dirt has been shown to be beneficial in building up resistance to germs. *Private Eye*'s verdict on the iPhone 5 as only being different from the iPhone 4 because 'It's more expensive' provides an exemplar message to begin to tackle the waste of consumerism driven purely by keeping up with the Joneses, reminding people that research suggests that this kind of consumerism is self-defeating as the latest gadget rapidly becomes a disappointment when it is overtaken by yet another new model.

Of course, tackling consumerism begins to question the whole basis for economic growth. Yet, perhaps surprisingly, the coalition government has actually suggested that the traditional measure of economic growth, GDP, is not the best measure of success. Early in its life, the coalition instructed the Office for National Statistics to develop a measure for well-being, David Cameron suggesting that this would measure 'Our progress as a country, not just by how our economy is growing, but by how our lives are improving; not just by our standard of living, but by our quality of life'.[14] The new measure is based on individual well-being; health; jobs and leisure etc.; personal finance; education and skills; the economy; governance; and the natural environment. The 2012 results, published at the end of 2012, showed an average 'life satisfaction' rating of 7.4 out of 10. The *Measuring National Well-being* report showed, to the surprise of many, that people were just as happy in 2012 as they had been before the recession, despite a significant reduction in average incomes.[15] Economist and chief economics commentator for *The Independent*, Hamish McRae, concluded that: 'Time spent finding ways of increasing people's well-being is a lot better spent than time calculating GDP'.[16]

This 'happiness index', as it has predictably been named, has the potential, at the very least, to send the message that behaviour based entirely on seeking financial reward is not the best way to achieve satisfaction. There is already plenty of evidence that, beyond a certain fairly modest level, increases in individual income do not bring increased happiness and that life satisfaction does not rely on consuming ever more goods and services. However, this message has clearly not got through to many politicians or to the media who, every three months, treat the publication of the quarterly GDP figures as the prime measure of the government's success or failure. One change that could help to alter this perception would be for the well-being index to be published alongside the quarterly GDP figures and for the government to give both measures the same prominence.

Of course, this would only provide background noise for programmes aiming to persuading people to act more sustainably. But it would be a start.

Changing people's behaviour is an important component in moving towards a more sustainable future. But behavioural change is not easy and policies must be based on the evidence of what works and what doesn't. And perhaps even more crucially, politicians and governments need to recognise the limitations of trying to change people's behaviour; there are real constraints on how much difference policies aimed at changing behaviour can make. Persuading people to change their behaviour is, in general, only likely to succeed when it goes with the grain of the lifestyles and beliefs of individuals and their peers.

Where change is really important to sustainability, regulation, standards, and use of technology that minimise human intervention are likely to be far more effective than trying to persuade millions of humans to change their behaviour individually. Thus upgrading the energy efficiency standards of products and homes is far more certain to deliver climate change benefits than labelling or providing information in other ways. Smart meters that provide information about the energy use of individual appliances in the home may persuade a few green enthusiasts to change their ways but are unlikely to have any lasting effect on the great majority of people; but using this technology to automatically control appliances, heating and lighting is guaranteed to deliver real benefits.

Regulation and standards can be unpopular, which is why politicians tend to prefer behavioural change options. But a 2011 report published by the Joseph Rowntree Foundation demonstrates how even potentially unpopular regulatory actions can win support.[17] Research for the report was carried out by the Fabian Society through a series of focus groups; one of its key conclusions is the importance of understanding the difference between people liking a policy and supporting it because they see it as legitimate. The report concludes that people will support policies aimed at sustainable consumption if they understand the issues and believe that the policies are fair – a key finding that will chime with Liberal Democrats. Addressing people as consumers and appealing to their self interest – the usual tactic used by government – may not be the most effective approach.

Four key points are highlighted in the report to persuade people that a policy is fair:

- Ensuring that everyone cooperates, which may make regulation and enforcement crucial.
- Where compulsion is used, measures to target a product or activity rather than the individual are preferred.
- Sustainability policies should be progressive: the greatest burdens of behaviour change should be on those with the greatest ability to reduce their consumption.
- 'Economic' approaches, and specifically taxation, are often seen to fail the fairness test.

Behavioural change is just one of the tools needed to achieve sustainability and in many circumstances it may not be the most effective. So it is crucial that behavioural change is not seen as a soft option to avoid taking hard decisions and is only used where there is real evidence that it can deliver the necessary change.

Notes

1   See http://www.cabinetoffice.gov.uk/behavioural-insights-team
2   House of Lords Science and Technology Committee, *Behaviour Change* (July 2011).
3   American Psychological Association, *Psychology and Global Climate Change* (2010).
4   See http://www.monash.edu.au/news/show/
    understanding-habits-key-to-sustainable-behaviour

5   Joseph Rowntree Foundation, *Tackling Alcohol Harm: Lessons from Other Fields* (2009).

6   TRL, *The Role of Social Networking sites in Changing Travel Behaviours* (2012).

7   Dora L. Costa and Matthew E. Kahn, *Energy Conservation 'Nudges' and Environmentalist Ideology* (working paper published by the National Bureau of Economic Research, 2010).

8   Paul Bain, 'Promoting pro-environmental action in climate change deniers', Nature.com, June 2010.

9   Christopher R. Jones and J. Richard Eiser, 'Identifying predictors of attitudes towards local onshore wind development', *Energy Policy*, June 2009.

10   Debika Shome and Sabine Marx, *The Psychology of Climate Change Communication* (Center for Research on Environmental Decisions, Columbia University, 2009).

11   Rachel James, *Sustainable Behavior – A Guide to successful Communication* (University of California, Berkeley, 2010).

12   Sarah Darby, *The Effectiveness of Feedback on Energy Consumption* (Environmental Change Institute, 2006).

13   House of Lords, *Behaviour Change*.

14   David Cameron, speaking on 25 November 2010 at the launch of the well-being index.

15   Office of National Statistics, *Measuring National Well-Being: Life in the UK* (2012).

16   Hamish McRae, *The Independent* 20 November 2012.

17   Joseph Rowntree Foundation, *Climate Change and Sustainable Consumption: What do the public think is fair?* (2011).

Chapter 10

Embedding Sustainability in Government

Simon Wright MP

Within weeks of the 2010 general election, the coalition government announced that it would cease funding the Sustainable Development Commission. Since 2000, the Commission had advised the four UK governments (UK, Northern Ireland, Scotland and Wales) on policy and helped government departments to develop the expertise they needed to make more sustainable decisions. From 2005, the Commission also reported on the sustainability of government operations and policies. The decision to axe the Commission led to intense criticism of the government and raised early questions over its commitment to be the 'greenest government ever'.

In practice, all governments face a significant challenge in pursuing environmental goals throughout their departmental structure. The actions and decisions of a wide range of ministers and departments are relevant to the achievement of environmental policy goals – including, for example, those covering business, finance, transport, housing, planning, agriculture and international development – but are rarely a high priority for many of them. Furthermore, environment departments are often smaller, in terms of staff and funding, and of lower perceived political status than, for example, economic, finance, industry or trade departments. As a result, many countries have found it difficult to ensure that environmental objectives are pursued consistently across government.

Over the last twenty years a range of different models has been deployed in the UK. These include a small internal committee and secretariat (the UK Panel on Sustainable Development, 1994–2000), a much larger external advisory outfit (the Sustainable Development Commission, 2000–11), and a Parliamentary scrutiny body (the House of Commons Environmental Audit Committee (EAC), from 1997). Although progress has been made, none of these models has worked to fully embed sustainable development objectives at the heart of government. The main reason, as the EAC observed in 2011, has been that 'sustainable development has not been fully embedded into Government because the political will to do this has not been maintained'.[1]

The withdrawal of funding for the Sustainable Development Commission was poorly handled; it was announced, in 2010, as part of the government's review of quangos, making it look as though the coalition put cost-cutting ahead of a commitment to sustainable development. Nevertheless, although the Commission had done much valuable work, it had increasingly come to operate essentially as a (high-quality) external pressure group, too easily overlooked or ignored by ministers. As the Commission itself indicated before its closure, weak governance arrangements had held back the progress of sustainable development as a driver of government policy and practice.[2] It was probably more effective in helping government departments manage their own operations sustainably, often generating cost savings in the process.

Coalition ministers were therefore not wrong to say that the closure of the Commission provided an opportunity for government itself to take the lead on sustainable development, strengthening democratic accountability, rather than delegating responsibility to an arms-length body. This chapter will look at whether the government has yet achieved this, whether it has moved sustainable development beyond being seen as a priority for only a few departments and pushed it into mainstream thinking and practice across the whole of government.

Embedding sustainable development in policy-making: the coalition's record

Several months after announcing the end of the Sustainable Development Commission, the coalition government published its vision for sustainable development, *Mainstreaming Sustainable Development*.[3] It defines its aim as 'stimulating economic growth and tackling the deficit, maximising well-being and protecting our environment, without negatively impacting on the ability of future generations to do the same'.

The emphasis on economic growth and tackling the deficit raised concerns that the balance of the three pillars of sustainable development risked being weighted against the social and environmental, in favour of the economic. These concerns were reinforced in July 2011, on the publication of the draft National Planning Policy Framework, which included an inadequate definition of sustainable development, and confusing statements emphasising economic growth over other considerations of sustainability; fortunately, and partly thanks to Liberal Democrat ministers, the final Framework was much better.

In August 2011 the government published *Enabling the Transition to a Green Economy: Government and business working together*.[4] Originally intended as a roadmap for business and government to develop a green economy, the document was a disappointment: it simply restated existing policies and suggested that businesses take voluntary action. As highlighted in the EAC report, *A Green Economy*,[5] the government did not fully embrace the principles of sustainability in its definition of the green economy. *Enabling the Transition* is predominantly concerned simply with growing the environmental goods and services sector, and in doing so does not adequately consider social justice, well-being or environmental limits and opportunities across the whole economy.

What the vision document, *Mainstreaming Sustainable Development*, did do, however, was to announce laudable intentions for clearer ministerial and Cabinet-level oversight for mainstreaming sustainable development. The Cabinet Office, working alongside the Department for Environment, Food and Rural Affairs (Defra), has responsibility for reviewing departmental business plans (which set out the actions required to deliver on the commitments in the coalition programme) in relation to the principles of sustainable development. The Minister of State for Government Policy, currently Oliver Letwin, reviews business plans on a quarterly basis, and oversees their revision; this gives him the power, at least in theory, to hold departments to account for their performance on integrating sustainable development.

The Sustainable Development Team within Defra provides expertise to support the Cabinet Office's review of business plans in relation to sustainable development. In addition, the Secretary of State for Environment, Food and Rural Affairs now sits on key Cabinet committees, including the Home Affairs, Economic Affairs and Reducing Regulation Committees, with the aim of providing a clear voice for sustainability across government policy-making. While this input is valuable, this is not a post which normally carries much political influence, and in areas of dispute it is far from clear that the arguments for sustainable development will prevail.

Defra staff also work with other government departments, helping them to ensure that tools such as impact assessments are applied consistently, and that policy training reflects sustainable development priorities. Although some former Sustainable Development Commission staff have been recruited to Defra, these activities represent only a small part of the service that the Commission was previously able to provide.

Departmental annual reports and accounts, which are presented to Parliament, now include information on how they have integrated sustainable development into policy, procurement and operations, together with commitments on mainstreaming sustainable development for the following year. It is still too early to judge whether this system works effectively, but the lack of a common format for reporting hardly helps.

These are all welcome initiatives as far as they go, but has the coalition demonstrated a clear cross-governmental commitment to sustainable development? The evidence suggests otherwise. While *Mainstreaming Sustainable Development* provides a brief overview of how the government seeks to 'build on the principles' of the 2005 Sustainable Development Strategy, it neither provides a new overarching strategy nor explains how sustainable development should be integrated into other priority policy themes, such as localism or infrastructure development. In the absence of a single government strategy for sustainable development, there is likely to be a tendency for departments to look for ongoing direction from Defra and Cabinet Office ministers – or to ignore the issue entirely.

As mentioned, the Department for Communities and Local Government's draft National Planning Policy Framework, published just five months after *Mainstreaming Sustainable Development*, failed adequately to incorporate sustainable development. The Treasury, while committed under the coalition programme to raise the proportion of government revenue deriving from green taxes, has unilaterally, and without any consultation, redefined the concept to exclude transport taxation (which accounts for more than 90 per cent of the total), allowing itself to cut fuel duty and air passenger duty without, on paper, breaching the commitment.

In reality, only a small number of the current crop of ministers are genuinely committed to the sustainability agenda; they are inevitably limited by their capacity to deliver, and there is of course no guarantee that future holders of their office would be equally committed. Ministers not normally identified as 'green', however, can still be motivated by a clear lead from the top. The initial success of David Cameron, before the general election, in apparently moving the Conservative Party in a greener direction, followed by his early commitment in government to cut the energy use of departments by 10 per cent, achieved results. Sadly, those achievements have not been built upon by Mr Cameron, who has, more than halfway through the Parliament, yet to give any major speech on environmental issues.

While the record of the Prime Minister may be disappointing, the impression given by the Chancellor, George Osborne, is too often one of hostility. The language of his 2011 Autumn Statement to the House of Commons was of particular concern to many, with green policies seemingly dismissed as a burden and a cost to British businesses. The impression left was potentially damaging, and is hardly likely to inspire ministers to progress sustainable development objectives in their departments.

Equally damaging has been the frequent reports of rows between departments, generally involving the Treasury, over environmental policies such as the fourth carbon budget, mandatory reporting of corporate carbon emissions, and borrowing powers for the Green Investment Bank. Proposals to reform the electricity market have also been obstructed, with the Treasury pushing back a decision on a 2030 decarbonisation target for the power sector until after the next election – though Liberal Democrat ministers won an important victory in the agreement for £7.6 billion of financial support for renewables.

Embedding sustainable development in policy-making: the future

It is clear that the current government has not succeeded in mainstreaming sustainable development objectives across all departments – just like Conservative and Labour governments of the past. It is clear that a more radical approach is needed. In reality, a combination of five key elements is necessary:

1. An agreed set of objectives across government
2. One or more departments giving a strong policy lead
3. An internal institutional set-up to (a) monitor all departments' adherence to agreed policies; and (b) question any department's decisions which impact negatively on agreed policies and objectives
4. An external scrutiny body
5. Strong, consistent and obvious support from the Prime Minister and/or other senior government figures

An agreed set of objectives across government

As noted, the publication of *Mainstreaming Sustainable Development* was a missed opportunity to update the previous government's approach – now eight years out of date – and develop a single new strategy for sustainable development to provide a clear point of reference for all departments in setting their policies and practices. In fact elements of this already exist, particularly in the *Carbon Plan* put together mainly by the Department of Energy and Climate Change (DECC) in 2011, explaining how the government as a whole intends to meet the targets set out in the successive carbon budgets.[6] Defra's Natural Environment White Paper, the Treasury's National Infrastructure Plan and other key documents can also be drawn on, but what is still missing is a strategic document which sets out the government's commitment to sustainable development, explains how it will be achieved and sets a framework within which specific strategies published by individual departments can be developed.

One or more departments giving a strong policy lead

Neither of the two key environmental policy departments in government – DECC and Defra – are particularly influential, though in the lifetime of the coalition, DECC has had a much better record of achieving its policy objectives. But both are small in terms both of numbers of officials and budgets, and sit relatively far down the Whitehall hierarchy.

Although the Labour government's habit of repeatedly reorganising government departments is not to be emulated, environmental policy did have something of a higher profile over the period (1997–2001) in which it was located in the Department of Environment, Transport and the Regions with John Prescott as Secretary of State. Partly this was due to the size of the department and partly to his status as Deputy Prime Minister.

Creating one larger environmental department by itself will not solve the problem of lack of commitment across government, but it would create a stronger champion to lead the fight. Consideration should therefore be given to merging either the environmental policy sections of Defra or the whole of the department with DECC, and possibly the Department of Transport and some elements of the Department for Business, Innovation and Skills (BIS). The Secretary of State for the new department could also regularly be the Deputy Prime Minister, placing them in the front rank of the Cabinet alongside the Prime Minister, Chancellor and Foreign Secretary.

Some kind of cross-departmental body is also likely to be needed to bring together ministers to discuss sustainable development priorities. Under the current government this function is supposed to fall under the remit of the Home Affairs Committee, but it does fit well with the existing Cabinet Committee structure, and a separate dedicated Cabinet Committee should be established, chaired by the Secretary of State for the new environment department. Other countries have this kind of structure. In Germany the State Secretary Committee for Sustainable Development, on which all ministries are represented, has responsibility for implementing the national sustainability strategy; it is chaired by the Head of the Federal Chancellery. In the US, the White House Council on Environmental Quality coordinates federal environmental efforts and works closely with agencies and other offices in the development of environmental policies and initiatives.

An internal institutional set-up to (a) monitor all departments' adherence to agreed policies; and (b) question any department's decisions which impact negatively on agreed policies and objectives

This is the function that the Government Panel on Sustainable Development, which preceded the Sustainable Development Commission, carried out. Established by John Major in January 1994, the Panel comprised five non-government experts, and was chaired by Sir Crispin Tickell; it had administrative support from the Cabinet Office. It produced four short reports each year, on topics of its own choosing, and all relevant departments were required to respond to them; it also reviewed progress against the recommendations in its previous reports. It had the power to examine any relevant papers from within departments, though it did not, in general, scrutinise previous decisions; rather, it produced recommendations for future action in what it considered to be priority areas. Its reports and the government's responses were all in due course made public.

Although the Commission was a much larger and well-resourced body, it lost this function of internal pressure and oversight, and it is not clear that the Cabinet Office and Defra between them really fulfil this function under the new arrangements. A new Panel for Sustainability Across Government, comprising of experts appointed by the Prime Minister, could provide oversight of government performance. This Panel would report regularly to the Prime Minister and Deputy Prime Minister, publishing recommendations on improving sustainable development across government to which they would provide a formal published response, helping to become a political driver for change across government.

An external scrutiny body

A strong internal scrutiny process is not in itself sufficient. External (from government) scrutiny and accountability to Parliament is also essential. With the demise of the Sustainable Development Commission, the Environmental Audit Committee, first established in 1997, will play an increasingly important role as a recognised 'green watchdog' of the government. Its resources, currently far less than those enjoyed by the Commission, should be expanded.

Indeed, the committee has already appointed additional expert advisers and is developing links with the academic community. With its wide ranging cross-government scrutiny role, it should explore establishing specialist standing sub-committees, with support from specialist staff and advisers, to avoid over-stretching committee members.

The National Audit Office (NAO) currently works with the Environmental Audit Committee on a case-by-case basis as required. The original model envisaged for the EAC suggested an enhanced NAO acting as an environmental auditor of government in support of the committee, with rights of access and resources. In the absence of the Commission, a better resourced NAO with a strengthened mandate in relation to its work with the EAC has the potential to provide a strong model of external scrutiny.

In addition, government also needs to provide further clarity for how so-called 'armchair auditors' and society as a whole are intended to scrutinise government performance. The revision of performance indicators, the publication of real-time data on websites, and inclusion of more data in departmental annual reports and accounts may help the government to argue that it is being transparent, but without a framework to assist auditing processes, including clear targets, there is a risk that publishing data will not lead to more meaningful scrutiny from outside.

Strong, consistent and obvious support from the Prime Minister and/or other senior government figures

All of the above institutional reforms should prove useful in helping to mainstream sustainable development more consistently across government, but none of them will substitute for a lack of leadership. As outlined above, the coalition government has so far failed to display this; indeed, it has demonstrated almost the reverse, with ministers clearly at odds over key elements of policy. Much of what has been achieved has been thanks to Liberal Democrat ministers, with a tiny handful of their Conservative partners in support. In this sense the government is little different from its Labour predecessor, which also saw the small number of ministers who understood and were committed to the sustainable development agenda struggle to make progress against their indifferent or actively hostile colleagues, with only a few instances of real leadership from the top. We will not make progress in this area until the Prime Minister gives a consistent lead and ensures that all government departments and policies adhere to the imperatives of sustainable development.

Leading by example

As well as the policies it develops and implements, government has a major role to play in making sure its own operations are sustainable. Central government is a significant player in the economy, employing over 450,000 civil servants and owning or managing the thousands of buildings and facilities they work in. The wider public sector, including the NHS, armed forces, prison service, public corporations and local government, is even larger, employing over 5.5 million.[7] Public procurement – the purchasing of third-party goods and services – amounts to over 10 per cent of the economy.

In attempting to ensure that these staff and buildings are employed and run in as sustainable a manner as possible, the coalition government got off to a good start. Within days of taking office, the coalition defined its ambition to reduce carbon emissions from central government departments by 10 per cent within a year: a clear demonstration that the new government would put its own house in order. The target was comfortably exceeded, with a 13.8 per cent reduction by May 2011, saving 100,000 tonnes of CO_2 and £13 million on energy bills across departments.[8] A new target was adopted of a 25 per cent reduction in emissions by 2015. Clearly this will prove more challenging to meet, but also provide the opportunity to implement more long-lasting measures.

The success of the emissions reduction target was in large part the result of strong political leadership. The previous government had also included targets, but made relatively little progress. The Prime Minister's personal commitment to deliver on the 10 per cent target was a key factor in seeing it met, but sadly has been seen on very few other environmental matters.

Real-time data of energy usage at the headquarters of all nineteen government departments in Whitehall, as well as Number 10, is now published online through departmental websites. By making this data available, departments can be held to account for behaviour that would otherwise be hidden in annual reports. (Indeed, one senior official at DECC is reported to have received enquiries from the public about the firing up of the building's heating system during bank holidays![9]) Transparency of performance is vital if the government is to show real leadership on sustainability; the vision held by ministers of 'armchair auditors' up and down the country holding public bodies to account can be realised only through the publication of relevant and comprehensive data.

As mentioned above, the government is the UK's biggest customer of goods and services. Total public sector spend on procurement was £238 billion in 2010–11.[10] This level of spend applied through the practice of sustainable procurement has the potential to be a significant driver for the green economy, stimulating industry innovation and reducing costs to the public sector. Indeed, in some areas this is already the case. For example, UK procurement policy for timber and timber products (including paper and packaging, wooden furniture and timber for construction) has, for almost ten years required that all the products must be legally and sustainably sourced, or recycled. In turn this has had a significant impact on the UK market (both public and private sector) for timber products certified as sustainably produced; by 2008 certified products accounted for over 80 per cent of the market (both domestic production and imports), having grown by about 10 per cent a year for several years.[11]

New and revised Government Buying Standards have been published to support the public sector in buying goods and services that are more sustainable. Government departments and their agencies must meet minimum mandatory specifications when buying products and services, while higher voluntary best practice standards are also defined. Products that meet the criteria will save more money over their lifetime (compared to the immediate cost), as well as reducing carbon and delivering other environmental benefits. The Standards do not yet apply to every area of procurement spend, but are steadily being extended.

While the Standards apply to central government departments and their agencies, this only accounts for about one-third of public sector purchasing power. Public institutions, including schools, hospitals, and even the House of Commons, are not covered. Given the benefits that can be brought to the green economy, the government should now consider extending the Government Buying Standards to the whole of the public sector.

The government should also set out how it will use spending on procurement to develop wider markets for sustainable goods and services, and how it will monitor the progress that it makes. The Cabinet Office is responsible for managing the performance across government of delivering the Greening Government Commitments on operations and procurement. Published in 2011, these cover greenhouse gas emissions (discussed above), waste, water consumption and procurement. Departments submit their plans for delivering operational and procurement targets to the Cabinet Office – which provides support, challenges data, and publishes the progress of departments. In general this is a good approach, though it could be pushed forward more quickly and given a higher profile within government.

Conclusions

The objective of mainstreaming sustainable development across government has been an objective of the Liberal Democrats since the foundation of the party, and has featured in every election manifesto. The party's 2011 policy development programme, *Facing the Future*, reinforced the idea that sustainable development lies at the heart of our thinking.

Liberal Democrat ministers in the coalition have achieved much on individual policies, and the government has a respectable record on – slowly – greening its own operations. Yet the coalition has clearly failed, as yet, to mainstream sustainable development objectives and policies across all departments. Clear and consistent political leadership, together with strengthened arrangements for scrutiny, remain objectives that have not yet been delivered.

Liberal Democrats know that sustainable development is neither optional nor something that can be bolted onto policies. It must lie at the heart of everything we do. Many of our actions in coalition have put this government on course for being the greenest ever, but to complete the job we have to make sure that sustainable development becomes an integral part of all policy-making and departmental planning.

Notes

1 House of Commons Environmental Audit Committee, *Embedding Sustainable Development Across Government, After the Secretary of State's Announcement on the Future of the Sustainable Development Commission* (HC504, 10 January 2011), p. 3.

2 Written evidence submitted by the Sustainable Development Commission to the Environmental Audit Committee during the inquiry into embedding sustainable development across Government; ibid., pp. Ev70–Ev99.

3 Defra, *Mainstreaming Sustainable Development – the Government's vision and what this means in practice* (February 2011).

4 HM Government, *Enabling the Transition to a Green Economy: Government and business working together* (2011).

5 House of Commons Environmental Audit Committee, *A Green Economy* (HC 1025, 21 May 2012).

6 HM Government, *The Carbon Plan: Delivering Our Long-Term Future* (December 2011).

7 All figures: Office for National Statistics, *Public Sector Employment*, Q2 2012 (12 September 2012).

8 See http://www.number10.gov.uk/news/whitehall-exceeds-10-carbon-reduction-target/

9 From the minutes of oral evidence provided to the Environmental Audit Committee, 3 November 2010, by William Jordan, Chief Sustainability Officer of the Efficiency and Reform Group, Cabinet Office.

10 House of Commons Library: *Public Procurement: Small Businesses and Savings* (January 2012).

11   Duncan Brack and Jon Buckrell, *Controlling Illegal Logging: Consumer-Country Measures* (Chatham House, March 2011), p. 11.

Chapter 11

Green Growth

Chris Huhne

The idea that growing and greening our economy are at odds, that we must plump for one or the other, is a classic false choice. In reality, as we invest to decarbonise our economy, we also grow it. Green investments – whether in resource efficiency or substitution for polluting processes – create jobs, raise incomes, and prop up demand. They produce *green growth*.

The years to come may well be different. It won't just be that we *can* have green growth; it will probably be that we can *only* have green growth. On market fundamentals, now and into the future, the prospects for high-carbon growth do not look good. This chapter looks at why this is – and why, perhaps more so than ever before, this is the green economy's moment.

This chapter advances a twin argument: a greener economy would enjoy lower resource costs and higher resilience to shocks. It would protect demand and investment when global prices rise, and thereby protect jobs and livelihoods. It would provide a more stable, stronger economy, less likely to topple into recession or suffer lost periods of growth. It is how we raise standards of living without creating systemic risk, and how we tease out growth in an age of scarcity. At one time, the green sector may have merely been a strand of growth. Now it is the new frontier. The raw economics are telling us this has to be our first priority, our prime strategy for growth. It is, perhaps, all there is.

Winds from the East

In early 1999, a barrel of oil cost just over US$10.[1] In March that year *The Economist* ran a leader article titled 'Drowning in Oil', contemplating the dangers of an oil price that could sink too low. Plainly, that particular danger was averted. After a nine-year surge, the barrel price of crude hit US$147 in July 2008. Though recession in the first quarters of 2009 cooled demand, the price was back over US$100 by January 2011.[2] For the first time in the post-war period, energy and other commodity prices are abnormally high for this point of a recovery. Usually the cost of basic materials falls in real terms for two years after the recovery begins, boosting real incomes and supporting spending.[3] This time we have a different phenomenon in the old developed regions of Europe, Japan and America: the 'squeezed middle'. Not only have we missed the boost to incomes and spending, but high energy and material prices have been pummelling a recovery already weakened by financial crises and the legacy of debt. The contrast is huge, and has enormous consequences for the future. We must grapple with the implications.

Since 1970, there have been four big global recessions. As noted earlier, if we take the first three, energy prices in the two years after the US recession ended were flat; on average, the rise was just 1 per cent. Allowing for the general rise in earnings and other prices, the cost of energy fell in real terms, bringing down petrol prices, cutting household bills, and raising disposable income. Twenty-four months after the 2008 financial crisis struck, energy prices were up 63 per cent. For non-energy commodities, including food, the past rise during those three global recoveries averaged just 11 per cent. This time it was nearly five times that, at a fraction below 52 per cent.[4]

It is sometimes claimed that this is due to speculation. But this is at most a contributory factor. As the International Energy Agency finds, 'commodities not traded in exchanges experienced similar fluctuations and price surges' in the latter half of the 2000s.[5]

The real cause is the extraordinary growth of Asia. This has a direct impact through the needs of manufacturing for energy and metals, and an indirect impact through the new demand for cars and other high-carbon consumer products. It has also been impacting heavily on food. As wealth flows to the new middle classes of China and India, people are eating more, and eating differently. This is nothing to regret. The pace at which living standards have improved in recent years is fantastic. But there are inevitably consequences for resources; meat consumption especially is on the rise, with well-known spillover effects for arable products – a kilo of meat takes many more kilos of grain to produce. One mainstream forecaster expects an 85 per cent increase in global meat production by 2050.[6]

In 1975, China accounted for barely over 5 per cent of global primary energy consumption. By 2010, it used a fifth of world energy.[7] The impact on trade was even greater, as China swung to being a substantial net importer of fuels. China accounted for less than 1 per cent of fuel and mineral product imports in 1985, but 12 per cent by 2010.

The trend is not slowing. Over the next twenty-five years, 60 per cent of new energy demand will probably come from China, India, and the Middle East, and total demand will be up by a third.[8] Almost all net oil demand is driven by the transport sector in emerging economies.[9] A thousand new cars join China's roads every day, and in the next two decades the global car fleet is forecast to double, meaning a car population of 1.7 billion by 2030.[10] The global middle class, meanwhile, is going to more than double, by most estimates swelling from around 2 billion today to 5 billion in 2030.[11] Again, this is in one sense an amazing development, banishing poverty, widening opportunity, and helping to spread democracy and the rule of law. But it does also mean an unprecedented demand for physical resources. Billions and billions of consumers now have the purchasing power for travel, air conditioning, meat, and many other high-carbon comforts. In that context, it is very hard to see how prices will be anything other than high and volatile.

Shock-proofing

The problem is not just demand. Even if global growth slows – as it did in 2012, and is forecast to do in 2013 – we need to worry about supply. As oil prices rocketed upwards in the 2000s, supplies grew at just 1 per cent a year.[12] Energy security has clambered quickly up the political agenda in many countries, not just because prices are high, but because they are skittish. Volatility is greater than at any time since the oil shocks of the 1970s.[13] Maplecroft's short-term Energy Security Index classifies the UK as 'high risk', more vulnerable than Germany, France, and the US, and only marginally more secure than Japan.[14] That reflects, at least in part, Germany's bigger stock of renewable energy, the French embrace of nuclear power, and US development of shale gas. Meanwhile, the UK has become a net importer of fossil fuels. North Sea oil and gas, experiencing one of the highest global rates of decline, cannot provide a buffer for Britain's balance of payments as it used to.[15] Only Yemen and Libya saw a bigger drop in production recently, and the latter had a civil war. Our failure to adapt, to green our energy supplies and cut dependency on fossil fuels, has left us dangerously exposed to shocks.

This is not just about Russian pipelines. A far more worrying prospect is Iran intervening in the Strait of Hormuz. A fifth of the world's oil is transported along this stretch of the Iranian coastline, and there is no guarantee that tensions in the region can be contained. Furthermore, many oil producers are pumping oil at the limits of capacity. Even Saudi Arabia is producing at near-record levels, leaving little manoeuvrability when supplies tighten or demand spikes.[16] When the Arab Spring broke out early in 2011, the price of crude oil soared 35 per cent in three months.[17] Within limits, the economy can absorb higher energy prices. A sustained 10 per cent rise in the oil price drags global growth down by an estimated 0.2 per cent.[18] But big shocks hurt. Sudden jolts can too easily throw advanced economies into recession.

Indeed, the rise of the crude oil price in 2011 was a significant factor in the global slowdown.

In the 21st century we are going to need a much more energy-resilient economy, insulated from the wavering price of fossil fuels. This isn't just an insurance policy. Shock-proofing the economy breeds confidence, supporting domestic and inward investment. This is why stability is not just a platform for growth, but a *driver* of growth. That case isn't always easy to make. Often stability brings an invisible dividend, sparing us growth we *would* have lost. Oxford Economics has modelled the impact of oil and gas shocks over the next few decades, contrasting a low-carbon scenario with 'business as usual'.[19] The low-carbon scenario reduces the impact of a fossil fuel shock by 60 per cent in 2050, with transport and manufacturing particularly benefiting from the change.

Cautious pessimism

Of course, we need to be wary of forecasts. The only good forecast is of history, and it is lined with resource-scarcity prophets who have been embarrassed before. The Victorian economist W. S. Jevons was so sure that we would run out of coal that when he died lumps of it were found stuffed into every cranny of his home. Thomas Malthus famously thought that food production could not keep up with population growth, and devastating famines would break out. In the late 1960s, Paul Ehrlich of Stanford University co-founded 'Zero Population Growth', warning again that the planet could not cope with so many people on it; humanitarian disaster was inevitable, and imminent. A few years later the Club of Rome forecast that resource consumption would impose an upper limit to economic growth, coinciding with the 1970s oil shocks that rocked global confidence. In 1980, Ehrlich was confident enough to bet the economist Julian Simon that commodity prices would go up; this is now known, naturally, as the Simon-Ehrlich wager. With an agreed measure of resource scarcity, they set a ten-year period to see how the prices of copper, nickel, tin, chromium and tungsten would play out. This was a decade when the global population boomed by 800 million. Still, Ehrlich lost, and badly. After ten years had elapsed, all five metals were cheaper, leaving the Stanford professor almost US$600 worse off.[20]

So we ought to be cautiously pessimistic. Whatever you make of the 'genius' of markets, supply squeezes in the past led not to famine, or economic disaster, or even war. They drove innovation. In the 20th century, while demand shot up twenty-fold, the index of critical commodities sunk by almost half.[21] We might achieve such a feat again. There may be new reserves of productivity in agriculture, or new ways of finding and exploiting minerals. In energy the obvious candidate is unconventional gas, where rock formations are split or 'fracked' by injecting water and chemicals at high pressure to release the gas inside. Natural gas is cleaner than coal or oil, and can also be used to generate low-carbon electricity, so long as the carbon is captured and stored. However, the speed of the US exploitation of shale gas is unlikely to be repeated in more densely populated regions like Europe. The footprint of shale wells is relatively large, and environmental concerns about water pollution have already led to bans, not just in France but also in US states like New Jersey and New York. Outside the US, mineral rights usually reside in the state, rather than the landowners, reducing incentives to drill and increasing reasons to say: 'not in my back yard'. What is more, many areas (such as China) where shale may be abundant lack the water needed for fracking.

In the short term at least, we have hit what may be a commodity price speed limit: where if the rate of supply cannot accelerate, growth must slow. In the past this reflected temporary inelasticity, the lag-time between spikes in demand and new exploration or innovation. This time we may be experiencing something different: we may well be undergoing, as GMO's Jeremy Grantham has argued, a 'paradigm shift' in energy and other commodity prices. The GMO index of thirty-three commodities shows that until 2002, commodity prices were on a 110-year slide, dipping on average 1.2 per cent a year – a 70 per cent decline over the entire period.[22] In the last decade that entire drop was reversed. Analysis from McKinsey warns that on current trends there is a significant risk of commodity prices remaining high and volatile, and that a completely unprecedented rise in resource productivity is needed. It is going to take an extra trillion dollars of investment, 175 million hectares of extra deforestation, 30 per cent more water, three times as much new land. And CO_2 emissions of up to 66 gigatonnes (more than twice the IPCC target), throwing the planet far beyond a 2°C temperature rise.[23]

The problem is that much of the easy extraction – the open mining, the shallow drilling – has already been done. From here on resources are likely to be harder, riskier, costlier and more controversial to access: across the steppe, out to sea, under the ice cap. As the CEO at Glencore, the world's largest commodities trading company, put it: 'Unfortunately, God put the minerals in different parts of the world. We took the nice, simple, easy stuff first from Australia, we took it from the US, we went to South America and we dug it out of the ground there. Now we have to go to more remote places'.[25] That should not surprise us. Growth always slows after the opening stages. At first

Fig. 11.1 Commodity prices 1900–2011[24]

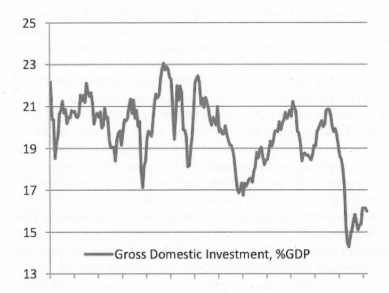

you take the best resources, the best land, the cheapest labour. After that, things get harder. You can raise productivity, invest in technology, skill up your workers; but it is a slower process. Diminishing returns may finally be setting in with commodities. Faced with this development, the safe national strategy is surely to hope for the best but prepare for the worst: to encourage resource-efficient growth. The more we save energy and the more we shift to renewables, the less dependent we are on whatever happens to fossil fuel markets. And in the immediate future, we release a badly needed wave of demand to help spur our sluggish recovery.

The great green market
After all, the green economy is no longer a cottage industry. It employs more than a million people in Britain. Across the globe there is a £3.3 trillion market for low-carbon products and services.[26] Governments, businesses, and individuals are buying up green goods and services at such a pace that in the UK the sector is growing at 4.9 per cent a year, and predicted to grow faster still in the years to come – 5.5 per cent by 2014–15.[27]

What has really been firing 'green demand' is cost-saving. All the analyses on energy supply and demand show that the most cost-effective way to close the gap is not to use energy in the first place. Investment in energy saving is more cost-effective than any investment in energy production.

There is also an increasing commitment to low-carbon electricity generation across the world, especially renewables. We have already passed the cross-over point when renewables investment exceeded that in fossil fuels. This is not because the costs are currently lower, but because the trajectory of cost reduction is clear. In just four years, solar panels (solar photovoltaics) have tumbled in cost from more than US$4 per watt in 2008 to less than US$1, and the cost is still falling, at around 10 per cent a year.[28] The cost of onshore wind has been coming down too. Wind is now competing, on cost, with conventional fossil fuels if the location is right. At a recent auction in Brazil, onshore wind beat conventional combined-cycle gas turbine plants on cost, offering electricity at US$61 per MWh, 24 per cent less than the year before.[29]

This has not gone unnoticed. China has nominated a quarter of its regions as low-carbon pilots. Ethiopia, as a low-income country, has embarked on a strategy for green growth.[30] Korea is powering ahead with a Green New Deal worth 10 per cent of GDP, investing in energy efficiency, recycling, and renewables, and expected to boost employment 10 per cent by 2013.[31] China's ambitions, unsurprisingly, are on an awesome scale. In fewer than eight years it wants 100 extra gigawatts of hydropower and 200 more gigawatts of wind power.[32] On top of that, its nuclear capacity is planned to rise from 10 GW to 80 GW. The Chinese are building more than twenty nuclear reactors in the time it will take us to build one, and laying 16,000 km of high-speed rail in the time it will take us to get HS2 from London to Birmingham.

It is often claimed that we should wait until the cost of green investment falls even more, or that the investments are simply too expensive. But in truth, the low-carbon future is cutting household bills even in the short term. The Department of Energy and Climate Change calculates the cross-over point at about US$100 a barrel (and the equivalent for gas). If world prices are higher than that, then the whole portfolio of UK low-carbon policies, including energy saving and support for low-carbon generation, pay for themselves and save businesses and consumers money.

These are not fringe savings. By one estimate, UK firms could recoup £23 billion a year.[33] One vehicle assembly plant wiped 28 per cent off its energy bill in one year, saving £2.3 million. It did so with minimal investment: it turned off unused machines and repaired the holes in compressed air pipes. More and more, selling cost-savings is good business. SPI Lasers in Hedge End produces rare earth lasers that save 90 per cent of the energy used by traditional carbon lasers, now the workhorse of world metal-bashing. Meanwhile, the lift industry is enjoying a small renaissance. The world's largest manufacturer, Otis, has just released the Gen2, and it has become its fastest-selling line ever because it uses as much as 75 per cent less energy.[34] The same thing is happening with LED bulbs. They consume 1 watt of electricity where 35 watts was needed before. If we want to roll out these savings more quickly, we need to make it easier for consumers to invest in energy efficiency through the Green Deal, and we need a powerful Green Investment Bank to lead business.

The green market in the UK is worth an estimated £122.2 billion a year, and it is expected to be £155 billion in 2014.[35] Plainly, this is now serious business. As the market in energy efficiency blossoms we are expecting significant expansion in employment in insulation alone.[36] Companies wanting to trumpet their green credentials are playing a bigger and bigger role too, responding both to the social responsibility of their customers and their employees. Companies that want to win loyalty have to behave like good citizens – and more and more are. Nearly 65 per cent of CEOs worldwide say their response to climate change initiatives gives them a reputational advantage.[37] Fewer than 25 per cent believe that such initiatives would slow growth in their industry. More importantly, nearly half of CEOs think new product and service opportunities lie in these efforts.

What is more, this is the sort of investment that sets innovation alight. In the past, the upfront-cost problem made greentech a specialist market, a preserve of the wealthy. Today, the green market is quickly creating the economies of scale to pull prices down and release full-scale competition. It is now supermarkets that are tussling for supremacy on insulation or smart meters or microgeneration. Not only is that attracting a wave of green innovation, it is making innovations a whole lot more accessible. And if we are to survive the 'paradigm shift' in commodities ahead, innovation is precisely what we are going to need.

Conclusion

There is little doubt about the trajectory of the developing world. China's growth has not stopped, and it is not going to stop. The increase in China's demand for natural resources will slow down or accelerate with the rhythm of its economy, but it will go on growing. We may be struggling through the worst economic crisis for three-quarters of a century, but emerging economies are still upping their exports, raising their incomes, and sucking in more and more commodities. For all the sluggishness of the developed world, the commodity price trends of the past decade are not about to reverse. This is supercharging the case for green growth like never before.

It will take an awesome expansion of production to bring commodity prices back to twentieth-century levels. Shale gas may take the edge off gas price rises, and help fill the hole as Germany and others go non-nuclear. But it is unlikely – at global level – to be a game-changer. On oil, there may be dips in oil prices from year to year, but the age of cheap oil now looks like a misty dream. For the next few years at the very least, we can expect a high floor price and a Saudi policy determined first to ensure that the Kingdom's budget balances. As for non-fuel commodities the prospects are none too bright. Extraction is getting harder and harder, and demand is growing faster than ever. New innovations will raise productivity, but they are very unlikely to reverse the long-term trend. The transition has happened. From now on steel and iron and copper and chemicals and other key commodities are going to cost more. If we want growth back, we simply have to adapt.

As long as high commodity prices are crimping demand, a part of our new prosperity must be created by cutting resource costs. The new markets in fuel-efficiency, renewable energy and resource-productivity are what will increase business margins, boost sales, and create jobs. As commodities veer unpredictably from one new height to another, the folly of having chosen excessive reliance on high-carbon is horribly clear. There may be a long-term role for gas with carbon capture and storage, but we mustn't make the same mistake of over-reliance on one resource again. In hard times, the worst thing the green agenda can do is slink back, awaiting the return of growth. We need, quite simply, to go as green as we can as quickly as we can.

The policy instruments have largely been laid out. The UK has a clear framework for cutting carbon in the Climate Change Act. We have the tools to encourage the shift to low-carbon transport through vehicle standards (on emissions) and subsidies for electric vehicles. The Green Deal will allow consumers to pay for energy-saving measures in their homes from the energy savings on their household bills. The government's new Energy Bill will provide investors in all the low-carbon families of electricity generation – renewables, nuclear and carbon capture and storage of fossil fuels – with certainty by means of fixed prices in contracts for difference. Any short-term competitive difficulties for energy-intensive industries should be met with special assistance, but the EU framework will help. The prospects for US leadership have increased markedly with President Obama's second term.

In theory, all three major British parties now share a cross-party consensus towards decarbonisation. However, the danger is that differences in enthusiasm between the Treasury and the Department of Energy and

Climate Change have become exposed, and that those mixed messages worry investors about staking their money on a low-carbon future. Investors abhor uncertainty, particularly in an area where government taxes or subsidies are crucial in offsetting the failure of the market to take into account the impact of carbon emissions. Policy matters. Mood music counts. When green growth is so crucial, and is responsible for so much of the increased activity in the UK economy, ministers need to show a united front. The future is green.

Margaret Thatcher was a Prime Minister who had been trained as a scientist, and perhaps as a result was the first world leader to highlight climate change as an important global challenge. As she might have said, there is no alternative. Either we will grow in a green way, or we will not grow at all.

Notes

1   IEA, *Monthly Oil Market Report*, March 1999.
2   IEA, *Monthly Oil Market Report*, February 2011.
3   In 2012, as some commodity prices dipped, there was speculation that we were experiencing a commodities super-cycle, which was coming to an end. However, as J. P. Morgan's commodities head Colin Fenton warns, this may be 'confusing a temporary consumption slump linked to the shorter business cycle with the "conclusion of a multi-decade investment boom" in the natural resources industry' (*Financial Times*, 'Iron ore prices climb 60% in four months', 28 December 2012), while the IMF notes in its October 2012 *World Economic Outlook* regarding oil that 'reflecting physical market (for example, North Sea) disruptions, ongoing geopolitical risks and concern about associated supply disruptions, and expectations of stimulus in China, the United States, and Europe, the risk to oil prices is tilted to the upside'.
4   World Bank, *GEM commodity price index*, 2012.
5   IEA, *Monthly Oil Market Report*, March 2011.
6   PwC, World Economic Forum Knowledge Concierge: *Sustainability, Environment, and Natural Resources*, 2012 .
7   BP, *Statistical Review of World Energy*, 2011.
8   International Energy Agency, *World Energy Outlook*, 2012.
9   Ibid.
10 Thomas L. Friedman, *Hot, Flat, and Crowded* (Picador, 2009); McKinsey, *A new era for commodities*, November 2011.
11 McKinsey Global Institute, *Resource Revolution: Meeting the world's energy, materials, food, and water needs* (2011).

12 Martin Wolf, 'Prepare for a new era of oil shocks', *Financial Times*, 27 March 2012.

13 McKinsey, *A new era for commodities*, November 2011.

14 Maplecroft, *Energy Security Index*, 2011.

15 BP, *Statistical Review of World Energy*, 2012.

16 Bloomberg, 'Saudi Oil Output in January Was Near 31-Year High', March 2012.

17 *The Economist*, 'Another oil shock?', March 2012.

18 IMF, *World Economic Outlook: Oil Scarcity, Growth, and Global Imbalances*, May 2011.

19 Oxford Economics, *Fossil fuel price shocks and a low carbon economy*, May 2012.

20 John Tierney, 'Betting on the Planet', *New York Times*, 2 December 1990.

21 McKinsey, *Resource Revolution*.

22 GMO, *GMO Commodity Index: The Great Paradigm Shift*, 2011.

23 McKinsey, *Resource Revolution*.

24 Source: ibid.

25 Javier Blas, 'Commodities: Into the spotlight', *Financial Times*, 10 April 2011.

26 BIS, 'Low Carbon and Environmental Goods and Services: an industry analysis', June 2012.

27 Ibid.

28 McKinsey, 'Solar power: Darkest before dawn', August 2012.

29 Bloomberg, 'Wind Cheaper Than Natural Gas, Hydro in Brazil Power Auction', August 2011.

30 OECD, *Towards green growth: A summary for policy makers*, 2011.

31 *OECD Economic Surveys, Korea*, 2012.

32 *The Economist, Special Report on Nuclear Energy*, March 2012.

33 Oakdene Hollins-Defra, *The Further Benefits of Business Resource Efficiency*, 2011.

34 McKinsey, *Resource Revolution*.

35 BIS, 'Low Carbon and Environmental Goods and Services: an industry analysis', June 2012.

36 DECC, *Final Stage Impact Assessment for the Green Deal and Energy Company Obligation*, 2012.

37 PwC, World Economic Forum Knowledge Concierge: *Sustainability, Environment, and Natural Resources*, 2012.

Chapter 12

Driving Growth through Green Innovation

Dimitri Zenghelis

Why the green time is now

The current period of low confidence and stagnating private investment presents a unique opportunity for the UK to boost employment and stimulate economic growth, while encouraging competition and innovation. By kick-starting investment now through strong, clear and credible green policy measures, policy can mobilise private savings and make green investment a safer bet for business. Such action can crowd in tax revenues and address public indebtedness. At the same time, the UK can meet tough emissions targets cost-effectively and leave a long-lasting legacy in the transition to a resource-efficient green economy.

Structural reform of the UK economy to increase productivity is essential, but it takes time. Without recovery any attempt to achieve fiscal sustainability any time soon will be unacceptably destructive, both economically and politically – as recent events in Europe have demonstrated. Enduring growth requires investment. But investment has slumped to record lows mainly because households, businesses and banks are nervous about future demand, and have responded by forgoing more risky investment in physical capital.

Figure 12.1: Fixed investment: United States (left); United Kingdom (right)[1]

Figure 12.2: Sector financial balances (net lending): US (left); UK (right)[1]

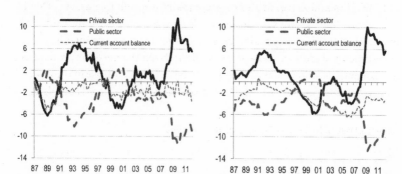

Instead, companies and households are squirrelling away private saving into 'risk-free' assets such as solvent sovereign bonds. As a result, annual private sector surpluses – the difference between saving and investment – have swollen to record levels over the past few years, amounting to £99 billion in 2011, equivalent to 6 per cent of UK GDP.

So how did the private sector come to accumulate such enormous saving surpluses? After the financial crash – which many governments helped fuel through excess fiscal borrowing at the peak of the economic cycle – households, businesses and banks undertook necessary and unavoidable long-run stock readjustments in their balance sheets. This required additional saving: a reduction in private spending in order to restore private sector net worth. A slowdown in growth, or even recession, was an inevitable consequence of this balance-sheet adjustment.

The problem is that many Western economies are now trapped in a classic 'paradox of thrift', in which greater saving and cost-cutting is the rational response to economic gloom at the level of an individual business (which also sheds labour), bank (which restricts credit) or household. But when everyone retrenches simultaneously, fear of extended recession becomes a self-fulfilling prophecy. This yields a vicious circle of low demand and low investment that affects the whole economy; and the longer recovery is delayed and capital sits idle, the more skills are lost, and the higher the misallocation of resources, making it harder to restore growth.

Desired saving has exceeded desired investment in many advanced economies to such a degree that global real 'risk-free' interest rates for the next twenty years have been pushed to zero and below. The collapse in US

Treasury bill rates offers the benchmark for 'risk free' returns (Table 12.1) but UK gilts and German Bunds are equally unprofitable assets. This is remarkable. Our savings are losing value by the day as pension funds and financial institutions pay real interest to (rather than receive interest from) governments; a truly perverse state of affairs given the need for productive investment. These low rates cannot and do not reflect a collapse in the under-lying returns to capital; instead they reflect desperately depleted confidence[3].

Table 12.1. Daily United States Treasury yield curve rates[4]

Date	1 m	3 m	6 m	1 y	2 y	3 y	5 y	7 y	10 y	20 y
29/10/12	0.13	0.14	0.16	0.18	0.30	0.40	0.74	1.16	1.74	2.48

With short-term interest rates close to zero, the effectiveness of monetary policy to stimulate growth is reaching its limits; and fiscal policy is tightly constrained. Some have argued that deregulation will help stimulate business activity. Deregulation is necessary in the long run, but it may not have much effect in a severely demand-deficient environment. What is needed to restore confidence is a clear strategic vision with supporting policies to guide investors. In the past, we have seen Roosevelt's New Deal, or rearmament for war. In this case, recognising the inevitable transition to a low-carbon economy, and helping to drive forward investment in resource-efficient, innovative sectors, could both restore growth and leave a lasting legacy. As well as achieving energy security, tackling climate change, and saving con-sumers and businesses costs in the long run, these sectors offer long-term returns for investors. Of course, all investment and employment raises costs, by definition: resources must be paid for. And these costs will be borne by consumers, but they are part of the process of generating economic surplus and restoring economic health. It is worth bearing in mind that the simulta-neous attempt to cut costs by households, businesses and banks is precisely what has prolonged this recession.

Standard macroeconomics tells us that the best time to support invest-ment is during a protracted economic slowdown. Resource costs are low, people are unemployed and the potential to crowd out alternative investment and employment is minimal compared with when the economy is operating at full capacity in a tight labour market. In addition, although public budg-ets are stretched, there is no shortage either of private capital available for investment, or of investment opportunities with the potential for profitable returns. The current opportunity should not be missed.

But why green? For one thing, unlike much conventional infrastructure investment which requires large sums of public spending, private green investment can be leveraged through coherent policy signals such as standards and regulations, which costs the exchequer little, or carbon pricing, which raises revenues. Investment in the sector is credible in the long run because a transition to resource efficiency is widely recognised as inevitable. It will be transformative, creating sizable new markets in all the world's economic sectors: buildings, transport, agriculture, manufacturing and communications.

The green sector is one of the few vibrant parts of the global economy at the moment. The most recent figures published by the Department for Business, Innovation and Skills show that the UK low-carbon and environmental goods and services sector had sales of £116.8 billion in 2009–10, growing 4.3 per cent from the previous year and placing the UK sixth in the global league table. But the private sector is not investing as heavily as it could in green innovation and infrastructure because of a lack of confidence in future returns in this policy-driven sector. The lack of confidence is due to uncertainties surrounding current energy and environment policy.

The reliance on policy to drive this market has advantages in the current fragile economic environment. Cautious investors can be driven to act now by correctly priced public resources, sweeping standards, regulations and technology support without relying on private sector sentiment to drive demand. Governments can provide clarity on their vision of the future, defining outcomes and letting entrepreneurs figure out how to get there. Korea and China have understood the logic of this approach. China has moved decisively to champion high technology low-carbon growth, both in its stimulus package of 2008–09 but also in its twelfth five-year plan, which sets strong targets.[5] China and other countries recognise that investment flows to the pioneers of the revolutions.[6]

Recognising and correcting market failures

Policies to encourage low-carbon investment would provide new business opportunities and generate income for investors. These markets are credible in the long term precisely because they address growing global resource challenges, so tapping into a fast-growing global market for resource-efficient activities. But what form should public intervention take? For all the failures of the financial sector in recent years, the market remains the most efficient way to coordinate the vast amount of information needed to match scare resources with the things consumers want to buy. Competitive markets, free from protectionism, create the disciplines that will drive success in global trade. Markets work best when power is diffused and information is symmetric – that is, when buyers and sellers both know what they are getting into. Markets are most dynamic when barriers to entry and to hiring people are low, and where prices reflect all the costs of production, including social and environmental costs.

But global integration and accelerating consumption have led to a growing number of market failures and missing markets, which require public intervention to become economically viable. These occur when uncoordinated markets driven by individuals pursuing their own self-interest are unwilling, or unable, to undertake the requisite investments alone. At the heart of these 'failures' lie information and ownership issues which prevent the setting up of a working market. These require coordinated public intervention to establish property rights and provide incentives to spur markets and foster innovation.[7]

For the most part, markets do not fail, but where they do, the consequences in terms of eroding welfare and efficiency can be dramatic. Moreover, different market failures point to different instruments, so long as the collection is mutually reinforcing. For example, without properly valuing natural assets, it is hard to prevent over-consumption and the depletion of scarce resources, especially ones that are owned in common, such as fish in the ocean, or clean air. This has distorted the development of advanced economies to make them far too hungry for such resources.

In addition to mispriced resources, policy-makers need to tackle market failures relating to information and ownership that yield insufficient research and development spending by the private sector, as investors fear that they will fail to capture the full returns to innovation because knowledge is free.

There are also a growing number of network externalities. These occur where the value of joining a network depends on how many others are on it, such as telephones, public transport, fast broadband, electricity grids and community-based insulation schemes. These increasingly require government frameworks to help firms reap increasing returns to scale by supporting new networks.

When standard economic cost-benefit analyses are not 'fit for purpose'

So what can economics tell us about the long-run opportunities and costs of resource-efficient investment? Will we need to trade off growth in order to preserve the environment? It is clear that standard narrow cost-benefit analysis can provide only part of the story.[8]

Where non-marginal, low-probability, high-impact, potentially irreversible events such as climate risks and species loss are involved, a broad risk-management approach to decision-making under uncertainty may be more appropriate than a deterministic cost-benefit assessment. This includes being prepared to pay a premium to guard against low-probability but possibly catastrophic events. It also means recognising the market failures listed above and the 'co-benefits' associated with green policies, including energy and resource efficiency gains,[9] valuing ecosystems and biodiversity, valuing energy security, and the regulation of dirty and more dangerous technologies.

Many standard models also ignore the complex dynamics of the problem, where delaying or postponing green policies is dangerous. As the stock of greenhouse gases continues to mount, the annual emissions reductions necessary to stabilise at a particular temperature become ever larger and more costly to achieve, while irreplaceable and non-substitutable resources are depleted forever. At the same time, the risk of crossing dangerous system thresholds increases. And delayed action means that society continues to lock in resource-intensive infrastructure and behaviours which are hard or costly to unwind later. Installing renewable technologies that have not been given a chance to mature in a desperate last-minute dash will also raise costs. It is far more cost-effective to manage the transition and work with the investment-depreciation cycle.

General Equilibrium models which assume optimisation by definition (i.e. all agents are rational utility-maximisers; there is no waste) cannot account for these crucial elements. Under these models, any departure from the current equilibrium is scored as a distortion with a cost. Thus they assume that resource-efficient investment is detrimental to growth and deduce that any action is simply a cost. This re-orients the discussion to 'affordability' while making for weak economics. Dynamic public policy analysis is required to understand innovation and learning and the creation of benefits beyond narrow GDP. The expenditure involved in making the transition to a resource-efficient economy must be assessed as an investment and an insurance option, rather than a cost net of benefits.

Innovation will be the driver of green growth

With billions of people in Asia and other developing regions rightly aspiring to the living standards and consumption levels of the rich world, investment in resource efficiency and renewables will be the only way to raise productivity while cutting resource use, waste and inefficiency. Thankfully, output and growth are functions not just of the amount of people, capital and materials thrown into the production process, but also innovation in the processes, techniques, and technologies with which these inputs are used. This element is termed total factor productivity (TFP). Growth accounting shows clearly that economic growth in most rich countries stems almost entirely from growth in TFP. And knowledge and ideas build on each other; new equipment enables new ideas and better technologies. For example, investing in computers induces bright ideas on how to use them.

This fuels increasing returns to scale in production, where investment in knowledge begets increased output and resources for further investment: a virtuous-growth spiral known as endogenous growth.[10] This means that policymakers can steer growth by focusing on the factors that drive innovation.[11]

The impacts of information and communications technology are comparable and probably bigger than those of steam or electricity. There is no previous example of a new technology whose price has fallen so fast, or which has diffused through the economy as rapidly, as innovations in computers and mobile communication. This can vastly increase resource efficiency through better use, monitoring and management.

Some sectors, such as energy, are already witnessing a technology revolution that, after an initial investment phase, is likely to bring down the cost of energy generation based on abundant renewable sources. Many renewable technologies such as solar PV will become competitive with conventional fuels in the next few decades. Some, such as onshore wind, already are. The benefits of learning have already helped costs of solar photovoltaic fall by a factor of five or six in the last five years or so.

This process of induced innovation is a key part of understanding true long-run costs. Improved efficiency will also continue to reduce the amount of energy required to create economic output. Pricing damaging emissions will not only incentivise the development of these technologies, it will also help staunch the so-called 'rebound effect' whereby extra disposable income from efficiency gains is channelled into additional resource-depleting consumption.

Outside the field of energy, some of the resource challenges are more pressing. Unlike conventional energy sources, essential 'elements' (minerals like phosphorus, potassium, arable land, soil, biodiversity, water) are hard to substitute. Until a decade ago, there appeared to be empirical support for the view that commodities were becoming more economically abundant,[12] given the long-term trend of declining commodity, food, mineral and energy prices over the twentieth century.[13] However, the welcome rise of a growing middle class in populous developing countries has over the past decade clearly reversed century-long price declines across a swathe of commodities, as supply struggles to keep pace with demand.

But there is plenty of scope to use resources more productively. McKinsey highlights fifteen areas where there is great scope for improvement in efficiency, including energy efficiency in the built environment, increasing yields on large-scale farms, reducing food waste, reducing municipal water leakage, increasing transport fuel efficiency, reducing land degradation, improving irrigation techniques, and improving the efficiency of power plants.[14]

Investment can need strategic direction

So the path of technological innovation matters. This means that policy must be about more than correcting market failures; government has a significant role in determining the strategic direction of an economy by demonstrating its commitment to a sector. This can give companies the confidence to invest in physical capital, and individuals the confidence to invest in skills development. Moreover, the commercial opportunities are magnified by the fact that the necessary change will be transformative. It will require major investment in all regions of the world and in all economic sectors, including buildings, transport, agriculture, manufacturing and communications. Just as a space race, the military-industrial commitment or the 'war on cancer' can induce innovation, so the setting of smart connectivity or green innovation challenges can be expected to create substantial knowledge spillovers, boosting Schumpeterian 'creative destruction', innovation and productivity across a broad number of sectors.[15]

Economic history tells us that these periods of change are characterised by two types of countries, 'those where the new industries are being deployed, and those areas of the world that are left out and falling behind'.[16] As Perez notes, 'Investment concentrates in these core countries, where the whole economy is flourishing and opportunities across the complete industrial spectrum now abound. It is the time of aggressive exports from the core countries.'[17]

Like business, governments need to be allowed to take risks

Innovation relies on risk being taken by the public sector too. Much of the innovation funded by the US government after 1945 was a by-product of the space race and the Cold War. The US government played a central role in financing or buying many of the innovations behind the ICT revolution; Silicon Valley venture capitalists took the credit, but they were standing on the shoulders of federal government investment and support over many years. Americans have made huge interventions in markets through vehicles such as DARPA, the US National Science Foundation, the Small Business Innovation Research programme, and the National Institutes of Health.

Companies like Apple, Google, Intel, GSK and Pfizer all benefited from crucial public sector support in developing their key technologies.

What Mazzucato has dubbed the 'entrepreneurial state' often takes on the greatest risk long before the private sector dares to enter. In the UK and elsewhere, incentives in the public sector often militate against risk-taking, which relies on a willingness to fail. The competence of policy-makers and public officials is commonly judged on how well they avoid expensive disasters. Indeed, the UK public sector seems to have been particularly conservative by international standards – with some notable exceptions, such as the NHS which, with a clear national mission, supported innovation on pharmaceuticals, helping make this one of the most innovative and successful sectors in the UK. Partly as a result, the UK languishes low in the OECD rankings for research and development spending as a proportion of GDP.[18] As in the private sector, there is a balance to be struck between risk and reward.[19]

Most importantly, policy must be credible, transparent and flexible

Intervention needs to be carefully designed in order to avoid replacing market failure with policy failure.[20] Expectations play a crucial role in influencing investor behaviour and establishing credibility takes time, so it is critical that policy-makers think carefully about policy design.

In a rapidly changing economic environment, policy-makers must embrace uncertainty on a number of fronts: technology costs, tastes and preferences, resource depletion rates and climate science, to name a few. So policy must be sufficiently stringent to change behaviour, predictable in order to contain policy risk, yet simple and flexible in evolving to changing circumstances while limiting compliance costs.[21] This requires that it be based on clear rules for review and revision, where the public sector responds to surprises in a predictable manner. Most importantly, stable rules that are not changed retroactively are a necessary condition in order to provide an appropriate return to induce private capital to flow into risky technological sectors. The government must convince businesses that it will not renege on its commitments once investment costs are sunk.[22]

Policies should be as neutral as possible, to allow a broad range of technologies to emerge and compete, and to avoid the problem of 'picking winners'. For example, price signals limit the scope for rent-seeking by avoiding discrimination between technologies and processes, while encouraging competition within sectors. However, governments cannot avoid making choices, given that there are a range of technological options that will be available over the coming decades, with specific barriers and opportunities that may require targeted assistance.[23] So choices should be well-informed, open and transparent, in collaboration with civil society and the private sector.

The role of environmental policies in setting expectations and providing incentives to induce innovation cannot be underestimated. Even modest and uncertain movement has generated a strong response.[24]

Policy risk requires public 'skin in the game'

The private sector is not investing as heavily as it could in green innovation and infrastructure because of a lack of confidence in future returns in this policy-driven sector. Only the government can reduce this policy risk. Thus, by backing its own green policies, the government can stimulate additional net private-sector investment, and make a significant contribution to economic growth and employment.

The government can do this, for instance, by allowing a well-capitalised Green Investment Bank to operate as a lending institution, sharing some of the risk of private investments in green infrastructure. The UK should also work with European Union member states to increase the target for emissions reductions for 2020 to 30 per cent from 20 per cent, supporting the carbon price within the Emissions Trading System. Promoting future growth also requires a shift in the tax base towards materials and resources, and away from intellectual activity. Finally, the Prime Minister and his Cabinet colleagues need to be clear advocates for the green economy. If they convey the false impression that we have to make a choice between environmental responsibility and economic growth, they will undermine the confidence of private sector investors in the direction and consistency of future policy, raising the risk premium on such projects. Loose talk costs jobs.

Rapid technical change is always disruptive, but by boosting productivity and resource efficiency, new technologies afford a welcome opportunity to promote sustainable growth. Although harnessing this revolution will be beneficial to society, like most 'change', it is not all 'win-win' and there will be losers and dislocation. Policy-makers must resist the temptation to respond to lobbying skewed in the interests of existing companies resistant to change as opposed to young companies (or companies that do not yet exist) who threaten to destroy them. Institutions must be designed to resist pressures for protectionism, from vocal 'merchants of doubt'. Policy must practically manage change, support, re-skill and retool threatened sectors.

But leadership and political will require public support and pressure. Changing social norms takes time – witness the initial response to smoking, seatbelts and drink-driving. But people are ready to act responsibly if they understand the scale of risks to future generations and have a clear vision of what can be done. Open public discussion and engagement and the building of a common understanding of the challenges is essential for democratic choice and the sustainability of actions. Policies must be explained clearly and made attractive and convenient rather than coercive and complex.

Conclusion

Public policy must be examined in the context of a collection of market failures, and designed to reinforce business confidence and spur innovation. To fail to correct market failures is to distort markets. The most urgent market failure is macroeconomic and is exemplified by the collapse in confidence which has driven an explosion in net saving, pushing real risk-free interest rates to less than zero – truly perverse at a time when physical investment is desperately needed. In the longer term, policy must account for the dynamics of change and learning and the risk of climate change and resource depletion. It needs to be informed by a rich economic analysis of risks, uncertainty, the costs of delay and the impact of technological lock-in and path dependency. Narrow cost-benefit modelling will not suffice.

The setting of green innovation challenges can be expected to create substantial knowledge spillovers, boosting innovation and productivity across a broad number of sectors. But policy that is not credible or clear will raise costs. Indecision risks the double failure of missing an opportunity to lock in to low-carbon resource-efficient infrastructure and unnecessarily extend the economic crisis. The adjustment will be disruptive and it will require bold leadership and substantial early investment. But in the world of innovation, policy choices made today will determine the shape of institutions, technologies and infrastructures that drive our economies for decades. There is no lack of private money, just a perceived lack of opportunity. Credible green innovation policy can reduce uncertainty, restore growth and leave a dynamic and resource-efficient legacy.

Notes

1   Source: Bureau of Economic Analysis/Office of National Statistics, quarterly data to second quarter of 2012.

2   Ibid.

3   Dimitri Zenghelis, 'A strategy for restoring confidence and economic growth through green investment and innovation' (Grantham Institute, 2012).

4   Source: United States Treasury.

5   Of the seven 'Magic Growth sectors' identified in the Twelfth Five-Year Plan, three are low-carbon industries (clean energy, energy efficiency, clean energy vehicles), and the others are high-end manufacturing.

6   C. Perez, *Technological Revolutions and Financial Capital: The Dynamics of Bubbles and Golden Ages* (Edward Elgar, 2002).

7   Zenghelis,'A strategy for restoring confidence and economic growth through green investment and innovation', Annex table 1 provides a list of pervasive market failures which justify public intervention.

8   M. Romani, N. Stern and D. Zenghelis, 'The basic economics of low-carbon growth in the UK' (Grantham Research Institute on Climate Change and the Environment, 2011).

9   McKinsey, *Resource Revolution: Meeting the world's energy, materials, food, and water needs* (McKinsey Global Institute, November 2011).

10 See Dimitri Zenghelis, 'The Economics of Network-Powered Growth' (Cisco, 2011).

11 See Dimitri Zenghelis, 'Networked Solutions for 21st-Century Challenges' (Cisco, 2011).

12 See D. Johnson, 'Population, Food, and Knowledge', *American Economic Review* 2000.

13 See R. Dobbs, J. Oppenheim and F. Thompson, 'A new era for commodities', *McKinsey Quarterly*, November 2011.

14 McKinsey, *Resource Revolution*.

15 See M. Mazzucato, 'The entrepreneurial state' (Demos, 2011); and C. Perez, 'The double bubble at the turn of the century: technological roots and structural implications' (*Cambridge Journal of Economics* 33(4), 2009).

16 See Perez's assessment of the next 'Golden Age' in *Inside Track* 30 (winter 2012).

17 Perez, *Technological Revolutions and Financial Capital*.

18 OECD Science, Technology and Industry Scoreboard 2011.

19 Institutional reform to enable greater public risk-taking in support of vital innovation may require distancing key institutions from politics. Even in the US, public sector risk-taking takes place strategically at arm's length from federal and state government – one reason why its significance is so often overlooked.

20 Hepburn, 'Environmental policy, government, and the market', *Oxford Review of Economic Policy* 2010.

21 Dieter Helm, 'Government failure, rent-seeking, and capture: the design of climate change policy', *Oxford Review of Economic Policy*, 2010.

22 Recent examples of retrospective changes to feed-in tariffs in the UK and Spain provide a case in point.

23 Fisher, 'The role of technology policies in climate mitigation' (Resources for the Future, 2009).

24 See EPO/OECD World Patent Statistics database (PATSTAT), OECD (2010).

Chapter 13

Supporting Innovation and Jobs

Dr Patrick Sheehan and Shas Sheehan

The issues of climate change, energy security, urbanisation, and population growth are posing fundamental challenges to today's societies. They will push the world towards a new resource- and energy-efficient economy – and this is essential if we are to meet the needs of emergent industrial nations. Humanity has the ability to meet its present and future needs by implementing sustainable development. However, building a sustainable green future will require large-scale changes across many industries.

There are of course many obstacles to environmental solutions. Not least, the word 'green' itself has become burdened with negative connotations over the last twenty years. Environmentalism has been seen by some as naive and impractical. It has been argued that a balance has to be struck between financial and environmental responsibility, that the two are naturally in conflict.

This chapter argues that such an approach is outdated. Today a range of new resource- and energy-efficient technologies (REETs) are being developed which offer the prospect of delivering major environmental benefits and at the same time delivering economic growth. There is a powerful message here: modern green companies can be practical, profitable, and have the potential to greatly improve the economy of a country wise enough to invest in them.

This chapter focuses on REETs and what the UK should do to enable them to prosper. The UK has historically been good at early-stage innovation, at generating ideas and inventions, and in the past decade or so has become far better at starting promising, innovative companies. However, it still struggles to help grow promising companies into viable global champions. We therefore focus here on what government can do to help those companies which have succeeded in commercialising a technology, but are in danger of failing due to lack of capital investment or access to markets.

This is not just about new government initiatives. There is also a strong case for a fundamental overhaul of the way government organises itself so that government departments and industry work together to develop a

Fig. 13.1 Development of the future green economy

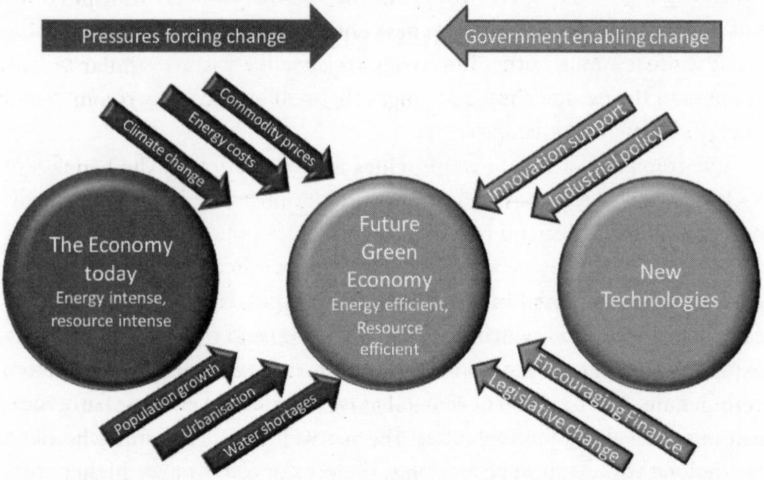

sustainable green economy in Britain – amounting to nothing less than an industrial policy.

A brave new world – moving towards a resource- and energy-efficient economy

Whether we like it or not, climate change, looming resource scarcity and other environmental pressures are forcing change. One response has been to suggest that society accepts higher costs and, in effect, a lower standard of living. This is defeatist and at the same time oddly optimistic – you would have to be an optimist to ask the public to vote for an ever-lower standard of living, and a defeatist to deny the power of innovation. The solution lies, as it did at the time of the industrial revolution, in embracing new technologies.

In order to realise the Liberal Democrat ambition of a zero-carbon future for Britain we must of course press ahead with developing the renewable energy sector, but on its own this is not enough. The economy as a whole must also become far less energy-intensive. Energy efficiency technology must be an essential element of national energy strategy. Saving energy is, after all, the most environmentally benign 'source' of energy, and has the crucial benefit of reducing costs.

Focusing solely on energy is still too limited, as we need to use all natural resources more efficiently. We need to move to a 'resource-efficient economy', not just a 'low-carbon economy'. It is not just the energy generation industry that will feel the impact. The automotive industry is also on the cusp of radical change as it experiments with the electrification of transport; the building industry is adapting to new environmental standards, as is the waste industry. Many other industries are also likely to see similar radical changes in the decade ahead – changes that will be driven by resource and energy efficiency technologies.

The graph below (Fig. 13.2) provides an illustration of the benefits of REETs.[1] It gives a summary of the contribution made by different technologies, both REETs and renewable energies, to potential greenhouse gas abatement. Each measure is ranked according to whether it saves money or costs money and placed in order from left to right, starting with the most cost-effective (such as switching to LED lighting) and ending with the more expensive measures (such as retrofitting power plants to capture and store carbon emissions). On the horizontal axis, the width of each measure indicates its CO_2 abatement potential. The vertical axis then shows whether a technology will result in cost savings (below the zero line) or higher costs (above the line).[2]

'Right-hand side measures' require investment of large amounts of capital, making a big and necessary impact, but at significant cost. In practice these investments are made by government in the form of subsidies to large infrastructure companies such as the energy companies. The 'polluter pays'

Fig. 13.2 Greenhouse gas abatment cost curve[3]

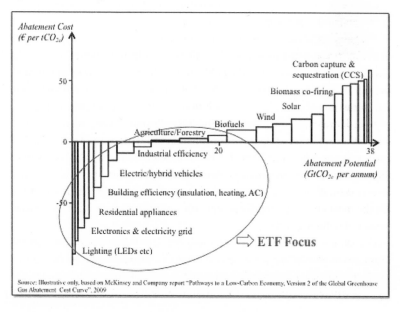

Source: Illustrative only, based on McKinsey and Company report "Pathways to a Low-Carbon Economy, Version 2 of the Global Greenhouse Gas Abatement Cost Curve", 2009

principle, although now established, does not motivate the energy companies to invest in technologies that produce more costly energy and which impact adversely on their profitability. Although the potential of these solutions is large, they require heavy long-term government subsidy or higher energy prices. While these approaches, such as carbon capture and storage, are of strategic long-term importance, deployment is not happening quickly.

REETs are quite different. They are defined as those companies that appear in the left-hand side of the curve, typically characterised by the use of cutting-edge technology, with the potential to reduce significantly greenhouse gas emissions and/or use resources more efficiently. They cover a broad spectrum of new technologies that bring costs down because they use resources more efficiently. They can usually be deployed relatively quickly because it is far easier to roll out a new technology that saves money, even in recession. Furthermore, the overall potential of REETs is broadly similar to that of alternative generation technologies. The catch is that it can take time and money to develop them initially, and individually their development is risky. Their commercialisation is typically led by the private sector, often by small entrepreneurial companies. Government is not normally involved, which is one of the reasons why these companies are generally overlooked when evaluating energy policy – even though their cumulative potential impact is very large, and their 'bang for the buck' of support from government is huge. Another reason is that quantifying this 'bang for the buck' is pretty difficult.

New resource-efficient technologies can be 'deep green'

Measuring the carbon footprint of a large and mature company is hard enough. Measuring the potential beneficial impact of a new technology that has not yet been widely deployed and is not yet mature is fraught with problems. Nevertheless, the Environmental Technologies Fund (ETF) set out to do this a couple of years ago, working with Trucost, a specialist consultancy.[4] ETF examined the technologies of ten of its portfolio companies, detailed in the table overleaf (Table 13.1), and their potential impacts.

As a result we think that if the technology developed by just these ten small companies was deployed globally, the environmental benefit would equate to 10 per cent (or 0.5 GtCO2e) of the EU's total carbon footprint; i.e. *half of the EU 2020 reduction target*. This is a huge figure. It should of course be treated with caution, as there are inevitable limitations in the methodology[5] (see below), and in practice not all ten technologies are likely to succeed globally. However those that do will probably be very widely deployed *without* any government subsidy. To create the same scale of impact (albeit with greater certainty) by investing in offshore wind, for example, would require investment of a totally different order, around £200 billion.

This list, among other things, illustrates clearly that 'green' is not a sector. Innovations creating big environmental impacts are found in many industrial sectors. In essence the underlying message is simple: investing in REETs can produce huge environmental benefits, at relatively low cost compared to the alternatives. The alternatives, such as offshore wind, are absolutely still needed – they are lower risk, and REETs alone cannot get us to zero-carbon – but far more effort should go into supporting innovation.

It must be stressed that more work needs to go into developing robust ways to assess the benefits of new technologies. One of the barriers these young innovative companies face is that they are not immediately recognised as being 'green' because there is no industry standard that they can be measured against. While Trucost and ETF have developed one meaningful methodology (the CO_2 impact on an industrial value chain caused by a new technology – hence the globally addressable potential market impact) more work needs to be done and a more standard and universally applicable methodology would be a big step forward.

The UK needs to lead

The UK government cannot afford to stand by and allow other governments to lead the charge in the development of green technologies.

Other countries are spending heavily on the development and deployment of such technologies across a whole range of industries. Their governments understand that the countries that host the new technologies will gain enormously when the rest of the world adopts them, as was the case in the industrial revolution. The only difference now is that global adoption of superior technologies will happen far, far faster. The UK is well positioned to lead in the development of REETs, especially as it holds the advantage of being home to much relevant early-stage innovation. Six of the companies listed above are British, underlining the fact that the UK produces innovative technologies in quantity as well as quality.

As is often said, the UK is good at early-stage innovation, but historically has been far less effective in building businesses based on it. One recent example of this is the development of graphene, a virtually two-dimensional carbon sheet that has revolutionary properties. Discovered at Manchester University less than ten years ago, several other countries acted faster and deployed far greater resources into the commercialisation of graphene than

Table 13.1 Environmental Technology Fund – selected ten portfolio companies

Company name and target sector(s)	New green technology
4energy Telecommunications	Highly efficient cooling solutions suitable for wireless network providers, e.g. Vodafone
Metalysis Metal refining	A breakthrough process for refining high-value metals (such as tantalum and titanium)
Compact Power Motors Electric vehicles	Arguably the most compact and efficient electric power motors in the world
Elstat Smart refrigeration	Energy management devices which enable commercial fridges to adapt according to their usage and environment
Novel Polymer Solutions Polymer manufacture	Polymer coatings which help to bond substances to each other more easily
Nujira Wireless network efficiency	'Envelope tracking' enables power amplifiers, used to generate radio signals, to operate far more efficiently
Perpetuum Industrial process monitoring, rail transport	An appliance that can harvest the energy from small levels of vibration and convert it into electricity
Chemrec Paper and pulp, biofuels	Turns paper-manufacturing waste into biofuels, enabling pulp and paper mills to become secondary bio-refineries
Kebony Hardwoods	Changes the cellular structure of wood, enabling rapidly growing softwoods to become hardwood
Industrial Origami Sheet metal manufacture	Unique technology which allows metal to be folded very accurately, without losing its strength

Environmental impact	Commercial impact
Halving the energy used for cooling in wireless networks	Energy is a significant cost for the rapidly expanding wireless industry, and it is putting significant effort into reducing usage.
Typically, metal refining is a dirty, energy-hungry business. Metalysis uses far less energy and no hazardous chemicals	Significantly reduces refining costs, and also potentially allows materials like titanium to be far more widely used
20 per cent of all the energy generated in the world is consumed by electric motors	Particularly important to the automotive industry as it begins to introduce electric scooters and cars
Can deliver energy savings of up to 60 per cent	Applicable to millions of drink cooling machines, vending machines and industrial fridges worldwide
Facilitates use of modern, environmentally friendly materials	Opens up the possibility of using modern materials in a variety of applications
Nujira's technology reduces energy consumed in wireless network operation by c.40 per cent	The technology has been adapted for use in mobile phones, highlighting its broad potential
Enables the practical use of wireless sensor networks, which then improve efficiency and safety	Enables the practical use of wireless sensor networks for monitoring industrial processes
Turns a large-scale source of waste into a fuel, at the point where the waste is created	The scale of the industry is such that this technology could potentially satisfy 2 per cent of current global fuel demand
Diminishes demand for irreplaceable tropical hardwood. Softwoods are far more sustainable	Softwood, which is relatively cheap and quick to grow, can be converted into more expensive high-quality hard wood
Reduces metal consumption by up to 50 per cent in products such as white goods, greatly reducing the environmental footprint	Sheet metal manufacturing is greatly simplified, dramatically reducing costs and improving productivity

the UK. While UK government did finally respond, late in the day, this example illustrates a real problem which is being made more acute by the ongoing financial crisis.

Smoothing the path of the cleantech revolution

So, what exactly can we do to help these companies at the stage when capital investment is needed?

Firstly, we should acknowledge that action is required on a large scale. We are not talking about small initiatives, or a good bit of PR. The Green Investment Bank is a good first step – but only that – and in practice it is quite focused on renewable energy funding, with only a nod towards energy efficiency and energy from waste. And in any case, the bank's capital is only £3 billion which, even taking into account its leverage potential, is a small fraction of the money required to fund a large scale shift to renewables. It does not really address the broader and more radical theme of a cleantech revolution across many industrial sectors. The Green Investment Bank needs a multiple of its current capital and a significant part of its remit – say, in proportion to the two sides of the graph above – should be the support and promotion of REETs.

Secondly, government can promote investment from other sources – a lower cost option for it. Below we suggest some ways this could be done (from companies, institutions and private individuals). Our suggestions are not comprehensive, and a greater dialogue is needed.

Thirdly, government can also change legislation in industrial sectors directly – the lowest cost option of all. We also discuss this below.

Encouraging investment

Encouraging investment by institutional investors and banks

The UK and European governments have, quite rightly, sought to clamp down on excessive risk-taking by banks. One unintended consequence, however, is to make it harder for banks and other institutions to take the type of risk desired and needed to support younger innovative companies. This problem needs to be addressed. On top of this, much of the legislation we do have, though implemented with good intention, often seems little more than a bureaucratic impediment. Take the example of Silicon Valley Bank, probably the leading global bank specialising in lending to young technology companies. It has had to fight for two years to be allowed a banking licence to do business in the UK. In China the same process took only six months.

We should explore how to create incentives for institutional investors to favour funds investing in innovative young companies, and 'green funds' over more general funds. Other European countries are looking into this, and the French have had perhaps the most creative and progressive debate. One proposal considered there is for the government to underwrite a proportion of the capital an institution assigns specifically for investment in young innovative companies. This guarantee would be small relative to the total invested, so a call on that guarantee would only occur in the case of very poor performance. The impact, though, could be to direct far larger sums into areas where such guarantees exist.

Encouraging and enabling private investment

Private investor behaviour is already deliberately shaped by government schemes. A savings and investment culture is promoted, for example, via ISAs (such investments are typically made via funds that invest in large, normally multinational, companies). Venture Capital Trusts (VCTs) and Enterprise Investment Schemes (EIS) are, in contrast, used to promote investment in smaller UK companies that many studies show are the engine of innovation and job creation. There are, however, no specific incentives for investing in 'green technologies' or REETs. There is, again, room for a more creative debate in this area; ideas include:

- Enabling individual private investors to invest their capital more easily, and more safely, into smaller UK private companies, the engines of growth. They should be encouraged to spread their risk around many companies, just as a professional investor would do. In other words, it should be made possible for individuals to have VCT/EIS tax breaks when investing in a wider range of collective investment vehicles.
- Specifically, VCT/EIS funds should be allowed to invest as 'funds of funds' into professional venture capital funds that focus on job-creating companies. Such venture capital companies currently only find it practical to raise funds from larger institutions, but could deal with a collective fund of VCT/EIS investors just as it would with any other institution. VCT/EIS rules would have to be relaxed marginally to fit into line with what works commercially for such funds, but this would only require a small amendment to existing legislation. Similarly, ISA collective investment vehicles could be allowed to invest in such 'institutional quality' venture capital funds.
- Create additional 'green ISAs' and 'green VCT/EIS' schemes, in addition to existing ISA and VCT/EIS schemes. Since it is hard to define 'green' effectively, an expert panel could be created that would 'kitemark' approved funds as having qualifying investment strategies. Consideration would then need to be given to subsequent auditing (though without trying to

encourage bureaucracy). Again, this should include access to traditional venture capital funds that are currently institutionally orientated.

Encouraging investment by companies

The various measures that have been used to encourage investment by individual companies could be applied specifically to encourage green investment. Examples to consider include:

- Enhancing R&D tax credits for 'green' R&D (both in terms of amount and by making such payments more rapid, or even enabling companies to claim 'on account').
- A special programme of capital allowances against tax for 'green' capital expenditure.
- A programme of capital allowances for investment by corporations into green venture capital funds.

Careful legislation can be used to stimulate innovation

In a number of industrial sectors it is also possible to use legislation, rather than subsidy, to promote change. Legislation has the huge advantage, to the government and taxpayer, of being free. National legislation is often viewed by business as a potential obstacle to international competitiveness, but certain types of legislation can aid competitiveness in the medium and longer term – specifically, legislation that acts to promote, or even force, innovation. For example, energy efficiency legislation for new buildings and anti-pollution legislation in the car industry have each stimulated innovation and international competitiveness.

So, consideration could be given to the more strategic use of legislation of products and markets to promote green innovation. Clearly this should focus on areas where environmental benefits are clear. Equally clearly, care would need to be taken not to be seen to impose short-term costs that are unaffordable or that do not result in significant longer-term competitive advantage. Any legislation should be implemented in such a way as to promote the rise of new industries, particularly industries that can then export their superior technologies to the rest of the world.

Green begins with government

The suggestions we make above are individually worthwhile, but they are only part of the solution.

Decades of industrial malaise on the one hand, and a laissez-faire drift towards a financially dominated economy on the other, have led the UK to a position where a focused environmental industrial policy is needed. But an overarching industrial policy without a working mechanism to deliver it is useless, and therefore government must change.

The UK needs a system in which the industrial planning and decision-making processes of government are integrated. As stated in the 1987 Brundtland Report, *Our Common Future*, government departments tend to be independent and fragmented, working to relatively narrow mandates with closed decision-making processes.[6] This is exacerbated by the fact that those responsible for managing energy needs and protecting the environment are institutionally separated from those responsible for managing the economy.

In order for an environmental industrial policy to have a clear focus, this needs to change. Specifically, three government departments must work together closely: the Department for Energy and Climate Change (DECC), the Department for Business, Innovation and Skills (BIS) and the Treasury.

DECC combines energy and climate change into one governmental organisation, inevitably then seeing climate change as one of a number of energy problems. Within this remit it does have a clear focus and appears to be doing a good job, and we would not want its efforts reduced. However, climate change is not a sub-sector of energy, so should not be represented solely within and by DECC.

BIS should have at least as great an interest in what we see as an industrial revolution. While it theoretically has an important role in shaping future government policy regarding green issues, it appears relatively unfocused and ineffectual. BIS should not be restructured in a manner which would amount to merely a cosmetic exercise of 'rearranging deckchairs'. Nor should it simply be abolished. BIS has a vital role to play, but needs a genuine and radical overhaul, with the clear purpose of creatively and assertively implementing a long-term programme to create a green economy which promotes growth and jobs. If BIS is to lead a green revolution it must be revolutionised.

It goes without saying that without the close cooperation of the Treasury, change will be impossible. To get these three arms of government to work together constructively will require strong leadership; responsibility for this agenda must rest with a high-profile individual from the highest echelons of government. This should be a specific appointment.

Conclusion

Green is not a single sector, it is an 'impact' that is found across all sectors
Attempting to deal with green issues as if independent from the rest of life is the wrong way to address the issues, and creates a disconnect between

environmentalism and economic realities. All industries can benefit from increased resource and energy efficiency.

Resource- and energy-efficient technologies are a vital part of the green solution

These companies can deliver both green and economic benefits. They enable 'green growth' and job creation.

Growth should be enabled by emphasising investment in green technology

Both large institutions and private investors have a role to play in supporting resource- and energy-efficient technologies (REETs), and this role should be encouraged by incentivising investments that are deemed 'green'. Government should also use legislation to enable green growth.

The UK should take a bold lead

Without a focus on developing technological innovation, the UK will fall behind other countries. Britain will be far better off as a country in the vanguard of a technological revolution, rather than subsequently importing the results of one that has happened elsewhere.

The UK government must refocus itself

The UK government's approach to such green issues is too departmentalised, fractured and lacks direction. As a minimum, inter-departmental communication and cooperation regarding this should be increased, and the Department for Business, Innovation and Skills in particular needs to place this issue far higher up its agenda. If BIS is to lead a green revolution it needs to be revolutionised.

Notes

1   The graph is not intended to be definitive, both because costs, particularly of new technologies, tend to change over time and because it only shows examples of some technologies (for example this version omits tidal and wave, as well as nuclear, power).

2   CO_2 abatement is measured in billions of metric tonnes of CO_2 equivalent per year ($GtCO_2e$ per annum). The cumulative potential of each of these measures if pursued to their full potential would be 38 $GtCO_2e$ per year. As a reference point, global greenhouse gas emissions may increase to around 56 $GtCO_2e$ in

2020 according to business-as-usual projections (United Nations Environment Programme).

3   Source: Environmental Technologies Fund illustration, based on McKinsey & Co., *Pathways to a Low-Carbon Economy: Version 2 of the Global Greenhouse Gas Cost Abatement Curve* (2009).

4   One of the authors, Patrick Sheehan, is a founding partner of the Environmental Technologies Fund.

5   It must be stressed that more work needs to go into developing robust ways to assess the benefits of new technologies. One of the barriers these young innovative companies face is that they are not immediately recognised as being 'green' because there is no industry standard that they can be measured against. While Trucost and ETF have developed one meaningful methodology (the CO_2 impact on an industrial value chain caused by a new technology – hence the globally addressable potential market impact), more work needs to be done and a more standard and universally applicable methodology would be a big step forward.

6   World Commission on Environment and Development, *Our Common Future* (Oxford University Press, 1987).

Chapter 14

Green and Growing – The Importance of Cleantech

Julian Huppert MP[1]

With a mountain of debt and low growth weighing heavily on our country, this decade could well become a lost opportunity for environmental policy. Liberal Democrats continue to call for proper action over climate change, but the temptation to dilute our commitment has increased as 'green government' has been portrayed as an unaffordable barrier to growth.

Lib Dems must reclaim environmental protection as a clear and necessary policy which benefits British society now and in the future. But we must also make the case for green growth – for an industrial policy which incubates economic growth by supporting climate change mitigation. We need an unambiguous vision of what green growth looks like: one we can put to the public in 2015, and one we can build on beyond the next election.

The UK clean technology sector (here referred to as 'cleantech') is already one of the key drivers for job creation and growth. The myriad of emerging cleantech companies, such as those clustered around Cambridge, point the way to green growth, and should provide a guiding light for liberal policy-making. Cleantech is a trillion-pound global industry, in which the UK has already excelled. It has the potential to create wealth and jobs, and help combat climate change. We must support it as a central plank of our green growth policy.

However, as will be discussed, there are also many obstacles standing in the way of a flourishing cleantech industry in this country. Decisive leadership and coordinated policies are needed to enable the UK to overcome these barriers and become a world leader in the field.

The cleantech industry

Cleantech is any new technology that helps to reduce our carbon footprint and use energy sustainably; it covers both sources of renewable energy and ways of using energy more efficiently.[2]

Fig. 14.1 Definition of Cleantech

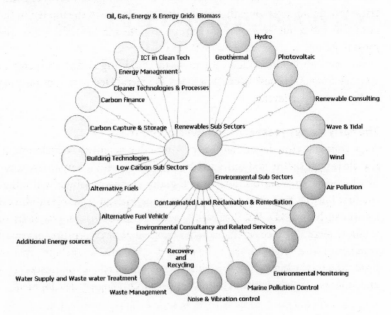

The global cleantech market already has a market value of £4.3 trillion and is forecast to grow 5 per cent each year for the next five years. The rising price of fossil fuels has played a key part in this.[3] Public attitudes are also shifting; consumers are increasingly demanding products which are environmentally friendly. Finally, governments are competing to put their country on the cleantech map and create jobs.[4]

Many British companies are already profiting from the shift towards sustainable technologies. The UK has been reasonably successful in carving out a place for itself in this emerging industry, and constitutes 3-4 per cent of the global cleantech industry. According to the 2012 Global Cleantech Innovation Index, the UK ranks tenth in the world for providing the best conditions for cleantech start-up creation.[5] Cambridge, in particular, has a thriving cleantech sector and is home to many leading businesses in the industry, such as AlertMe, Breathing Buildings, Eight19, Cambridge Carbon Capture, PolySolar and CamSemi.

Despite this strong potential, however, there are several challenges facing the development of the cleantech industry. The research and development (R&D) of new technology, the growth of new companies into national businesses, strong national demand and access to foreign markets are all critical for green growth. The UK is in danger of falling behind other countries if we do not overcome these barriers – we may be in the top ten in the cleantech index but we are fifth in Europe, and the market leaders have the most to gain.

So how can public policy contribute to a budding cleantech sector in strained financial times? What should we, as Liberal Democrats, be pushing for at government level?

The early stages – research and development

As a young sector dependent on cutting-edge scientific development, the cleantech sector is dominated by small emerging companies, some of which will grow into international giants, many of which will fall at the first hurdle. Few of these companies have enough resources to invest significantly in R&D. But there are benefits from having a multiplicity of small- to medium-sized enterprises. In particular, if we can ensure that small companies with bright ideas can be supported at the earliest stages, we can foster exactly the kind of creative thinking – with its concomitant successes and failures – which is critical to cutting-edge technological development.

Finance

Financial obstacles are particularly significant in this young industry. Research is capital-intensive; new cleantech companies need to secure a large amount of capital in order to carry out their projects. At the same time, financiers can be asked to wait a long time for a return on their investment, which can be a deterrent.

A recent report from Taylor Wessing, the Cleantech Group and Real Deals found that both venture capital and private equity investors are turning to firms with innovations which are reaching the end of the R&D phase. A 2010 report by the Greater Cambridge Partnership found that just 3 per cent of cleantech companies in the Cambridge cluster had received venture capital; comparable sectors such as ICT were 40 per cent and healthcare and biotechnologies 36 per cent.[6] A 2011 survey of 312 UK cleantech companies showed that 29 per cent of companies interviewed 'cited a lack of access to finance as the main obstacle to expansion'.[7]

As a consequence, many cleantech businesses rely on subsidies and grants, from the UK government or from the EU. The Taylor Wessing report highlighted that corporate investors and public funds are therefore providing a disproportionate level of funding, which punishes riskier early-stage R&D in younger companies. Uncertainty over the future of this assistance, particularly during a period of economic austerity, has created additional risk.[8]

The lack of public funding for R&D to fill this gap, when considered against the situation in comparable economies, is particularly worrying. A recovery in green investment has been seen since 2010, with a 35 per cent increase in investment in the clean energy sector in 2011. But the UK's investment is failing to grow as fast as some of its rivals. In terms of investment growth over the last year, the UK comes sixth behind Indonesia, India, the US, Italy and France. A report from the Pew Environment Group in 2011 also showed that the UK has failed to make the top ten in investment growth over the last five years.[9]

The coalition government is establishing the Green Investment Bank to fund green projects in the UK – a crucial Lib Dem success. Funding of £1 billion for the bank was announced in the 2010 Spending Review and a further £2 billion in the 2011 Budget. The ambition is to grow the Green Investment Bank over time. With the government in extraordinarily tight fiscal circumstances, the priority for Liberal Democrats now should be to enable this bank to borrow in order to lend, and this must be underwritten by the government.

This policy is, however, by no means a silver bullet. The UK's credit rating is predicated on the security of the public finances, which may not be helped by underwriting investment in green industries. But as the Stern Review so clearly showed, the cost of doing nothing on climate change outweighs the costs of acting now. While the UK government would be underwriting a wide portfolio of green industries – some of which will succeed and some will not – the sector is forecast to grow every year in spite of the recession.[10] For that reason, it should be able to borrow to lend, and restrictions on venture capital funding should be lifted.

In addition, the scale of investment in comparable economies, and the underlying cost of greening our economy in order to meet our carbon targets, necessitates either an extremely large level of investment or an industrial policy which underwrites and underpins new investment. Estimates of the costs of meeting UK carbon targets range from £200 billion to £1 trillion. We can either act now to develop the technology to help mitigate those costs, or we can delay our actions, damage our environment and spend vast sums buying new technologies later from countries which did invest in cleantech.[11]

Clusters, deregulation and government policy

Having said that, the government cannot just underwrite the entire sector without initiating significant structural reforms and providing consistent support for the clusters which do exist.

The first priority should be to leverage private-sector investment.[12] Of course, loans from the GIB will signal confidence in the sector and in cleantech companies; there is no better way of showing venture capitalists and private equity firms that cleantech is a safe bet than a loan from the independent GIB underwritten by the government. But the cleantech sector must become an attractive hub for entrepreneurial investors in its own right.

In order to achieve this, the government should also target existing funding streams to entrench cleantech 'incubators'. The Cambridge area benefits from several business 'incubators' which help cleantech companies get off the ground. For example, Cambridge Cleantech[13] offers clients access to finance, advice from experts in the field, opportunities to promote their business internationally and advice on government regulations. Other groups such as the Technology Partnership offer similar services. The government's priority should be to direct existing funding streams towards these clusters.

In addition, tax credits are an effective way of supporting companies willing to risk their own capital in R&D. Since coming into office, the coalition has increased the rate of relief available for small and medium-sized enterprise (SMEs). The system could be further targeted towards high-tech environmental companies by offering a higher rate for environmentally beneficial schemes. According to the OECD, in 2011 the UK ranked nineteenth in terms of the attractiveness of its tax system incentives for R&D.[4]

Support for cleantech clusters

To maximise the potential benefit to the economy of the cleantech sector in the current climate of limited public funding, existing economic development budgets should be partly refocused to support the sector. This could include:

- Targeted cleantech sector programmes initiated by the Technology Strategy Board.
- The cleantech sector prioritised in the allocation criteria for the Regional Growth Fund.
- Government loan funding for SMEs via the clearing banks to include cleantech as a priority sector.

To help boost growth in the economy, a more radical solution would be to focus Department for Business funding on the cleantech sector as one of a small number of high-priority growth sectors.

Martin Garratt, Chief Executive, Cambridge Cleantech

Consistent policy-making

From feed-in tariffs to zero-carbon new build home requirements by 2016 and to domestic smart metering requirements by 2019, the cleantech sector is driven by government regulations and incentives. More clearly defined and consistent regulation was the second highest concern in the survey of cleantech companies conducted in 2011. (Cleantech Group and The Carbon Trust, 'Bullish UK cleantech entrepreneurs confident of green growth').

While no cleantech company business plan will be totally reliant on government regulation, there is a reasonable expectation that it should be clear to understand and be consistent over time. The recent debacle over reducing feed-in tariffs for solar PV at very short notice is a case in point of how not to regulate and incentivise the sector. Such 'moving of the goalposts' makes for very difficult business planning. Government should instead set out a clear plan, which may involve reducing tariffs over several years, but which would be clear and consistent and not subject to short-term changes.

Martin Garratt, Chief Executive, Cambridge Cleantech

Finally, the government should take extreme care, that, whatever funding streams, tax incentives or policy initiatives it implements, the application is consistent and the deadlines are clear.

Universities and immigration – fostering ideas and attracting talent
The cleantech sector is heavily dependent on a very close interaction between businesses and universities, while the success of budding companies is dependent on the talents of the people who run them. The co-location of the Cambridge cluster and the University is critical to its recent success.

It is crucial, therefore, that in the next budget the government ring-fences – and increases – the existing science research budget. This was a particular success in the Comprehensive Spending Review; the government agreed to freeze the £4.6 billion revenue science budget for the rest of the Parliament. But the slower than expected pace of deficit reduction may result in further spending cuts. This must not fall on the science budget, which is a key driver of growth, ideas and, ultimately, tax receipts.[15]

Talent is also vital for success in the cleantech industry. For that reason, the government must change course on immigration policy. Current Home Office policy is to reduce immigration to the tens of thousands. To achieve that, almost all non-EU economic migrants are now effectively treated as 'guest workers', and economic migrants coming from outside the EU to fill skills shortages are to be expected to stay no longer than five years, with the exception of those who earn more than £150,000 per year or who work in the sports sector.

This provides a clear disincentive for scientists and industry leaders to come and live and work here. Nearly half of all UK researchers collaborate with overseas colleagues, while a number of foreign scientists have won Nobel prizes while working in British labs. A recent report by the Breakthrough Institute set out a clear path for the US to grow their own cleantech industry by removing barriers to immigration for foreign scientists and engineers who wish to work in the US. The UK must provide similar exceptions for talented scientists, and we must do so as soon as possible.[16]

The co-terminosity of finance, ideas and people is absolutely critical. This three-pronged strategy will help get cleantech off the ground in the UK. Increased government support, policies designed to leverage more private sector investment and tax breaks for start-ups are all necessary. But it is not just this initial phase where there are problems to overcome.

Scaling-up – creating demand at the earliest stages

Following the development of a new product, there are challenges involved in scaling up a business from serving a niche market to a national one. This stage has been found to be a particular stumbling block for British cleantech businesses. According to the 2012 Global Cleantech Innovation Index, Britain does well at encouraging innovation but poorly at commercialising this innovation:

> Evidence of commercialised cleantech innovation measures the ability of a country to scale up innovations developed by cleantech start-ups. The increasingly global nature of the cleantech industry means that this is not necessarily a measure of where those innovations originated; however, a domestic market does help drive innovation and provide a test-bed where products and companies can develop before efforts begin to build an international customer base … The UK performed less well on commercialised cleantech innovation due to low renewable energy consumption and cleantech company revenues.[17]

This implies that although innovation exists and companies are being created, we are failing to scale up effectively due to low demand for cleantech products, relative to other countries.

Successes so far

Liberal Democrats in government have created a solid base from which domestic demand will emerge – our first priority should be to highlight the successes of these policies and argue for their retention.

The Green Deal is encouraging energy efficiency improvements in homes, paid for by savings from energy bills. This has already created demand for clean technology, such as solid wall insulation. Steps have also been taken to increase the UK's capacity for microgeneration through the use of feed-in tariffs, which has provided significant demand for cleantech companies, while the Electricity Market Reform Bill will give greater certainty to developers of renewable electricity technologies. Finally, the Renewable Heat Incentive is further stoking demand for climate mitigation tools.

Already this has borne fruit. Cambridge Retrofit, a scheme aimed to make Cambridge the first city to meet the 2050 carbon reduction target, has enabled private and public sector organisations to team up to create a city-wide carbon reduction scheme. This, in turn, has provided a large market for local cleantech companies to provide sustainable services and technologies, which will ultimately allow these companies to grow and export.[18]

Public procurement and green growth

The Liberal Democrats should look to further demand-side reforms to supplement this growth. Government procurement contracts can provide companies, particularly new start-ups, with a powerful incentive to develop new technologies. However the UK's track record of using procurement to stimulate innovation is poor compared to countries with thriving high-tech sectors like the United States or Finland.[19]

The government has made clear its aspiration that 25 per cent of government contracts should be awarded to SMEs, compared to just 12 per cent currently.[20] This has the potential to benefit new cleantech companies because the sector is dominated by smaller enterprises. But the government should do more to specifically target cleantech.

Two areas where demand could drive the cleantech sector, through a combination of procurement and changes to existing regulations, are transport and housing.

Iarla Kilbane-Dawe, Liberal Democrat candidate for Edmonton in 2010, recently worked on a procurement strategy for electric vehicles (EVs). His work showed how the government could use sustainability criteria to create a preference in government service procurement for competitive bidders who use EVs. For example, reform of the conditions attached to the Bus Service Operating Grant could supplement the Green Bus Fund by incentivising procurement of low-emissions buses.

In addition, the government should further consider high-visibility pilot schemes to generate confidence in UK electric vehicle production and identify gaps in knowledge. One example is the Big Switch, advocated by former Liberal Democrat London Assembly Member Mike Tuffrey, which would require London buses, taxis and vans to convert to electric power by 2020. While the scheme seems ambitious, Tuffrey showed how the entire scheme could be cash-positive by 2023 due to the rising price of fuel and the falling cost of battery technology. Sainsbury's are already considering changing all their urban deliveries to electric vehicles for cost reasons.[21]

Sustainable building technologies are also an integral area of the UK cleantech industry, and one which we must incentivise. A proper housing policy is one way in which we can both promote this sector and solve the country's housing crisis. One way of doing so could be a combination of continued low interest rates and planning reforms to incentivise building; Tim Leunig, former Chief Economist at CentreForum, identified the benefits of such a policy for our housing crisis, our unemployment and our lack of growth.[22]

If this policy was combined with tough new criteria in the National Planning Policy Framework about the sustainability of the construction process and the final buildings, rather than their location, we could use this solution to address the UK's housing crisis and spur the cleantech industry. Together these policies have the potential to create truly green growth in the UK.

Making carbon pay

Support for particular sectors, such as transport and housing, must be coupled with proper carbon pricing. It is important that the cleantech industry is free to think holistically about how carbon can be reduced in every single sector.

Following the Climate Change Act 2008, the UK now has binding carbon budgets which ensure that where emissions rise in one sector, corresponding falls will need to be achieved in another. The Act also established unilateral legally binding greenhouse gas emissions reduction targets of at least 34 per cent by 2020 (from 1990) and at least 80 per cent by 2050. Further, the Electricity Market Reform Bill and the carbon price floor for the electricity generation industry, which will be introduced from April 2013, will help to promote renewable electricity production.

While these policies provide a framework for action, and set out our overall targets, it is critical that investors are provided with a guarantee that, in whatever industry they choose to invest, the price of carbon will ultimately rise, and there will be a market for low-carbon alternatives. For that to happen, Liberal Democrats should look to create a proper carbon price with a trading scheme in the medium to long term.

We must pay close attention to how the scheme works in Australia. They have already introduced a price of A\$23 per tonne for carbon, with substantial compensation for consumers and companies exposed to foreign trade. The price is due to rise each year until 2015, when it will be set by the market.

Under the European scheme, the price is set by the number of carbon credits available. To date, the market has been flooded, keeping the price below the necessary level to meet carbon reduction targets, creating an uncertain climate for investors. The carbon price floor being introduced by the Chancellor from April 2013 in an attempt to meet this problem is an unsatisfactory solution – since it is being introduced unilaterally in the UK, an unintended consequence will be a surplus of allowances becoming available from UK enterprises, thus driving the price down in the EU even further. There is no substitute for reducing the total number of allowances available at an EU level, which means arguing for a more ambitious EU emissions target – creating a clear market incentive to switch to renewable technologies.

Finally, a border tax on carbon-heavy imports could also reflect the damage caused by cheap, unsustainable production methods in some countries from which the UK imports. Similar ideas have been proposed in the US and in the EU. Although no agreement has been reached in the European Commission, the UK could support a limited measure requiring industries to buy some credits in the Emission Trading Scheme if their country has no carbon abatement programme.

Export-led recovery

UK green growth policies should focus on R&D, scaling up and boosting domestic demand. But we must capitalise on domestic developments as soon as possible if we are to grow our cleantech companies, grow our economy and become world leaders in sustainable technologies. That requires substantial support for cleantech exports.

UK Export Finance, the operating name of the Export Credits Guarantee Department (ECGD), is the UK's export credit agency under the auspices of the Department of Business, Innovation and Skills. Its role is to support UK companies to export, by providing guarantees, insurance and reinsurance against loss. However, reform of the agency is urgently needed to provide the best service for UK business and cleantech in particular.

Virtually all the ECGD's support goes to a handful of large companies. The ECGD has great potential to support and promote new, green industries, but at present it supports proportionally more carbon-intensive industries than any other EU country. In 2009–10, 90 per cent of ECGD's portfolio concentrated on the commercial airline industry. Worse than that, its non-aerospace activities declined by nearly 90 per cent, while over the last decade overall business declined by 70 per cent.

The coalition has said that ECGD and UK Trade and Investment (UKTI) will not support 'dirty fossil-fuel energy production', but this commitment has yet to be implemented. We must go further, by changing the statutory footing of UK Export Finance to make it more accountable and more open, and also to include a presumption in favour of sustainable technologies when it is considering which exports to support. Fifty million pounds a year was ring-fenced in 2003 for supporting renewable energy, but this money was never spent.[23] The whole ethos and purpose of the organisation must change if we are to support the greener industries which are destined for long-term growth rather than short-term gain.[24]

In addition to financial support from the ECGD, British companies can receive export advice and assistance from UKTI. UKTI already organises promotional activities to reach SMEs and cleantech organisations, as well as assisting in press and marketing. But the focus must be on cleantech. Again, greater accountability and a statutory focus on sustainable technologies would provide UKTI with the tools and direction it needs to support green growth.[25]

Conclusions

The expansion of the cleantech sector in the UK is something Liberal Democrats naturally support. As fossil fuel prices continue to rise, renewable energy and energy-saving technologies will grow. Countries that invest now will reap the rewards in the years to come.

As Liberal Democrats, we have already played a key role in reforming barriers to success for fledgling cleantech companies. Increasing investment through the Green Investment Bank, making funds available so that banks can lend with confidence, and ring-fencing science research funding are all coalition policies of which the Lib Dems can be proud.

But over the coming years we need to make the case that the less the country invests in the cleantech sector, the more it will cost us in the future. We can do this by promoting existing cleantech clusters, such as in Cambridge, but we also have to ensure that there is a growing domestic market for carbon reduction technologies – a market which our companies can thrive in, before exporting across the globe.

I strongly believe that the liberal choice is to make carbon pay, and allow our scientists and small companies to innovate and grow. It is hard to imagine that, by 2050, the choice will be between green or growth. The sooner we encourage British cleantech companies to emerge and grow, the faster we will capitalise on the greening of the global economy. There is a palpable lack of a clear industrial policy to place our country on a sustainable footing. I firmly believe that liberals everywhere should look to the thriving cleantech sector as a crucible for action over the coming decade.

Notes

1   With thanks to Martin Garratt, Chief Executive, Cambridge Cleantech, for his contribution.
2   Cambridge Clean Tech, 'Definition of Cleantech', May 2010; http://www.cambridgecleantech.org.uk/definition-of-cleantech
3   Greater Cambridge Partnership, *Cleantech Strategy and Action Plan* (May 2010).
4   Ron Pernick and Clint Wilder, *The Cleantech Revolution* (Collins, 2007).
5   Stefan Henningsson, Richard Youngman and Amanda Faulkner, *Coming Clean: The Global Cleantech Innovation Index 2012* (Cleantech Group and WWF, February 2012).
6   Taylor Wessing, 'Capital-intensive cleantech innovations may lose out in battle to secure funding', 7 May 2009.
7   Cleantech Group and The Carbon Trust, 'Bullish UK cleantech entrepreneurs confident of green growth', *International Sustainable Energy Review*, April 2011.
8   Oxford Capital Partners, *Supporting Cleantech Enterprise in the UK: The Role of Incubators* (December 2008).
9   The Pew Environment Group, *Who's Winning the Clean Energy Race?* (April 2012).
10 Environmental Audit Committee, *The Green Investment Bank: Second Report of Session 2010–11*, 3 March 2011.
11 Henningsson et al., *Coming Clean*.
12 James Dyson, *Ingenious Britain – Making the UK the Leading High Tech Exporter in Europe* (March 2010).
13 Cambridge Cleantech website, 'Business Support'; http://www.cambridgecleantech.org.uk/business-support
14 Confederation of British Industry, *Making the UK the Best Place to Invest* (April 2011).

15 Nick Hall, 'Fresh concern over immigration restrictions', Campaign for Science and Engineering, November 2011; http://sciencecampaign.org.uk/?p=7867

16 Jesse Jenkins, Mark Muro, Ted Nordhaus, Michael Shellenberger, Letha Tawney and Alex Trembath, *Beyond Boom and Bust: Putting cleantech on a path to subsidy independence* (Breakthrough Institute, April 2012).

17 Henningsson et al., *Coming Clean.*

18 Pew Environment Group, *Who's Winning the Clean Energy Race?*

19 Dyson, *Ingenious Britain.*

20 Department for Business, Innovation and Skills, *Blueprint for Technology* (November 2010).

21 Mike Tuffrey, 'The Big Switch: Turning London's buses and taxis electric', Lib Dem Voice, 25 July 2011.

22 Tim Leunig, 'We need to learn from the 1930s', *Daily Telegraph*, 25 April 2012.

23 WWF, *A Dirty Business?: Manifesto for Action on the ECGD* (2011).

24 Department for Business, Innovation and Skills, *Rebalancing the Economy: Trade and Investment* (June 2011).

25 Dyson, *Ingenious Britain.*

Chapter 15

Revitalising the Green Investment Bank

Christopher J. Wigley

O ther chapters have highlighted the environmental challenges the UK is facing. Alongside these we have the challenge of designing and implementing an innovative energy policy, providing both energy security and a transition to a low-carbon economy, and of seeking hundreds of billions of pounds of investments to fund this critical transition.

We also face financial challenges. As the government observes in its National Infrastructure Plan, the next decade in finance will be different to the last decade: 'ongoing instability in financial markets could disrupt the supply of long-term bank lending for project finance'.[1] Additionally, 'the principal sources of private finance for the UK's existing infrastructure pipeline – the balance sheets of utility companies and commercial banks – may be facing growing pressures in the medium to long term'.[2] Indeed, due to changes in the regulatory environment such as Basel III,[3] banks may not be able to dominate the financing landscape in the same way as before. Similarly, Solvency II may change the asset mix for insurance companies.[4] Recognising this, the UK government has adopted the strategy of bringing in institutional investors such as UK pension funds to provide finance. This is logical: following the financial and economic crisis the government cannot afford to fund long-term projects as it did before, while pension funds do need to find long-term assets to match their long-term liabilities.

There is also a need to mobilise finance at scale from institutional investors. The UK Green Investment Bank (GIB) is intended to accelerate investment in green technologies and infrastructure. By providing a focal point for green finance, the GIB can help to attract and facilitate private-sector investment flows to green projects. Its positive attributes include critical mass and a government mandate. It possesses a critical role and must be innovative and creative to meet the challenge of the transition to a lower carbon economy, with the accompanying rewards of green growth and jobs.

The Green Investment Bank: history and outlook

The adoption of the Climate Change Act 2008 stimulated debate on ideas for the transition to a low-carbon economy. In March 2009, Climate Change Capital and E3G recommended the creation of a Green Investment Bank to catalyse private-sector investment, while in September of the same year, Policy Exchange called for the establishment of an Infrastructure Bank mandated by national priorities.[5] In 2010, all three main political parties included in their general election manifestos pledges to establish either a Green Investment Bank or an Infrastructure Bank. After the election, in June 2010 the 'Green Investment Bank Commission' – established by the Conservative Party while in opposition – recommended the creation of a Green Investment Bank within a year. In October the government announced plans for its creation.

In October 2012 the European Commission granted state-aid approval for the Bank; it has already started to operate as a grant-making fund as UK Green Investments. In November 2012 it was formally launched by the Secretary of State, Vince Cable. While it is a relief that the GIB is now up and running, there are concerns that its operations may not be optimal or resourced adequately to meet the challenge.

The GIB is commencing operations with just £3 billion of capital to 2015–16 – which seems unambitious given the scale of the challenges. An Ernst & Young report estimated that the UK funding gap for low-carbon technologies alone to 2025 is £330 billion – £360 billion.[6] In light of this, it is also a concern to hear GIB's comments on its strategy – which include being cautious and seeing profitability as an important objective.[7]

GIB has made some positive first steps but could do more. In April 2012 the GIB team started investment, with up to £180 million for specialist fund managers to co-invest equity into waste and non-domestic energy efficiency infrastructure projects.[8] Although in December 2012 the GIB additionally lent £45m for an offshore wind facility, the particular focus on equity investment is not promising.[9]

A recent interview in the *Financial Times* with the GIB's Chief Executive illuminates the issue. Shaun Kingsbury was reported as saying, 'I'm not a green activist. I'm an investor … it's really important for me to do the thing I know how to do best, which is to make money'.[10] Of course, wealth creation is to be encouraged, but profit targets or an overly cautious approach should not be allowed to become obstacles to the transition to a low-carbon economy. GIB should not be loss-making but a not-for-profit organisation seems to be more appropriate.

The prime environmental objective must be the raising of hundreds of billions of pounds for green investment. It seems inconceivable that a fund structure similar to Investors in Industry (3i), for example, could provide finance on the scale necessary. While GIB is now indeed a bank, not just a fund, it is significant to see how many of its senior personnel are from 3i,[11] the fund specialist. 3i has been criticised in the City. They threw themselves into the paradigm of a new economy in the late 1990s and their funds disappointed investors as the tech bubble burst. An additional concern is that equity finance provided with co-investors may not necessarily deliver the desired levels of transparency expected.

Further, much of the senior expertise at GIB appears to be in 3i's specialist field, that of private and listed equity.[12] As at December 2012, there does not seem to be any senior member executive with specialist experience in bond finance. This is a serious concern, as bond finance is lower cost than equity, both to the government and to potential green corporate borrowers.

The Green Investment Bank: potential

As mentioned above, the government has tried to attract private finance for infrastructure from the pension funds. However, they are targeting just £20 billion – tiny in the context of what is needed. And the pension funds are proving reluctant to invest even this amount due to the government's unconvincing commitment to policy stability.

There is, however, tremendous potential for investment through bond finance. Global bond markets currently amount to US$99 trillion,[13] twice the size of global equity markets (US$49 trillion).[14] Bonds are a frequent and important funding vehicle used by governments and companies across the world, from the US Treasury to Toyota to Network Rail. They are a core asset class for all institutional investors, accounting for about 43 per cent of assets for pension funds, more than equities.[15] With bond markets being so large, the largest investors in the world continually need to reinvest in new bonds as their existing bonds reach maturity.

Global institutional investors cover a massive universe. In the UK, the largest pension funds include BT Pension Scheme (US$58.0 billion), Universities Superannuation Scheme (US$50.3 billion), Electricity Supply Pension (US$39.9 billion), Royal Bank of Scotland Pension Fund (US$35.6 billion) and Railpen (US$27.8 billion).[16] Other large UK institutional investors include insurance companies such as Prudential, Aviva and Standard Life. Large global pension funds which have an interest in investing in infrastructure around the globe include California Public Employees Retirement

System (US$214.4 billion), California State Teachers Retirement System (US$138.9 billion), Ontario Teachers' Pension Plan (US$108.1 billion) and Australian Super (US$37.8 billion).[17]

However, possibly the largest investors in the world are the sovereign wealth funds who have hundreds of billions of dollars invested. These include the Government Pension Fund of Norway (US$611.0 billion), the Abu Dhabi Investment Authority (US$627 billion), the Chinese SAFE Investment Company (US$567.9 billion), Saudi Arabia's SAMA Foreign Holdings (US$532.8 billion) and Government of Singapore Investment Corporation (US$247.5 billion).[18]

Bonds are a natural investment vehicle. Institutional investors, particularly pension funds, often look for long-term assets to match their long-term liabilities. Long-term infrastructure assets are therefore ideal. For responsible investors, green infrastructure is even better. For a facilitator such as the Green Investment Bank, this is a good time to seek finance – as it is for any borrower who is not overly indebted. Due to the economic crisis, the Bank of England's base rate is at the lowest level for more than 300 years. Similarly, due to the Bank's programme of quantitative easing, long-term interest rates are also at historically low levels of between 2 per cent and 4 per cent.[19]

Agency banks and the asset-backed security model

Government agency banks have existed for about 150 years. Credit Agricole was established in 1860 with a primary remit to supply credit to the French agricultural industry. In 1958, the European Investment Bank (EIB) was established to facilitate the integration, balanced development and economic and social cohesion of EU member states. EIB raises substantial funds on the capital markets which it then uses to provide loans and other financial products to projects furthering EU policy objectives.

Possibly the most commonly cited example is Kreditanstalt für Wiederaufbau (KfW), the agency bank set up by the Marshall Plan in 1948 for the reconstruction of Germany. It is 80 per cent owned by the German government and 20 per cent by the Länder. Significantly, it has a large presence in residential energy efficiency, renewable energy and municipal public transport and sanitation. KfW is able to provide lower than normal interest rates. The German government guarantees by law all existing and future obligations in relation to funds borrowed, bonds issued, obligations guaranteed and derivative transactions entered into by KfW. It borrows approximately €80 billion a year from the capital markets but its debt is not consolidated into that of the government.

While it is not recommended that GIB's direct debt is similarly unconsolidated with that of the UK government's, it is not a huge leap to explore the possibility that the agency status of the GIB may also bring benefits to infrastructure and a green economy in the UK. Significantly, there is a way in which the GIB may borrow from capital markets, lend to the green economy and yet not increase liabilities for the UK government.

The GIB could, using funds already available, make high-quality secured loans to the green sector.[20] It can then use these loans as collateral to back global bonds. In this way, acting as an intermediary, GIB could access more finance, not from the government but from the global investment community such as pension funds, insurance companies and sovereign wealth funds.

The GIB could use its loans to issue global bonds on a secured basis through, for example, an asset-backed security (ABS) or covered bond, which should receive high ratings from the credit agencies due to the high quality of the collateral and bond structure. Once such bonds had been issued and the funds received, GIB's balance sheet is freed up to make additional loans to the green sector, and so the cycle may continue. It is not continually drawing on the government's capital; it is, rather, efficiently recycling it.

Fig. 15.1 The model

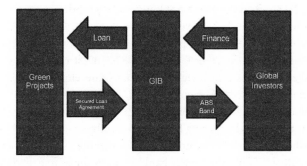

There is currently high demand from UK and global pension funds, insurance companies and sovereign wealth funds for such highly rated, long-term infrastructure bonds. The GIB should, over time, foster expertise to develop other specific financial instruments focused on the green sector, to provide additional finance by appealing to additional long-term investors.

The investment priorities for the GIB for the period to 2015–16 include support for the Green Deal and non-domestic energy efficiency, commercial and industrial waste processing and recycling, and offshore wind power.

All would benefit from this innovative and low-cost financing. However, the restrictions on borrowing placed on the GIB by the Treasury – which is that it will not be able to borrow before 2014–15, and then only if public sector debt is falling as a percentage of GDP – are a serious constraint. In fact current Office of Budget Responsibility projections indicate that public sector debt will not be falling by then, so the ability of the GIB to borrow in its own name or on an unsecured basis from the financial markets will be delayed.

An Agency/ABS model may, however, provide a solution. Borrowing through an ABS, and not in the name of the GIB, means that should the ABS fail to pay its annual interest or full value at maturity for any reason, then investors seek compensation in the value of the collateral rather than from the UK government. For this reason, ABS are considered 'off-balance sheet' for the issuer, or unconsolidated with existing debt as a result. Consequently, it is logical that ABS issuance should not contribute to the UK public sector deficit, allowing the GIB to access financing earlier than currently planned.

A similar proposal was made by Ernst & Young in 2010.[21] However in that case, banks would have originated the loans which would then have been sold to GIB to be pooled together as collateral for the issuance of a bond. The problem with this structure – and perhaps why the government did not adopt it – was the lack of control GIB would have had over the quality of the loans. But events have moved on since then: banks are not lending to the degree desired and GIB is starting to lend direct itself. GIB can then control the quality of the collateral and, using the Agency/ABS model, can use that collateral to borrow from the capital markets independently of the UK government.

Other potential innovations

Should the GIB follow the Agency/ABS model there would also be other positive impacts. In theory there is no limit to the amount of funds global investors could provide and pass on to green companies in the UK. This may also have the benefit of providing credit to smaller and middle-sized UK green companies, currently starved of credit by UK banks. It carries with it at least the hint of greater economic growth, green growth and more jobs.

In addition to borrowing on a collateralised basis (Agency/ABS), the GIB could also enable other financially sound companies to borrow at a lower cost than normal with a GIB guarantee. The GIB could hold a portfolio of guarantees which, because they are diversified, would be considered lower risk than borrowing in its own name. In this way, it could guarantee a larger amount and attract more private finance to the green sector. This avenue is worth exploring further.

There seem to be two current concerns within government regarding the GIB's powers to lend and to guarantee debt. The first is that in providing debt and equity finance, GIB may crowd out commercial banks once they are able to return to the market. Secondly, GIB may become an enduring public sector bank, less well run than a private sector bank.

There is one solution that may meet both these concerns: the possibility of a sunset clause. The GIB's investment banking operations (debt and equity finance) could be privatised after, say, ten years, if there is no longer a public need for a green investment bank with agency status – i.e. if major green infrastructure funding was completed and it was believed that commercial banks could meet the new green challenges on their own. Green finance would be fully integrated into commercial banks' operations. Any direct GIB debt could be grandfathered to avoid disruption.

However, the path ahead is not smooth. The EU has authorised the GIB to lend for low-carbon investment only for four years. Additionally, some may be concerned that the green companies the GIB assists may be regarded as receiving state aid. However, the GIB is acting solely as a catalyst for private finance, making loans when commercial loans are not available. Additionally, the GIB is only lending as the banks are constrained by the financial crisis and Basel III risk restraints. Further, the GIB would only be providing low-cost finance because it is more efficient for it to fund this way, in a similar vein to KfW. Finally in the context of state aid, it is important to retain sight of the big picture – which is that all the UK is aiming to do is transition to a low-carbon economy and mitigate the impact of climate change.

Adapting to climate change and new norms of energy provision is not easy. It requires a change of mindset and new modes of thinking and operating. It additionally requires substantial new infrastructure investment, including energy infrastructure which will not only provide low-carbon but also lower cost energy. Overcoming this challenge requires having the courage to be a leader, and the GIB is best placed to provide that example. Being prepared to do this means that it will also secure globally the benefit of first-mover advantage.

National Infrastructure Bank

The government's National Infrastructure Plan outlines a vision and six areas of commitments: transport, including aviation, energy supply, broadband, water, flooding and coastal erosion, and waste.[22] Significantly, these are all green issues. An alternative option to privatising the GIB in the future would be to bring the National Infrastructure Plan under the wing of the Green Investment Bank.

Long-term investment in the UK's infrastructure requires policy stability, consistency and continuity. A plan overseen by an independent agency such as the GIB should help to ensure exactly that stability, putting an end to the volatility and uncertainty of different political parties in successive governments following different agendas.

Public participation
Sourcing finance for the UK's transition to a low-carbon economy is critical. Agency/ABS funding may do the heavy lifting but the public can contribute too. Indeed it would be very positive for the public to participate in this transformation as much as possible.

Green cash ISAs
Banks and building societies could offer green cash ISAs, with the funds feeding directly to the GIB; the customer would know that their funds would be fully applied to environmental projects. To attract this investment, the government would provide ISA status and so there would be a tax benefit to the deposit returns.

Green energy victory bonds (National Savings Bonds)
The struggle to mitigate climate change can be seen as a war; 'green energy victory bonds' could be as relevant today as the Victory Bonds that were offered during the world wars. In fact legislation is currently being proposed in the US for Clean Energy Victory Bonds. These would be similar to green cash ISAs, with the funds going directly again to the GIB for green projects. They would be issued by National Savings and Investments (NS&I) and, with longer maturity dates than ISAs, would carry a higher yield. They too would carry a tax lift to attract investment.

Local authority infrastructure bonds with tax incentives
In 2011 the Chancellor suggested that financially sound local authorities should be encouraged to borrow more from capital markets. The funds raised by the bonds issued could be used for local infrastructure projects. The bonds could appeal to investors because they fund local projects, directly benefiting local people. Additionally, because they invest in green infrastructure, they could be provided with a tax incentive. In this way they would be similar to

the Build America Bonds recently made available in the US. The GIB could play a role in coordinating these projects.

Infrastructure bond funds

Should the GIB be able to access substantial long-term funds from the global capital markets, and should other countries' green investment banks, or similar, be able to do the same, there will be liquid financial markets for green infrastructure bonds of various maturities. National Savings and Investments (NS&I) and possibly high street banks may want to market to the public funds that invest in green infrastructure bonds, thereby establishing another source of funding for the government. Such funds may well be attractive to the public, not only because they would be green and finance worthwhile projects, but also because paying an interest rate of 2 per cent to 4 per cent and backed by a government agency, they would be a relatively high-yield and low-risk product – more attractive than the 0.1 per cent most savers receive ordinarily on their deposits at banks. An additional attraction could be ISA status, providing a tax incentive or tax treatment similar to Venture Capital Trusts (VCTs).

Conclusion

No one is under any illusion that the challenges of the low-carbon transition are substantial. However, for an innovative and creative Green Investment Bank, the potential rewards are great. Not only could the GIB source hundreds of billions of pounds of green investments, it could also become the custodian for a stable and consistent National Infrastructure Plan. Through developing an innovative Agency/ABS model, it could access hundreds of billions of pounds without increasing the budget deficit. It could help to ensure energy security and build a low-carbon economy while also providing the private sector with high-quality, long-term infrastructure assets. Through, for example, the provision of guarantees, the GIB could not only foster green growth and green jobs, it could also provide credit to smaller and medium-sized green companies in the UK.

To achieve all this, the GIB needs to be ambitious and in terms of funding, it needs to think globally. Now is not the time to think of reasons not to act; rather it is a time to be innovative and to lead.

Notes

1   HM Treasury, *National Infrastructure Plan* (2011), p. 7.
2   Ibid., p. 97.
3   Basel III is a global regulatory standard on bank capital adequacy, stress testing and market liquidity risk agreed by the committee of global banking supervisory authorities.
4   Solvency II is an EU Directive that codifies and harmonises the EU insurance regulation. Primarily this concerns the amount of capital that EU insurance companies must hold to reduce the risk of insolvency.
5   Climate Change Capital and E3G, *Accelerating Green Infrastructure Financing: Outline proposals for UK green bonds and infrastructure bank* (March 2009); Policy Exchange, *Delivering a 21st Century Infrastructure for Britain* (September 2009).
6   Ernst & Young, *Capitalising the Green Investment Bank* (October 2010), p. 5.
7   At the All-Party Parliamentary Group on Climate Change discussion on 'The Future of Green Infrastructure Investment' on 21 November 2012, Ian Nolan (CIO) stated that the GIB aimed to be an 'enduring institution' and so the early years were important.
8   Written Ministerial Statement by Vince Cable MP, Secretary of State for Business, Innovation and Skills, 30 October 2012.
9   Sally Bakewell, 'UK Green Investment Bank strikes its first offshore deal', Bloomberg, 20 December 2012.
10 'Green bank powers up', *Financial Times*, 29 November 2012.
11 Lord Smith of Kelvin (Chairman) was at ICFC (now 3i) until 1982. Sir Adrian Montague (Vice Chairman) is the current Chairman of 3i. Shaun Kingsbury is the new Chief Executive of GIB and was an adviser to 3i. Ian Nolan (Chief Investment Officer) was also CIO at 3i.
12 Shaun Kingsbury came from Hudson Clean Energy Partners. Tom Murley (non-executive director) is at HgCapital. Also, Tessa Tennant (non-executive director) co-founded the equity Jupiter Ecology Fund.
13 Bank for International Settlements, *International Debt Securities* (June 2012) and *Domestic Debt Securities* (March 2012).
14 World Federation of Exchanges, *Market Highlights for the First Half Year 2012* (23 July 2012).
15 'Bonds switch signals end of cult of equity', *Financial Times*, 19 November 2012.
16 Towers Watson, *Top 300 Pension Funds*, September 2011.
17 Ibid.
18 Steve Johnson, 'SWFs go shopping for managers' FTfm, 16 July 2012.
19 The ten-year gilt currently yields just 2.11 per cent while the thirty-year yields just 3.32 per cent (4 January 2013).
20 Possibly secured in a similar way to a project finance loan.
21 Ernst & Young, *Capitalising the Green Investment Bank*, p. 14.
22 HM Treasury, *National Infrastructure Plan*, p. 6.

Chapter 16

Empowering a Shift to a More Circular Economy

Ben Earl

We are at the beginning of a resource revolution. The decline in commodity prices seen over the whole of the twentieth century has been completely reversed in just the first ten years of the twenty-first. The limits of finite fossil fuels, combined with the end of an era of cheap labour and abundant materials, mean that traditional models of wealth creation need revisiting. With a projected 9 billion people on the planet by 2050 a resource crunch is looming.

Much is made about how the economy can be lifted out of recession. The debate centres around the degree of austerity needed to cut the deficit versus the amount of fiscal stimulus needed to promote growth. What is plain to see is that high oil and commodity prices are a significant factor associated with the flatlining of the UK economy. If you compare the current economic cycle to the end of the 1930s' recession then it is these high prices that are seriously hampering a traditional economic recovery.

The green movement of course has been predicting this for some time. The oil shock of the 1970s was an early pointer, but through initiatives such as 'One Planet Living' and other sustainability programmes the alarm bells have been ringing over rampant consumption of natural resources. Despite this, the drive for change in consumer behaviour has had limited success. If we take the challenge of waste in society as an example, huge strides have been made through recycling to reduce the amount of waste sent to landfill. The landfill tax has been the crucial driver here. For business, the landfill tax regulation, with annual increases and fiscal certainty, has been understood and responded to. However, this shift happens at the 'end of pipe', and we remain constrained by operating within an economy which is take-make-dispose, and therefore linear in its make-up.

What would happen, however, if we focused on redesigning products and business models to reflect these modern realities? Instead of waste products, items would be made that could be easily disassembled and regenerated. Business systems would emulate living systems and collaborate to cycle materials and components, meaning waste would be eliminated by design. Householders would receive the latest styles and gadgets through rental or performance contracts that would encourage trends to be easily refreshed while energy and resource productivity was integrated from the start.

Progressive thinkers have long championed different economic models that reflect 'quality of life' indicators. There is evidence that shifting taxation on to polluting, non-renewable resources and removing it from low-carbon or sustainable technologies may provide a powerful lever for accelerating progress in these models. Progress towards these goals has been slow. The Treasury has not yet embraced the 'green economy' in a meaningful enough way, and as such, for example, the Green Investment Bank is unable to use its own capital to borrow.

A shift in system thinking

Policy-makers have legislated to place limits at the end of linear systems for decades. Examples include discharge limits to air, land and sea, disposal bans and taxes. These limits have driven necessary change and go to the very heart of what standards responsible government believe are necessary. In recent years significant consideration has been applied to rethinking the product supply system. The notion of the 'circular economy' allows maximum resource productivity alongside built-in waste reduction. By changing the very nature of our relationship with products and services it requires a parallel shift in perception, economic incentives and behaviour.

A circular economy is one that works on the principles of the natural world. Products are made from natural raw materials being endlessly reused from creation to disposal, with few ill-effects. If you think of a rainforest, the complexity of the ecosystem is sustained by the constant use and reuse of available resources. Strip back to the soil, and the foundation of the rain-forest is actually quite thin. The ecosystem is so efficient that waste is at a minimum, yet just look at the abundance of life it supports. For so much of our current economic activity unsustainable systems are maintained which ultimately degrade life support systems over time.

The use of instruments to promote such a system shift requires some progressive and potentially radical thinking. In a Green Alliance report at the time of the last election the Liberal Democrats received three green lights by offering the strongest set of policies on climate change, green taxation and greener living. Most famous was the strand of environmental policy running through each chapter of the party's manifesto. It is once again time for the Liberal Democrats to exhibit new thinking and put in place policies that encourage action to address the worst prognosis of environmental degradation ever reported in recent months.

Economic instruments, along with suitable technical requirements, could play a crucial role in laying the foundations to enable a substantial shift to take place in business thinking. Reflecting the challenges posed by the nature of globalised markets, international agreement and partnership is needed. Tax incentives leveraged into research and development, alongside the development of 'waste hierarchy taxes', would effectively shift the economy to address the increasingly efficient use of resources – similar in outline to the progress seen as a result of the landfill tax.

It is well known that reuse is the most sustainable waste option – yet economic levers do not reflect this. By using these instruments, factors such as product take-back become even more attractive to business. Taking those increasing commodity prices into consideration, it is already starting to be acknowledged that recovering raw materials is cost-effective. The complicated construction of many products, including the large number of raw materials in trace form they contain, makes reprocessing very complicated. Designing products with eco-design in mind will not only aid the material recovery process but also lead to a clearer understanding of key issues such as water and carbon usage at various points in the supply chain.

The circular economy, however, also requires different ways of working. It is perhaps obvious to see how retailers can work with suppliers to deliver new methods of resource efficiency – but what happens when companies deem it most efficient to work with their competitors? This may be seen as an unusual step in our highly competitive market, and may pose competition issues which will need to be addressed. Most likely are shared facilities, involving different tiers of the supply chain to enable close collaboration. Government can play a role here with an industrial policy designed to promote this collaboration. Financial incentives in planning policy would help shape the industrial parks of the future, built with more resilience and collaboration as fundamental to sustainable business practice.

The changing nature of taxation

The Liberal Democrats already believe that a key step in creating an environmentally sustainable economy is to establish a system of taxation which rewards activities which are non-polluting and resource-productive, achieved through a gradual switch from taxation on income and employment to taxation on pollution and resource depletion. At recent conferences the party has reaffirmed this commitment, with a call for the government to set a target of securing not less than 10 per cent of its revenue from environmental taxes by 2015, thus positioning the UK among the better performing members of the EU.

Speed is of the essence here, particularly as sectors of society such as those exploiting traditional fossil fuel sources will seek to challenge this shift to a more sustainable trajectory. The December 2012 Autumn Statement contained an announcement of a consultation on new tax incentives for shale gas, despite the Climate Change Committee (who advise on the legally binding climate targets within the Climate Change Act) stating that a high-gas scenario would be 'completely incompatible with climate change targets'.

Walter Stahel is credited as being one of the founding fathers of industrial sustainability. Coining the phrase 'cradle to cradle' in the late 1970s, Stahel has called for a shift from labour to resources. He argues that this shift is good for employment as less than a quarter of overall employment is dedicated to the procurement of resources, with a subsequent three-quarters employed in the manufacture of the product itself. The reverse is true for energy; three times as much energy is used to extract virgin or primary materials than in the manufacturing process. Placing reused rather than virgin components in manufacturing products can therefore use less energy through a dynamic supply chain which, by the nature of the associated value-added processes, can provide more employment opportunities.[1]

A logical argument then follows that taxing the consumption of non-renewable resources instead of labour will promote a circular regional economy instead of a linear global one; increasing the costs of fuel-based transport by road, air and sea will favour local and regional solutions. In the same way, the local reuse of components will reinforce the competitiveness of these value-preserving business models. In the UK this thinking needs to be injected into the industrial policy led by the Department for Business, Innovation and Skills (BIS).

Government policy in the UK and across the developed world is, however, in most cases heading in the opposite direction. According to an International Energy Agency report in 2010, fossil fuel subsidies across the world in 2008 amounted to US$557 billion compared to just US$46 billion for renewables. The report argues that a phase-out of fossil fuel subsidies would enhance energy security, reduce greenhouse gas emissions and bring immediate economic gains.[2]

Product rental and collaborative consumption
Dame Ellen MacArthur famously gave up her sailing career to, in her words, 'rethink the future', quoting the resource constraints of long-distance

sailing as a clear parallel to the challenges outlined here. The retailer B&Q has signed up as a founding partner of the Ellen MacArthur Foundation, recognising the need to invest in new business models such as product rental and collaborative consumption.

Applying rental models to power tools or appliances builds on the success of the mobile phone operators and delivers to the customer a quality, ready-to-use product at point of need. Using a power drill as an example, the average use is just ten minutes per customer, per year, so why do we all need to own one? Renting a drill for each use makes much more sense. Renting products and using refurbishment on returned products, alongside other new models such as collaborative consumption, means that efficiencies are maximised. This process emulates nature by ensuring that the manufacture of products minimises the loss of energy and materials, while concentrating on convenience of service and lowering costs to the consumer. These proposed changes partly reflect the degree of risk that exists to global supply chains, demonstrated by volatile commodity prices, but also a desire to remain ahead in effective business planning. A circular economy therefore is a more predictable industrial system that is restorative in its design.

The washing machine provides a good example. B&Q has for some time had an A-rated appliance policy, only stocking a number of appliances (including washing machines) with a minimum energy efficiency rating of A, to aid the customer in keeping energy bills lower. With the introduction of even higher standards (up to A+++) the business is now looking at ratcheting up those standards. The problem is that the purchase price also increases – yet higher end washing machines (those facilitating 10,000 wash cycles instead of just on average 2,000) in more households would save the consumer around 30 per cent in washing costs and the manufacturer about 180kg of steel and 2.5 tonnes of carbon over a twenty-year period.[3] A rental model for washing machines could therefore lead to lower wash costs for each customer and an efficient material recovery process for the manufacturer.

A mindset change needs to be demonstrated through a model where access shifts from simple ownership to one where buying performance becomes a key driver. The retailer makes a profit on the contract formula and the consumer ensures they are a recipient of a higher efficiency, top-quality model in perpetuity. Progress has been made in a perhaps more obscure market, that of carpet tiles. Desso, a carpet tile manufacturer, has introduced a rental model for carpet tiles that ensures that returned tiles are reused in new products with attention paid to different stages of the supply chain to ensure a sustainable approach. The floor covering is provided with upgrades to ensure customer satisfaction. The company continues to generate profits and deliver high levels of customer service. Indeed Desso wants to go further, and by 2020 it is aiming to have its processing and manufacturing processes completely powered by renewable energy.

Accelerating the transition

The Ellen MacArthur Foundation believes that inspiring a generation of young people to grasp the opportunities of the future and become excited about subjects like science, technology, engineering, maths and design lies at the heart of the transition. They believe that the circular economy offers a coherent framework in which young people are inspired to design things differently and revolutionise our economy to one in which the long term will be more effective and efficient.

This turns what is often currently seen as an insurmountable challenge into future innovation and employment opportunities. The challenge is that this often comes up against the narrow restraints of the National Curriculum. New thinking is needed to equip young people with the skills to become creators of the new business models of tomorrow. The circular economy should therefore be included in existing curriculum activities through new educational initiatives with economic and environmental sustainability intertwined.

Internal communication within the business sector is equally important from the board room to the shop floor. Too often leadership occurs at the top of an organisation, but this is not supported at the grassroots level. Employees need to understand the reason for different models and to be inspired in the implementation of the subsequent changes that follow. With the economy having been awash with cheaply produced and supplied products with scant regard to resource efficiency, the need to make store staff aware of the challenges we face on resource costs and to inform them of solutions such as new rental models becomes very important. A clear reason to move shop floor staff, buyers and other procurement teams to a new 'normal' requires thinking and reward. A clear example is in relation to chemical additives that might work against the ease of reusability in future disassembly. Assembling a truly 'cradle-to-cradle' product involves ensuring that its content and components can be fully disassembled and that its chemical contents do not pose blocks in this process. Buyers that have been used to (what is on paper) the cheapest ingredients will not have factored in the next stage of the process beyond the sale of the product.

This comes back to leadership, catalysing the mindset change needed by business. Much recent work on 'followership' has suggested that the act of leadership is less about instructing or even inspiring; it is more about ensuring that those under your direction have the tools to make the changes. This is particularly challenging in the current economic climate of job insecurity, flat retail sales and wider eurozone instability. Most boardrooms facing these headwinds have rightly focused on daily essential spending, and in many cases investment for new business innovation has been particularly badly hit.

Innovation therefore requires suitable investment, again related to the business strategy to improve skills, enable new methods of collaborating and ensure a sustainable transition to a more resilient economic model. The recent report to government by former UK Deputy Prime Minister Michael Heseltine[4] once again made the case for tax credits for research and development. The circular economy and the new investment models needed to accompany it are important to be part of this R&D call to arms. Business spend in this area of the economy will build resilience to price and resource volatility and once again be good for employment.

Marketing the change

Inspiring consumers is an equally important part of the challenge. A decade of education around the resource, ecological and climate-related problems faced across the world has been followed by a decade of persuading people to do something about them. Awareness has been seen as the easier part, probably because action is often perceived as being against consumers' interests; mass market transition has been slow.

A new era of communication with consumers is therefore important. We need to shift expectations about the level of change needed in society. In the 2008 WWF publication *Weathercocks and Signposts*, the authors concluded that any adequate strategy for tackling environmental challenges will demand engagement with the values that shape the decisions we make.[5] Underpinning the shift to a circular economy is the notion of a 'new norm', based on a rational argument. Clear explanation of the current linear nature of supply chains and its obvious vulnerability provides a logical argument to illustrate the need for change.

Crucial to any changes is the perception of greener products. We need to shift expectations in the performance of so called 'eco' products. Indeed, we need to go further. The words 'eco' or 'green' need to be dropped in favour of terms such as 'optimal' or 'innovative'. In most cases eco-products have been seen to be poor substitutes; studies have shown that they often deter more consumers than they inspire. The environmental movement has often painted a picture of retreat from modern living and a climate of sacrifice.

The circular economy, in contrast, paints a very positive picture for consumers: better-performing products, including more beneficial features, rented or purchased through more user-friendly business models. Correctly positioned and effectively marketed, this vision can be sold to an audience that understands the limitations of the way we currently do things. Recycling has been embraced as a mainstream activity and so can the concepts laid out here. No one questions the mobile phone rental model, for example, and so new thinking can be applied to line up better-performing products, cheaper production models and profits generated in different ways.

Action by government

Recent acknowledgement by government of a potential resource problem has come in the form of the Resource Security Action Plan jointly produced by Defra and BIS.[6] Framed very much with 'opportunity' rather than 'risk' in mind, the document focuses on the need for resilience, recognising the serious threat to economic recovery that stems from our wasteful linear economy. It is welcome that the government is working with the Circular Economy Taskforce. Set up with the support of leading businesses such as Unilever and BASF, and managed by the Green Alliance along with WRAP, this body is clearly framed to produce practical recommendations that aim to shift thinking and policy-making.

It is clear that pressures on natural resources are already concentrating minds within business. The role of government is to help remove barriers to good practice, particularly where it may not be in a company's own direct interests to act – for example in the complex regulations around waste handling, even if the waste is destined for reuse. As in many emerging technologies the early pioneers need supporting to build well-constructed markets. Priorities for future Liberal Democrat policies include:

- A shift in taxation from employment to resource use – through the reduction of employers' national insurance, making it cheaper to hire staff, and a corresponding increase in taxation on raw materials. This combination will accelerate the price differential in favour of closed-loop models while at the same time being potentially fiscally neutral.
- The transition of the landfill tax into a 'waste hierarchy tax'. This hybrid version of a waste tax will progressively increase as you move down the waste hierarchy, ensuring that the more environmentally responsible options, such as 'closed loop' and product reuse are more financially attractive, while at the same time penalising the most polluting options such as incineration and landfill.

- Support for new innovative business models through a cut in VAT for closed-loop products – products designed to be reused, with future reassembly designed into the process, or which are as close to fully recycled content as possible. This will be a significant driver in the creation of new markets for recycled materials.
- Opening up the National Curriculum to new thinking to enable the designers and brand consultants of tomorrow to recognise the shift towards a closed-loop economic system. This will need to influence science, IT, marketing and economics to truly reflect the business models of tomorrow.
- Further work on the 'Green Claims Code', with measures to ensure that business adheres to clear terminology. Developed in partnership between BIS and Defra, these guidelines should eradicate 'greenwash'.
- The phasing-out of fossil fuel subsidies to ensure a smooth but clear direction of travel towards a low-carbon economy. A review of field allowances, the tax breaks given in recent budgets to develop oil and gas fields in the North Sea, is one example.
- A change in industrial policy to encourage greater supply chain collaboration between SMEs and the larger companies they supply. A review of competition law to ensure that logical collaboration between different business sectors is not inhibited, while ensuring suitable safeguards to prevent cartel activity.
- Tax breaks to promote research and development into the circular economy. Although capital allowances for suitable investment are already available, in future these should be clearly focused on promoting 'closed-loop' activity.

Conclusions

The onset of increasingly volatile energy and resource costs, coupled with a rapidly increasing number of global consumers, is driving a significant change in the way in which business will be conducted in the future. Policymakers have responded, often in isolation, to each of the employment, growth, climate and resource scarcity challenges without joining up their measures. The corresponding models and rules by which our economy works therefore need significant adjustment to turn the new approach into an advantage for the UK.

The circular economy by its very design offers the opportunity to paint a positive picture for manufacturing – which, at its heart, contains the ability to create jobs, deliver resilient economic growth and mitigate resource and environmental risks. But to get there we need a gear change in terminology and business innovation. Government can play an active part by providing tax breaks and shifting taxation on to those things we want to reduce and away from those that as a society we need more of.

Walter Stahel describes the circular economy as 'symbiotic', aligning a series of levers that naturally build in the positive features that politicians of all colours increasingly espouse for the economy. Perhaps just as crucially, it makes common sense to the public at large and still leaves room for the progressive innovation that inspires the consumer and ensures that business can prosper.

Bold leadership on industrial policy is required by all involved. This call has been answered by Kingfisher plc, the owner of B&Q. As part of the Net Positive business plan a target has been set to deliver 1,000 products with closed-loop credentials by 2020. This is a significant challenge as the business seeks to define, implement and report on these changes. The other founding partners of the Ellen MacArthur Foundation are setting similar goals; together, this will help to set a clear blueprint showing the way to the low-carbon economy that needs to be developed.

Set out in this chapter are pointers to some practical interventions that politicians can design to aid this process. BIS has already shown that longer term thinking is needed in relation to the banking sector; the splitting of the functions of the retail and investment banking arms will ensure more stability to taxpayers. Will a similar shift in industrial policy lead to adequate support being given to wean the nation off short-term models that lead ultimately to higher prices and longer term economic decline? Is new thinking to fully embrace the circular economy a real possibility? The Liberal Democrats within the coalition have the radical thinking and environmental heritage to ensure this shift takes place, but they need to make the case loud and clear to ensure that it does.

Notes

1   Stahel, *The Performance Economy* (2010).
2   IEA, OECD, World Bank Joint Report, *The Scope of Fossil-Fuel Subsidies and A Roadmap for Phasing Out Fossil-Fuel subsidies* (2009).
3   McKinsey, *Towards a Circular Economy* (2012).
4   Heseltine, *No Stone Unturned* (2012).
5   WWF, *Weathercocks and Signposts* (2008).
6   Defra, *Resource Security Action Plan – Making the most of valuable materials* (2012).

Chapter 17

A World Without Waste – Achieving a More Resource-Efficient Country

Susan Juned

The demand for resources is increasing. As the rest of the world strives and achieves the standards of living that we take for granted, consumption levels and price levels will continue to rise. Meanwhile climate change and environmental degradation are realities that can only become worse. The conundrum is how to achieve a competitive economy that continues to provide a high standard of living for our residents but also addresses climate change and lowers environmental impacts.

What is resource efficiency and why is it important?

The UK has high imported material and energy dependency. As a result, access to adequate sources of raw materials and recycled materials and the security of energy supplies will have an increasing impact on future economic growth. Environmental policy that is designed to prevent waste and conserve resources should therefore not be seen as a constraint on business, but rather as an essential part of ensuring future competitiveness and resilience. Using resources more efficiently produces savings that can be reinvested and prevents over-dependence on particular sources of raw materials.

The business practices of the future have to consider ways to use resources such as metals, minerals, water and fuels in a more sustainable manner. The consumption of all these is a part of the standard of life that we have come to expect, but they must be conserved and used efficiently, or be replaced by more sustainable alternatives if that standard is not to be eroded for ourselves and future generations.

Across the world competition is increasing for many of the resources that we currently use in manufacturing products. It has been estimated that by 2030, the world will need at least 50 per cent more food, 45 per cent more energy and 30 per cent more water than it currently uses – all at a time when environmental boundaries are throwing up new limits to supply.[1]

A 2011 article in the *European Financial Review* claimed that there are increasing signs of a crisis in natural resources being shown by the Commodity Price Index.[2] The index is a measure of price movements for twenty-two basic commodities and has more than tripled since 2002. Price volatility, upward price trends and growing scarcities pose a serious challenge for the security of global supply chains. In addition, the treatment of waste, the extraction and processing of raw materials and the generation of energy from fossil fuels all impact negatively upon the environment and add to the dangers of climate change.

Recognising the importance of resource efficiency is essential as the start of the journey required to address the whole-life impacts of the products we use and to find sustainable solutions. Government policy needs to set the UK firmly on the journey towards a zero-waste low-carbon society where resources are valued and efficiently used. This journey should aim to see waste production and water use minimised, successful resource-efficient yet cost-effective businesses encouraged, the environment protected and resource and energy security ensured.

What types of benefits can resource efficiency bring?

A report from the EU in 2011 recommended that increasing resource efficiency will be the 'key to securing growth and jobs for Europe'.[3] A strategy has been agreed that aims to make the EU a 'circular economy', based on a recycling society where waste generation is reduced or used as a resource. Taking a similar route in the UK to improve resource efficiency is one way of limiting the growing economic costs to business of importing materials and sending too many usable materials to landfill.

A 2011 Defra-commissioned study into business resource efficiency identified that UK business could make significant savings by being more efficient in the use of raw materials and by preventing waste – often for a relatively small-scale level of investment.[4] The study recognised that the efficient management of resources will protect industry from shortage and security threats and will also protect the environment and reduce the impacts of climate change. However, the study also noted that there are often difficulties involved in estimating the hidden costs of resource efficiency measures, which emphasises the need for specialist advice and assistance.

Using resources more efficiently has clear economic benefits for companies, and an environmental policy that supports resource efficiency is an essential ingredient in ensuring the future competitiveness and resilience of the UK economy as a whole. Businesses understand that they can make savings by using resources more efficiently and more are recognising that they should plan to avoid an over-dependence on those raw materials that are likely to be in short supply in the future or originate from an insecure source.

Small businesses may have an even higher level of exposure to rising resource costs and will need specific support and access to credit to enable them to invest in measures that mitigate the risk of higher bills for energy for power, heat and transport, leading to reduced competitiveness. Larger process industries that are heavily dependent on power are also vulnerable to price increases in fuel as well as other resource costs. These larger businesses should be considered as key partners in disseminating best practice to their supply chain in areas such as industrial water management, energy efficiency, zero-waste concepts, recycling and reuse and more resource-efficient technologies and production systems.

Government can ensure that data and information is freely available to business and that considered regulation is put in place. Government will play a vital role in ensuring that the development of resource management policy is twin-tracked with innovative research into the low-impact materials of the future and the engineering solutions required to reduce the materials used in products and find substitute materials. This has to be done with some urgency to prevent the shortage of materials becoming an insurmountable problem.

The material we waste

The UK lacks reliable waste data, with the exception of the waste (mainly from households) collected by local authorities. However, the best estimates from Defra indicate that the UK produces about 280 million tonnes of 'waste' materials every year. The amount is declining but the UK still produces more waste than the top performing European nations.

Local authorities collected a total of 23.5 million tonnes of household waste in England in 2010–11, of which 41.2 per cent was recycled, composted or reused.[5] The amount sent to landfill has fallen in recent years, but 11.4 million tonnes is still disposed of in this way each year. However, household waste accounts for a small fraction of the total waste stream.[6] The commercial and industrial (C&I) sectors produce approximately 24 million tonnes each per year. The volume being recycled by this sector has risen but 24 per cent of C&I waste was still being sent to landfill in 2009. Small businesses employing less than fifty people are estimated to account for 35 per cent of the waste in this sector.[7] None of these figures take into account the whole-life resource cost incurred through the volume of waste materials produced or water or energy used in the countries which produce the goods we buy or in their transport to the UK.

The cost of dealing with materials as waste is huge. According to WRAP the cost of disposing of the 18.4 million tonnes of food- and drink-related waste produced by the UK food and drink industry and UK households each year is around £17bn.[8] And the breakdown of food and other biodegradable waste contributes to emissions which are a significant component of climate change.

Protecting our raw materials

The security of our future resource supply is an area of critical concern for the economy. For example, the so-called rare earth elements are a group of naturally occurring metallic elements that are used in a range of the technologies we take for granted. Their use in wind turbines and hybrid petrol-electric cars are particularly crucial to the development of the low-carbon, energy-efficient economy.

Organisations such as the Royal Society for Chemistry have warned for some time that there needs to be an increase in the recycling rates of speciality metals such as lithium if we are not to face the danger of a shortage of supplies in the future as the result of higher international demand, reducing supplies, unstable countries and the rise of Chinese domestic manufacturing and export quotas.[9]

These concerns have been echoed by several EU reports on the supply of rare earths used in magnets and electronics as well as materials used in agriculture and other industries. A list of fourteen economically important raw materials which are subject to a high risk of supply interruption has been identified,[10] and initiatives to set targeted measures to secure and improve access to raw materials for the EU have been undertaken.[11]

Increased efficiency of use, more recycling and the development of alternatives are necessary, but even if such actions are undertaken immediately there is likely to be a short-term gap in supply. Such a gap could have serious economic and business resilience implications if not addressed.

Managing our water

Water is essential to every aspect of our lives. The more volatile weather patterns associated with climate change heighten the need to reduce leakage, find ways to use water more efficiently and assess any future pressure on supplies. New water resources will need to be developed, and storage and transport addressed.

After two winters of below-average rainfall, large areas of the UK faced drought in early 2012 and then had to cope with excess. The measures taken early in 2012, when water companies, farmers, businesses and consumers were requested to take action to prevent shortages, may become more common in the future.[12] Short-term measures such as hosepipe bans and other restrictions will not solve the long-term issue of water shortages caused by a growing population, changing weather patterns and commercial decisions.

Every person in the UK uses an average of 150 litres of water per day.[13] By contrast, the amounts used in Germany and France are 125 and 110 litres per person per day. The Environment Agency estimates that water bills for manufacturing industry could be costing over 1 per cent of business turnover. The UK also has an ageing utility service infrastructure. Water leakage is a problem, but the ability to assess the condition of buried pipelines and cables without undue excavation of the ground in which they are buried is complex, and likely to become more so as the climate changes. Further research on assessing the condition of underground service infrastructure is required.

An approach that moves from considering water use in a linear fashion – in which water is imported, processed and exported as wastewater and storm water – to a more cyclic model of water management, with reduced import of water, high rates of recycling and reduced wastewater and storm water has been analysed and discussed as part of the Urban Futures research.[14] Such approaches can offer water efficiency solutions provided that they are acceptable to people and take account of human behaviour. Greater awareness and information on methods to save water and an increase in responsible metering can help people and companies measure and manage their water usage effectively.

Energy security

The UK is facing a rising dependence on imported energy. Energy security will become of increased importance when the closure of ageing electricity generating plants is added to the impacts of climate change and increased competition for dwindling reserves as other countries improve their own standards of living. Reduced energy supplies or higher prices would affect all aspects of life in this country, from the services provided to the most vulnerable in our communities through to the ability to maintain competitive industry.

Government policy can be highly influential in encouraging investment in infrastructure and ensuring that energy generation capacity (including renewables) continues to be developed. Government can also do more to prepare business and the public sector to audit and address energy efficiency, introduce behavioural and operational change and use low-carbon replacements. At a local government level, planning policy as well as other policies and emergency plans have to anticipate the potential impacts of reduced energy supplies and increased climate change instability.

Whatever solutions are proposed they must be tested for resilience to ensure that they remain resistant to sudden change, take into account human behaviour and do not yield an unexpected negative legacy.

UK policy on material resources

The 2011 Waste Review was seen by many within industry to be lacking in aspiration, with an absence of targets and an over-reliance on voluntary agreements and responsibility deals as an alternative to regulation.[15] The Review presented a move towards zero waste as simply an aspiration, even though the Scottish government is planning its zero-waste regulations in a bid to make Scotland one of the highest performing countries for recycling in Europe. Included is a complete ban on municipal biodegradable waste to be sent to landfill by 2020, and requirements on businesses to present recyclable materials for collection.

Past government policies have concentrated on 'end of life' and have been too narrowly focused on local authority-collected waste. This focus on the collection and disposal of municipal waste has delayed the development of policy and data on business and industry waste; knowledge of the amounts, types and destination of waste materials from this sector remains limited. Landfill Tax has been a major driver for all businesses to reduce their waste, and there appears to be a marked decline in waste from the industrial sector. However, the trend is less clear in the commercial sector, and particularly the small business sector.

Many leading retailers are aiming for zero waste to landfill but small businesses struggle for assistance to support a recycling infrastructure that meets their needs and lack knowledge of the costs, opportunities and solutions available to them. The launch of a Business Waste and Recycling Collection Commitment by Defra in 2011 was designed to encourage local authorities to collect waste and recyclable materials from small businesses, open up household recycling centres to trade waste and work with commercial operators to develop contracts that cover small businesses in their areas. However, in a time of economic constraints on local government, further financial incentives would be usefully directed to encourage this sector. The former Business Resource Efficiency and Waste (BREW) Centre for Local Authorities (now a part of WRAP) worked to develop infrastructure and guidance and case studies using the vast experience available in local authorities.

The separation of the collection and disposal functions between two-tier local authorities and the reluctance of some councils to work across their administrative boundaries has encouraged more expensive and less efficient collection services. In much of Europe commercial and industrial waste is not separated from household waste when it is of similar composition. Collecting small business-separated waste along with household-separated waste would allow for increased economies of scale and a better infrastructure to be developed.

A new approach to the use of all resources and the role of economic instruments in promoting a more circular economy is required. A report from the Green Alliance called for a greater emphasis on recovering and recycling materials, and also greater resource efficiency, improved design and durability of consumer products to assist resource recovery as a way of avoiding some of the damaging, environmental impacts of extracting resources and the negative aspects of waste.[16]

Zero waste is a concept that takes a closed-loop 'cradle-to-cradle' approach rather than a linear approach to the use and disposal of resources and takes nature as a model. Flows of energy, water and materials through the economy are mapped to preserve the value of resources wherever possible. A circular economy approach to resource use and developing innovation is a model that has been developed by the UK's NISP (National Industrial Symbiosis Programme) organisation. By working with industry, the waste of one company can become the resource of another. The UK is recognised globally as a centre of excellence in the development of industrial symbiosis as a business model.

Resource efficiency was recognised by the EU as an essential part of their roadmap for the future.[17] Future government policy must build on this roadmap approach.

Waste, resource management and planning

In their State of the Nation report 2010 the Institute of Civil Engineers concluded that the waste infrastructure of the UK was 'requiring attention', and that there was no excess capacity. Significant investment was required in the next five years.[18] The government's new National Planning Policy Framework (NPPF) proposals do not address waste or resource management, so further guidance on waste will not emerge until the government publishes its National Waste Management Plan in 2013. This lack of clarity could delay the delivery of essential waste management facilities.

Many local authorities do not serve a large enough population to justify planning for their own resource management facilities, and developing partnerships across administrative boundaries makes economic sense. The ability to plan for facilities that are of a larger than local significance and the co-location of facilities has to be considered. Under previous regional arrangements, Regional Technical Advisory Boards (RTABs) consisting of local authority officers, businesses and environmental groups became repositories of expertise. The current remaining RTABs offer the opportunity for local authorities to utilise this expertise and demonstrate the 'duty to cooperate' requirement introduced by the government. However there needs to be further clarity about their role and funding.

Alongside a local approach there remains a vital need for strategic waste and resource planning and representative bodies, such as the RTABs, that can raise the profile of resource issues, focus on skills, investment, data-gathering and research and provide the vital policy-making advice and coordination that is required to build the green infrastructure economy. Such a body would need to work with Local Enterprise Partnerships and local authorities in each area to integrate infrastructure into local economies and encourage innovative UK manufacturers into the market.

A lack of good-quality reliable resource data makes it difficult to plan and finance innovative infrastructure. Much of the data for the commercial and industrial sector is estimated or extrapolated, and there is no ability to determine the type of industry producing materials or where they are located. Developing the ability to map where waste is being produced, by material type, geography and sector would assist the efficient exchange and utilisation of resources.

How do we become better at managing our resources?

An EU report on resource efficiency concluded that: 'it is perfectly possible to produce more value with fewer inputs, to lessen our impact on the environment, and to consume in a more intelligent fashion'.[19] But it also recognised that 'millions of firms and consumers will need to be mobilised' to achieve the required innovation and economic benefit.

The problems are compounded because the full costs of production and consumption are rarely reflected in the prices consumers pay for goods – which reduce the incentives to producers and consumers to innovate or change their behaviour. Information and science-based labelling, while useful for consumers, are not thought to be sufficient without other measures to reinforce the decision-making process.[20]

Support for and the development of the concept of the circular economy will assist UK businesses to become more resource-efficient. The ability to bring together traditionally separate industries and organisations from all business sectors with the aim of improving cross-industry resource efficiency and sustainability, involving the physical exchange of materials, energy, water and/or by-products together with the shared use of assets, logistics and expertise has the potential to boost economic prosperity.

A fundamental challenge to becoming resource-efficient is that waste, water and energy are currently perceived to be a small percentage of the overall costs of a business, and therefore managing them often takes second place to developing the core business, despite the fact that relatively simple measures can boost profitability. This is hard enough for large companies with dedicated staff, and even harder for small companies. Small businesses have particular problems which can include a lack of access to information, infrastructure, investment capital and management capability. Addressing these needs must be a priority.

The journey forward

The UK is on a journey towards a zero-waste and low-carbon society where resources are valued and reused and waste is only sent to landfill if there is absolutely no alternative. Preventing wastage of materials, energy or water has to become the norm.

The UK must develop a resource (rather than just a waste) strategy, where energy policy and climate change are taken into account and where the ensuing policy is tested for resilience to ensure that all solutions are resistant to change.[21] Such a policy has to consider the whole supply network and ways to reduce dependence on a small number of suppliers. Boosting awareness of the need for resource efficiency in business processes and the recovery of materials from discarded goods is also required. Further development of closed-loop economic models has to be addressed.

An integrated approach must deal with all material resources, including collection, sorting, reprocessing and reuse mechanisms to ensure high-quality recycled materials. Cross-sector working and a holistic approach that considers all resources has to be encouraged across all industrial sectors, with a partnership between industry and government agencies to smooth out the inevitable barriers.

Future policy should include the complete ban of biodegradable waste to landfill, and a target to halve residual wastes from households and businesses. Such a target would require an increase in the capacity and infrastructure to handle resource recovery, and small and medium size businesses to recycle. Clarity is needed on the future of the Landfill Tax, with an extension that ties in with a ban on biodegradable waste to landfill and the drive to reduce carbon emissions. Hypothecating the tax revenue to provide the finance required for waste minimisation and new infrastructure, through the Green Investment Bank, would benefit economic development.

The costs of acquiring and disposing of materials, water and energy are providing a strong incentive to businesses to improve their processes. However, more research and support for businesses would be welcome, as would more support and encouragement for ongoing UK university research to improve the recovery of rare earths from the waste stream and develop the materials and technologies of the future.

Resource efficiency requires an increase in capacity and infrastructure and adequate support from the planning framework for investment and innovation. Planning has to tackle the need for innovative closed waste facilities such as anaerobic digestion. Waste regulations have to be reviewed to encourage resource management and remove existing anomalies while safeguarding human health and the environment.

There is an increasingly urgent need to communicate the fact that resource efficiency is an economic opportunity that needs to be supported by a planning and strategy framework if it is to attract the investment and innovation required. Consideration has to be given to how materials are moved, what sites are available for facilities, what technologies and industries are available to handle the materials and how to ensure robust markets that are properly sustainable and resilient whatever the future brings. Real change, not tinkering around the edges, is required; consumers and businesses alike cannot afford a continued lack of action.

Notes

1   United Nations Secretary-General's High-level Panel on Global Sustainability, *Resilient People, Resilient Planet: A future worth choosing* (United Nations, 2012).

2   Chris Laszlo and Nadya Zhexembayeva, 'Embedded Sustainability: A Strategy for Market Leaders', *The European Financial Review*, April – May 2011.

3   European Commission, *A Resource-Efficient Europe – Flagship Initiative under the Europe 2020 Strategy* (2011).

4   Defra, *The Economics of Waste and Waste Policy* (June 2011).

5   Defra Statistical Release, 'Local Authority Collected Waste Management Statistics for England – Final Release of Quarters 1, 2, 3 and 4, 2010/11' (November 2011).

6   Ibid.

7   Ibid.

8   WRAP, *Waste Arisings in the Supply of Food and Drink to UK Households* (March 2010).

9   Emily Davies, 'Endangered elements: Critical thinking', *Chemistry World* (January 2011).

10   European Commission, *Critical Raw Materials for the EU, Report of the ad-hoc working group on defining critical raw materials* (July 2010).

11   European Commission, *Tackling the Challenges in Commodity Markets and on raw materials* (February 2011).

12   Environment Agency, *Review of the 2010–2012 drought and prospects for water resources in 2013* (March 2012).

13   See www.waterwise.org.uk

14   D. R. Lombardi, J. M. Leach, C. D. F. Rogers and the Urban Futures team, *Designing Resilient Cities: A Guide to Good Practice* (IHS BRE Press, 2012).

15   Beasley Associates and RGR, *The Defra Waste Review 2011: Reflections from the Industry* (September 2011).

16   Green Alliance, *Reinventing the Wheel: A Circular Economy for Resource Security* (2011).

17   European Commission, *A Resource-Efficient Europe*.

18   Institution of Civil Engineers, *The State of the Nation: Waste and Resource Management* (2010).

19   European Commission, *Roadmap for a Resource-Efficient Europe* (September 2011).

20   European Commission, *Lags in the EU Economy's response to change, Communication on a Resource-Efficient Europe Final Report* (2011).

21   Lombardi et al., *Designing Resilient Cities*.

Chapter 18

The Choice –
Energy Policy in a Changing Climate

Tom Burke

It is not yet widely understood by politicians, policy-makers or the public alike that climate change will lead to a complete transformation of the human prospect. This is true whether climate policy succeeds or fails. If it succeeds, the transformation will take place over the next thirty years. If it fails, a very different transformation – one that is already under way – will accelerate and become dramatic in the thirty years after that.

Success will mean that the way we produce and use energy will change totally, as we create a carbon-neutral global energy system. Failure will mean a world that becomes inexorably warmer and, as it warms, becomes ever more unstable – economically, socially, politically and environmentally.

The choice is whether events or people drive this transformation. If people drive it, then over the next thirty years the technologies we use to make energy available for daily use will change completely. This will bring with it a wide range of co-benefits in terms both of economic efficiency and human health. Food security and water security will be maintained. Economic and political stability will be retained.

If events drive the transformation then the technologies we use to make energy available will remain much as they are now. But the global temperature will rise relentlessly and, for all practical purposes, irreversibly. Food security and water security will be undermined and ever larger numbers of people will be displaced, exposed to conflict and disease and subject to deeper climate-induced poverty.

In these circumstances preserving political support for the international institutions, including the United Nations and the European Union, that have sustained the prosperity and security of billions of people for more than sixty years will become progressively more difficult. There will be a retreat into the aggressive nationalism that so limited human development for much of history.

The political choice

Politics is the art of making choices together. It is the antithesis of the radical individualism that has come to dominate public life in recent times. For Liberal Democrats, it is the art of making those collective choices that best preserve the liberty of individuals to realise their aspirations. There has been no political choice in the whole of human history more significant than the choice we must now make about climate change. This is the choice about whether we determine for ourselves the climate in which we live, or whether that climate determines for us and our successors what kind of lives it will be possible for us to live.

Climate policy and energy policy are two sides of the same coin. For all practical purposes, energy policy *is* climate policy. It is the only tool we have to manage the climate. There are some who fantasise that if the climate changes as dramatically and as quickly as projected by climate science we can use novel technologies to remove carbon from the atmosphere. But even were all of the huge problems of using geo-engineering on the necessary scale to be solved, no one has yet explained why it would be any easier to get two hundred countries to agree to do something we do not know how to do than it has proved to be so far to get them to agree to do something we *do* know how to do.

There are others who believe that we can rely on the great capacity of human beings to adapt to a changing climate. They are not heeding the lessons from Superstorm Sandy and Hurricane Katrina about the vulnerability of the cities in which half of us already live. Nor are they grasping the reality of the progressive loss of food and water security, in both rich and poor worlds, that will accompany climate change.

These are false prospects, offered by those who seek to avoid the responsibility of facing up to the choice we must make if we are to preserve the values for which Liberal Democrats stand. A world that allows events to determine the future will not be friendly to civil liberties, human rights or the rule of law. It will be four degrees warmer by soon after the middle of the century. Liberty will not be its watchword. To keep a climate in which our values can thrive we must adopt a carbon-neutral energy policy.

It is not an accident that climate-deniers are to be found almost wholly on the political right. If your core political beliefs are in smaller government, less regulation, lower taxes and an ever expanding realm of personal choice for individuals, if you believe that markets are always wiser than governments, then you cannot accept the existence of climate change. Its solution requires the defeat of your core beliefs.

The political left is also compromised by its core beliefs. It is committed to making the economy grow as much and as fast as possible in order to create the economic resources to improve public services and alleviate poverty at home and abroad. Policies which might put economic growth at risk are anathema to these beliefs. They do not require climate denial but they do inhibit timely action on the scale required.

Climate change pays no regard to these ideological preoccupations. It will overwhelm the defining ideas of both right and left equally. There is much to be said for keeping governments out of people's lives and for making full use of the power of markets to innovate. The relief of poverty is a moral as well as a political imperative, better public services is a goal we all share, and there is nothing wrong with the aspiration to share the benefits of a growing economy.

The problem with a changing climate is that it will destroy markets, and communities and families with them. It will spread poverty more widely, and more certainly, than any other phenomenon in human experience. It will confine personal choices and it will destroy the infrastructure on which public services depend faster than it can be rebuilt. Dealing with it requires politics that grasp the difference between principle and dogma.

Systemic risks and the duties of government

The world has just had a brutal lesson in the consequences of failing to understand and deal with systemic risks: risks to an entire system rather than to any particular part of it. Systemic risks are not well understood by politicians, nor by the economists who advise them. They arise from the interdependencies between the elements of a system such that a failure of a single element can lead to a cascade of failures that brings down the whole system. Such were the interdependencies in the global financial system that the failure of one bank came within a whisker of bringing down the entire global economy.

The central role of the financial system in underpinning the global economy is now widely recognised. Without huge flows of private and public capital it cannot function. It was the threat to these flows of capital that made the financial crisis so urgent and action to tackle it so rapid. It is less well understood that those flows of capital also depend on political stability. Without the confidence that comes with political stability, investors will not invest. Without investment, there is no economic growth. Lack of growth in an expanding population with rising aspirations threatens to further undermine political stability, triggering another downward ratchet in investment.

It is barely grasped at all that a stable climate is a prerequisite for political stability. Climate change is a systemic risk that, if not managed effectively, threatens to bring down the post-war economic and political system that has brought unprecedented prosperity and security to billions of people and still offers that prospect to billions more. In a world that is four degrees warmer, crop productivity will be falling at a time of rapidly rising demand for food. Water scarcity, already a chronic problem for nearly half the world's people, will become acute. This strategic loss of food and water security will be accompanied by many other stresses, as extreme weather events increasingly take their toll on homes, businesses and infrastructure.

We will not begin to deal properly with climate change until we grasp that the stable climate we have taken for granted throughout history and the global economy are a single system. The stable climate provides the context within which all economic activity takes place. The global economic system, the financial system which underpins it, the political system which supports it and the climate system are interdependent, subject to exactly the same kind of systemic risk that brought the world's banks to the edge of collapse.

We must stop thinking about climate change as an 'environmental problem'. This is not an issue we can put off until after the economy recovers. The desire to defer climate action, a view strongly held by the current Chancellor and his officials, is mistaken. It fails to grasp that the climate defines the realm of the possible for the economy, not the other way round.

It is the first duty of any government to maintain territorial integrity; clearly, governments which fail in this duty are no longer governments. Its second duty is to maintain internal stability; if it cannot do that it rapidly becomes unable to discharge its first duty. The third duty of a government is to maintain food, energy and water security for its citizens; if it is unable to do this then it will not be able to maintain internal stability and thus to preserve territorial integrity.

We have all witnessed on the nightly news over the last three years the fate of governments unable to meet these imperatives. In Tunisia, food price spikes resulting from extreme weather events were a trigger for the Arab Spring. Drought played a part in the social stresses which set off the explosion of violence in Syria. Food, energy and water security are the pillars of prosperity. They support the political stability on which economic success depends. The changing climate is already undermining the integrity of these pillars in some parts of the world. As the change accelerates it will make this task progressively more difficult everywhere. Eventually it will become impossible.

No government will put at risk energy, water or food security in order to achieve climate security. These are more familiar risks for governments to manage, and issues where policy failure has very immediate political consequences. Not surprisingly, for a majority of governments they appear more pressing than climate security. However, allowing the more immediate to obscure the more urgent is a common cause of policy failure. We know from experience that it is possible for nations to recover from a loss of energy, water or food security, albeit it at great human and economic cost. The same is not true for climate security. Once lost it cannot be regained. There is no recovery, no return to business as usual.

If climate security is lost, it brings down the other pillars of prosperity with it. Unlike the other challenges we face in the twenty-first century, climate change is time-bound. Not only do we have to achieve a certain goal – a carbon-neutral global energy system – but we must get there by a certain time. The build-up of carbon in the atmosphere is cumulative and effectively irreversible. To keep the change we are experiencing within the bounds of the manageable, we need to have achieved carbon neutrality by about the middle of this century.

Maintaining security

There are some more hard truths that we must grasp. The first priority for our economy must become the maintenance of food, energy, water and climate security. Unless they are maintained successfully in an increasingly stressed world then all other political, social and personal priorities are put at risk. Subordinating climate policy to the short-term exigencies of the economy is a prime example of the penny-wise, pound-foolish policies for which the Treasury has become notorious.

The economic policy favoured by the deficit hawks is failing. It has assumed that rapid deficit reduction accompanied by aggressive deregulation would be enough to restore growth. But it has never been obvious why destroying the planning system and trashing environmental laws would accomplish what £350 billion of quantitative easing has failed to achieve. We clearly do have a demand problem. The construction industry is not building houses because there are too few people who can afford to buy them, not because there is too little land available.

The capital markets know the difference between borrowing to invest and borrowing to spend on entitlements. Interest rates for public borrowing are now so low that this is the best possible time for government to make the essential investments in the energy-efficient smart infrastructure required to build a low-carbon energy system. We would be foolish and irresponsible to miss this chance.

Typically, energy, water, food and climate are each dealt with by different government departments and agencies. Each has a separate constellation of supporting professionals and clusters of related businesses. This significantly increases the risk of policy cannibalism as the solutions to one problem add to the difficulties of another. Successive British governments have consistently sought to drive energy prices down to deal with competitiveness and fuel poverty issues while driving them up to tackle climate change – leaving investors bewildered.

Threats to water security can be addressed by energy-intensive desalination and water transfer projects, but at the risk of undermining energy security by increasing dependence on expensive imports. If the extra energy is provided by the combustion of fossil fuels then that will undermine climate security and eventually water security. If lower water security threatens food security by climate-altered precipitation this can be compensated for by the use of energy-intensive agrochemicals and water transfer projects. But if this additional energy is provided from fossil fuels it increases the risk of further altering precipitation patterns and raising temperatures – undermining both water and food security.

Little is gained if the policy effort to strengthen one of the pillars of prosperity simply weakens another. In particular, poor policy coherence undermines the ability of the business world to make confident and timely investment decisions. This means that we must place a powerful mechanism at the heart of government, able to ensure that other public policy goals do not conflict with achieving climate – and therefore food, energy and water – security. Britain's Climate Change Act leads the world in providing a potent legislative framework, but it lacks sufficiently strong support from the machinery of government to achieve its goals expeditiously.

Winners and losers

Another hard truth that we must grasp is that, as with any transformation, there will be winners and losers. There is no pain-free solution to the climate crisis. Choosing where gains and losses fall as the world changes is a primary task of politics. It is our responsibility as a political party to strike the fairest possible allocation of those gains and losses. This question is the most difficult part of the whole climate problem.

We know what we need to do to build a carbon-neutral global energy system. All the technologies and engineering knowledge we need to get there in time is already available. We also know that we can afford to do it, both globally and as a nation. The International Energy Agency has pointed out that when you net out the avoided cost of unused fossil fuels the additional cost of a carbon-neutral future is only a relatively small addition to what we will be investing in energy anyway. What we do not know how to do is to put the technology and capital together on the scale and timescale that is necessary. That is a political problem. Its solution will require the political will that has so far been lacking. And that, in its turn, requires political leadership. Politics is often said to be the art of the possible. This is correct. But political leadership is the art of expanding the realm of the possible.

If we, as Liberal Democrats, are unable to provide that political leadership then events, not people, will determine the outcome. If they do so then we will all be losers, but those of us under forty will be the biggest losers, as societies everywhere struggle to come to terms with a world that is at least four degrees warmer.

Building a low-carbon economy in Britain will not undermine our economy but it will change the pattern of winners and losers. The new economy will be rich in jobs and opportunities, but they will not be the same jobs and opportunities, in the same places, for the same people with the same skills. The energy transition necessary for climate security will be accompanied by a social transition. There will be a social adjustment cost that will not be paid by the market as we retrain workers and regenerate the places that support our current high carbon economy. We must be honest about these costs, and fully prepared to meet them.

Working with others

There is a final hard truth that we must come to terms with if we are to succeed. Climate change is not a problem that Britain can solve on its own. Others must act too. But a certain recipe for disaster is to let the global debate on climate change degenerate into a 'you first' discussion. Fine words will not be persuasive. It is actions that will count. If we want others to build a low-carbon economy we must build one ourselves. If we cannot summon the political will to do so, why would we imagine that others would?

Furthermore, we must do so as a fully committed member of the EU. Britain has played a central role in alerting the world to the magnitude of the risks posed by a changing climate. British initiatives in science, economics, diplomacy and legislation have fundamentally shaped the global debate on the issue. But it has been our ability to leverage the weight of the twenty-seven members of the EU behind these initiatives that has given us such disproportionate influence. Those siren voices arguing that somehow Britain would be better off outside the EU turn out to be the same voices casting doubt on the existence of climate change. In reality, without the weight of the EU behind it no government of Britain would be able to properly protect its 60 million citizens from the risks of climate change.

Those same siren voices frequently invoke the word 'freedom' to defend their indifference to a changing climate. Markets must be left 'free' to seek opportunities. Individuals must be 'free' to choose. Businesses must be 'freed' from government regulation. This is an ideologically tainted use of the word. All too often it translates in practice to meaning that companies and some individuals should be 'free' to pursue their selfish interests at the expense of everyone else.

For Liberal Democrats an essential role of government is to ensure its citizens are free from the blight on their lives that will result from climate change; free from ever-more intense floods and droughts of the kind we have so recently experienced; free from ever-rising food prices and free from the threats of an increasingly insecure world, as climate change causes more states to fail. Another key task for Liberal Democrats is to free families and communities to be able to do more to ensure their own energy security. This will mean tackling the pernicious influence of the energy lobbies and freeing local government from the dead hand of the Treasury.

Our energy policy – our climate policy by another name – must fully recognise the scale and urgency of the challenge we face. It must recognise that the necessary technology transition will be accompanied by a social transition that must also be thought through. It must meet three tests that are now often mentioned: build a low-carbon economy by 2050; ensure security of energy supply for our homes and businesses; and be affordable. It must also meet another test that is too rarely mentioned in the policy debates: it must be fair and be felt to be fair.

Meeting these tests is well within our engineering and economic competence. But they cannot be met without a clear and stable framework of public policy. The current lack of enthusiasm for energy investment of any kind is predominantly a result of the incoherence of successive governments, including the present government. These have all tried vainly to please everyone, often letting headlines rather than analysis drive decisions. The result of trying to do a bit of everything is that we are not doing enough of anything, and consumers are increasingly distressed by ever-rising bills.

Political imperatives

There are seven political imperatives for an energy policy that will provide secure and affordable low-carbon energy for Britain. A stable policy informed by these imperatives will ensure that Britain plays its full part in tackling climate change. It will also enhance the competitiveness of Britain's businesses and contain the pressure on household incomes. It will limit the power of the energy lobbies and it will free individuals, families and communities to take more control of their own energy supply. And it will provide a crucial stimulus to the demand necessary to restore growth.

The first imperative is to recognise the prime political importance of separating bills from prices. The price of the fossil fuels that currently provide the bulk of our energy are determined globally. There is little any government can do to manage those prices. But there is a great deal that governments can do to ensure that those global prices do not translate inexorably into rising bills for home-owners and businesses. Two of the most important measures are making sure that demand management measures are prioritised in the Energy Bill to avoid the higher costs of new generation of any kind, and to begin a national programme to deploy charging infrastructure for electric vehicles.

The second imperative is to get serious about energy efficiency. Setting up the Green Deal has been a useful first step but the programme has been widely criticised for its lack of ambition. Energy efficiency improvements are, by a long way, the largest, fastest and cheapest source of carbon reductions. They are also the most effective way to ensure that rising global prices do not translate into rising domestic bills. The impact of the Green Deal could be hugely increased simply by overturning the dogmatic and inexplicable opposition of the Treasury to letting the Green Investment Bank borrow from the capital markets immediately.

The third imperative is to halt the Treasury's theft of green taxes for disguised revenue-raising. Contrary to the government mantra the carbon price floor to be introduced in April is not a floor price on the emissions trading market. It is simply a progressive carbon tax, exactly like the much-maligned vehicle fuel duty escalator. Outside the Treasury's models, in the real world of energy investors it will do nothing to incentivise the low-carbon transition. It simply raises revenues for the government and justifies public cynicism about stealth taxes. The revenues from this tax should be recycled directly into financing the low-carbon transition. This would be both honest and make a real difference to both the climate and our energy security. These revenues should be used to pay for three things: to incentivise the rapid deployment of the infrastructure for a low-carbon energy system; to alleviate fuel poverty; and to help pay for the social adjustment costs of the energy transition. This would go a long way to ensuring that our energy policy met the fairness test.

The fourth imperative is to stimulate much wider participation in community energy projects. There is considerable, as yet untapped, scope for local communities in Britain to play a role in ensuring their own energy security – much as is done widely elsewhere in Europe. The keys to unlocking this potential are to create a more supportive regime for managing our electricity grid and giving local councils more fiscal freedom to initiate and support community energy projects. Working at the community level allows for a much greater integration of energy policies than can be achieved by Whitehall and has the considerable advantage of keeping the revenues from energy bills in the local economy rather than exporting them to remote, often foreign, companies.

The fifth imperative is to stop dithering about renewables. DECC has belatedly woken up to the fact that solar power can play a key role in ensuring Britain's low-carbon energy security, especially in community energy projects. We already know how much both on- and off-shore wind power are capable of contributing if only the government would provide a stable enough energy policy to keep investment flowing. The cost of both wind and solar are falling rapidly, allowing the current level of subsidy to decline to nothing over time. There is a real danger of Britain missing out on the renewables revolution under way elsewhere simply because DECC, Number 10 and the Treasury cannot make up their mind who is in charge of energy policy.

The sixth imperative is to move forward urgently on carbon capture and storage (CCS). Gas has a central role to play in our energy future; it is an essential complement to renewables for electricity generation. But if we are to avoid an unacceptable conflict between energy security and climate security then that gas must be accompanied by CCS. The current government lethargy on this issue is disgraceful. It has meant we have missed out on getting European funding and have deterred investors with meaningless – and expensive – competitions for public financing. In any case, it is hugely in the economic interest of Shell and the gas suppliers to see CCS demonstrated, to secure their long-run access to markets. Arguably, there is no compelling argument for public finance at all and the gas suppliers should pay for its demonstration themselves.

The seventh imperative is to work vigorously with our partners in the EU to build an integrated electricity grid and gas supply networks that would hugely increase our energy security and accelerate further the falling costs of the renewables. Building this physical infrastructure would also further the integration of European energy markets, boosting the competitiveness of Britain's businesses both within and beyond the EU.

Chapter 19

Only Connect

Fiona Hall MEP[1]

'In order to have a 50 per cent chance of keeping the global mean temperature rise below 2°C relative to pre-industrial levels, atmospheric greenhouse gas (GHG) concentrations must stabilise below 450ppm CO_2 equivalence. Global GHG emissions should peak by 2020 at the latest and then be more than halved by 2050 relative to 1990.'[2]

This is the science which drives global and European decision-making on energy and climate change. In March 2007, EU leaders agreed the 20-20-20 targets: a 20 per cent reduction in EU GHG emissions from 1990 levels, 20 per cent of EU energy to come from renewable resources and a 20 per cent improvement in the EU's energy efficiency. In July 2009, the leaders of the European Union and the G8 announced an objective to reduce greenhouse gas emissions by at least 80 per cent below 1990 levels by 2050.

In the UK, the Climate Change Act 2008 set a legally binding target to reduce UK greenhouse gas emissions by 80 per cent from 1990 levels by the year 2050.[3] As a result of decisions taken by the Liberal Democrats in government, the carbon budgets established under the Climate Change Act now require the UK to cut its greenhouse gas emissions by around half 1990 levels by the year 2025.

Achieving those targets will require a major change in the UK energy system. The government sees electricity coming from three low-carbon sources by 2050: renewable energy, especially onshore and offshore wind, a new tranche of nuclear power stations, and gas and coal-fired power stations fitted with carbon capture and storage (CCS) technology. Continuing the policy espoused by the previous Labour government of not picking winners, the coalition government maintains that competition between the low-carbon sources – renewables, nuclear and CCS – will drive innovation and lower costs. This is known as the 'basket' approach to delivering low-carbon electricity technologies.

In applying this approach, the coalition government has continued with the twin assumptions taken by its predecessors: that 110 GW of installed generating capacity will be needed by 2025, compared to 85 GW in 2011;[4] and that 60 GW will need to be new build.[5]

Crucially, the UK's policies to promote low-carbon energy continue to focus heavily on supply-side measures, rather than the demand side. Moreover, UK climate change policy focuses on reducing CO_2 emissions, rather than on reducing energy use. The UK carbon budgets lay down limits on the amount of carbon that can be emitted into the atmosphere in a given timeframe, in order to set a trajectory to achieve at least an 80 per cent reduction from 1990 levels by 2050. But there are no targets or clear projections with regard to the amount of future energy use or of energy savings.

This chapter argues that the government's apparently cautious and neutral strategy is, in fact, flawed. First, the focus on supply-side options means that the benefits of managing energy demand are severely undervalued. Second, as we pursue a low-carbon future, the 'basket' of UK energy policy contains few viable options. The chapter goes on to suggest that UK energy policy needs to be considered in its wider European context and will propose a different approach to meeting UK energy needs and GHG reduction commitments over the next forty years.

The potential role of demand-side measures

Successive studies, including modelling by the Committee on Climate Change, have shown that reducing demand for electricity – through, for example, improved energy efficiency – will play a key role in minimising the costs of meeting the UK's emissions targets.

A 2012 report by McKinsey, commissioned by the Department of Energy and Climate Change (DECC), shows that electricity use could be reduced by the equivalent of 40 per cent of total electricity demand by 2030, a massive 155 TWh, by implementing electricity-saving measures in the domestic, commercial and industrial sectors.[6] The existing policy framework is, however, insufficient to deliver this. McKinsey estimates that existing policy will only deliver savings of 14 per cent, or 54 TWh, which is only a third of the total potential.

Yet the fundamental policy question underpinning all others has been: 'how do we ensure enough (low-carbon) energy supply?', not: 'how do we match supply and demand?' The consequences have been significant. The assumption that the UK would require 110 GW of total electricity capacity by 2025 was key to the decision in 2005 (under Tony Blair) that the UK needed a new fleet of nuclear power stations. In 2005, with renewables at only 3 per cent of electricity supply, a forward low-carbon scenario based heavily on renewable energy sources alone, without nuclear, hardly looked credible. Had already planned and achievable reductions in energy consumption been taken into account, a very different figure for total electricity demand in 2025 would have formed the basis of discussions even in 2005. Moreover, significant energy efficiency measures have been put in place nationally and at a European level since that decision was taken.

The assumptions about future UK energy demand have never been challenged. A report from the UK Association for the Conservation of Energy (ACE), *A Corruption of Governance?* has revealed that ministers asked for scenarios of how such a level of demand could be met in compliance with carbon emission reduction targets, but they did not question the assumed level of demand itself.[7] Nor was any cost-benefit analysis carried out as to whether demand management through implementation of energy efficiency measures would be cheaper than increasing capacity on the supply side.

The absence of any questioning of the likely future level of UK electricity demand is particularly remarkable given the divergence of UK assumptions from EU-wide predictions. In 2010, the European Commission calculated that, considering the role of electricity in decarbonising the transport and heating sectors, EU electricity consumption would rise by 24 per cent, from 243,907 Ktoe in 2010 to 303,526 Ktoe in 2020.[8] This calculation takes into account energy efficiency measures already under way or in the pipeline, but not the potential effects of the 2012 Energy Efficiency Directive. For the UK, the Commission calculation shows a mere 15 per cent rise in electricity consumption, from 28,230 Ktoe in 2010 to 32,400 Ktoe in 2020.[9] According to the European Network of Transmission System Operators for Electricity (ENTSO-E), from 2020 to 2025 a slower increase in the rate of consumption (by only about 0.8 per cent a year) is expected.[10] These figures contrast starkly with the 37 per cent rise in electricity consumption by 2025 assumed by successive UK governments, and, at the time of writing, not yet adjusted in light of the 2012 McKinsey report. A DECC consultation on demand management closed on 31 January 2013.

Across the EU, reducing primary energy consumption is now understood as an economic as much as an environmental imperative. The '20 per cent by 2020' target equates to slashing energy imports by some €38 billion annually.[11] According to European Commission calculations, achieving the 2020 target also yields avoided costs for investment in energy generation and distribution of an average of €6 billion annually[12] – assuming, of course, that member states adjust their new-build plans downwards to take account of efficiency gains. If the UK continues to disregard demand-side management, it will be forced to invest in extra generating capacity and new grid connections the need for which could have been avoided. It would be an extraordinarily expensive mistake, not only in terms of the cost of the investment itself but also because of the knock-on effect on the UK's global competitiveness.

The low-carbon electricity supply options: renewables

On the supply side of low-carbon electricity, let us consider first the renewable electricity technologies. Of all EU member states, the UK has arguably the greatest potential in wind and marine renewables. If the right decisions are taken early enough, the UK could become the world leader, and a net exporter not only of energy itself, but also of cutting-edge energy technology.

Onshore wind is the cheapest sustainable technology today, and the UK still has considerable unused potential. By developing onshore wind, the UK can decarbonise its power sector quickly and at least cost. Unfortunately, reasonable local concern about the appropriateness of one or other specific site has been transformed into an orchestrated resistance to onshore wind in general by a combination of climate-change deniers and a populist right-wing press. But opinion polls continue to show a clear majority in favour of wind power. In a YouGov poll commissioned by *The Sunday Times* in October 2012, 55 per cent of those questioned said there should be more wind farms, while a ComRes poll for *The Independent* in June 2012 showed 68 per cent in favour, including 58 per cent of Conservative voters.

However, offshore wind is where the biggest potential for the UK lies. The European Environmental Agency has assessed the wind energy potential of the North Sea as sufficient to power the European Union four times over[13] – in other words, to provide electricity for two billion of the seven billion people on the planet. The UK has the potential to become the market leader, a position taken by Denmark and Germany in the onshore sector.

Offshore wind presents much bigger technical challenges than onshore wind, but the UK has the necessary offshore expertise, as well as good ports and skilled personnel. The development of sites and of the supply chain is underway, along with research and testing in centres such as Narec in Blyth, Northumberland. Offshore wind can be the driver of an industrial renaissance in regions such as the north-east of England. For this potential to be fully realised there will need to be commitment and investment certainty, otherwise the UK will again lose out to its neighbours around the North Sea. The UK could also be a world leader in wave energy, but this technology is still some way from commercial exploitation and will require strong and stable support if its considerable potential contribution is to be realised.

Turning to land-based renewable resources, biomass energy has the advantage of being cheap and available at any time. Solid biomass – wood or plants such as miscanthus – can be used to generate electricity as an alternative to fossil fuels or can be co-fired with coal to reduce overall CO_2 emissions. Biomass can also be used to produce biofuel, either ethanol from sugar or cereal crops such as wheat and maize, or biodiesel from oil seed such as rape.

Unlike wind energy, biomass is a limited resource, within the UK and globally. Biomass crops may compete with food for land use. Moreover, to be sustainable, biomass must not be burnt at a rate faster than it can be regrown. Expanding the cultivation of bioenergy crops is likely to have a detrimental effect on overall GHG emissions if associated with deforestation. Indirect land use change (ILUC) can be as important in this respect as direct land use change – for example if bioenergy crops are planted on grazing land and forest elsewhere is cut down to provide replacement grazing.

Whereas small-scale biomass plants may source wood locally from timber yard offcuts or trimmings from forests, wood for large biomass power stations has to be imported by sea from sustainably managed northern forests in Canada and Scandinavia. Here, the slow growth rate of the replacement trees means that decades will pass before new trees have absorbed the CO_2 released when the old trees were burnt. In other words, there is an initial burst of CO_2 and a long tail of re-absorption. This is of concern because of the need to reduce GHG emissions *now* rather than in 2100. What is more, burning biomass for electricity has a very poor rate of energy conversion and is below 35 per cent efficient on current technology.[14]

Biomass cannot, therefore, be a silver bullet, but it has a role to play if used in moderation, from sustainable sources, and in the most efficient way possible – namely in combined heat and power (CHP) plants rather than to generate electricity alone.

While the northerly latitude of the UK means that the potential of photovoltaics (PV) is less than in southern Europe, solar power can nevertheless make a useful contribution on a domestic scale. A well-insulated building with solar panels on its roof can become a 'positive energy' building producing, overall, more electricity than it uses. In Germany, which has scarcely more sun than Britain, PV now produces 5 per cent of electricity.[15] Crucial to the expansion of PV has been the offer of a feed-in tariff (FiT). This has stimulated the market for PV, causing costs to fall dramatically. Indeed prices have dropped so much that PV is set to be competitive without subsidy by 2020.[16]

The low-carbon electricity supply options: CCS

The second component of the UK government's 'basket' approach to low-carbon electricity technology envisages an ongoing role for fossil fuels provided that the CO_2 emitted is neutralised through carbon capture and storage (CCS). Using pre- and post-combustion CCS would allow Britain to continue to exploit its considerable coal and gas reserves. But CCS is proving not to be the magic solution to decarbonisation that it was originally hyped up to be. There is huge uncertainty about the cost, and with British and EU commercial-scale projects yet to get under way it is hard to predict how quickly there could be a move to mainstream CCS use. It will be at least 2030 before CCS is commercially available. This poses a practical dilemma, since existing fossil fuel installations will need to be replaced before that date. If they are replaced with new fossil plants, the UK will become locked into high-carbon electricity generation, either in the short term until CCS is ready, or potentially long term should CCS turn out not to be viable.

CCS promises a CO2-free way of continuing to use gas. Gas-fired power stations can be cranked up and down extremely quickly, so are an attractive option for balancing variable renewable energy sources, particularly wind. Unfortunately, current research on CCS indicates that gas-fired plant can *either* be used for fast balancing of renewables *or* coupled with CCS to remove the carbon, but not both together, because the CCS process itself is not stop/start. It is possible that the true value of CCS will prove more to be in capturing CO2 from the chemical industry and from industrial processes such as cement-making and aluminium smelting.

The low-carbon electricity supply options: nuclear

The third component, nuclear, is a low-carbon energy source, but it fits awkwardly into the low-carbon energy basket. The arguments against a new fleet of nuclear power stations are well rehearsed. The nuclear process produces waste which is radioactive for thousands of years and structures which have to be decommissioned at eye-watering cost. In three years the estimated cost of decommissioning the Nuclear Decommissioning Authority (NDA) sites rose from around £56 billion (2005)[17] to £73.6 billion (2008).[18]

Since Windscale, the nuclear industry in Britain has had a good safety record, but accidents in other countries – Three Mile Island, Chernobyl, Fukushima – are a reminder of the inherent instability of the nuclear fission process. Nor does nuclear fit well with other low-carbon energy sources. It is highly inflexible and so needs to run as the base load electricity supply and, unlike gas, cannot be used to balance variable renewables. Indeed it is nuclear rather than wind which is an intermittent (as opposed to a variable) source of power. A nuclear power station is either on or off, and when one or more stations is off for an extended period of time because of safety concerns, a multi-gigawatt supply gap opens up.

But the major obstacle to the building of a new generation of nuclear reactors is cost. According to the Cour des Comptes, French nuclear reactor costs have increased by more than 300 per cent in real terms since the 1970s. At the end of the 1970s an average French nuclear reactor cost around €1 billion, but by 2010 this had gone up to almost €4 billion,[19] or even €6 billion, according to some estimates,[20] a four-to-six-fold rise in the headline cost over thirty years and a tripling of the real cost, accounting for inflation. The rising cost of nuclear power is particularly striking because it is the opposite of the downward cost curve characteristic of a mature technology. Today, no one argues that new nuclear is cheaper than onshore wind, let alone 'too cheap to meter', as originally claimed.

For the UK government, the rising cost of nuclear is particularly uncomfortable. The EPR reactor under construction in Finland is expected to be completed eleven years late and at double the original budget. A similar plant being built by EDF at Flamanville in France is also at double its budget and running four years late. The EPR is the leading contender for new nuclear build in the UK. But following Fukushima, EDF is reported to have raised its estimate of the cost of building a new nuclear reactor in the UK from £4.5 billion to £7 billion.[21]

The UK government is left with three options with regard to nuclear. First, it could persuade the nuclear industry to go ahead with building new reactors by subsidising the spiralling cost. But the coalition government has signed up to *not* giving public subsidies to nuclear new build, and therefore would have to put in place a covert subsidy through the mechanisms of electricity market reform. Second, the government can allow existing nuclear stations to continue operating beyond their planned lifetime, even though half are due to be replaced by 2020. This inevitably raises some safety questions, but would allow existing nuclear operators to rack up substantial windfall profits through the carbon floor price. Third, the government could accept that nuclear is not economically viable, and rethink its energy policy.

The low-carbon energy mix

To summarise: nuclear should be ruled out simply on cost grounds. Gas with its carbon removed by CCS cannot work flexibly to balance variable renewable sources, on present technology. Sustainable biomass is a limited resource. Only wind, onshore and particularly offshore, offers the prospect of sustainable low-carbon electricity in abundance, supported by other marine technologies as they come on stream.

The future for low-carbon electricity in the UK lies, therefore, in renewables. This has important consequences for energy policy. The UK government to date has been unsupportive of EU-wide renewable targets beyond 2020, arguing that a technology-neutral approach to low-carbon energy sources should be maintained. But if nuclear and CCS are out of the frame, and the UK (and the EU as a whole) is going to rely on renewable energy, the industry needs the stable investment framework that will enable rapid growth and expansion. A decarbonisation target alone does not give the clear signal that investors crave, particularly investors in associated long-term developments such as port infrastructure, for whom 2030 is tomorrow. The UK, with its massive potential in a technology – offshore wind – which is not yet competitive but will be, stands to benefit more than any other member state from the mooted post-2020 EU renewables target. It would be bizarre if the UK government blocked a target which favoured the UK's own strengths in energy production while supporting a subsidy demanded essentially by the nuclear industry of a neighbouring member state.

Certainty and stability is what markets need most. Offshore wind is in urgent need of new investors such as pension funds, but they need to know what the market will look like tomorrow before they put their money in. The faster offshore wind can develop, the quicker it will reach the economies of scale which will bring the price down. It is time to put down the basket of hedged low-carbon technologies and back the winner.

Unfortunately, the government's proposals for electricity market reform are not particularly helpful in this respect. The introduction of a British price floor for carbon, which is ostensibly being pursued to incentivise new low-carbon generation, both nuclear and renewable, will, in practice, produce a huge windfall profit for *existing* nuclear plants, while at the same time creating the UK's very own carbon leakage problem. British energy-intensive industries are now at a competitive disadvantage within Europe and are having to be compensated by a generous package of measures from BIS and the Treasury. Moreover, since the UK is operating within the EU Emissions Trading Scheme (ETS), raising the carbon price artificially in the UK has the effect of making more ETS allowances available, and thus unhelpfully *lowers* the EU ETS carbon price.

The proposed contracts for difference (CfDs) offer a guaranteed 'strike' price for low-carbon electricity. In theory, if the market price exceeds the strike price then the government claws back the difference. In practice, CfDs are more likely to work like the feed-in premium (FiP) used in a number of other EU states, with the government topping up the market price to the level of the strike price.[22] This will create a subsidy not only for new low-carbon technologies such as renewables and CCS but also for nuclear. EU state aid policy does not allow mature technologies to be subsidised and CfDs are currently under review by the European Commission. Furthermore, there is the political difficulty that the coalition agreement promises that there will be 'no public subsidy' for new nuclear power stations.

The EU context

In March 2011, the European Commission published a low-carbon roadmap, with a 80–95 per cent CO_2 reduction objective, mirroring the UK's commitment.[23] This was followed in December 2011 by the *Energy Roadmap 2050*, seeking to illustrate how an 85 per cent CO_2 reduction compared to 1990 levels can be achieved in the EU's energy sector and on EU territory (i.e. without offsetting).[24]

Because energy mix is a member state competence, the Roadmap does not propose any particular combination of energy sources or lay down an ideal percentage mix, but outlines different decarbonisation scenarios with varying proportions of renewables, CCS, nuclear and energy efficiency, alongside 'business as usual'.

Underpinning the scenarios is an assumption that substantial electrification of energy is necessary for decarbonisation. In transport, electric vehicles using a range of technologies, from batteries to hydrogen-powered fuel cells, are assumed to play a significant role by 2050, alongside conventional engines running on sustainable biofuels. Forms of electric heating such as air- and ground-source heat pumps are assumed to be in operation alongside thermal renewable energy sources such as geothermal heat, solar heating panels and biomass-fuelled boilers.

The Roadmap scenarios throw up some interesting conclusions. First, energy efficiency needs to remain the prime focus of any long-term energy policy. But even without taking into account the savings to be made from combining a high-energy-efficiency approach with high renewables (a glaring omission), the Roadmap shows that decarbonising Europe's energy supply is viable and no more costly than business-as-usual non-decarbonisation, because the enormous saving in fuel costs offsets the higher capital investments.

Second, the Roadmap shows that decarbonisation can be achieved while maintaining the same levels of security in the energy system. Indeed decarbonisation is shown to increase energy security in the geopolitical context. because of higher EU energy independence.

Third, the Roadmap concludes that whatever the scenario – even the 'high nuclear' or 'high CCS' scenarios – renewable energy will have a huge role to play, ranging from a 54.6 per cent to a 75.2 share of consumption by 2050. Renewable *electricity* is set to provide between 59.9 per cent and 86.3 per cent of production. The Roadmap therefore recognises that 'the second major prerequisite for a more sustainable and secure energy system is a higher share of renewable energy beyond 2020'.[25] And while gas can play a key transitional role in the energy mix because of its flexibility, its long-term future will be dependent on the availability of CCS technology.

Overall, the very different scenarios that the Roadmap considers lead towards the same conclusion, that energy efficiency, renewable energy – plus much higher levels of interconnection – are the 'no regrets' choices. There is no case at an EU level for maintaining a 'full basket' of energy options.

Only connect

Perhaps the prospect of a UK increasingly dependent on variable renewables creates too much anxiety about keeping the lights on for the 'basket of technologies' to be easily discarded. Certainty about security of supply will, understandably, always be a key energy policy objective. Something needs to be in place to ensure that the lights are still on when the wind is not blowing.

Fortunately, there are a number of ways to deliver such flexibility. Gas-powered turbines can come on stream in seconds when renewable sources need to be topped up – but at a high cost in terms of both CO_2 emissions and investment, since a plant used only for balancing will for the most part lie idle.

Aggregated demand-side management is a second option. This means dealing with peak electricity consumption by an 'offer' of temporary demand reduction totalling many megawatts or even gigawatts. But demand-side management can only help with short-term balancing of renewables. It is not enough to deal with a worst-case scenario in which a long period of still weather leads to sustained under-performance of the UK's wind turbines. Batteries, fuel cells, fly wheels and compressed air systems all offer the possibility for energy storage, but currently all have limitations in terms of capacity, cost and availability.

However, a cost-efficient solution to balancing varying renewables exists, is already under development and has the potential to keep the lights on in even the worst-case scenarios. The UK needs to be connected to its neighbours, and in particular to Norway, in order to be able to utilise Norwegian hydro storage.

Great Britain is still virtually an energy island, with very limited links to the wider European electricity market. The 2 GW interconnector to France was built as long ago as 1986, and the Moyle interconnector to Northern Ireland in 2002, followed in 2011 by the BritNed interconnector to the Netherlands. But the UK still has an interconnection capacity of only 3.5 GW – less than 5 per cent of its installed capacity, despite being signed up to a European target of having interconnection equivalent to at least 10 per cent.[26]

Two interconnectors to Norway are currently at the planning stage and are set to be operational around 2020: a link from Blyth in Northumberland under National Grid and Statnett, and a private-sector 'merchant' cable from Peterhead in Scotland involving several utilities. In May 2012 a memorandum of understanding was signed between the UK and Icelandic governments on a possible 1,500 km interconnector to Iceland, which would be the longest in the world and would give the UK access to electricity generated from Icelandic geothermal sources.

Interconnection to the wider European electricity market brings the immediate advantage of any market: the ability to buy and sell. If UK electricity generation falls below demand the difference can be made up by importing electricity. Conversely, the UK can sell to the continent at times of surplus. But interconnection to Norway opens up access to the electricity storage capabilities of Norwegian hydropower. Norway has 29 GW of installed capacity and a massive 84 TWh of storage capacity, the equivalent of over a thousand hours of peak UK electricity demand.[27]

At times of low electricity demand or high levels of wind production, Norway could cut back its production of hydro electricity and import the UK's excess. Conversely, when there was little wind or demand was high, more water could be released from Norwegian reservoirs, generating extra hydro electricity to export to the UK and make up the shortfall. In practice, the flow of electricity would go in the direction of the higher price of the two markets, to the extent that there was interconnector capacity in place.

But the flexibility offered by Norwegian hydropower goes considerably beyond the simple process of balancing. Storage capacity is increased by building more pumped storage plants between existing hydro reservoirs, so that surplus electricity can be used to pump water uphill from a lower to a higher reservoir.

The cost of a 1.4 GW interconnector between the UK and Norway is £660 million – 880 million.[28] By comparison, as stated above, a 1.4 GW nuclear reactor post-Fukushima costs £7 billion simply to build, without factoring in the cost of decommissioning and dealing with the radioactive waste. The money needed to construct just one nuclear power station could thus build nine interconnectors and give the UK around an extra 12 GW of dispatchable generation capacity while still making use of only a fraction of Norway's potential balancing power.

So the lights will stay on in the UK provided that adequate interconnection is put in place between the UK and other European countries, especially Norway. The precise level of interconnection required will depend on a number of factors such as the percentage of dispatchable generation in the mix, but as an indication, analysis by Imperial College suggests something in the region of 23–37 GW would be beneficial by 2050.[29] A 2011 report from WWF UK suggests that the UK would need 27–35 GW of interconnection to supply 87 per cent of UK electricity from renewables in 2030, depending on the level of energy efficiency improvement and therefore the level of overall electricity demand.[30] For optimal connectivity, the UK government should also back investment in a 'super grid' linking wind farm hubs around the North Sea and the development of transnational networks across the continent – so that southern sun and northern wind are ultimately feeding into the same grid.

Summary

For too long, energy policy in the UK has been blinkered and inward-looking. Successive governments have failed to assess or exploit the potential for controlling energy demand and have treated UK security of supply as an issue to be solved on national soil by means of an expensive basket of options – despite the development of a European energy market. The UK government should:

- Make energy efficiency and energy demand management its first and top priority, on economic grounds.
- Reassess how much electricity capacity will be needed to 2050 taking account of demand-side savings.
- Abandon the 'basket' approach to energy supply.
- Encourage a favourable investment climate for renewables, acknowledging that this primarily means wind. Electricity market reform must not act as a covert subsidy for nuclear.
- Support the introduction of EU 2030 targets for renewables and energy efficiency.

- Integrate the UK fully into the European internal energy market by optimising interconnection to other countries.
- Work closely with Norway to exploit the additional balancing capacity of hydropower, including pumped storage.

As positive partners in Europe, it is the Liberal Democrats who can be relied upon to deliver this open, outward-looking and green approach to UK security of supply.

Notes

1   The author would like to thank Stéphane Bourgeois, Håvard Vaggen Malvik and Jūlija Poliscanova, without whose input and support this chapter could not have been written.

2   EU Climate Change Expert Group 'EG Science', *The 2°C target* (Version 9.1, 9 July 2008).

3   HMG, *Climate Change Act 2008* (November 2008).

4   Department of Energy and Climate Change, *Planning our Electric Future: a White Paper for Secure, Affordable and Low-Carbon Electricity* (July 2011).

5   Department of Energy and Climate Change, *Overarching National Policy Statement for Energy (EN-1)* (July 2011).

6   McKinsey and Co, *Capturing the Full Electricity Efficiency Potential of the UK* (Department of Energy and Climate Change, November 2012).

7   Unlock Democracy and The Association for the Conservation of Energy, *A Corruption of Governance?* (January 2012).

8   Eurostat, *Final Energy Consumption of Electricity* (November 2012); European Research Centre of the Netherlands and European Environment Agency, *Renewable Energy Projections as Published in the National Renewable Energy Action Plans of the European Member States* (November 2011).

9   Ibid.

10 ENTSO-E, *Scenario Outlook and System Adequacy Forecast 2011–2025* (2012).

11 European Commission, *Non-paper of the Services of the European Commission on Energy Efficiency Directive* (April 2012).

12 Ibid.

13 European Environment Agency, *Europe's Onshore and Offshore Wind Energy Potential* (June 2009).

14 International Energy Agency, *Biomass for Power Generation and CHP* (January 2007).

15 Fraunhofer Institute for Solar Energy Systems ISE, *Electricity Production from Solar and Wind in Germany in 2012* (May 2012).

16 International Energy Agency, *Technology Roadmap: Solar Photovoltaic Energy* (May 2010).

17 'Nuclear clean-up cost up to £56bn', BBC News, 11 August 2005.

18 Nuclear Decommissioning Authority, *Annual Report and Accounts 2007/8* (July 2008).

19 La Cour des Comptes, *The Costs of the Nuclear Power Sector* (January 2012).

20 Greenpeace, *The EPR Nuclear Reactor: A Dangerous Waste of Time and Money* (January 2012).

21 'UK nuclear build requires taxpayer rescue – Citi', Reuters, 8 May 2012.

22 Currently, in the Czech Republic, Finland, Germany, Netherlands, Slovenia, Spain. Presentation by Dr Mario Ragwitz, 'Quota systems: The right tool to promote renewables?' (Fraunhofer Institute, 12 December 2012).

23 European Commission, *A Roadmap for Moving to a Competitive Low-Carbon Economy in 2050* (8 March 2011).

24 European Commission, *Energy Roadmap 2050* (15 December 2011).

25 Ibid., p. 10

26 Department of Energy and Climate Change and Office of the Gas and Electricity Markets (Ofgem), *Statutory Security of Supply Report* (DECC, November 2012).

27 Leonardo Energy, *Supporting Wind Development with Hydro Balancing Services* (June 2012).

28 Letter from Statnett to the Norwegian Water Resources and Energy Directorate (29 September 2012); http://www.statnett.no/Documents/Nyheter_og_media/ Nyhetsarkiv/2012/Investeringsplan per cent20for per cent20sentralnettet per cent202012.pdf

29 Department of Energy and Climate Change, *Electricity System: Assessment of Future Challenges - Summary* (August 2012).

30 WWF, *Positive Energy: How Renewable Electricity can Transform the UK by 2030* (October 2011).

Chapter 20

A Liberal and Democratic Energy Market

Dr Mark Hinnells

O ver the last two decades, the UK has been developing a policy frame-work to reduce greenhouse gas emissions, culminating in the Climate Change Act 2008, which aims at a cut of at least 80 per cent by 2050, and puts in place a budgeting process to achieve the target. It is already widely accepted that to deliver on the target, the current energy policy landscape is not fit for purpose. However, the current business landscape in which energy is delivered and used also requires a radical overhaul, given that the market is operated by a cartel, and also that consumers do not know how much energy costs, where it comes from or how much they use. Instead, a new set of business relationships and models is needed, based on liberal and democratic principles, to deliver low-carbon energy use in homes, commer-cial buildings, and industry, which together account for around two-thirds of UK carbon emissions. In terms of energy markets, this equates to almost all electricity use, most gas use, and some oil and other fuels.

An energy market based on liberal and democratic principles

The energy-producing infrastructure in the UK has been highly centralised since nationalisation in 1949. Even privatisation created an oligopoly bor-dering on a cartel. Other countries have followed different historical paths. In Denmark and Germany there has always been much more municipal involvement in production of heat and power, and in the US, energy markets are organised along state lines, producing a much more regional market.

In the UK, the electricity and gas markets were privatised in the late 1980s, and generation, distribution and supply of electricity and gas are now regu-lated by OFGEM. Energy supply is dominated by six major players (the 'big six'), serving 26 million homes and around 2 million non-domestic consum-ers. To date, very few UK homes and businesses generate their own energy. In Germany, on the other hand, 51 per cent of renewables are owned (or part owned) by individuals or communities (amounting to 53 GW of power, almost equivalent to UK peak demand), representing £100 billion of investment.[1] The

German model puts power (literally) in the hands of citizens, and is much more open to innovation, compared to the UK, where a limited number of increasingly multinational corporations dominate. The UK structure is thus not easily amenable to socially driven change to drive lower carbon.

A liberalised market would be more competitive and democratic: consumers would be participative, involved and understand the market, and providers would be more answerable for their decisions. The indicators of a functioning liberal and democratic market might include:

- Significant new entrants, with the power of the incumbents reduced.
- Innovative business models.
- A very different political dialogue in Westminster and Whitehall, and wider participation in political decisions.
- Diverse investment, including self-investment (by both households and businesses), community ownership, and municipal involvement, with less dependence on non-UK capital, ownership, fuel supply and technology.

Opportunities for innovation

There is a wide gamut of technological solutions available, from energy efficiency to renewable energy generation and Combined Heat and Power (CHP). Energy efficiency encompasses reducing heat loss in a building through fabric measures to walls, floors, windows and roofs, and also includes generating heat more efficiently in a boiler or from heat pumps, or controlling heat use more efficiently. Renewable energy includes generating heat or power from resources which will not run out in the timescale of human existence, such as wind, sun, waves and tides, or which are regenerated in a short period, such as biomass from wood products, energy crops and biological or agricultural wastes. CHP is the simultaneous generation of electricity and heat in a single process, with the heat then supplied to industrial processes or space heating, in doing so achieving efficiencies of 70 per cent or more. This offers significant energy cost and carbon savings over conventional power generation.

There is also a revolution in metering under way, with electro-mechanical meters read manually being replaced by internet-connected digital meters. These 'smart meters' can help consumers understand their electricity usage and feedback can reduce demand by 5–15 per cent[2]); but beyond this, technology offers the opportunity of real progress towards balancing demand and supply by directly controlling such uses as water heating and refrigeration, where a delay of an hour or two may be acceptable.

Researchers have explored the technical, economic and social potential of these innovations, together with a variety of scenarios for the uptake of low-carbon solutions.[3] If anything even similar to these scenarios came to fruition, the nature of the relationship between customer and supplier would fundamentally change. Instead of the utility company selling as much power as possible, and having no real interest in saving energy, much of the investment to deliver low-carbon might happen on the customers' side of the meter; this would involve users needing a much greater understanding of their own energy consumption, of their opportunities to reduce consumption, and of opportunities to generate their own power. In any such scenario there are new roles for the installers, financiers and operators of such equipment.

What gets in the way of innovation?

So what are the barriers preventing consumers, commercial or domestic, investing in their own energy generation and efficiency? For the necessary change to take place, policy needs to understand and change to address these barriers. As long ago as 1996, Golove, and Eto identified a range of barriers to energy efficiency, including transaction costs (understanding and concluding a 'deal'); asymmetric information between customers and energy providers (energy users often have no idea of their energy usage, the price of energy, or the available alternatives); lack of capital; lack of management time; lack of knowledge; and, perhaps because of this, a risk-averse attitude to investment.[4] In addition, energy is often seen as a low priority because it is a small proportion of the annual expenditure of a household or business. Barriers are compounded when the occupier of a property is not the property owner but a tenant (whether residential or commercial); there is at present no incentive for the landlord to improve the property as it is the tenant who benefits, and no incentive for the tenant to invest as they would never see a return on that investment.

Emerging business models

Table 20.1 shows a typology of emerging business models which is explored further elsewhere.[5] Service models include the introduction of on-site (embedded) energy generation or a portfolio of energy efficiency solutions. Where investments are large in scale, there is sufficient return for the provider to be able to both finance debt and set up costs off the balance sheet of the customer and recover the investment through service charges or payment for units of energy provided. Where they are smaller – homes or small businesses – the customer would usually provide or borrow the finance themselves and then benefit directly from the ongoing cost savings. Some business models are market makers, often based on information or resale of power, and this is explored further below. There are also new investors, both individuals and communities, with different aims and objectives.

Several key models for the delivery of the Climate Change Act target are briefly explored below. These models struggle to emerge and flourish in the context of a cartel energy market; policy therefore needs to break open the market.

Embedded generation

Embedded generation opportunities include CHP, wind, solar photovoltaic (PV) and energy from waste.

The growth of CHP is well documented in government statistics[6] and elsewhere.[7] In the UK approximately £6 billion has been invested in 1,600 schemes, of which around 1,100 are in buildings and 500 meet process heat needs in industry in sectors such as chemicals, pharmaceuticals, paper, food and drink. Buildings tend to be those with a large heat demand (such as hospitals or universities) or groups of buildings connected by a heat network. In the UK, CHP has seen an average 5 per cent growth p.a. over the last fifteen years but with significant annual variations. Less than a third of the potential for CHP is thought to have been accessed.

There is a growing portfolio of wind turbines on industrial and commercial sites (such as food, distribution, car industry, chemicals, dockyards or ports as well as some in the public sector); together, around 270 MW of wind power capacity across around seventy industrial and commercial sites, an investment of over £300 million.[8] There is potential for up to an order of magnitude more.

In the UK there has been much interest in large-scale PV in solar parks (ground-mounted), and on the roofs of factories and other large commercial buildings, as well as on car parks following US and European models. While this market has been heavily constrained following the reviews of both feed-in tariff and renewable obligation certificates, a mature and stable support regime, together with a rapid fall in the cost of PV, will see much more development.

Energy Services Companies (ESCos)

An Energy Service Company (ESCo) is a commercial business providing a range of energy solutions including an in-depth analysis of the site, the design of energy efficiency, heating and sometimes power generation solutions, installation of the required elements, and maintenance of the system to ensure energy savings. Often the ESCo also provides 'off balance sheet' finance with the savings in energy costs used to pay back the capital investment of the project over a five- to twenty-year period. If the project does

Table 20.1 A typology of new business models

	Type	Example	Business model	Main drivers
Service models	Embedded generation	Ecotricity, Wind Direct, Susenco	Financing a single asset (renewables or CHP) off balance sheet	Energy prices, Climate Change Levy, FITs
	Energy Services Companies (ESCo)	MITIE	Financing a portfolio of energy efficiency measures, renewables and CHP off balance sheet	Energy prices, Climate Change Levy, FITs, RHI, Green Deal for business and local authorities
	Renewable installers	EnergyMyWay, JoJu, Econergy	Installing small-scale renewables into homes or small businesses, e.g. farms, often starting with one technology and broadening to include more	RHI, FITs
	Home refurbishment	Carillion Energy Services, Mark Group, Parity Projects	Financing a portfolio of energy efficiency measures	Green Deal for homes
Market making	Green energy supply	Good Energy, Ecotricity	Buying power from renewable sources only for sale to households and businesses	ROCs
	Metering	Still emergent	Smart meters provide an entry point for mobile phone providers or sellers, together with internet ISPs, to break into the energy market.	Government and OFGEM have worked with energy suppliers to roll out smart metering by 2019
	Networking	2degrees	A managed networking service for businesses to fast track low-carbon solutions	A wide variety of policy
Investment	Finance	Octopus VCT	Investment opportunities for low-carbon, fast change, appropriate balance of risk and reward.	FITs, EIS
	Community	West Oxford Community Renewables	To engage and motivate a local community to invest in community-scale projects or refurbishing their own home	FITs, EIS

not provide returns on the investment, the provider is often contractually required to pay the difference between promised and actual savings.

An ESCo addresses the barriers to investment by providing investment, managing risk, and reducing transaction costs. It allows someone else with the time, money, knowledge and risk appetite to deliver a solution that the host would not have been able to deliver alone. Bringing in a third party may be a particular advantage where there is a landlord-and-tenant arrangement, and where the changes may survive more than one tenant.

This model has been seen across both Western and Eastern Europe as well as the US since the 1970s.[9] It is a model which has hitherto struggled in the UK, but is now beginning to establish itself in the public estate. In 2010–11 the UK government achieved an average 13 per cent cut in emissions in its own buildings in one year; while much of this derived from simple measures, it is now aiming for a 25 per cent saving in all civil and operational estates by 2015, which is likely to require finance off balance sheet.[10] Similarly, the London Mayor is targeting 600 public buildings in London. These policies are helping to create a new energy services industry in the UK. These are new entrants to the energy services market, but they have an established base in a related market, stemming from a construction background (such as Balfour Beatty), an energy background (such as EDF), a building services background (such as HurleyPalmerFlatt) or an outsourcing and facilities management background (such as MITIE). Although there are many European or US ESCOs, they are not yet entering the UK in a meaningful way, since the market is considered too small at present.

Community financing

A final and very interesting new model is community financing. Strachan and Lal note that local involvement in the ownership of turbines can play an important role in reducing opposition, and both the Danish and German governments have made local ownership an important dimension of implementation strategy.[11] UK examples range from co-operatives issuing shares in large solar farms (such as the 5 MW 30-acre solar farm costing £14m set up by Westmill Solar Co-operative Limited in 2012), or Industrial and Provident Societies investing in 50 kW of PV on commercial roofs, to community buying groups purchasing residential rooftop PV installations. UK-based community investment in renewables also includes wind and hydro schemes, as well as groups of farmers coming together to invest in anaerobic digestion, using a mix of crops and animal slurries. Community financing of renewables is the subject of ongoing research by the author.

Policy implications

Embedded generation, energy services and community financing are three models that allow consumers of all types to participate in the energy market. The process of engaging is also educative, and those who produce their own power understand energy use and thus energy efficiency.[12] These models struggle to emerge and flourish in the context of a cartel energy market, however, and policy needs to break open the market.

Government can act as market maker and can be key to opening the doors to innovation and to the development of new business models. There are a range of opportunities.

First, with regard to buildings:

- Through websites such as zoopla, we know the prices houses sell for. The information about energy performance (available at www.epcregister. com) could be used to create a market in energy efficiency. Energy performance certificate (EPC) records should be live, and could be simply updated by accredited installers when a new boiler or new windows are installed.

- The government should aim to move the property market from one where property agents apologise for having to charge for an EPC then forget about it to one where the market is incentivised to develop a relationship between energy performance and value, for example, through education programmes for agents and buyers, encouraged by a lower rate of stamp duty for homes with better energy ratings.

- The government has announced changes to the Energy Bill to include a new law introducing a legal minimum energy efficiency standard for homes rented from a landlord from 2018, so why not extend this to home-owners and the commercial sector?[13] Retrospective standards would need to be appropriate to different types and ages of buildings, and raised over time. They could be based around the energy label, so homes that are F and G rated could not be offered for sale or rent from a certain date. The standard could be increased incrementally. Government also has a key role in providing guidance and case studies. This process could provide entry points for energy services or off-balance-sheet finance.

- Passivhaus standards (where heat gains from lights and appliances, metabolism, and solar reduce the need for a heating system, nearly to zero) need to be much more widely understood and become the norm for new build, as well as retrofits. Equipment buyers need to be helped to pay as much attention to the lifetime costs of ownership as to the initial capital cost.

The second group of policy issues are around finance:

- Off-balance-sheet finance solutions are key to the government delivering on its targets. Government must create exemplars in its own estate and, more importantly, in how it sets market rules; off-balance-sheet financing needs to become the norm. This allows someone else with the time, money, knowledge and risk appetite to deliver a solution that the host would not have been able to deliver alone.
- The government's Green Investment Bank is at an early stage and could take on a clear role in supporting the expansion of providers in the market delivering innovative solutions, including third-party or community-based solutions, in line with the models explored in this chapter.
- UK feed-in tariffs were designed to deliver a return on investment of 5–8 per cent p.a. This is too low in the commercial sector, where companies will look for higher returns from internal capital, and where many companies will be in leased premises with a likelihood that the remaining lease period will be shorter than the payback period of the investment. To deliver large-scale uptake will require higher feed-in tariffs, but delivered over a shorter period. This would result in the same cost to government, but would be more attractive to commercial organisations.

The third group of policy issues is around innovation. Government has failed to manage its knowledge of the energy market, and has become reliant on big business to help design policy. In consequence government does not understand new solutions, technologies and business models, or what is needed for their introduction. Progress has also been inhibited by inconsistency and lack of clarity in policy over many years: we have gone from Clear Skies to the Low-Carbon Building Programme to the Feed-In Tariff and the Renewable Heat Incentive. And, even now, the Renewable Heat Incentive for the domestic sector has been on and off and is again delayed, possibly indefinitely.

One form of support for business model or service innovation is to create markets (such as through the Green Deal) or provide tax incentives. However, investors in projects whose main income was feed-in tariffs have recently been excluded from tax relief under the Enterprise Investment scheme (EIS), unless they are community groups, meaning that government has given with one hand and taken with the other. Those trying to build a business go from feast to famine, which makes the changes needed more expensive and painful than they would otherwise be, with people laid off and re-employed and laid off again. In addition to consistency, there needs to be specific support for innovation in both technology and service models. There is already support made available for *technical* innovation through the Energy Technology Institute and Technology Strategy Board, and to an extent through the Carbon Trust. However, there is little support available through these routes to explore and develop *business models or service* innovation, and there needs to be.

Government needs to better understand the relative roles of incumbents and newcomers in delivering innovation. While some innovations (especially technical) can originate in start-up businesses, some originate in businesses with significant resource in one area and then move into a new area (such as ESCos). Large organisations are often not good at innovation (particularly service innovation) because they risk stranding existing investments, assets and business models. Large business is often a latecomer and acquires innovation by buying into an existing technology or business, as has happened to firms such as Econergy (biomass boiler installers) and Ceres Power (developers of fuel cells). Government needs to appreciate that it is easier for large companies to manipulate the policy process through the lobbying process, which puts innovation at risk.

The fourth group of policy issues are for the wider energy market. Ultimately to achieve the targets set, a complete new market framework is needed which moves power from the hands of a few large utility companies and creates a market of literally millions of embedded generators deploying a range of technologies. This means measures which make small generation more competitive with large centralised supply. It also means a market framework which makes demand reduction more competitive with energy supply. An ambitious target could be to see half of UK homes and businesses generating their own renewables in some form.

Steps towards this in the UK include encouraging significant new entry beyond the 'Big Six'. In 1998 the then director of the energy regulator, Stephen Littlechild, forced National Power and PowerGen to cut their market share to about 40 percent from 80 percent through a series of forced disposals and new entries to the market. Has the time come to do this again, both in generation and supply?

The offshore renewables industry needs to be opened up to new entry beyond the 'Big Six', for example, through looking again at the role of the Crown Estate in consenting offshore renewables. Exploitation of offshore is currently restricted to organisations or consortiums with very large balance sheets, much more so than onshore development.

There is also a role for planning policy. Over the last twenty years, various states in the US have operated integrated resource planning frameworks which require all options to be explored (including investments in energy efficiency) before new power stations can be built.[14] In an era when new power stations are controversial and expensive, it makes sense to prioritise cheaper and less controversial energy efficiency investment through the regulatory regime. In addition to this, even if new plant is built, some technologies are better than others.

In the UK in 1997 the government, for a period, operated a 'stricter consents' regime, whereby new power stations could not be built unless they were either CHP or based on renewable energy. This incentivises power generators to find ways of capturing and supplying the heat, driving them to work with large industrial heat users to deliver off-balance-sheet solutions for those heat users. And some locations are more sensitive than others. Planning policy on wind power and energy from waste could clearly indicate a presumption in favour of schemes on industrial sites (where the landscape is already man-made and where background noise would mask turbine noise).

Ultimately, too much of UK government policy is implemented though obligations on existing market players (e.g. the Renewables Obligation and the Energy Company Obligation which finances Green Deal). This reinforces the dominance of the existing players and makes new market entry very difficult. It is very easy to be lobbied by large organisations with strong policy and lobby teams: their reach is such that from at least 1997 (when Enron drove a coach and horses through the Labour government's stricter consents policy) to recent decisions on nuclear power, government policy is what the 'Big Six' want it to be. Government needs to make greater efforts to listen to organisations such as start-ups or small businesses that do not have the resources to lobby. Policy-making needs continually to create opportunities for new market entry.

Conclusions

If the UK carbon target is to be met, and in a timely way, it is key for government to realise that the business landscape needs to change to be more inclusive of new technologies and business models. Government has a key role in enabling this change, since the rules of the market are under government control. Three key models – embedded generation, Energy Service Companies and community investment – in particular, need positive encouragement.

Government can be a market maker, not only by way of creating exemplars in the government estate, but in how it sets a range of market rules. In particular, mechanisms to drive new entrants are needed, and energy demand and energy supply need to be treated as equally important parts of the energy market and energy policy. Ownership of energy generation also needs diversifying, with potentially more than half of households and businesses generating their own renewable electricity or heat in the next decade or so, with all users becoming much more aware of how they use energy. These and other key changes would imply a very different balance of market power and thus political discourse from today. Such a market would be a much more liberal and democratic market rather one which continues to operate as a cartel.

Notes

1 Paul Gipe, '51 per cent of German renewables now owned by its own citizens', Wind-Works.org, 5 January 2012; http://www.wind-works.org/coopwind/ CitizenPowerConferencetobeheldinHistoricChamber.html

2 Sarah Darby, *The Effectiveness of Feedback on Energy Consumption: A review for Defra of the literature on metering, billing and direct displays* (Environmental Change Institute, University of Oxford, 2006).

3 Mark Hinnells, 'Technologies to achieve demand reduction and microgeneration in buildings', *Energy Policy* 36, 2008; Brenda Boardman, *Home Truths: A low-carbon strategy to reduce UK housing emissions by 80 per cent by 2050* (Environmental Change Institute, University of Oxford, 2007); Brenda Boardman, *Achieving Zero: Delivering future-friendly buildings* (Environmental Change Institute, University of Oxford, 2012); David Mackay *Sustainable Energy – without the hot air* (UIT, 2009); Centre for Alternative Technology, *Zero Carbon Britain: A new energy strategy report* (2012).

4 W. Golove and J. Eto, *Market Barriers to Energy Efficiency: A Critical Reappraisal of the Rationale for Public Policies to Promote Energy Efficiency* (Lawrence Berkeley National Laboratory, 1996).

5 Mark Hinnells and Isobel O'Neil, 'Reflections on new business models for a low-carbon future: case studies from the energy sector', in Sarah Underwood, Richard Blundel, Fergus Lyon and Anja Schaefer (eds.), *Contemporary Issues in Entrepreneurship Research Volume II: Social and Sustainable Enterprise: Changing the Nature of Business* (Emerald, 2012).

6 DECC, *Digest of UK Energy Statistics*, Chapter 6: 'Combined heat and power' (2011).

7 Mark Hinnells, 'Combined heat and power in industry and buildings', *Energy Policy* 36, 2008.

8 Mark Hinnells, *Wind Energy in the Industrial Landscape in the UK: Does Evidence to Date Suggest Significant Further Potential?* MSc thesis, University of East London (2013).

9   P. Bertoldi, B. Boza-Kiss and S. Rezessy, *Latest Development of Energy Service Companies across Europe – A European ESCO Update* (Institute for Environment and Sustainability, Joint Research Centre of the European Union, 2007); A. Satchwel, C. Goldman, P. Larsen, D. Gilligan and T. Singer, *A Survey of the US ESCO Industry: Market Growth and Development from 2008 to 2011* (Lawrence Berkeley National Laboratory, 2010).

10   Camco, *Wider Public Sector Emissions Reduction Potential: Research Report by Camco to Department of Energy and Climate Change* (2011).

11   P. Strachan and D. Lal, 'Wind Energy Policy, Planning and Management Practice in the UK: Hot Air or a Gathering Storm?', *Regional Studies* 38.5, July 2004.

12   James Keirstead, 'Behavioural responses to photovoltaic systems in the UK domestic sector', *Energy Policy* 35.8, August 2007.

13   See Boardman, *Achieving zero: delivering future-friendly buildings.*

14   Synapse Energy (2011) *A Brief Survey of State Integrated Resource Planning Rules and Requirements* (prepared for the American Clean Skies Foundation, April 2011).

Chapter 21

A Green Deal for Transport

Stephen Potter

Transport policy objectives

Transport is a policy area that seems to have somewhat lost its way. The last Labour administration's attempt at an integrated and sustainable transport policy[1] never took root and eventually degenerated into the fractured, virtually strategy-free 'policy' of today. Yet transport remains a major and important area that needs to be at the heart of government. It is this very centrality of transport to a range of policy areas that results in tensions and conflicts that have led to our inconsistent and fragmented approach. Although the environmental impacts of transport (CO_2, air quality emissions and land take) have attracted considerable attention, transport is key to the powerful political drivers of economic development (witness the Heathrow third runway/'Boris Island' debate) and energy security. Policy responses to transport's environmental impacts have thus tended to be add-ons to fundamentally unsustainable systems rather than means of seeking a systemic solution, and so have failed to construct a coherent transport policy structure that simultaneously achieves social and economic sustainability as well as environmental sustainability. A theme of this chapter is that a more systemic approach will not only deliver a greener transport system, but one that better addresses the economic and social functions of transport as well.

Along with other countries, the UK Transport sector has failed to cut CO_2 emissions; indeed it was only the recession that meant that emissions in 2009 were the same as 1990 (previously they had risen above 1990 levels). With other sectors reducing their CO_2 emissions, the proportion coming from transport has grown from 15.6 per cent in 1990 to 21.7 per cent in 2009 (Table 21.1). Passenger cars remain the biggest source of CO_2, but road freight emissions are significant and those for light vans have risen substantially. Rail produces only 1.7 per cent of transport's CO_2 emissions, despite substantial rises in passenger-kilometres and freight carried.

Table 21.1: UK CO2 emissions by source (Mt CO2) 1990 and 2009[2]

		1990	2009
Aviation	Civil aviation (domestic only)	1.4	2.0
Road	Passenger cars	73.1	70.9
	Light duty vehicles	9.4	15.3
	Buses	3.8	5.3
	HGVs	24.0	21.0
	Mopeds and motorcycles	0.6	0.6
	LPG emissions (all vehicles)	0.0	0.3
	Other (road vehicle engines)	0.3	0.1
Railways	Railways	2.1	2.1
Shipping	National navigation	1.8	1.5
Other mobile	Military aircraft and shipping	5.3	2.5
Other transport	Aircraft - support vehicles	0.3	0.5
Transport total		**122.1**	**122.2**
Transport as percentage of total		*15.6%*	*21.7%*
Total UK emissions		*781.6*	*563.6*

Within this recent trend of little change in CO_2 emissions, it is notable that emissions from cars have dropped slightly, but there has been a strong rise in emissions from light duty vehicles (which coincides with the rise in internet shopping deliveries). Table 21.1 covers domestic emissions but excludes some sources, notably international aviation. Between 1990 and 2009, CO_2 emissions from UK-based aviation (both domestic and UK-based international flights) more than doubled to 33 million tonnes CO_2-equivalent.[3] At current growth rates, aviation will make up about a third of the total UK climate change impact by 2050. So air travel is a key environmental issue for the twenty-first century.

Energy security and energy shortage were issues that attracted much attention in the 1970s, but came to be overshadowed as attention shifted to the environmental impacts of transport. However, this issue has returned to the geopolitical agenda. In early 2007, the price of a barrel of Brent Crude was around US$70; by mid-2008 the price had shot up to US$140, but then dipped to around US$50 as the recession hit. Since then, the price has steadily risen again to stand, by late 2012, at around US$120 a barrel. Short-term economic factors produce price volatility, but the long-term trend is steadily upwards.

However, responses to energy security and shortage can be less than compatible with environmental requirements. The easiest and most secure way may not be to develop clean energy. This is typified by the burgeoning interest in and development of oil and gas shale reserves that can economically outcompete renewable energy. It is difficult to see how environmental concerns will moderate such a powerful economic and political combination.

For sustainable transport, the strategic challenge is to simultaneously achieve a low-carbon transport future that links to adequate and secure supplies of energy. Although it is crucial to cut transport's CO_2 emissions, any approach that does not also deliver economic, political and social sustainability will be entirely sidelined.

Low carbon and high mobility

The issues discussed above have led to the emergence of a particular meaning of 'sustainable transport'. This is not defined purely in terms of environmental sustainability, but has become part of the conceptual and ideological mantra of 'sustainable development'. Sustainable development is the ideology that carbon reduction is an opportunity to be realised through 'greening' economic growth. For transport, this philosophy is epitomised by the 2011 UK White Paper, *Creating Growth, Cutting Carbon*.[4] This set out a vision (p. 7): 'for a transport system that is an engine for economic growth, but one that is also greener and safer and improves quality of life in our communities'.

Thus highly motorised but low-carbon mobility is seen as the way forward. This could involve the widespread use of very low-carbon vehicles coupled with a continued rise in mobility amidst the population and settlement dispersal – i.e. roughly business as usual but with clean technology vehicles. You still build lots of new roads and suburbanisation continues, but congestion remains intense and a substantial economic and social cost, and so it will need to be managed by advanced information technologies.

But this is not the only way in which sustainable transport could be achieved. There could be an alternative sustainable transport future of active travel demand management, with cities and towns reconfigured around high-capacity electrified public transport systems, where walking and cycling dominates and car use is restricted to a minority of trips (Fig 21.1). This is an alternative green growth sustainable development vision, but a very different one, as epitomised by Newman and Kenworthy's seminal *Overcoming Automobile Dependence* study[5]). Either end of this spectrum (and anything in between) could be claimed to represent 'sustainable transport'. This poses a key question: could 'sustainable transport' manifest itself

Figure 21.1: A walk- and public transport-oriented city design

in a series of different ways, or can only a particular combination of measures deliver a low-carbon future?

Whether there is only a single way to achieve sustainable transport is a crucial question because we appear to be entering a new stage in the transport energy debate. Despite rearguard actions from those who benefit from fostering climate change denial, it is clear that we cannot continue transport's hydrocarbon-intensive regime for much longer. Quite aside from climate change, energy economics, supply and security issues will require an alternative approach. We now need to explore questions around what sort of transport regime represents a viable future and how the transition to this future may be achieved. Under the 2008 Climate Change Act, Britain has set legally binding 'carbon budgets', to cut UK emissions by 34 per cent by 2020 and at least 80 per cent by 2050. These CO_2 cuts can be taken as a reasonable working definition of the level of environmental improvement needed to achieve a 'sustainable transport' system.

Approaches to sustainable transport

A list of greener transport initiatives is not difficult to compile, but how far they take us towards a low-carbon and more energy-secure future is debatable. Compared to conventional petrol and diesel-engined cars, hybrid cars can cut carbon emissions by around 20 per cent. Low-carbon fuels offer greater improvements; bioethanol can cut CO_2 emissions by 25 per cent, bio-diesel by 45 per cent and hydrogen by 40 per cent or more. These fuels can also address fuel security concerns, although whether they can be produced in sufficient volume is open to question, and any carbon improvements depend heavily on the production methods used.[6]

The promotion of electric road vehicles (Fig 21.2) has achieved prominence in the last few years, including a longer-term transition path outlined in DECC's 2009 Low-Carbon Transition Plan and BIS's 2009 New Automotive Innovation & Growth Team report on the future of the automotive industry.[7] This anticipates cleaner internal combustion technologies being joined by an initial widespread uptake of battery electric vehicles (including 'plug-in' hybrids) followed later by hydrogen fuel cell vehicles. The 2011 European Transport White Paper envisaged that by 2050 internal combustion engine cars will simply not be permitted in cities. But how viable is such a technical transition to a high-mobility low-carbon transport future? In practice, the uptake of battery and other low-carbon vehicles has been painfully slow.

It should be noted that the emphasis in all these reports and strategies is on switching to low-carbon fuels. An alternative technical approach is to use fuel more efficiently. Over a decade ago, Wemyss considered that advances in vehicle technologies should allow cars to achieve a fuel consumption of 1.9 litres/100km (150 mpg) within ten years.[8] Yet there are still no cars on the market that achieve anywhere near this technically possible performance. Although car manufacturers had developed a number of energy efficiency technologies, these largely remained unapplied until, in 2009, the European

Figure 21.2: A battery electric Leaf at an on-street charging point at Milton Keynes.

Commission announced its CO_2 emissions regulation.[9] This sets a sales-weighted CO_2 target for new passenger cars, with an average target of 130g/km by 2015 (a 9.8 per cent reduction on the 2010 level), proceeding to an average of 95g/km in 2020. This resulted in the sudden appearance of a range of 'eco' petrol and diesel cars incorporating a variety of fuel-efficient technologies.

All these strategies represent a low-carbon technical fix for a highly motorised mobility scenario. This can be contrasted with a separate range of measures that involve a demand management approach, advocating modal shift from cars to more energy-efficient forms of transport, including light rail and innovative public transport systems, public shared bicycle schemes, car pooling, car clubs and teleworking/shopping. This is often coupled with proposals for planning controls to produce settlement patterns and conditions that will cut trip length, favour sustainable modes and disadvantage car use. Such an approach involves very different processes and understandings to those needed and used for a technical-fix based approach.

In a comprehensive review of this and other demand management approaches, Banister cites case studies of cities that have achieved a 10 per cent drop in car use through approaches utilising planning controls and public transport development.[10] Using such techniques, Transport for London

Fig. 21.3: A variety of transport demand measures: Bristol's high-occupancy lane, London's congestion charging zone and a city bike hire station and bike lanes.

achieved a 15 per cent cut in central London traffic during the 2012 Olympics. The key thing about such an approach is that it seeks to 'lock in' the impact through travel patterns and behaviour.

A further demand management approach is that of pricing mechanisms. Economists such as Pearce, Maddison and Glaister have long argued that the environmental costs of road and air transport are under-priced, and that marginal cost pricing should be adopted.[11] The arguments and evidence for a tax-neutral programme of green fiscal reform was presented by the 2009 report of the UK Green Fiscal Commission, including a detailed briefing paper on transport taxation.[12] A shift from taxation on vehicles and fuel to one based on road use has long been advocated as necessary for a sustainable transport future. In the UK the first steps were the London and Durham congestion charging areas, but there has been no political will to build upon these successful pioneering schemes. Plans that tentatively emerged for lorry and generalised road user charging to replace existing fuel and excise duties lost momentum and were dropped. Marginal eco-taxation reform has replaced a systemic approach that alone would deliver the changes needed.

Overall, the sustainable transport debate has come to revolve around the relative roles of supply-side technical measures to promote cleaner fuels and fuel economy as opposed to modal shift and other demand management measures. What combination of factors is used involves a very different set of social and economic adjustments. This issue has been explored by a number of researchers who broadly conclude that you cannot achieve sustainable transport by using any one of these approaches in isolation.[13] For example, using technical measures in isolation means that to achieve a relatively modest 40 per cent cut in CO_2 emissions from cars (while not addressing behavioural demand-generating factors) would require doubling fuel economy and the widespread uptake of low-carbon fuels. This would require very substantial fiscal or regulatory actions that politically would be very difficult to deliver.

Equally, the studies above show that, alone, even a substantial modal shift to public transport cannot attain a sufficient CO_2 reduction. The energy efficiency improvements of public transport over cars do cut carbon emissions, but not enough to achieve sustainability if trends to higher motorised mobility continue. Indeed some public transport developments, like high-speed commuter railways, can lead to highly car-dependent sprawl and stimulate highly car-dependent lifestyles.

The need for a combined strategy is clear. If everything depends on one group of measures, then economic, socially and ecologically sustainable transport become unattainable, even if improvements are pushed to technically and politically unrealistic extremes. At the very least, low-carbon fuels must be introduced in conjunction with substantial improvements to fuel economy. Merely substituting petrol gas guzzlers by hydrogen guzzlers is no sustainable solution. The most viable combination is the integration of technical improvements with demand management that not merely seeks modal shift but also reduces trip lengths and promotes trip substitution. This would counteract rises in transport costs and so help increase political, economic and social acceptance.

Despite the case for a combined approach, there is a real danger that it may be politically easier to develop some technical measures (e.g. fuel switching) more readily than demand management. Any success of technical measures could result in the neglect or abandoning of demand management policies, particularly as the latter are perceived as politically difficult. In reality the magnitude of the challenge is that while 'quick wins' are being implemented, the foundations of longer term and more tricky measures need to be put into place. Transport policies at the local, national and international level need to blend technical improvements to vehicles with modal shift and other aspects of travel behaviour, such as trip length, frequency and vehicle occupancy. Transport's energy challenge is of such a magnitude that, unless substantial progress is made on all these fronts, we will inevitably fail to achieve environmental, economic and social sustainability.

Innovative low carbon transport systems

A transition to a transport system that is inherently energy-efficient and adaptable to future challenges could involve a variety of configurations that combine vehicle technical improvements with demand management. Indeed, a sustainable transport energy future may be far more open than we think. New transport technologies and service systems are emerging, and developments in IT have already had a major impact on travel behaviour (e.g. the growth in web-based shopping and home-based teleworking). These developments are likely to affect different places in different ways. For major cities there may be an emphasis on high-capacity, low-carbon public transport systems, roadspace reallocation to buses, cyclists and pedestrians and demand management through road and parking pricing. Behavioural measures to reduce and manage travel needs might include electronic substitution for commuting and business travel, distance access to services and education, workplace and leisure travel planning and a variety of new product-service systems such as car clubs and city electric car hire schemes such as the Paris Autolib and the UK's eCar Club.[14]

Some of these measures can work well in suburbs and smaller towns, but there is a danger of simply building in such places a lower-specification version of big city systems. Trams, metros and other high-capacity public transport systems are inappropriate and unaffordable, but there are newer transport systems emerging that could work very well in such contexts. For example advanced guided bus systems can provide the coverage and flexibility needed for cross-suburban travel or, as being applied in Cambridge, to provide a city link corridor serving a mix of established and new settlements.

There are also important emerging designs and technologies that have the potential to provide entirely new sorts of transport service. Demand-responsive transport (DRT), such as shared taxis or using small vehicles to take people door to door, is increasingly viable using modern 'smart' IT systems. These are well suited to the dispersed pattern of transport demand found in suburbs, towns and rural areas. There are examples of successful systems in a number of countries and in some places in the UK. Several Canadian, Dutch, French and German suburban-style towns have entirely replaced their conventional bus routes by semi-scheduled DRT systems.[15] Advances in IT now make it possible for a hybrid taxicab/minibus DRT service to provide a considerably better service than conventional bus or even light rail services, but the main barriers are regulatory and financial, in that existing institutional structures do not recognise such a fusion of service systems. Addressing this should be a priority for transport policy.

Personalised rapid transit (PRT) perhaps represents a vision of a long-term low-carbon public transport system that has all the characteristics

Fig. 21.4 Heathrow PRT pods at a station.

needed to provide a high-quality low-carbon service in suburbs and towns. PRT uses small automated battery electric vehicles running on lightweight guideways that make up a network taking people directly between their origin stop to their final destination stop. People do not wait for a service to turn up, but the service is there 24/7 when they arrive at a station. The first PRT system in the UK has been built at Heathrow Airport to link the car parks to Terminal 5 (see Fig. 21.4). Such systems are yet to be proven outside the sheltered operating environment of an airport, but a hybrid taxicab/minibus DRT service could develop the service system in readiness for when it might be automated into PRT.

The potential exists for future transport systems to be very different to those of today. It is not just a matter of new technologies and designs substituting current vehicles, or of policies to encourage people to shift between traditional transport modes, but of different business models for a new transport product-service system. So a possible future may be one where many people may not buy one or two multi-purpose vehicles, but have a 'mobility package' whereby they have a lease car, plus the availability of specialist vehicles for specific uses coupled with 'add-ons' like discounted rail or public transport passes through integrated smart cards. If internal combustion-engined cars are to be phased out in cities, car access may be through schemes like Paris' Autolib city car hire scheme rather than individual car ownership. Much wider options are opening up to obtain car use, and the distinction between 'public' and 'private' transport could well become blurred.

The real barriers to a green deal for transport

The sort of technical and service system developments outlined above, together with behavioural measures that allow people to explore transport alternatives, suggest that customised packages of measures will need to vary by different types of settlements and patterns of travel demand. We could have a much more diversified transport future. However, the transition to a flexible and appropriate sustainable transport system requires more than developing a range of service and technical designs. Traditional transport and planning policy measures need to be combined with other initiatives. Indeed, the key to transport sustainability may lie in finding alliances with social and economic trends towards the information society, leading to the reinvention of how access is achieved.

This has major implications for the nature of transport policy, which needs to shift towards a focus on service development, delivery and social marking. Indeed the very concept of transport planning may cease to have much meaning in a low-carbon society. Thus transport policy needs to engage with different players; not so much with the civil engineering and automotive industries, but with business development, IT services, marketing and education.

A new business model for sustainable transport needs a new policy model as well. Our institutional, regulatory and assessment structures are built around the existing models of transport provision and make it difficult, if not impossible, for new design configurations to emerge. This key obstacle largely goes unrecognised, but is an utterly crucial part of the formula to deliver sustainable transport.

This institutional inertia is deeply rooted in the way in which transport policy is conceived and articulated. Transport policy has long been a supply-led process, built around interactions with, and the management of, the specialist professions to deliver transport projects. Indeed, even when the need for transport demand management emerged in the early 1990s, this was done in a way that was compliant with such an approach. So instead of building roads, the civil engineering project approach shifted attention to building new metro and tram systems and upgrading the railways.

This highlights a key institutional issue that shifting the transport policy focus also requires a change in the regulatory and professional structures of transport policy. In the UK, public transport privatisation and deregulation in the 1980s and 1990s produced an institutional context that makes major new public transport investments risky and expensive, and innovations such as the taxi-bus fusion difficult to introduce other than for small niche markets. Indeed, it is notable that, rather than addressing the key barriers of the institutional and regulatory structures, policy-makers in the UK have sought to find projects that can be implemented within the existing structure. Transport demand management has been deemed 'too hard', and building tram systems are going this way too. This probably means that many effective transport solutions will see little application in Britain, and there is a real danger that our old governance structures and processes could jeopardise the viability of many of the new innovative systems and technologies needed to radically decarbonise the transport system. The barriers to achieving a green deal for transport are not just technical, social or economic, but are very much about the institutional way in which we do transport policy.

How might this institutional situation be addressed? The first step is to recognise that transport's institutions and governance structures are inhibiting the implementation of effective transport policy. It needs to be accepted that we do not know exactly what the desired structures should be. There is a danger in introducing big ideologically driven structural change, and many of our public institutions are suffering from ill-conceived reorganisations. We need the traditional supply-side implementation skills, and must not jeopardise their functioning in developing good demand management skills, professional structures and culture. This suggests a programme to develop capability and to explore how a transition to a new transport policy approach can be achieved.

This can build on the approach adopted in Liberal Democrat minister Norman Baker's Local Sustainable Transport Fund, which has set particular criteria to stimulate new thinking and approaches. A programme for learning and developing skills in effective demand management might be a Smart Choices Transport Fund. Managed jointly by the Department for Transport and the Department for Business, Innovation and Skills, this would identify programmes of user and partner engagement to complement more traditional policies through which capability and professional skills can be developed and enhanced. This sort of approach has also been adopted in a parallel sector by the Low-Carbon Network Fund for Smart Grid developments. This substantial research and knowledge transfer programme acknowledges that, as well as technical projects, effective demand management is needed and the electricity industry needs new skills and user engagement partnerships to deliver this. A DfT/BIS Smart Choices Transport Fund would not only deliver some useful programmes, but crucially also deliver learning in a form that allows knowledge transfer to take place across the transport planning profession.

Notes

1   Department of the Environment, Transport, and the Regions, *A New Deal for Transport – Better for Everyone: White Paper on Transport Policy* (1998).

2   Source: Department of Energy and Climate Change.

3   Department of Energy and Climate Change: *2009 Final Greenhouse Gas Emissions* (2011).

4   Department for Transport, *Creating Growth, Cutting Carbon – Making Sustainable Local Transport Happen* (2011).

5   P. Newman and J. R. Kenworthy, *Sustainability and Cities: Overcoming Automobile Dependence* (Island Press, 1999).

6   For details, see *Transport and Sustainability* at http://openlearn.open.ac.uk/course/view.php?id=4575

7   NAIGT, *An Independent Report on the Future of the Automotive Industry in the UK* (2009).

8   N. Wemyss, *Solving the Urban Transport Dilemma – The Motor Industry's Approach* (FT Newsletters and Management Reports, 1996).

9   EC443/2009.

10 D. Banister, *Unsustainable Transport* (Taylor and Francis, 2005).

11 For example, D. Pearce and R. Turner, *Economics of Natural Resources and the Environment* (Harvester Wheatsheaf, 1990) and D. Maddison, D. Pearce, O. Johansson, E. Calthrop, T. Litman and E. Verhoef, *The True Costs of Road Travel, Blueprint 5* (Earthscan, 1996).

12 *Reducing Carbon Emissions through Transport Taxation, Green Fiscal Commission Briefing Paper 6* (Green Fiscal Commission, 2009).

13 S. Potter, 'Exploring approaches towards a sustainable transport system', *International Journal of Sustainable Transportation*, Vol. 1 No 2, 2007, pp. 115–31.

14 http://www.nef.org.uk/e-carclub/

15 Marcus Enoch, Stephen Potter, Graham Parkhurst and Mark Smith, *Intermode: Innovations in Demand Responsive Transport* (Department for Transport and Greater Manchester Passenger Transport Executive, 2004).

Chapter 22

Reducing Emissions from Transport: The Role of Taxation

Tim Leunig

This chapter looks at how we can use a more intelligent tax system to reduce the carbon intensity of travel. In this context, an intelligent green tax is one that persuades people to change their behaviour. A good green tax has both short-run and long-run effects, and persuades both individuals and firms to change their behaviour. Thus, for example, a green tax on cars both induces people to buy lower-emission cars from the current selection, and persuades firms to produce even lower-emission cars in future.

This chapter does not look at how we can cut the amount we travel. This is because the author is sceptical of claims that we will travel less in future, and because even if we did travel less, reducing the carbon intensity of the travel that remains would still make a useful contribution to reducing carbon emissions.

Most people think that reducing the carbon intensity of transport means persuading people to take the train rather than to fly, or to cycle rather than to use the car in town. There is sometimes merit in these ideas, but the likely effect on aggregate carbon emissions is very limited. Even in the Netherlands, the poster child for cycle use, the average person travels 9,900 km by car per year, far in excess of any estimate of the distance travelled by bicycle.[1] In any case, the relative importance of different types of transport has remained almost constant over time in almost every country in recent years.[2] 'Modal shift' is a slogan, not a policy.

Cars

The reality is that cars work best for most journeys. And cars are liberal and liberating: people who have access to a car can choose when and where to travel. That is a fundamentally liberating principle and since ownership is the best – and in general the only practical – way to guarantee access, liberals should be extremely enthusiastic about car ownership. Of course, cars have their downsides: they kill an unacceptably large number of people each year, and badly designed roads can divide communities. There are sensible policies to tackle each of these issues, but here we look simply at cars and carbon.

It is easy but wrong to see electric cars as the answer. In reality electric cars are almost useless because batteries are feeble. 1 kg of diesel fuel contains 13 kW of energy. In contrast, 1 kg of battery will rarely contain more than 0.14 kW of energy.[3] It would take a two-tonne battery to store as much energy as can be found in the fuel tank of a typical car, even taking into account the greater efficiency of electric cars. A two-tonne battery would be extremely expensive, and the weight of the car would make the car much less energy-efficient. Battery cars also perform very badly in even mildly cold weather. *Autocar* magazine has found that their Nissan Leaf's range falls by around one half in winter, to well under fifty miles. That is a pretty short range, even for a second car. No one thinks that the amount of energy a battery can store will increase by the necessary fifty to a hundred times in the next decade or even two.

Cars will, therefore, continue to contain internal combustion engines for as far as the eye can see. We therefore need to get petrol and diesel cars to be as efficient as possible. There has already been considerable progress. In 1990 the average new car sold emitted 190 grams of carbon dioxide per kilometre travelled.[4] By 2011, figures from the Society of Motor Manufacturers and Trader show that that figure had fallen to 138.[5] This fall has been caused by improvements in fuel efficiency within all sizes of car, rather than by people purchasing smaller cars.

We can reform the vehicle excise duty system to go much further, much faster. At the moment we have thirteen different bands of vehicle excise duty, plus a different rate of duty in the first year compared with subsequent years. It is hard to think of a worse designed green tax. Green taxes only deserve the name when they are levied at a point at which someone can alter their behaviour. Increasing or reducing the vehicle excise duty for the driver of a seven-year-old Ford Mondeo is pointless: the car exists, and it is unlikely to make environmental sense to scrap it.

We should replace annual vehicle excise duty with an upfront first registration fee, levied when a car is purchased or imported. The average car in Britain lasts for thirteen years before being scrapped.[6] Increases in reliability and reductions in rust make it likely that cars bought this year will last for around fifteen years. We therefore propose replacing annual vehicle excise duty for all new cars with an upfront first registration fee equal on average to fifteen times the current vehicle excise duty. Since this is an environmental tax it would be set in accordance with the car's estimated emissions per kilometre driven. Today virtually no cars have emissions lower than 90g CO_2/km and so it would be sensible to tax cars on emissions above this level. Above this rate the duty would be set at, say, £35 per gram. (Cars emitting less than 90g of carbon dioxide per kilometre would receive a rebate of £35 per gram). At the time of writing the average car sold averages around 138g, and would thus pay tax on the 50g above the 90g threshold. At £35 per gram the average car would therefore be liable for a tax of £1,680, which is the equivalent to £112 per year over fifteen years. This scheme would strongly incentivise reductions in carbon emissions. As a result we would expect the carbon emissions of cars sold to fall by at least 10 per cent very quickly. This would imply average emissions of around 125g, carrying an average tax charge of £1,225. This equates to around £82 over fifteen years. As cars become more efficient the threshold would fall.

Every car manufacturer would immediately make small tweaks to their cars to cut carbon dioxide. Volkswagen, for example, produce the Mark 6 2-litre diesel Golf in regular and 'BlueMotion' formats, with the BlueMotion model cutting 12g of carbon dioxide per kilometre driven. This is achieved by slightly lowering the suspension to improve the aerodynamics, fitting a slightly different front grille and tyres, slightly altering the gearing, and adding regenerative braking. The acceleration and top speeds are identical. As *Top Gear* magazine remarked: it 'makes you wonder why more cars don't get the eco treatment as standard'.[7] This proposal would give the BlueMotion model a £420 tax break compared with the regular model, which is more than sufficient to offset the current price premium of £410. In reality every car firm would make these small alterations to their cars, cutting carbon dioxide emissions of every new car sold by around 12g. This represents an immediate 8 per cent cut in new car emissions.

We would also expect features such as 'stop start', which turns the engine off when the car is stationary, to be adopted more rapidly. This cuts 5 to 10g of carbon dioxide from emissions, and would clearly be economic for car firms to fit to all cars that are currently suited to it, and to ensure that all future cars were equipped with this feature. It seems plausible to anticipate a further 5 per cent saving within five years.

Second, every car manufacturer would have an incentive to design more efficient cars and engines. Vauxhall, for example, offers the Insignia with both 1.4 turbo and 1.8 litre conventional engines. They both produce 138hp, but the 1.4 model emits 45g of carbon dioxide less per kilometre driven. It is currently £900 more expensive to purchase, but under this proposal it would have a £1,575 tax advantage, making it the cheaper car to purchase. Clearly Vauxhall would withdraw the 1.8 litre engine immediately, as no one would buy it, and more generally this demonstrates just how big an incentive car firms would have to produce more fuel-efficient engines.

Third, it will give individuals a great incentive to buy cars that are fuel-efficient. This will give a further boost to diesel cars at the expense of petrol cars. At the time of writing, the cheapest Peugeot 207 costs £10,000 to buy, but emits 145g of carbon dioxide. An extra £1,300 buys you the cheapest diesel, which cuts 35g of carbon dioxide from emissions. Under this proposal the petrol engine would attract an additional £1,225 in tax, making the diesel almost the same price to buy and cheaper to run than the petrol. It is hard to imagine anyone buying the standard petrol engine in the circumstances, and again we would expect Peugeot to either withdraw the petrol model, or replace it with a much more efficient engine.

As well as giving people an incentive to drive a more fuel-efficient version of the same car, it will also give them an incentive to buy a more efficient car altogether. The Chrysler Grand Voyager diesel emits 222g of carbon dioxide, whereas the similarly powered Ford Galaxy emits only 149g, and the Volkswagen Sharan 152g. All three cars currently cost £28,000, but under this proposal the Chrysler will attract a tax of £4,620, the Ford £2,065 and the Volkswagen £2,170. This means that the Chrysler will be £2,500 more expensive to buy than either of the other cars. The result is that people are more likely to buy its more fuel-efficient rivals. This directly improves the average fuel efficiency of the cars on Britain's roads, as well as giving Chrysler a huge incentive to install a more efficient engine in their car.

This proposal will not give people a particularly large incentive to drive small or boring cars. BMW, for example, produce a 184hp 5-series saloon that will accelerate to 60mph in just over eight seconds and yet has emissions of just 119g of carbon dioxide per kilometre driven.[8] That is just 4g more than the smallest, cheapest car produced by Ford, the 68hp tiny Ford Ka.[9] This tax proposal is not about eliminating the pleasure of driving a decent car, or about trying to get everyone into tiny little cars. It is about giving all car manufacturers an incentive to produce really efficient cars.

There are, of course, general European targets for fuel economy that car manufacturers have to reach. This tax policy complements these targets by giving car manufacturers an incentive not only to hit the target but to hit it faster, and to go further.

As the fuel efficiency of cars improves, the point at which the tax is levied would change. Initially the first 90g of carbon per kilometre would be tax-free, but this would fall as cars became more efficient in future, so that manufacturers always have an incentive to strive to reduce carbon dioxide. A sensible approach would be to link the free allowance to existing best practice.

This tax would be based on official fuel economy figures. It is well known that these figures are generally optimistic, and Britain should work with other European nations to revise the test. The test should cover a wider range of driving styles, including motorway cruising, they should take into account hills, and cars should be laden with weight equivalent to typical loads for people, luggage and fuel. Rates of acceleration should also be those typical of everyday driving. This will give manufacturers an incentive to produce cars that are actually efficient on the road rather than efficient in a rather artificial test.

In the case of electric-only cars we need to take into account the carbon produced in power stations when setting the tax. In the case of hybrid cars we need a much better sense of the proportion of their journeys that are actually under electric power. The current European test is very short, and thus allows hybrid cars to travel for a longer period on electric power than is likely to be the case in everyday driving.

The government should also consider offering a small tax break if manufacturers can prove that innovations that they make increase actual fuel economy, even if they do not increase test fuel economy. For example, it is now relatively common for manual cars to have an indicator urging the driver to change gear if the gear they're using is not the most fuel-efficient. If there is good evidence that this changes behaviour it would be worth a small tax incentive – say £50 – in order to ensure that this feature becomes universal.

This proposal also increases the incentive to keep cars going a little bit longer; the abolition of annual vehicle excise duty, combined with an increase in the price of new cars, makes it more likely that it will be sensible to keep an existing car for slightly longer. Although fuel efficiency is on a downward trend, it will still generally be more environmentally efficient to keep a car for an extra year than to scrap it and produce another one in its place.

This policy is progressive. The price of new cars goes up, and the cost of running an old car falls. Generally speaking, rich people drive new cars and poor people drive older cars. As a result the policy fits with a commitment to social justice. It will also allow more people to own a car: the annual cost will fall because there will be no annual vehicle excise duty to pay. As a result we would expect car ownership to increase slightly, which liberals should welcome. The increase in miles driven is likely to be very small.

Other road vehicles

An equivalent policy should be introduced for mopeds, motorcycles, vans and trucks. All can and should be tested for fuel economy, at which point it is straightforward to introduce equivalent schemes. Since we know that speed is important in determining fuel economy for less aerodynamic vehicles, it would be sensible to incentivise the fitting of devices that limit the top speed. These are already universal in trucks, but an incentive to make them more common in vans would almost certainly reduce actual carbon emissions.

Driving styles

Everyone knows that driving styles can dramatically alter fuel consumption. The Co-op has created an insurance policy for young people that puts a small GPS receiver in the car. This analyses how you drive, and alters your premiums according to whether you are driving in a risky or a sensible manner. The government could consider offering – though not compelling – people to have such a box in their car. If they drive well they would be given a discount card which they would present at the garage each time they bought petrol. It would entitle them to a reduction of, say, up to 10p a litre on the price of fuel.

We know that people are remarkably aware of and sensitive to the price of fuel. As a result, it would be worth piloting a scheme like this to see how it alters people's driving style. It is not difficult to analyse acceleration, braking and top speeds, as well as the extent of stop-start (urban) motoring. This would give people an incentive to drive carefully when they drive, and to consider whether very short urban journeys that almost always involve poor fuel economy are actually worth doing. Clearly some people will see civil liberties issues here, which is why the scheme would need to be voluntary.

Effects

Taken as a package these policies would aim to reduce the official carbon intensity of new cars by 10 per cent almost immediately and to no more than 80g of carbon dioxide per kilometre within ten years. Given that there are many cars with emissions under 100g at present, and that the lowest emission Toyota Yaris is already under 80g this seems a plausible target.

Buses

As with cars, it would make sense to tax buses at first registration in proportion to their fuel efficiency. This would give bus companies a strong incentive to improve the carbon efficiency of their fleet. We know that small batteries, installed in cars as part of a 'mild hybrid' system, can offer useful advantages in stop-start urban driving. Electric power offers particularly high levels of torque, and is very efficient at moving a vehicle from a standing start. In addition, the battery can be recharged when the engine is not under load, that is, when the vehicle is travelling at a steady speed or is braking. In addition, it is possible to capture some of the energy lost in braking back to the battery. For these reasons it is plausible that 'mild hybrid' buses would offer significant carbon savings compared to regular diesel buses. This sort of innovation would be given a strong incentive were we to tax the first registration of buses in line with an assessment of their fuel efficiency.

It is also imperative that bus companies are given an incentive to ensure that their buses are well maintained, and that their drivers drive as efficiently as possible. Given the buses are extremely un-aerodynamic, it is even more important that they pull away steadily, and do not accelerate and then brake a few yards down the line. At the moment, perversely, bus companies receive a refund on the fuel that they use: the Bus Service Operator's Grant. At the moment the rebate is 81 per cent of the duty levied on diesel. At present that means the bus companies pay approximately £1 per litre (including VAT) rather than £1.45. This clearly reduces their incentive to buy fuel-efficient vehicles, and to work with their drivers in developing more fuel-efficient styles of driving. The coalition government is reducing the extent of this rebate by 20 per cent between now and 2015.

This rebate currently costs £147 million per year.[10] It should be abolished immediately. If the government wishes to maintain the current level of subsidy to the bus industry it would be better to subsidise either passengers, passenger-miles, or bus-miles. Subsidising passengers gives companies an incentive to attract people onto their buses, particularly for short-distance journeys where cars are exceptionally inefficient. Subsidising passenger-miles would be a good way of rewarding bus companies that persuade people to travel by bus for a decent distance, implicitly reducing the total number of miles travelled by car. Subsidising bus-miles risks subsidising empty buses, but can be justified in terms of providing a service that is available. Any of these three, or more likely some combination of these three, would be better than subsidising fuel use.

Trains

Trains are divided into two types: electric trains and diesel trains. In each case the tax should be levied on the carbon emitted – by the power station for electric trains, and by the train itself in the case of diesel trains. The tax rate in each case should be based on the price of carbon in international markets.

Making energy more expensive gives train companies an incentive to be more efficient with power. Commuter train companies, for example, would have a greater incentive to run shorter trains off-peak, rather than running heavier, 'commuter-length', trains all day.

Second, train companies would have an incentive to consider acceleration rates and top speeds. Clearly, passengers like short journey times, but railway companies would have to weigh up people's preference for arriving a couple of minutes earlier with their preference for a lower fare. It is unlikely the trains will travel significantly slower as a result of this change, but at the margin we may find small adjustments to the timetable that yield moderate savings in energy used.

Third, train companies would have an incentive to consider fuel efficiency to a much greater extent when purchasing new trains. Trains last much longer than cars, so a more rational price for energy will take much longer to have an effect, but the effect will be very long-lasting once it occurs. Train companies could also look to retro-fitting energy-saving technology to existing trains.

Given that trains account for a relatively small proportion of total miles travelled, increasing their fuel efficiency will only ever play a small part in reducing the carbon intensity of the economy. That said, just as low fuel prices have led US drivers to drive exceptionally inefficient cars that offer little or no performance benefits, it is likely that low energy prices paid by train companies in Britain have also led to trains being much less efficient than they could be. It is plausible that we could see significant reductions in energy use in future, as our train fleet is gradually replaced.

Finally, train companies using electric trains would be able to avoid the tax by generating their own electricity – say by adding photovoltaic cells to station canopies, or even – when they become light enough and cheap enough – to the tops of trains.

Clearly this proposal increases the cost of travelling by train. If the government does not wish to make trains less economic it should compensate train companies with additional grants unrelated to fuel use.

Planes

Travel by plane does not attract VAT, and fuel used by airlines is not taxed. The only duty levied is the air passenger duty. The government should replace this with a tax on the plane, which is related to the likely carbon emissions created by that plane on that route.

A per-plane tax offers many advantages. First, provided that the tax is related to the estimated fuel efficiency of the particular plane on the particular route it gives airlines an incentive to use more efficient planes. Second, it gives airlines a very strong incentive to fill the plane. This is environmentally friendly as it makes it much more likely that airlines will withdraw underused services. Third, it gives airlines an incentive to consider using larger but less frequent planes if that is more fuel-efficient. Fourth, it rewards airlines that cram passengers in. Although this may be unpleasant for passengers it is very good for the environment. Airlines can then make a sensible trade-off between people's willingness to pay for space and the additional tax per person that that implies. Finally, it would end the idiocy through which a transfer passenger from Mexico to Rome via London pays no tax at all on the flight from London.

Both the Conservatives and Liberal Democrats were committed to this policy prior to the election, and the policy appeared in the coalition agreement, but it has been abandoned, for reasons that are at best obscure.[11] Nor is it operationally difficult to implement, particularly for short-haul flights where people are unlikely to change planes in Paris to avoid the duty. (It is worth noting that there is little evidence that people are choosing to change planes in Paris to avoid the relatively high rates of long-haul air passenger duty that are already currently levied).

The current policy exempts transfer passengers. This disproportionately benefits British Airways, and it is at least possible that the reason for government backsliding is successful lobbying by our national flag carrier. This would not be a good reason for failing to proceed with a good policy.

Note too that this policy would be popular. Assuming it was introduced on a revenue-neutral basis it would lead to a fall in the taxes levied on British passengers, to the extent that the total tax burden would be paid in part by transit passengers. Furthermore, given that the airline has to pay the tax whether the plane is full or empty it will make sense for the airline to sell seats that might otherwise be empty at very low cost. This would increase the number of genuine bargains available.

Shipping

Travelling by water generally uses a lot of energy – as any swimmer knows. Yet again, fuel use is essentially untaxed. The government should therefore look to create the equivalent of the per-plane duty outlined above for shipping. Clearly this would not work for direct shipments from say, China, which would simply choose to go to Rotterdam and unload their British cargo on to a smaller ship that would then come across the Channel. But at the very least we can implement this sort of duty for passenger ferries, river ferries, and coastal shipping. Again the duty would be based on an estimate of typical fuel use for a given journey and schedule. The duty would be based on the internationally traded price of carbon.

As ever, this has two effects: it gives companies an incentive to use fuel-efficient ships, and it gives companies an incentive to run them in a fuel-efficient manner. In particular, given that fuel costs can rise dramatically with speed for waterborne transport, it will increase the incentive to travel at a slightly slower, but perhaps much more fuel-efficient pace.

Conclusion

The changes outlined here appear at first sight to be frighteningly mundane. There is no 'Brave New World' in which our eyes are suddenly opened, we abandon our cars and take to walking, cycling and travelling on solar-powered trains. Nor does it propose a world in which we all suddenly start working from home, using Skype and email to talk to colleagues and clients.

But the changes outlined here are straightforward to implement and would have real effects. It is easy to imagine that the efficiency of new cars would improve by 10 per cent within a year, and by perhaps 50 per cent within a decade. This would continue the major progress that we have seen in recent years, and could well deliver us a car fleet that is environmentally acceptable rather than a major environmental issue. Similar progress can probably be expected from motorcycles, vans and trucks. Progress on trains, buses, planes and shipping will be slower and more erratic, given that these are replaced less frequently.

The 2008 Climate Change Act requires Britain to reduce greenhouse gas emissions to 20 per cent of their 1990 levels by 2050. These changes will not lead to reductions of that size within the transport sector. This is because it is easier and cheaper to decarbonise static energy use than to decarbonise mobile energy use. Fossil fuels contain huge amounts of energy per kilogram. This makes them exceptionally well suited to transport, where it is necessary to carry the fuel. For that reason it is important to ensure that we use fossil fuels efficiently in transport, but it is likely to be much cheaper to replace fossil fuels in static uses than in mobile uses. A world in which houses and other buildings use little energy for space heating because they are well insulated, in which appliances are energy-efficient and powered by nuclear and/or renewable energy, and in which cars are still powered by petrol, but run more efficiently, is a sensible and deliverable environmental outcome entirely consistent with meeting our climate change objectives. And that world may even be able to cope with people flying around to see it!

Notes

1 OECD Joint Transport Research Centre online statistics; available at http://www.internationaltransportforum.org/jtrc/environment/CO2/Netherlands.xls.

2 OECD International Transport Federation online slide: 'Modal split of inland passenger-km has remained constant over time in the EU and the United States; available at http://www.internationaltransportforum.org/statistics/GlobalTrends/Passenger.pdf

3 Automotive Engineering Online, 'Leaf to be sold with battery pack at C-segment price', 20 March 2010.

4 Jonathan Murray, 'Car CO2 taxation and its impact on the British car fleet', Low Carbon Vehicle Partnership online presentation; available at http://www.lowcvp.org.uk/assets/presentations/Car CO2 tax in the UK 2011 – Jonathan Murray.pdf

5 SMMT, *New Car CO2 Report 2012*.

6 Murray, 'Car CO2 taxation and its impact on the British car fleet'.

7 *Top Gear* online review of Golf Bluemotion: http://www.topgear.com/uk/volkswagen/golf-6/road-test/bluemotion-5dr

8 BMW 520 efficient dynamics saloon data; available from BMW website, http://www.bmw.co.uk/en/new-vehicles/5/saloon/2010/technicaldata.html

9 Ford Ka 1.2 data; available from Ford website, http://www.ford.co.uk/Cars/Ka/EconomyAndEmissons

10 Department for Transport online table to BSOG grants; available at http://assets.dft.gov.uk/publications/bsog-grants-paid-to-20120331/bsog-grants-paid-2011.pdf

11 'Aviation is a global industry bound by international agreements. The UK is a signatory to the 1944 ICAO Chicago Convention and has Air Service Agreements (ASAs) with over 150 countries. Many stakeholders have expressed concerns about the legality and feasibility of introducing a per plane duty under current international rules. The Government wishes to proceed with consensus in this area and will not introduce a per plane duty in place of APD at the present time, but nevertheless will continue working with our international partners to build understanding and support for this approach in the future.' HM Treasury, *Reform of Air Passenger Duty: A Consultation* (2011).

Chapter 23

Going Green Has To Be Fair

Chris Huhne

Climate change is not an ordinary political issue. It is beset by collective-action problems, in which individuals acting in their self-interest condemn us collectively to a bad outcome for everyone. It involves huge sums of money. Debates are riddled with misinformation, often put out by or funded by groups with an interest in the status quo. There are virtually no solutions that some vociferous section of the country does not hate.

However, climate change is also set apart by its ticking clock. We are dangerously close to the 2°C point of no return, beyond which there is little humankind can do to prevent further temperature rises or stabilise global weather patterns. Yet the process of changing the energy infrastructure is tantalisingly slow, because so much capital has been committed to high energy demand and fossil fuel use. Rising energy costs have lashed disposable incomes for more than a decade, pushing many families into fuel poverty, and worsening an already brutal economic downturn. Yet in spite of the urgency, the process of building public support is painfully slow. Maslow's hierarchy of needs switches in during a period of squeezed living standards, focusing politics on the raw and short-term issue of family budgets. The sceptics argue that the poor cannot afford greenery.

If measures to attack climate change are to be sustained in the UK, this argument has to be tackled on two levels. The first is the evidence that climate policies promote growth, jobs and living standards. That set of issues is addressed elsewhere in this volume. The second level is that climate policies are fair. This is not just about fairness to future generations, but also fairness in the way that solutions are implemented today. At the very least, green policies must not worsen the distribution of income. They might even aim to improve it. Liberal Democrats, after all, believe in greater equality of outcomes, not just equality of opportunity. Even equality of opportunity is meaningless if a child's circumstances curtail its life chances.

Overall, climate change policies have to meet this equity test. Green efforts that hit poorer families and create real social injustices will not be seen as fair or legitimate, and they will gradually erode the coalition in favour of change. Some green enthusiasts are blind to the potential impact of some measures (such as a high carbon tax) on the poorest in society, yet this would fracture the key progressive cross-party coalition in favour of change and call into question our commitment to greater equality. This chapter is, in essence, about why the environmental agenda must complement the social agenda, and how to go about it.

Shelter from the storm

A little over a decade ago, the Labour government set out to abolish fuel poverty. At that time, when oil prices were us$10–15 a barrel, and disposable incomes were growing steadily year on year, more than 2 million UK households were still 'fuel poor': they had gas or electricity bills that swallowed more than a tenth of their income.[1] The government set itself a deadline of 2016 to wipe out this kind of hardship, launching new income-related benefits and a nationwide home improvement scheme to get demand for energy down and reduce the toll on disposable incomes.

It has not gone well. Huge sums were invested in the Winter Fuel Allowance and Warm Front, and yet the numbers of fuel-poor have gone up. They are on course to hit 8 million by 2016.[2]

The first problem is that energy prices have been bounding upwards for more than a decade, pulling more and more families into fuel poverty. Gas is the key fuel for domestic heating, but non-US gas prices still move with the oil price (and in some cases are explicitly linked to oil prices). Within eight years, an oil price of us$10 a barrel was replaced by one of us$147. The average gas bill in the UK doubled.[3]

The government's policy response was too slow and too untargeted. Part of the problem is the definition of the measure of fuel poverty, as John Hills' recent excellent review pointed out. When Her Majesty the Queen flirts with fuel poverty because her palace's furnaces burn nearly a tenth of her income, there is something wrong with the targeted definition. Hills rightly proposes that people should be considered fuel-poor if they have relatively high required fuel costs to maintain reasonable heating levels, and if they would be left below the official poverty line if they were to spend that amount. In addition, the government should concentrate hardest on those most in need. It should adopt a new indicator of the depth of fuel poverty – a 'fuel poverty gap' – which is the amount by which the energy needs of fuel-poor households exceed the threshold for reasonable costs. This government – any government – should set sensible targets for things it can actually affect.

There were other problems with the last government's efforts. The Warm Front scheme involved upgrading boilers for free, but the costs were often loaded up by the contractors so that the scheme was more expensive than it should have been, and householders sometimes had to top up the generous subsidies. More broadly, the government continues to support the costly Winter Fuel Allowance (at around £2 billion – £3 billion a year), handing payments to virtually all over-sixty-one-year-olds regardless of the efficiency of their home or even where they live; more than 60,000 British pensioners who are lucky enough to have retired to the Costa del Sol and other Mediterranean climes benefit as well.[4] Just 41 per cent is actually spent on heating (and some estimates put this much lower).[5]

However, the real enemy – both on costs and emissions – is leaky homes. Under-insulated, single-glazed, cavity-wall-less houses are the reason why fuel poverty stays stubbornly high, and indeed rose with the rise in fossil fuel prices. At the end of the 2000s, when fossil fuel prices were at their very highest, it was still efficiency rates that made the difference. Among the poorest fifth of the population, almost 90 per cent of those in very inefficient homes (with a Standard Assessment Procedure (SAP) rating of less than 30) were living in fuel poverty. For those in very efficient homes, in the same income group, just 10 per cent were fuel-poor.[6] Perhaps more intriguingly, only 40 per cent of those in fuel poverty are among the poorest 20 per cent by income. While there is obviously some overlap, nearly a quarter of the fuel-poor are found in the second-to-bottom income bracket.

Fig 23.1 Fuel poverty and energy efficiency ratings[7]

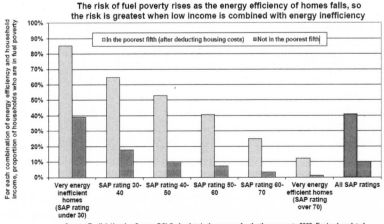

The risk of fuel poverty rises as the energy efficiency of homes falls, so the risk is greatest when low income is combined with energy inefficiency

Source: English Housing Survey, DCLG; the data is the average for the three years to 2009; England; updated Jul 2011

What is going on? In the post-war housing boom of the 1950s and 1960s, Britain built more than one in five of the homes standing today.[8] It was an amazing chance to design out fuel poverty, minimise fossil fuel use, and shore up the economy against energy shocks. We missed it. Houses were built at a tremendous pace, but mostly with lousy standards of efficiency, scarcely better than the older vintages of housing on which we also still rely. The typical British home is too cold in winter and too hot in summer.

Even though the continent tends to face much fiercer winters, other Europeans do not have anything like the UK's rate of fuel poverty. The Swedish winter is on average 7.24°C colder and lasts two to three months longer,[9] but at one point in recent years they actually used less energy for heating per dwelling.[10] This is mostly because the Swedes have already had their energy efficiency revolution; after the oil shocks of the 1970s, they made impressive efforts to conserve energy and switch away from high-carbon, reducing the use of fossil fuels and increasing renewables.

The second story is rather brighter. One of the big reasons why more low-income families have not tipped into fuel poverty is that social housing has been properly renovated. Some 92 per cent of social housing now meets the 'Decent Homes' standard for warmth,[11] and average SAP ratings for energy efficiency have jumped from 47 to 63 since 1996 – not a long way from the 'very efficient' marker of 70 plus.[12]

Not too surprisingly, the private rental sector is doing worse. Some 40 per cent of dwellings were built before 1919,[13] and 44 per cent are deemed 'not decent'.[14] It is the sector least likely to be upping efficiency, has an average SAP rank of 53,[15] and yet is growing rapidly because of increasingly unaffordable house prices.[16] And it is not well-suited to home improvements. Renters need permission to make any alterations – especially major retrofits – and since landlords don't usually pay the bills, they don't have much incentive to reduce them. Many people in rented houses do not plan to stay very long, so even loft insulation that pays for itself in less than a year does not get done; almost 40 per cent of all private renters leave after less than a year, and almost 60 per cent leave after fewer than two.[17]

The effects of all this are all too real. Low-grade homes are a serious economic drag, and they do terrible harm to the health and welfare of their occupants. In the midst of the worst cold snaps, some poorer elderly citizens find that they have to choose between eating and heating.[18] Energy use among the lowest income bracket can vary wildly, with the heaviest users consuming six times that of the lightest.[19] As the Hills Review of fuel poverty shows, a troubling number of low-income households are 'significantly under-consuming relative to need'.[20] In the colder regions of the UK, residents in poor housing are 45 per cent more likely to have high blood pressure,[21] and as many as 24,000 people are thought to die needlessly each winter from the cold.[22] The economic toll is fairly severe too. The Department of Health estimates that winter-related disease from cold private housing costs the NHS nearly £1 billion a year.[23]

The problems with price signals

This is all rather troublesome for some green propositions. So long as such a vast efficiency gap stretches between one dwelling and another, imaginative ideas that rely on people reducing their energy use are not going to work. The inefficient simply cannot get their usage down: they are locked into consumption that they often cannot control.

The theory of the carbon tax is marvellous. Put up the price of carbon – of coal, oil and gas – to capture the full extent of the damage that it inflicts on the environment, and the market economy will do the rest. Higher prices for carbon will curb demand, and encourage alternative low-carbon supply; and price signals will ensure that people tend to find the cheapest and therefore most economical way of dealing with the problem. A full-scale tax on the carbon cost of every transaction could be truly transformational, but it is also hugely risky.

For one thing, there are very real differences in need that cannot be lessened just by tweaking behaviour. Most senior citizens and many disabled people, for example, are going to be at home most of the time, in a room temperature several degrees higher than average. And as we saw above, low-income households often live in the worst-insulated homes that need to improve their energy efficiency just to get comfortable. They can't reasonably be expected to actually reduce energy consumption. The environmental justice of a 'polluter pays' response could provoke a gross social injustice, especially for those least able to pay.

Carbon taxing also rests on the premise that bill payers act rationally – and, for the most part, conventional economics is probably right to suggest that they do. Make it simple to choose cheaper providers, efficiency measures or renewable generators, and take-up will soar. But there are exceptions, and they tend to be among the most vulnerable. The green charity Groundwork, which installs free energy efficiency measures for poor households, disabled people, and the elderly, find that around a third do not know what energy efficiency is, refuse to believe that it saves money, and are unlikely to trust retailers unless the council authenticates them.[24] Elderly people very rarely switch energy supplier and can be wary of big changes to their living situation, even those scraping by on a low income.[25] Plenty of elderly home-owners would benefit greatly from an equity release scheme to pay for energy efficiency improvements, since a good many are income-poor but asset-rich, but in reality many are very reluctant to do it. Realistically, this sort of problem has to be addressed before a full-scale carbon tax could go ahead.

For the progressive case behind green energy to hold, it is essential for the state to play its role as the navigator of the 'information problem', directing people to markets, simplifying decision-making, and providing guarantees and reassurance to consumers. The number of people in the UK who change energy supplier each year hovers around a lowly one in five.[26] As energy prices spiked in 2011, switching actually fell to fewer than one in seven. Fully 64 per cent of householders have never switched.[27]

The poorest households take the biggest hit on energy, and yet are likely to overspend the most – by around £250 a year on some estimates.[28] On average, those on pre-payment meters pay an extra £125 a year. One analysis suggests that fuel poverty (on the old definition) would fall by 15 per cent if the lowest third of earners switched to the lowest tariffs.[29] Just as weights and measures legislation in the late nineteenth century allowed us to grumble over the price of beer, and go elsewhere agitating for a better deal, so electricity market reform has begun the much delayed process of simplifying energy choices. But there is some way to go on building a culture of choice on energy, or efficiency products, or domestic renewables. Unless the way in which we choose energy is completely rewired, cheaper, cleaner supply will continue to elude us.[30]

This is where there is a potential conflict between green and equity objectives which requires care to navigate. Abolishing fuel poverty is going to cost a lot[31] and cannot realistically be achieved through 'hands-off' market measures like the full carbon tax. Targeted measures are needed to deal with specific problems.

The government's Energy Company Obligation (ECO) has brought one stream of outside support which will supplement the Green Deal by about £1.3 billion a year; it will fund those who currently under-consume energy, where energy saving improvements tend to lead to more comfort and, consequentially, no saving in energy. It will also fund old houses that were built before the widespread use of cavity walls, and where insulation to the solid walls has to be applied internally or externally as cladding.

The amount allocated to ECO should be larger, not just on energy-saving and equity grounds but also because this is a particularly effective job-creating tool where a small amount of government funding releases a multiple of private spending. For example, a solid wall home may attract ECO subsidy, but the associated measures of draught-proofing, balloons in chimneys and so on, will all pay for themselves under Green Deal finance.

Transport

We have discussed the conflict between green and redistributive objectives when it comes to energy use in the home, and the problems that can be caused both by differing needs and by different levels of energy efficiency. There are also problems when we look at green objectives for transport, although arguably there are less acute side-effects for redistribution.

At the time of writing a litre of petrol costs £1.32. That was composed of 58p in fuel duty and 22p in VAT, leaving 52p for the actual fuel.[32] In the United States, the federal gas tax is just 18.4 cents a gallon.[33] The Treasury does not now classify fuel duty as an environmental tax, it falls under 'revenue-raising' – and it hauls in a little under £30 billion a year.[34] This has made it all too easy for the anti-green right-wing to claim progressive colours, and say that taxes on driving are a tax on the poor. There are plenty on the left who sympathise, worrying that fuel duty has become a closet flat tax. After all, rich and poor pay exactly the same levy with no consideration of ability to pay.

In rural areas, it is indeed true that virtually everyone needs a car, because bus and train services are so poor. But this is a problem for a minority, and there are other means of tackling it (like specially reduced rates of duty on petrol in remote rural areas). Taking the country as a whole, the poorest households often do without a car. Overall, 20 per cent of households have no access to a vehicle.[35] Half of low-income households (the bottom 20 per cent) do not have access to a vehicle, and for the average family in the bottom 10 per cent, transport takes up less than 9 per cent of weekly spending.[36] Most of the poorest use public transport. In principle, therefore, the use of price signals – green taxes on motoring – is a way of shifting behaviour, providing that some of the rural side-effects can be offset with lower fuel taxes or vouchers.

There are also strong reasons for doing so which do not just involve carbon emissions. Traffic is expected to rise by 44 per cent by 2025,[37] and already cars are responsible for 3,300 premature deaths every year – more than the numbers killed on the road – at an estimated cost of £6 billion, particularly thanks to the respiratory consequences of pollution.[38] London's roads regularly breach nitrogen dioxide pollution limits.[39] Overall, air pollution in the UK is thought to kill 29,000 each year.[40]

Partly because of the ratcheting up of fuel duty that began under Ken Clarke's chancellorship, the demand for rail travel has been soaring. Even though rail journeys are still very expensive in Britain compared with the Continent, Britain's railways are carrying more passengers than at any time since the 1940s, before Dr Beeching's cuts to the extent of the national network.

Tackling the problem: Green Deal

At this point, it is worth summarising the argument. There is indeed a potential conflict between green objectives and the objective of equality if simple solutions such as a carbon tax are relied upon. We have seen that consumer short-sightedness, differing needs, lack of access to capital, and the sunk capital in the housing stock all have their effects. Our homes are too draughty, our cars too dirty, our knowledge too patchy, and our investments too scary. Yet we ought not be discouraged. These are all solvable problems even if they will tend to complicate policy.

There have always been two problems with energy efficiency improvements. The first is that the cost has to be met upfront, which puts off some people who will nevertheless benefit. The second is that landlords of rental property have no incentive to improve given that the tenant reaps the benefit, while tenants have no interest in improving a property which is not theirs. Both of these issues are addressed by a 'pay as you save' scheme like Green Deal, which therefore creates the conditions for a sharp improvement in energy saving.

Under Green Deal, energy-saving measures are installed for free, and you pay back the cost out of the savings made on your bill. The scheme is designed so that savings always outweigh repayments; your bill will always be lower. The payments, moreover, are attached to the energy bill, so that it does not matter if the tenant moves; the cost will continue to be deducted from the electricity bill linked to the property until the repayments are complete.

The Green Deal scheme also avoids the problem of Warm Front locking in privileged suppliers: any householder can take their survey and get a competing quote. Competition will keep suppliers honest, and ensure that any subsidy goes to improving homes rather than suppliers' profit margins.

In a rational world, Green Deal should take off on its own, as its benefits outweigh its costs; householders should save money immediately by installing Green Deal measures. However, there is a long history of consumers failing to take up such measures, perhaps because of worries like clearing the attic, having the builders and their dirt in the house, or – as we saw above – not believing that the activity is worthwhile.

That is why it is crucial for the government to provide information, incentives and, where necessary, regulation to support the scheme. Already, private landlords will be required to undertake Green Deal by 2018 if their properties are F or G rated in their Energy Performance Certificate, affecting more than 600,000 of the least energy-efficient properties. This was not regarded as a regulatory burden because there is no cost to landlords, and indeed there may be a benefit if they are able to charge higher rents. There will certainly be a benefit to tenants who pay lower bills.

If Green Deal is to reach its full potential, however, the government will have to be much braver about driving demand, particularly among owner-occupiers, still the largest sector with the greatest number of leaky homes. The obvious solution is to make it particularly attractive to install Green Deal when a property changes hands, as this is the point at which most owner-occupiers repair, improve and decorate their property. Since the builders are going to be coming in anyway, it makes sense to get Green Deal done as well.

Two incentives would help. The first would be to require any buyer of a home without Green Deal to ask for a survey, and install the measures within a year, unless they specifically opted out of doing so. Such an arrangement is already being adopted by the government for private pensions, and there is no reason why it should not be extended. It would make sense to add an incentive: those who continue to opt in should benefit from a lower rate of stamp duty on the purchase price than those who decide to opt out.

Let us turn now to some of the potential impact on economic activity. The UK already has close to a million green-collar workers,[41] and Green Deal is estimated to add a further 39,000–60,000 in insulating jobs by 2015.[42] If Green Deal is pushed with regulation and tax incentives, it would be relatively easy to increase the employment impact sharply – possibly to 100,000 or more over a similar timeframe.

Green Deal jobs are created wherever there is old housing stock, which is pretty equally spread across the country in proportion to the population. Most other government measures tend to have much more localised employment impacts, depending largely on where the investment is required or where it can be built: an aircraft carrier in Rosyth, a motorway in the West Midlands and so on. Because Green Deal boosts construction, it is also particularly beneficial in absorbing young men who are often hard to employ, and it gives them important and useful skills.

A greener economy will go on creating jobs, stirring innovation, and raising incomes after the first wave of Green Deal improvements. Many of the early-stage technologies discussed here will quickly be eclipsed. The accelerating pace of cost reduction in solar panels is one example. Another is the improvement in lithium-ion vehicle batteries, extending range and cutting costs. The first low-energy lightbulbs, compact fluorescents, have now been bested by LEDs. The former uses 20 per cent of the electricity used by traditional incandescent bulbs,[43] but LEDs take a further leap, using just 10 per cent for the same amount of light.[44]

The green tax switch

We have already discussed the problems of a carbon tax, but there are green taxes which, if combined with tax cuts elsewhere, can have a progressive impact on the income distribution. Fuel duty tends to be progressive, because richer people tend to drive bigger cars, and poor people drive no cars at all (with the exception of rural areas, already noted, for which there are other solutions). There could also be a much more radical reform of car sales tax and Vehicle Excise Duty, with sharply graduated taxes according to the carbon emissions of vehicles, as I have argued elsewhere.[45] Air transport duties are also progressive, as only 32 per cent of leisure flights from UK airports are taken by the bottom two socio-economic groups.[46] The average income of those taking leisure flights is nearly £49,500, almost double the national average.[47] Revenue from such green taxes can be used to bolster low and middle incomes through rising personal allowances or even rising tax credits (which are in turn removed from the better-off).

The green tax switch, though, must be seen to involve tax cuts that offset the tax increases, or the public support for any such measures will dwindle. Voters are understandably suspicious of finance ministers who impose green taxes, thinking that this is just another revenue-raising gambit. However, a clear and transparent offsetting tax reduction can be popular, as the Scandinavians have proved. This is what the Swedish did with their green taxes in the 1990s. In France in 2009, voters were polled on whether they would back a carbon tax, with 74 per cent saying no; but when asked whether they would back one that is fiscally neutral for households, a majority said yes.[48]

The move to a low-carbon economy will be one of the dominating themes of the next few decades, and there is an understandable temptation in some parts of the green movement to look impatiently for simple and attractive solutions which will deliver major change. Hence the carbon tax, or the personal carbon allowance. However, these could have very dramatic adverse effects on equality, and could undermine the progressive political consensus in favour of a transition to a low-carbon world. It is crucial that policies are not just effective, but fair. It is therefore essential that there are targeted measures – such as Green Deal, supported by ECO, a green tax switch to low-income families, and support for low-carbon public transport – to tackle those difficulties. They must be bolstered by regulatory and other incentives. Decarbonisation policy will inevitably be complex, but the total package must be fair if radicals are to meet our objectives and public support is to be sustained.

Notes

1   DECC, *Fuel Poverty Statistics*, July 2012.

2   John Hills, *Getting The Measure of Fuel Poverty: Final Report of the Fuel Poverty Review* (Centre for Analysis of Social Exclusion, LSE, March 2012).

3   John Hills, *Fuel Poverty, The Problem and its Measurement, Interim Report of the Fuel Poverty Review* (Centre for Analysis of Social Exclusion, LSE, October 2011).

4   DWP, *Benefit Expenditure Tables*, 2012.

5   IFS, *Cash by any other name? Evidence on labelling from the UK Winter Fuel Payment* (May 2011).

6   Joseph Rowntree Foundation, *The Poverty Site: Fuel Poverty, 2011*.

7   Ibid.

8   DCLG, *English Housing Survey: Household Report 2010–11* (February 2012).

9   UK Meteorological Office, 2012; Sweden Meteorological Service, 2012.

10   ODYSSEE, *Consumption per dwelling for space heating* (2005).

11   Homes and Communities Agency, *Existing Housing Stock* (2012).

12   DCLG, *English Housing Survey* (2012).

13   DCLG, *English Housing Survey* (2010).

14   ONS, *Housing* (2011).

15   DCLG, *English Housing Survey* (2012).

16   IFS, *The spending patterns and inflation experience of low-income households over the past decade* (June 2011).

17   ONS, *Housing*.

18   IFS, *Is there a heat or eat trade-off in the UK?* (2011).

19   Ekins and Dresner, *Improving UK home energy efficiency without negative social impacts* (2006).

20   Hills, *Getting The Measure of Fuel Poverty*.

21   Imperial College London, *Elevated risk of high blood pressure: climate and the inverse housing law* (2002).

22   ONS, *Excess winter mortality in England and Wales* (2012).

23   Department of Health, *Cold Weather Plan for England – Making the Case: Why cold weather planning is essential to health and well-being* (November 2011).

24   Groundwork, *Leeds Green Doctor: Qualitative Survey* (2012).

25   Hills, *Fuel Poverty, The Problem and its Measurement*.

26   Ofgem, *The Retail Market Review – Findings and initial proposals* (2012).

27   Ipsos MORI, *Customer Engagement with the Energy Market – Tracking Survey* (2012).

28   Save the Children, *The UK Poverty Rip-Off: The poverty premium* (2010).

29   Hills, *Fuel Poverty, The Problem and its Measurement.*

30   Tim Leunig, 'People Power – How to Transform UK Energy', *Financial Times*, 9 September 2012.

31   IPPR and NEA, *The Long Cold Winter: Beating fuel poverty* (2010).

32   DECC, *Oil and Petroleum Product Price Statistics: Weekly fuel prices* (14 January 2013).

33   American Petroleum Institute, *Gasoline Taxes* (January 2013).

34   Department for Transport, *Transport Statistics Great Britain* (2011).

35   Joseph Rowntree Foundation, *The Poverty Site: UK Ability to Travel* (2012).

36   ONS, *Living Costs and Food Survey* (November 2011).

37   RAC Foundation, 'RACF backs Work Wise' (May 2012).

38   Steve H. L. Yim and Steven R. H. Barrett, *Public Health Impacts of Combustion Emissions in the United Kingdom* (2012).

39   Defra, *Air Quality* (2012); King's College London, *London Air* (2012); Environmental Research Group, King's College London, *Air Quality in London – briefing note to GLA Environment and Health Committee* (July 2012).

40   Committee on the Medical Effects of Air Pollutants, *The Mortality Effects of Long-Term Exposure to Particulate Air Pollution in the United Kingdom* (2009).

41   BIS, *Low Carbon and Environmental Goods and Services (LCEGS) Report for 2010/11* (July 2012).

42   DECC, *Final Stage Impact Assessment for the Green Deal and Energy Company Obligation* (2012).

43   Energy Saving Trust, *Lighting Products* (2012).

44   Energy Saving Trust, *Lit up: an LED lighting field trial* (2011).

45   IPPR, *Beyond Liberty: Is the Future of Liberalism Progressive?* (2007).

46   Civil Aviation Authority, *Trends in UK air passenger traffic* (2011).

47   Civil Aviation Authority, *Passenger Survey Report* (2011).

48   'France's Carbon Tax: Taming the Carbonivores', *The Economist*, September 2009.

Chapter 24

Planning for Sustainability and Green Growth

Paul Burall and Kate Parminter

England's planning system has always been controversial. Some have attacked it as an unnecessary obstacle to business and economic development. Others believe that it gives insufficient regard to protecting heritage and the natural environment. Local politicians and their communities often portray the system as being too top-down, with targets and policies dictated by central government. House-builders, farmers, energy providers and many others see the system as a bureaucratic nightmare that inhibits their ability to provide the services, goods and wealth that the nation needs.

The 2011 *British Social Attitudes* report illustrates the challenge for anyone expecting the planning system to be popular. For example, while 80 per cent of people believed that new homes are needed, 45 per cent opposed any new development near them, with opposition strongest in south-east England and other areas where property is in the shortest supply.

Any decision about development is in practice likely to require compromise, and the balance of such compromises will inevitably be influenced by the priorities of those making decisions about planning policy and its implementation.

Planning should be about meeting current needs without compromising the future. That means ensuring the quality of life of people in the long term, securing sustainable economic prosperity, and safeguarding the sustainability of the environment. Sacrificing these objectives in a quick-fix attempt to secure short-term economic growth can create problems requiring expensive correction in the future, as well as risking the destruction of valued landscapes and biodiversity. Planning, of course, has a role in job and wealth creation but this should not override other considerations, not least because good planning can help to reduce business costs and enhance opportunities for growth.

The ideal planning system should give everyone affected the opportunity to be involved, operate efficiently and not demand more time or cost than is essential, consider all significant impacts and options, be transparent so that everyone can follow the logic of decisions, and ensure that decisions support declared long-term objectives.

As for planning outcomes, the 2005 *Planning Policy Statement 1* set the objective as facilitating and promoting sustainable and inclusive patterns of development by:

- Making suitable land available for development, in line with economic, social and environmental objectives to improve people's quality of life;
- Contributing to sustainable economic development;
- Protecting and enhancing the natural and historic environment, the quality and character of the countryside, and existing communities;
- Ensuring high-quality development through good and inclusive design, and the efficient use of resources; and,
- Ensuring that development supports existing communities and contributes to the creation of safe, sustainable, liveable and mixed communities with good access to jobs and key services for all members of the community.

The National Planning Policy Framework

So how does the coalition government's National Planning Policy Framework measure up against these criteria? After a hard-fought battle against Treasury rhetoric claiming that planning was damaging its pro-growth agenda, victory was won by those, like Liberal Democrats, who believe that planning can and must arbitrate the competing interests over land use while creating economic prosperity, meeting the needs of all sectors of society and protecting our environment and its resources to provide a pathway to a low-carbon future. We especially welcome the inclusion of:

- A clearer definition of sustainable development;
- Democratic local plans as the fundamental building block of the planning system;
- Priority for using previously developed land before greenfield sites;
- Recognition of the value of the intrinsic character and beauty of the countryside;
- Explicitly making planning authorities responsible for taking account of the Climate Change Act and the target of an 80 per cent emissions cut by 2050.

But the way in which the NPPF will work in practice is still unclear. So we need close monitoring of its results, and a review of the impact of the NPPF in 2014.

The NPPF embraces genuine community engagement in decisions that shape their lives and their environment – a fundamental tenet of Liberal

Democrat beliefs. But making community involvement meaningful is not easy. We are therefore disappointed that the Localism Act failed to bring in a community right of appeal. While the Act ensures that local communities have the right to be consulted prior to the submission of some planning applications, the public – unlike developers – still does not have the right to appeal against applications which are contrary to the Local Plan or in which the local authority has an interest. It is therefore crucial that engagement by the local community in pre-application scrutiny is meaningful.

Involving the public

Large-scale developments often excite controversy, but they can offer the opportunity for local people to be genuinely engaged in shaping their local environment. One example is the Chichester Community Development Trust. This aims to help existing residents in the Graylingwell Park development – the UK's largest zero-carbon development – to inform the master planning of new homes and the services, open spaces and infrastructure; it will own and be responsible for any new community facilities as well as the large open green spaces, thus fostering a sense of community. Originally funded with pump-priming from a section 106 agreement between the developer and the planning authority, the Trust will become financially sustainable through a combination of income from assets, a resident levy and user charges.[1]

The neighbourhood planning concept introduced in the Localism Act is welcome; it gives people the power to develop a shared vision for their neighbourhood and deliver the sustainable development they need. The challenge is for local authorities to support a significant number of Neighbourhood Plans at any one time and to be able to provide not only the planning skills of a trained planning officer but also the community development skills necessary to ensure community engagement which is socially equitable. All local authorities should commit to providing such support for a reasonable number of plans.

There are already good examples of community engagement achieved by local authorities. For example, Liberal Democrat-controlled Bristol City Council has developed a unique Neighbourhood Planning Network. This supports, coordinates and promotes the work of around forty-five specific neighbourhood planning groups across the city and has resulted in several plans being supported by the City Council, initiated a rigorous process for pre-application engagement on applications above a specified (quite small) size, and enhanced engagement in the City Council's strategic planning.

Valuing open spaces

Neighbourhood planning reflects the fact that the quality of the local environment has a direct impact on people's lives. Living among attractive parks, gardens and streets and with access to unspoilt countryside does not merely lift the spirits, it has been shown to enhance health and well-being.[2] So the implementation of a key Liberal Democrat policy in the Localism Act that will allow the protection of allotments, playing fields and other green spaces of particular value to the health and well-being of local people is a move in the right direction. But there can be tensions between public access and enjoyment of open spaces and enhancing biodiversity and wildlife. An example where this has been sensitively managed is Cambourne, where the Wildlife Trust entered into a formal agreement in 1997 to manage 80 hectares of green space in a village where housing takes up 133 hectares. Residents now say that it is the ecology which is one of the best things about this new settlement in the East of England. The site is now far more biodiverse and Cambourne is especially attractive to young couples, leading to the village having the highest birth rate in Europe. Three things critical to the success of Cambourne – and indeed any similar future schemes – are a clear management plan at the outset of the development, the necessary funding to deliver that plan, and constant community engagement.

Food systems planning

Urban green spaces are also important as places to provide food, and in doing so often create opportunities for social cohesion. Liberal Democrats have a strong record in this area. Bristol, for example, is at the forefront of bringing a revolutionary concept of food systems planning, aiming to build a food culture for the city that has the health of people and the planet at its heart. The City Council and the local NHS commissioned research to gather baseline information about all aspects of the food on Bristol plates. The resulting report contained a wealth of facts, figures and case studies relating to production, processing, distribution, catering, retail, community food growing and waste.[3] This led to the setting up of an Advisory Food Policy Council with the aim of driving change and plugging food considerations into all areas of planning the city's future. The Council is now drawing up plans to make Bristol a city where eating and celebrating healthy and sustainably produced food becomes something that everyone is proud to be part of, land for food production is safeguarded, urban food production and distribution increases and key infrastructure for local food supply and the diversity of food retailing is safeguarded. It is a means to help build a green economy with food at its heart and build a mutually supportive relationship between the city and its hinterland, where a significant – and potentially increasing – amount of the food eaten is grown. It enables the development of 'productive green infrastructure', where green spaces have multiple benefits and can function as 'green corridors' linking the city with its rural surroundings.

Liberal Democrats want to see every council adopting a food policy and use a food systems planning process to help deliver it. But it doesn't just have to be in cities. In Todmorden, a Pennines town, an amazing project to involve local people in shaping their own environment and developing social cohesion has taken root. Literally. The 'Incredible Edible Todmorden' project aims to make the town self-sufficient in food by 2018 and to do so by improving the town environment through community action. Starting off with growing in raised beds around the town, it now includes growing plots at community service buildings, surgeries, the fire station and the police station. Many of the beds are adopted by local groups who do much of the planting and maintenance, although some in the town centre are cared for by an organising group. In three years over a thousand fruit trees have been planted and people can just help themselves to the produce. Local eggs and honey have now joined the fruit and vegetables and there are plans to expand the local food range to include fish.[4] Local and national government should look to this experience and implement similar approaches wherever practical.

Enhancing the natural environment

While these initiatives play an important role in promoting biodiversity and enhancing the environment, there is much more that the planning system needs to do, not least because the natural environment is crucial to the long-term health of the economy, from the pollination of crops to the treatment of waste. The loss of habitats and species reduces our options for the future, and we wholly support the government's commitment in the Natural Environment White Paper for a national green accounting system that puts a value on environmental assets as much as on economic output and their creation of the Natural Capital Committee to advise government on the state of natural capital in England.

But we need to go further. Currently, the planning system relies too much on mitigating the damage that development may have on environmental resources. We need to move instead to a system of identifying sites where the environmental capacity is sufficient to absorb development without too much damage. The factors involved in assessing environmental capacity are complex, and there is an urgent need for a national research programme to set guidance on environmental limits and then to initiate the necessary research to provide information at a local level so that policies affecting the natural environment can take full account of their environmental impacts.

In the meantime, there are some significant improvements that should be made to protect habitats and biodiversity:

- Local authorities should be given a positive duty to protect local biodiversity.
- Previously developed brownfield sites that are usually prioritised for redevelopment sometimes have significant biodiversity value, not least because they have frequently been left undisturbed for years; such sites should be protected.
- The same level of protection currently given to Sites of Special Scientific Interest should be given to irreplaceable natural habitats that are currently unprotected, including remaining areas of ancient woodland and upland moorland.

Housing and land availability

Of course, in planning terms, protecting the environment is often seen as protecting the countryside, and perhaps the most controversial planning issue of all is how to provide the huge numbers of new houses needed while minimising intrusion into the countryside. The most popular way of achieving this is to build on brownfield sites, but this is not always possible, especially in areas of high demand where much of the brownfield land has already been used. So we do need other measures to minimise the take of greenfield land.

One approach has been to increase housing density, which has too often led to some poorly designed developments with little greenery or amenity space. But this need not be so; good design can produce attractive and popular developments with high densities. For example, the Greenleys development in Milton Keynes has a comparatively low density of 25 dwellings per hectare but is much less attractive and has lower property values than the nearby Wolverton development which has a density of 52 dwellings per hectare; the major difference is that accommodating the car was a priority in Greenleys while Wolverton has given priority to walking.

We need more research into ways of minimising the land devoted to the car within residential areas. Key objectives should be to minimise the total space devoted to roads and parking, putting higher density housing nearer areas of good public transport to cut the demand for car ownership, and incorporating, as far as possible, roads and parking spaces into the community living space through genuine shared space design and landscaping.

One major hurdle to maximising the sustainability of new housing is the near-monopoly in the control of development land in many areas. In 2008, 47 per cent of all homes were built by just seven house-builders, and the large building companies held strategic land banks equivalent to more than fourteen years of development. In 2011, the Campaign to Protect Rural England estimated that the biggest developers held land with planning permission for more than 280,000 housing units. And at the beginning of 2012 one major house-builder held a land bank sufficient for 63,000 new homes – yet it had built fewer than 10,000 homes in 2011.

Land is, of course, a finite resource that cannot be moved from place to place. So when most of the land identified for development in a particular area has been bought up by just one or two developers, this near-monopoly inhibits the competition that should help drive higher sustainability and design standards, and may slow delivery as house-builders seek to keep market prices high. This near-monopoly has contributed to the demise of many of the small construction companies that have traditionally been important to their local economies and are often more sensitive to the local vernacular. Some of these smaller developers are also the leaders in sustainability and innovative design.

The huge land holdings of the big developers have also inhibited self-build: a report by the National Self Build Association in 2008 found that the major obstacle to increasing the number of self-build homes was the availability of land.[5] This matters because self-builders have been shown to drive significant improvements in housing design and performance, as well as providing more variety than is the norm on so many British estates.

Opening up the housing land supply to more competition would contribute to speeding up development, enhance design and sustainability standards, and develop local economies. We therefore welcome the recent IPPR report, *We Must Fix It*, which calls for the diversification of the industry, in particular by bringing in new entrants.[6]

One IPPR proposal that we would like to see implemented is the registration of all land ownerships (including options to purchase) with the Land Registry; this would reveal where competition is being inhibited by land banks held by the major developers. Where this is the case, any land disposal by a public authority should seek to favour small local builders and new entrants, learning from the Public Land Initiative piloted by the Homes & Communities Agency in 2010 which resulted in successful bids from construction firms prepared to accept lower profits and fast build-out rates rather than the traditional vertically integrated house-builders, which profit as much from land trading as from actually building homes.

To encourage self-build, we propose that a fifth of all public residential development land disposals should be allocated for self-builders, that Local Development Frameworks should include a policy allocating a percentage of all larger sites for self-build, and, in areas of high growth, that larger areas of land should be allocated for self-build. While the servicing of self-build plots and their subsequent sale could be left to the site developers, such projects are well-suited to community land trusts or other community-based groups and these should be encouraged through the neighbourhood planning process.

We also propose that the government should commission an independent study into the way in which land becomes available for development and how this might be improved; this should be wider than the 2007 Office of Fair Trading study and include such issues as the constraints that the system places on design quality, sustainability and innovation. It should also examine whether the huge increase in land values that results from the granting of planning permission is fairly distributed between landowners, developers and the community and how the financial gains might better be used to create sustainable communities. We would expect this study to examine such proposals as the IPPR's suggestion that the government should act as a clearing house for the land banks of failing house-builders, and those put forward by Dr Tim Leunig (when chief economist at Centre Forum) for using community land auctions to drive down market land prices while enabling local authorities to separate land trading from house-building.

Design and sustainability

Increasing competition between house-builders should encourage higher design and sustainability standards. But, with housing representing nearly 25 per cent of all current UK climate change emissions, it is clear that the UK's existing housing stock must also be tackled, as well as ensuring far higher standards of environmental performance in new developments. Building regulations provide a welcome floor, but not an incentive to go further. Planning authorities should insist on higher standards wherever possible, not least because the lifetime savings on energy bills are likely to more than offset any increased building costs.

A good incentive to increase the environmental performance of buildings is that of insisting on 'consequential improvements'. This is where anyone requiring planning permission to change or extend a building should, as a condition, apply cost-effective energy efficiency measures to the existing property. This was introduced in 2006 by Liberal Democrats-controlled Uttlesford Council for homes where it was 'possible and practical'. Key barriers to people undertaking energy efficiency work is the hassle and management of contractors involved. There are therefore good reasons to encourage people to think about energy efficiency when they are already undertaking construction work.

We also want better integration of highway planning into the design of new developments. Too often highway planning takes place in a silo, with the highways authority involved only as a statutory consultee when an application is submitted rather than being involved at the design stage with the planners, architects and designers to create clutter-free, liveable spaces. Exhibition Road in Kensington shows what can be achieved when highway engineers are part of the design process. Safety is important but so too are liveable, pleasant spaces.

Another initiative to improve sustainable development would be ensuring informed impartial review of the design of significant applications, through the kind of Regional Design Panels set up under the now defunct *Commission for Architecture and the Built Environment*. Not only would these deliver the capacity to review design but they would also provide planning staff with the opportunity to find out about best practice elsewhere and develop the knowledge and skill base within local authorities while helping to make a reality of integrating design into delivering sustainable development.

The issue of water resource efficiency needs far more attention, given the impacts of climate change and a rising population. Given regional variations in water scarcity, different areas will have different sustainability priorities. So local authorities in, for example, the East and South-East of England should be free to push for stricter standards than prescribed by building and other regulations.

All new housing developments in areas of water stress should become 'water neutral', with increased water usage offset by efficiencies elsewhere. We support the introduction of compulsory smart metering in water-stressed areas by 2020 and strengthening planning guidance in favour of compulsory rainwater harvesting, grey water recycling, green roofs and sustainable urban drainage systems where appropriate. This could be complemented by fiscal incentives such as preferential VAT rates for rainwater harvesting systems, as has been introduced in France.

Large-scale developments

A major advantage of planning a large-scale development is that low- and zero-carbon solutions can be laid across the whole town if financing and other barriers can be overcome. This can be part of the attraction of garden cities – in addition to the benefits of having places that are, as David Cameron has said, 'Green, planned, secure, with gardens, places to play and characterful houses, not just car-dominated concrete grids'.[7] The principles governing garden cities – that of stronger community engagement and ownership, long-term private sector commitment and visionary design – are applicable to different models of large-scale growth, from the free-standing to clusters of linked new towns and sustainable urban extensions.

But there are significant barriers to creating large-scale sustainable new communities based on garden city principles. The Town & Country Planning Association, in its recent report *Creating Garden Cities and Suburbs Today*, highlights the need for serious and sustained political commitment to deliver such schemes.[8] It identifies the potential of using surplus previously developed public land as a way of partly overcoming the issue of unlocking land for sustainable development, and has suggested that the Green Investment Bank could be used to provide low-cost, long-term loans to boost the sustainability of major housing developments and through local-authority-led partnership approaches.

Planning and business

While house-building and construction in general is important to the economy, the planning system is often seen as an obstacle to economic growth and being anti-business. A survey of 5,300 businesses carried out by the British Chambers of Commerce early in 2012 showed a general lack of confidence in the planning system, describing it as 'Beset by cost, complexity and inconsistency'.[9] One key improvement would be the universal availability of non-binding advice from planning authorities prior to the submission of a formal planning application, in order to clarify policy issues with which businesses, especially small businesses, are unlikely to be familiar; this is especially necessary for environmental protection policies. Providing such help ought to both improve the quality of applications and speed up decision-making by avoiding refusals on grounds that could have been averted.

Sensible compromises should be sought even where businesses and environmentalists usually take immutable stances, such as the interpretation of the Habitats Directive. One example is the blanket 1,500-metre buffer zone placed around Special Protection Areas (SPAs) to safeguard nesting stone curlews, preventing any development even where existing buildings and activities are present. In Norfolk, Natural England, the RSPB and local landowners have agreed a draft policy that would allow some development for existing businesses within the SPA, providing that measures are put in place to minimise disturbance to the birds – a compromise that goes some way to meet rural development needs while still protecting the birds.

But it would be wrong to see the planning system simply as a way of moderating economic development to protect the environment. Good planning contributes in many ways to the long-term health of businesses and the economy.

It does this both directly and indirectly. For example, setting high standards to ensure that new buildings use energy, water and other resources efficiently reduces business costs and usually provides a net financial gain for those occupying the building. This is especially important when those submitting planning applications are not those who will finally occupy it, as they have little incentive to invest the extra money to make the long-term savings.

At a wider level, good planning can encourage the development of communities with the high-quality environments demanded by the professional, skilled, creative and usually highly mobile staff so essential to growing businesses. And there are numerous studies demonstrating that the provision of high-quality open spaces within communities has significant physical and mental health benefits which, of course, have obvious benefits for employers.

Planning also has a key role in protecting the cultural, historic and landscape value that is so vital to tourism, an industry that already generates £97 billion each year and employs more than 2 million people in England, not far off the number employed in manufacturing.

Finally, in enforcing high sustainability standards, planning can enhance the demand for some of the green products that are so crucial to the growth of the economy.

We recognise the frustration felt by some green industries confronted with constant planning refusals on grounds that they consider to be dubious; King's Lynn & West Norfolk Borough Council has never approved an application for a wind turbine despite neighbouring authorities giving approvals for comparable sites with no resulting problems. Clearly, wind turbines should not be given permission in areas of outstanding landscape attractiveness, but they are a significant part of the mix of non-fossil fuel energy sources that the UK needs. We suggest that a system of financial incentives similar to that being provided by the government for new housing should be mandated for new wind farms to be paid by the developers to the individual households and communities directly affected, possibly through reduced energy bills.

Land values

Whether the new fiscal initiatives – the New Homes Bonus and Community Infrastructure Levy – will result in more development in areas of the country where more homes are required remains to be seen. For us what is key is ensuring that the capital gains from changes in land use are spread fairly, meet the identified needs of communities and provide for the ongoing upkeep costs of any infrastructure provided.

Land value taxation (LVT), which raises public revenue through an annual charge on the rental value of land, an idea long espoused by Liberal Democrats, could play a key role in capturing the increase in land values created by the community agreeing to allow its development. LVT would discourage speculative landholdings and encourage the redevelopment of brownfield sites and the efficient use of land, thus minimising the demand for greenfield development.

Until LVT is introduced, we should implement a Greenfield Development Levy to encourage the development of brownfield land and to pay for local infrastructure as a way of compensating communities for the loss of amenity.

There are two other fiscal measures that we believe are important. First, the Community Infrastructure Levy must be used to ensure the long-term maintenance of any new public facilities as well as providing new infrastructure. This would help overcome the lack of resources that is allowing too many public open spaces and other facilities to suffer from neglect. Second, VAT on new build and renovations should be equalised on a revenue neutral basis to remove the current disincentive to repair existing properties.

The proposals that we have outlined in this chapter will make the planning system more responsive to the needs of local communities and ensure that our countryside and towns and cities provide the economic, social and environmental setting necessary to provide people with a high-quality and sustainable quality of life.

Our proposals are based on the belief that investment in well-designed and sustainable developments will, over their lifetime, more than pay for any higher capital costs, as well as providing quality environments in which people can live, work and enjoy themselves. We believe that localism not only means giving communities greater control over what happens to them but also giving them more opportunities to maximise the benefits from the land around them.

Climate change, failing biodiversity, inadequate housing, environmental degradation and poor economic performance are enormously challenging. They can only be tackled by positive planning guided by a vision of what kind of future we want, a vision that must be long-term but must also be bought into by local communities.

Notes

1   See http://www:chichestercdt.org.uk

2   Study carried out by Richard Mitchell of Glasgow University and Frank Popper of the University of St Andrews, published in *The Lancet*, 7 November 2008.

3   See www.bristol.gov.uk/whofeedsbristol

4   For more information on this community-led project, which is re-engaging people with food and building community cohesion, see www.incredible-edible-todmorden.co.uk

5   National Self-Build Association, *Self Build as a Volume Housebuilding Solution* (October 2008).

6   Matt Griffith, *We Must Fix It* (IPPR, 2011).

7   Speech at the Institution of Civil Engineers, 19 March 2012.

8   Town and Country Planning Association, *Creating Garden Cities and Suburbs Today* (TCPA, May 2012).

9   See http://www.britishchambers.org.uk/press-office/press-releases/bcc-no-going-back-on-radical-planning-reform.html#.ULJfhIYlfUY

Chapter 25

How to Save Our Cities from Economic Collapse

David Boyle

When the first Liberal mayor of Birmingham, Joseph Chamberlain, addressed councillors in the 1870s, he told them to 'be more expensive'. This is not, of course, the kind of language you expect from local politicians these days, but in fact I suspect the meaning has changed. What Chamberlain meant was 'more ambitious'. Ambition was the cornerstone of his work in Birmingham, which his colleague Jesse Collings described as the business of having it 'parked, paved, assized, marketed, gas & watered and improved'.

At the end of 1873, Chamberlain had seized control of a city that was in a desperate state. The problem was not just extreme poverty as the premier city of the Industrial Revolution had burgeoned in size. It was environmental. The poisoned rivers, and dodgy, very occasional, water supplies were well known.

He and his Liberal colleagues took control of the city from a group of independent councillors who met regularly in a pub called 'The Woodman' and who prided themselves on their ability to avoid spending any money. They called themselves the 'Economists'. There has always been a very English strand of pragmatic economics which believed it was all about avoiding spending; that isn't the Liberal way.

I start with Chamberlain because he is in some ways a very modern hero. He revived Britain's second city, paved it, lit its streets, and infused it with enormous pride, and he built parks and galleries and concert halls. But the key point was that he did it using the assets at his disposal – the foul water, the money flowing through, the local people. He did not wait for central government grants or plead for corporate sponsorship. He used the assets he had.

That is important because in the new economic dispensation – a combination of dwindling resources and climate change – that is exactly what we are going to have to do ourselves.

A century of cheap energy has driven the shape of our cities. They are dependent on cars but they are also extremely dependent on imports. Development in most parts of the world has concentrated on transport infrastructure which has, among other effects, deepened this dependence. It has also encouraged cities to specialise, based on the economic doctrine of comparative advantage – an option that is simply not open to many, if not most, places in the world.

Since the 1920s, and the introduction of refrigeration, cities have become used to having their fresh milk and other food trucked in during the night, and the farms that used to be such a feature of city life until then have gone. We have also lived through a generation where environmentalists and architects have teamed up to call for denser cities on the grounds that they use less energy. It isn't so: dense cities are specialised cities where people live – sustainable cities will have to be spread out enough to produce their own food, deal with their own waste, make their own things. They need to be spread out enough to be green.

But the main reason why the shape of cities is going to have to change – economically as well as topographically – is the rising cost of energy. The Stern Report finally brought the business of global warming into the remit of old-style economists.[1] As we reach the peak of oil production, we can almost certainly expect major hikes in the price of oil, combined with enormous and unpredictable dips. This will turn all the assumptions of recent generations about the economics of local production on their heads.

We have developed many of our institutions in a period where energy was so cheap that it was worthwhile to truck a consignment of beans grown and picked in the Netherlands down to Italy – or further afield – just for packaging, and then send it all the way back again. Our just-in-time distribution systems depend on cheap energy. If energy becomes expensive, none of that works any more. We need to find not just decentralised sources of energy, which no longer waste a third in transmission, but decentralised food production systems too – and those are likely to include very small family production as well, which will increase access to land for the poorest.

The question is no longer whether aspects of this massive localisation is going to happen, but – if energy becomes expensive – *when* it will happen. That puts cities in the frontline of change. The problem is that some of them are not very well equipped to deal with it. Because local government has been so constrained over the past two generations by two generally accepted truths that were both completely wrong: one, that the economic levers have until recently all been in Whitehall; and two, that all they can do is to beg for government handouts or major corporate investment.

The first is wholly illiberal. In fact, there's really no point in decentralising political power to cities and communities if they remain supplicants to Tesco or Barclays. The second is unfortunately still the mindset of some parts of local government. Of course, outside investment is important, but cities will need to look increasingly to their own resources to feel their way into the new world. The coalition's Localism Act is an important first step, but how do they use it? What will sustainable economies look like in green cities?

The following are three propositions that I believe will need to guide cities and towns in the future, and they are all based on Joseph Chamberlain's approach of using what you have got.

It isn't how much money you have going into an area that counts, it's how you use it

This is one of the key insights of what I call the new economics.[2] It means that there might be places with the same amount of money coming in, but in one of them it gets spent in the supermarket and then it leaves the area straight away. But in another place, the income gets passed on from local business to local business, over and over again, like blood. It is the same money, but every time it changes hands, it creates local wealth. It is not the total amount of money that is important here. It is the diversity of business, and maybe even the diversity of people that matters – because they can keep money circulating.

Ten years ago, my colleagues in the New Economics Foundation were struggling to find a language to describe this idea so that anyone could understand it. We borrowed the idea of a leaky bucket to explain the way local economies worked.[3] The problem is that the bucket never stays full, but it can be made to leak less. We came up with a formula for estimating where local money gets spent, tracking it through three exchanges, and seeing how much of it stays put. We called it LM3 (Local Money 3), and you can use it online (lm3online.org). It is supposed to be a way in which cities can weigh up different investment options – or measure how healthy their local economy is, or businesses, or charities too. We found that spending £5 in a supermarket chain was about half as useful to the local economy as buying vegetables from a local farm.

The implications of this are pretty far-reaching. If you have a high street where all the stores are owned by big chains, you may be more vulnerable economically than a high street where there are many interdependent businesses trading with each other – though this might not be nearly as wealthy. One will survive an economic downturn; one may well not.

This is critical also to the way in which cities and towns spend their money, and who they commission to run local services. A small shift in the local government procurement spend that goes to local businesses and gets re-circulated locally by them can make a huge difference to the local economy.[4] It means that they can develop in the way that cities have always done historically, which is by finding ways to replace some key imports with local production. It also means there is less trucking around of resources, and it means that local resources – and local waste – can be used more efficiently. And it means that local money goes to local energy production, and local jobs, rather than to distant centralised utilities.

Of course, I am not arguing that it makes no difference at all how much money is coming in. It does. But it also matters very much where that money is going and how it is used. It therefore matters what size procurement contracts are (big contracts may have to go out of the area). It also matters that councils learn the difference between a fake anchor store which hoovers up local spending and corrodes the businesses around it and a real one which genuinely supports the surrounding local economy. It matters that they know how and where local money circulates.

Before William Harvey announced, in 1616, his theory about how blood works, most people thought it was made in the liver and the heart and swallowed up by the other organs. Harvey showed that it was the *circulation* of the blood that really mattered. If nothing circulates, the patient dies. It is the same with local economies. If the money goes round, the place lives. If it doesn't, it dies.

One city which has been running with this idea is Cleveland, Ohio, the US city most hit by the sub-prime mortgage crisis. There are two major economic players still active there: the university and the hospital. To put the hospital to better economic use, they have borrowed an idea from one of the great success stories of co-operative business, in Mondragon in Spain. The Mondragon story dates back to just after the Second World War, when the local Catholic priest founded the first worker's co-op to employ local people and meet local needs. Half a century on, there are now 256 linked co-operative businesses, employing nearly 100,000 people and with offshoots worldwide, and they have been doing even better during the global downturn – so much so that the US steelworkers union has signed a long-term agreement to do something similar in North America.

Now the Evergreen Project is doing this in Cleveland, but clustered around and dependent on the hospital, starting with a sustainable laundry business.[5] The second project is a renewable energy company, starting with installations on the hospital roof. So there are two elements to this innovation: new co-operatives that employ local people, and give them a real stake in their success, but which are also redirecting the spending power of the local hospital to launch them and underpin them.

The hospital has to agree that these contracts represent the best value to them, but of course hospitals have an interest in a thriving local economy, because it reduces acute demand.

Not all economic resources are monetary

The money already flowing through a local economy is not something that has exercised local authorities until recently. Nor has it exercised the Treasury, but it is an asset that can be used to rebuild thriving economies. So is wasted land, or wasted buildings. So too is the distinctiveness of the local area, because people want to live and invest in places they think are real. So is wasted furniture or reject white goods or other kinds of rubbish which might actually be turned into raw materials. So is compost and old food or old furniture, which can be used for training. And putting these wasted resources to better use is more sustainable.

The doctrine of comparative advantage suggests that cities must specialise. It makes sense to be aware of what you are best at for any town or city but, throughout history, cities have grown and developed by replacing their imports, by plugging those money leaks and by keeping the money circulating locally. That means they have to treat their diverse populations as assets, rather than as deadweight claimants on services – as brilliant, imaginative, determined people who can make things happen.

When my New Economics Foundation colleagues start work somewhere new, they don't say: 'what needs fixing here?' or 'what's the problem here?' They ask whether anyone has any ideas or dreams they want to achieve. If they do, they get linked up, not with the usual ubiquitous training programme to tell them how to write business plans – Labour's contribution to entrepreneurship – but with a coach. To be precise, an enterprise coach.

We called this approach, pioneered with the Civic Trust, BizFizz.[6] The coaches work with local people and ideas and do whatever is necessary to make them happen. If that means helping get childcare so that their client can go to the bank, that is what they do. They are backed up by a panel of local business people, bank managers and other local volunteers, who meet once a month and give the new enterprises advice. These panels behave like successful networks do in successful places. They explain that they have a cousin with a lock-up garage, or offer to put in a word with the local bank. They are absolutely critical resources – just like the empty garage is – and they are not monetary at all, like the wasteland that could grow things or the empty council office that could house start-ups, or the rubbish that is actually a resource for some other kind of business.

My favourite story about local assets is about the Marsh Farm estate on the edge of Luton. Marsh Farm was a symbol of a place where the money barely circulates. It comes in by benefits cheque and then goes straight out again. But they did one of our LM3 surveys and they found that, between all the households, they were spending a million pounds of their money every year on fast food outside the estate. That is a million pounds leaking out of the bucket.

So they started a new business, employing local people, to provide healthy fast food. Then they leased some unused fields next door from the council and grew some of the ingredients. And so it goes on. That is sustainability in practice: it means that local resources are used better, less has to be trucked in, and the local economy benefits too.

My colleagues have been doing similar things with immigrant groups outside Tel Aviv, in shanty towns in Honduras and Lima, and outside Durban in South Africa. What is fascinating is that we are often told by local development agencies that there is no entrepreneurial flair locally. Yet, in Durban, 174 people showed up at our event, and put forward 100 business ideas, and 82 were then supported by the business coach.

If we are honest, there has been a similar problem here. Whitehall has never really believed that our cities were enterprising places, so they have ignored this resource. Cities that waited as supplicants to Whitehall ignored these resources too. But the new low-energy cities will have to look to local resources that much more, and we can ignore them no longer.

Innovative local institutions matter

Why do regeneration agencies traditionally believe there are fewer entrepreneurs in economically disadvantaged communities? That has never been clear. Our experience has been that, despite what people say, there is rarely any shortage of people with ideas. But there *is* a shortage of confidence and a shortage of effective social networks. Most of all, there has been a shortage of local institutions, and the UK has been poor at borrowing the ideas for these local institutions from other countries.

Community-supported agriculture is a way of providing finance for small-scale local food, but it has been very slow to take off in the UK.[7] Small business currencies, or credit circle factoring, are both supported by the European Commission in Latin America, but there is almost nothing like them here.[8] Partnership banking, and other kinds of public sector banking

– like the Bank of North Dakota (see below) – are all emerging in the US, but there is little that is similar here.[9]

Most of all, productive and sustainable local economies require credit. The bad news is that the debate about the future of banking has got stuck in this country, as politicians try to find new ways to force the banks to lend to small business. Most bankers will agree privately that the problem is not that they are reluctant to lend to small business, but that they are no longer set up to lend effectively in that sector. Their systems don't allow it. They allow no useful local knowledge.

That means that the real issue is how we get that local lending infrastructure we need – and, once again, the issue is not really about new money. There is a great deal of money, some of it in local authority bank accounts which is currently invested in London or in the next asset bubble. What we lack is the local institutions capable of lending it profitably and investing it locally.

Here, Britain is different from other European countries. We all have our highly centralised banking oligopolies, focused on global speculative finance, but they have an effective, stable, community-based banking sector as well. We don't and we badly need one, especially if the sustainable new economy is to thrive here.[10] New businesses require finance to start with.

It may be that this urgent lending infrastructure can be created under US-style community reinvestment legislation. That means that the big banks will create the infrastructure to lend where they are unable to. It may be that this can be done voluntarily by the banks in order to end the damaging debate about whether they are lending to small business. But equally, the new banking sector could be set up by local authorities themselves as a place to keep some of their money, and to invest it locally – using local knowledge that the big banks don't have.

One model might be the Bank of North Dakota, set up by the state of North Dakota in 1919, the same year in which Neville Chamberlain launched the Birmingham Municipal Savings Bank. It is profit-making, and has contributed over US$300m in dividends to the state's coffers over the past decade. It works by partnering local banks to provide the loan finance for small business lending on specific deals. Their lending portfolio is mainly these participation loans, which allow local banks to lend more.

There have been no local bank failures since 2008 in North Dakota, and no bank in the state has more than 10 per cent of local deposits. The existence of a powerful 'partnership bank' has underpinned a diverse banking system there. In 2011 Oregon, Washington and Massachusetts introduced bills in their state legislatures to launch their own state banks. Maryland has followed suit since. Illinois, Hawaii and Virginia are already looking into the idea.

The point is that sustainable cities do not emerge by themselves, or just by cutting back the public sector. They require institutions that can put people and money together, either from business partners or from potential customers. Institutions are vital. If we want to use waste as raw materials, or drive the take-up of household energy saving and energy generation, it requires business to do it – and that requires credit, and we have allowed our credit institutions to atrophy or become too regional, or uselessly virtual. These trends will have to be reversed.

~

These are three propositions for the future. The key point is that we have to produce locally again if we are going to prevent places sliding into hopeless dependence. We also have to produce locally if we are to avoid the cost and the damage of increasing transport emissions. That means we have to use the resources we have got more effectively. Sustainable economies are much more local than they are now; they use resources more effectively and require less infrastructure.

But this is, in some ways, not such a revolutionary idea. Cities have always dragged themselves into viability by local production, whatever policy-makers tell you. They do so not by specialisation but by import replacement. They do so by recognising the assets they already have and putting them to work.

But there are important lessons here. The new economics is still feeling its way towards many of the answers, but it asks challenging questions of the status quo – the ruling elites with their creaking economic ideas – and those questions imply something about where the answers might lie. People are poor because the assets they need have been taken from them, or simply devalued, leaving them impoverished. It implies that if we can recognise those assets, measure them and put them to use, we might begin to make real, unambiguous progress.

If the legal and organisational economic institutions of the world are weighted in favour of the rich, then we need to reform and reorganise those institutions, whether they are international or local. Out of these questions, new directions and concepts begin to emerge – together with a whole raft of new, more difficult questions. How do we provide resources for welfare in a low-growth economy? How do we sell the new economics to those whose privileges will be undermined?

Many of the original campaigning demands of the new green economics, as set out in the 1980s, are also now mainstream. Green taxation is limited but is on the political agenda all over the world. The ideas behind environmental and social auditing of companies are widely accepted, and many companies produce reports even though their variable quality merely highlights the limits of voluntary approaches to corporate responsibility. Around £10 billion is invested ethically in the UK alone.[11] New ways of measuring that reveal the true environmental and social success or failure of the economy are starting to push older, cruder measures aside. There are anything up to 9,000 complementary currencies (parallel currencies denominated in values other the national currency) in the world.[12]

For the time being, the issues that have caused so many problems over the past half-century or so remain as powerful as ever. We still have the combination of implacable centralisation and an industrial policy gauged to suit the City of London – that is, low-to-zero regulation, massive political support, bailouts for failures. That is what has distorted the economy, undermined proper investment in sustainable transport infrastructure, and left us with the weak institutions that are unable to row against the tide that draws investment and people to London.

The horns of the dilemma we are now caught on is that central government thinks of economics as their remit, but they do not have the levers that can make a difference locally. Local government has some of the levers available but still believes, in some places, that they are dependent on the centre to shift their economic fortunes. What I have argued here is that, just as our cities have the power to bring their energy and imagination to bear on the problems of sustainable economics, we also increasingly understand what has to be done.

So here is my ten-step programme for the cities.[13]

Plug the leaks that are draining local money away: that means setting up sustainable businesses and social enterprises that can use local resources to replace some of the leaks in the local economy.

Local diversity and distinctiveness: places that feel authentic attract money and people.

Bust local monopolies to let enterprise flourish: when all the groceries are provided locally by one supermarket chain, or when the only available contractors for local waste contracts are the handful of national giants, then it will undermine the energy of the emerging sustainable local economies.

Enterprise coaching, support and advice in every neighbourhood: along the lines pioneered by BizFizz, to create new locally-owned businesses.

Build an effective new local lending infrastructure: we need local banks for the new sustainable businesses we need.

Invest in local energy and local food: these are two areas where local economies can replace scarce imports.

Use waste products as raw material for new enterprises: sustainable local economies are increasingly circular, but again that needs new social enterprises to make it happen.

Use public sector spending to maximise local money flows: in impoverished areas, it makes sense for local procurement to encourage local business, and green business in particular.

Experiment with new kinds of money to provide credit, like the new currencies of Latin America which are designed to tackle local poverty and provide credit to small business.

New credit creation for local public benefit: it is time to experiment with new ways of creating national currency that can provide a stream of quantitative easing, created by the central bank, not the commercial banks, which can provide the capital to underpin a Green New Deal that can build the new local energy infrastructure we need.

This last one is, in some ways, the odd one out because it requires central government to lead. I don't mean through mechanisms such as quantitative easing, which just drives money to the big banks and stays there. But it is becoming clear that relying on credit creation by banks – which are mainly geared up to produce the next mortgage bubble – to provide society with the means of exchange they need to make their economies work is not enough. We need a more effective and reliable way of creating money. We need publicly created money to grow the green, productive economy, and get people back to work.

That means that the Bank of England should exercise its power to create money to provide the loan finance for the new local lending or green infrastructure without wasteful payments to financial intermediaries. This should then be repaid, free of interest, when the task is complete, and then withdrawn from circulation.

~

So there we are: a ten-step programme for green cities. It is true that not all of these ideas can be organised tomorrow, at least without central government support. Getting the banks to fund a new community banking infrastructure – capable of supporting the small business market, as they do in the US

– depends on some co-operation between the banks. But most can be done by imaginative and forward-looking city leaders, and can be done immediately with the new powers under the Localism Act.

Most of these ideas have been put into practice somewhere already. What has not yet happened is for enlightened local government to knit all these approaches together and claw their way out of recession by doing so, and set their cities further along the path to sustainability. That is the challenge. This is a potential revival of the idea that cities can claw back some measure of self-determination and vision, not because someone can be persuaded to give them the money – but because they have the assets they need already. Because these are ordinary renewable assets, this agenda is about sustainability in its broadest sense.

Notes

1   Nicholas Stern, *The Economics of Climate Change* (HM Treasury, 2006).

2   See for example, David Boyle and Andrew Simms, *The New Economics: A Bigger Picture* (Earthscan, 2009).

3   Justin Saxchs et al., *The Money Trail* (New Economics Foundation, 2004).

4   See, for example, Matthew Jackson, *The Power of Procurement* (Centre for Local Economic Strategies, 2010).

5   See Gar Alperovitz et al., 'Cleveland's worker-owned boom' (*Yes!* Magazine, June 2009); http://www.yesmagazine.org/issues/the-new-economy/clevelands-worker-owned-boom

6   See Paul Squires et al., *Who's the Entrepreneur?* (New Economics Foundation, 2007).

7   See Steven McFadden, *The Call of the Land: An Agrarian Primer for the 21st Century*, NorLights Press, 2009).

8   See www.socialtrade.org

9   Jason Judd and Heather McGhee, *Banking on America* (Demos, 2011).

10 See David Boyle, *A Local Banking System: The urgent need to reinvigorate UK high street banking* (New Economics Foundation, 2011).

11 See www.eiris.org

12 Peter North, *Money and Liberation* (University of Minnesota Press, 2007).

13 See David Boyle, *Ten Steps to Save the Cities* (New Economics Foundation, 2011).

Chapter 26

Power to the People? The Case for Community-Owned Renewable Energy

Steve Bradley

If American psychologist Abraham Maslow was developing his famous hierarchy of needs today, he would surely consider adding 'energy' to his list of basic human requirements. Mankind has created societies whose orderly functioning is increasingly reliant upon technology, appliances and vehicles which all require some form of energy. It is difficult to comprehend how ill-prepared we would be for a prolonged and widespread outage of power or fuel, and the social and political consequences which that would trigger. Yet that is the 'do nothing' scenario predicted to be only a decade away if we fail to address the looming capacity problem in the UK's energy generating infrastructure.

Uniquely among the three main parties in Britain, the Liberal Democrat approach to politics is generally to strive for *local* solutions to problems – underpinned by a belief that issues are best addressed with reference to the communities and circumstances within which they manifest. So how can we address the large-scale national energy problem the UK faces without losing sight of our localist and liberal principles?

This chapter considers the challenge of moving towards zero-carbon energy provision in terms of its interface with principles of community, democracy and liberalism. It outlines the overall challenges and opportunities in our shift towards low-carbon energy, analyses and critiques the government's current approach, and signposts a number of ways in which liberal principles could direct future energy policy to ensure that it is not only technically appropriate but also supports the provision of community-owned renewable energy (CORE) infrastructure.

What is wrong with our current energy system?

The UK's energy system faces a number of fundamental and well-documented challenges, at the root of which lurks an impending capacity shortage. Almost a third of the nation's electricity comes from coal-fired power stations – infrastructure that is highly polluting and nearing the end of its lifespan. To keep the lights on while meeting carbon reduction commitments, these facilities need to be decommissioned within the next decade and their output shifted to less polluting infrastructure. Failure to ensure a seamless shift risks not just power cuts, but also serious economic, social and political consequences.

The replacement of our most polluting and outdated power plants would ordinarily be championed as a real opportunity to meet our carbon reduction targets. But the challenge of what form those replacements should take – or more precisely, what fuel source they should use – is the source of much controversy and debate.

When faced with a complex decision in government, one's political principles ideally offer a helpful compass with which to navigate the maze. For Liberal Democrats, that means asserting that individuals and communities should have the maximum freedom to decide and pursue their own priorities as best they can, while demanding an acceptance of individual responsibility and a sense of duty towards one's fellow citizens and community in return. It views the state's role as one primarily of enabling and informing, rather than controlling and directing, with its fundamental duty being to help create 'agency': the capacity for individuals and communities to make *meaningful* decisions about their circumstances and to influence the world around them.

But for proponents of liberalism and the quest for agency, our principles merely highlight a further problem with the UK's energy system. Viewed through the prism of individual and community agency, our energy system is the antithesis of liberal. It is anti-competitive, unaccountable, undemocratic and, by virtue of energy's necessity to modern existence, it greatly erodes the ability of individuals and communities to influence meaningfully their circumstances. In short, it is illiberal.

The uncompetitive nature of the UK's energy market is due to its domination by a de facto cartel of six huge mainly foreign-owned companies. Normal economic rules dictate that the presence of large financial returns should act as a stimulant for new providers to enter a market. With our energy system structured so heavily around large-scale centralised production, however, it has become a natural oligopoly which stifles genuine competition. Centralised energy production is the norm in the UK, and the cost of establishing a gas-fired or nuclear power plant is so huge that we can realistically expect no large-scale new entrants while it remains so.

The energy market lacks democracy and accountability because, as with all economic oligarchies, the UK's 'Big Six' operate in splendid isolation.

Occasionally they feign responsiveness to ward off the slim chance of significant government intervention in their cosy consensus. But despite the central role that energy plays in our modern society, they remain largely unaccountable to the society they serve simply because they can. After all, who else could we turn to for our heat and light?

In addition to these philosophical flaws with our centralised energy system, it is also unsatisfactory from an efficiency perspective. Few people want to live near a large power station, so we generate our electricity in huge quantities far away from where the output is most needed. That leads to two fundamental inefficiencies. Firstly, the production of electricity by gas, coal or nuclear power generates a large amount of heat as a by-product. Isolated power stations have few domestic or commercial neighbours to take advantage of this, so it disappears up the chimney as waste. While the latest gas power stations can achieve efficiencies of up to 60 per cent, in practice our power stations (and particularly the older ones) have efficiency levels nearer 40 per cent. That means that they convert less than half of all the energy they consume into electricity, with the rest being dumped as waste heat. And there is little thirst within the power sector to address this. A recent informal consultation with the Big Six energy companies by the Department for Energy and Climate Change showed that most were opposed to any suggestion that power generation should be made more efficient through the mandatory recycling of waste heat for buildings.

The second problem arises when this centrally produced electricity is transmitted to where it is needed. Transmitting electricity over long distances results in about 7 per cent of that power being lost naturally along the way. So we produce electricity centrally in vast quantities in isolated locations, waste half of it in the generation process, and then lose a further 7 per cent of what is left in transmission – all before it gets to the people it was created for in the first place.

Finally, centralised energy production is increasingly out of tune with a world where energy security is a growing issue. The political stability of the countries which supply our gas cannot be guaranteed. And our energy infrastructure (particularly nuclear) would be an obvious target for ideologically motivated terrorists. Dispersed energy generation would greatly reduce both these threats while also providing localised control over an essential commodity.

What is the alternative?

Combining the liberal principles of localism, agency and genuine competition with an acceptance that centralised energy generation is inherently unfit for purpose can only lead to one conclusion. We need to enable, as far as possible, the production and supply of our energy requirements to be taken back to the communities and the people for whom it is being created in the first place. We need a new era of localised community energy.

This suggestion is neither as novel nor as revolutionary as it may at first sound. As is outlined elsewhere in this book, community energy schemes have been a mainstream reality across a host of European countries for decades now.

What currently happens in the UK?

In recent years the UK has introduced a feed-in tariff programme for small-scale renewable energy. While this has led to a boost in renewable energy installations, it has been a rather different experience elsewhere. For example, the German FiT system operates on an open-ended budget, with consumers picking up the costs via their energy bills. The UK model, on the other hand, had a government-managed budget with a ceiling which was quickly exceeded. This led to a sudden and drastic adjustment in the level of FiTs on offer, which created huge uncertainty in this new and growing sector. And when a reduction in the FiT available for larger-scale solar installations was introduced, no attempt was made to differentiate between community groups and commercial operations. So while the German model provided a major stimulant for communities and individuals to invest in renewable energy, the UK FiTs approach has reduced the role of communities to a marginal one and limited the scale of involvement for individuals. We have missed an opportunity.

The UK has isolated pockets of district heating springing up, with local authorities like Woking and Birmingham providing a real leadership role. District heating involves a level of scale and complexity which demands the involvement of bodies like councils, who are certainly more democratic than large utilities and private developers. But if our underlying liberal desire is the quest for empowerment and 'agency' via a fully democratised energy system, we need to create an environment which encourages and enables communities and citizens to play a leading role in the creation and distribution of the energy that underpins their lives. Examples of how this has been achieved are given elsewhere in this book.

Encouraging community energy

If one accepts that our current centralised energy system is inefficient, unaccountable, undemocratic and illiberal, and that the development of community-owned renewable energy infrastructure could help tackle these ills while creating agency, then what is required to encourage that change? Different renewable energy sources present different challenges, necessitating a range of responses. As onshore wind is one of the more efficient and most controversial technologies accessible to communities, it offers a useful starting point.

Regardless of one's view on the merits or aesthetics of wind turbines, they undoubtedly have a significant visual impact upon areas in which they are located. It is therefore absolutely right that the surrounding community should receive direct benefits to acknowledge that fact. Yet the case for renewable energy in the UK has been undermined to date by a failure to ensure that those forced to live next to such infrastructure share directly in its benefits. In Germany one fifth of all electricity is generated renewably, with over 65 per cent of installed turbines and solar panels owned by individuals, land-owners or local communities. This high level of community and citizen ownership has had a transformational effect, as resistance eases greatly when it is 'our turbine' being proposed. Conversely, with less than 10 per cent of the UK's renewable energy infrastructure currently in local hands, resistance to specific wind farm proposals is often high, despite research indicating majority support for wind power nationally. The lesson is clear: by ensuring that host communities share substantially in the economic benefits of renewable infrastructure, the relationship between people and energy can be fundamentally changed from one of resentful consumption and opposition to one of empowered and involved self-provision. And with plans significantly to increase wind's contribution to the UK's total energy needs over the next decade, something must be done to address the opposition that it can often attract.

What is therefore required is a sufficiently motivating package of benefits from renewable energy projects which will make individuals and communities more accepting of them, if not actively supportive. And to create agency, such benefits should constitute more than just a minor and passive profit share. Communities should be positively enabled and encouraged to take a direct financial interest (to a suitable scale) in part of any renewable infrastructure located within their neighbourhood. This is particularly important in the case of wind, as the areas of the country with the strongest and most reliable wind source often tend to be isolated, relatively impoverished and limited in both population and economic opportunity. Localised energy offers a liberal route to empower such communities to reinvigorate themselves.

A significant legal barrier facing CORE projects is that they are currently unable to secure a license to sell the electricity they generate directly. Instead they are forced to sell it to the major utility companies at a significant discount on retail price (e.g. 4.5p p/kWh in the case of solar PV), who then in turn sell it to consumers at the significantly higher market price of 10–14p /kWh. This is an anti-competitive situation which further entrenches the power of large energy companies and prevents communities from providing lower cost energy to their own residents. Suggestions to abolish the mandatory obligation which forces utility companies to buy from micro-generators introduces the real risk that the Big Six will at best reduce the price they are prepared to pay micro-generators or at worst opt to kill off the small energy sector simply by refusing to buy from it.

We need to enable and encourage communities to participate in energy generation and supply consumers directly themselves, or provide an assurance that they can continue to sell to utilities at a fair price instead. In this way we would encourage localised mini-energy utilities to spring up, addressing fuel poverty and applying downward price pressure within the marketplace, along with new and innovative energy supply companies buying their electricity wholesale from a range of community producers before selling it on to consumers – all of which would help to tumble the huge barriers to entry which stifle innovation and competition in our current energy system.

Key government measures
As the above examples highlight, there are barriers which currently prevent CORE from reaching its full potential, or which fail to address the confrontational relationship that has developed towards certain infrastructure. There are six fundamental changes which government could implement which would help to address this situation overall.

First, the efficiency of renewable technology is advancing at a tremendous rate while the costs of the infrastructure (particularly solar PV) continue to plummet. This will escalate as demand for renewables increases, continually pushing the generation cost downwards. Meanwhile, the price of electricity from non-renewable sources is rising continuously, with the two likely to intersect at some point as they travel in opposite directions. To both expedite and reflect this dynamic, a new uncapped tapered FiTs arrangement should be introduced. At the point at which the cost of energy from a specific renewable source equals that from non-renewables, its FiT (and thereby its cost to consumers, going forward) should be zero. As in Germany, this change would maximise investor confidence and lead to a boom in individual and community involvement in renewable energy, while also ensuring better and more transparent control of the subsidies.

So while there would be a cost borne by consumer bills in the short- to medium-term by removing the current cap on the total levy, the boost it would give to the sector would bring nearer the point at which the cost per unit of electricity generated by renewables would be lower than that of fossil fuels, thereby helping drive prices further down in the longer term by cracking open the tough nut of competition in the UK energy market. And it would give a huge boost to the UK's prospects of becoming a major global player in the renewables sector.

Second, a model off-the-shelf Community-Owned Renewable Energy Supply Co-operative (or 'CORESCo') should be developed to reduce the legal costs and complexity for communities in establishing their own. To reflect the differing legal responsibilities of cooperative and commercial organisations (i.e. social responsibility versus profit maximisation), that model should include a distinct legal status for CORESCos. This would enable future differentiation in tax treatment to acknowledge their community value.

Third, to help CORESCos to access start-up capital the Green Investment Bank should have ring-fenced annual funding available on favourable terms for community-owned micro-generation schemes with a credible business and environmental case.

Fourth, CORESCos should be entitled and encouraged to be licensed as community utility companies, to enable them to supply their own residents or other wholesalers. To provide investor confidence, CORESCos that do not opt for direct supply should continue to have the right to supply major utilities at an agreed price beyond 2017.

Fifth, business rates applicable on the entirety of any localised renewable energy installation should be reallocated directly to the local authority concerned, to spend on environmental initiatives within the project area.

And finally, planning law should be altered to ensure that applications for micro-generation proposals (up to a certain capacity) which have the support and/or active involvement of a local CORESCo should include a presumption in favour of the development.

Wind

There are two further measures which would help ease host-community resistance that often arises towards wind installations. One is a requirement that all onshore wind energy schemes (or those within a certain distance of the shore line) should include an annual community payment based upon the size of the installation. These funds should then be locally managed, ideally prioritising energy efficiency measures for both residential homes and community buildings. A second is that local communities should have the power to purchase and own a certain maximum percentage of any wind infrastructure proposed within their area. These steps would empower communities to both access the benefits of and directly control any local wind installations, which should help remove some of the antagonism that can arise.

Solar

In many ways solar-based CORE projects present less of a challenge than wind. The installations are less visually intrusive, and the dispersed nature of their power source makes them viable across much broader swathes of the country. Unlike wind, solar is also much more suited and viable in urban areas, where electricity demand is the greatest. London and the south-east of England are the most densely populated regions of the UK, and also some of the sunniest and most sheltered. So while wind power would be a non-starter there, solar PV would offer a much more viable alternative, particularly in cities with swathes of south-facing roof tops. The lower scale requirement of solar power also makes it much more suited to individual as well as community investment. The downside with PV, however, is that it is much less efficient and harder to scale-up than wind. Nonetheless, as existing community-owned solar projects from Bath to Brixton have shown, there is an important role for solar PV installations in contributing to our renewable energy mix while empowering individuals and communities to participate in electricity generation.

Three additional government measures to acknowledge the community benefit role, and differentiated legal status, of CORESCos would greatly assist in encouraging more community solar. Firstly, a new higher-rate PV FiT should be introduced solely for CORESCos. Secondly, CORESCos should become eligible for larger scale installations at a more generous level of FiT than the current 50kWh cut-off point. And finally, a mechanism should be introduced whereby suitable publicly owned buildings would be required to host solar installations on their roofs if approached by a CORESCo with a viable proposal to do so.

Steps to support localised heating projects

In addition to community production of renewable electricity, central government can also encourage the growth of micro-generated heating infrastructure, particularly in urban areas. Local authorities should be encouraged to embrace their key leadership and enabling role in this technology. Councils have a variety of built infrastructure under their direct or indirect influence, including town halls, libraries, schools, leisure centres and housing estates, often located in close proximity in urban clusters. Connecting them together offers the potential base demand needed to make a district combined heat and power (CHP) system viable. As we have seen to date in the UK, however, very few local authorities will take the initiative on district heating projects of their own accord. Government therefore needs to use its wide range of policy, scrutiny, legal and fiscal levers to cajole and incentivise councils. As experience has shown elsewhere, once a solid core of municipalities are supplying their residents with lower-cost heating and electricity through CHP, it provides both positive role models and citizen pressure for schemes to be introduced into new areas.

Through the steps outlined above government could provide communities and individuals with incentives and entitlements that would empower, encourage and enable them to play a more active and constructive role in the production and supply of their own energy needs. The timescales and uncertainty involved in the implementation of some new renewable installations would be reduced. And a network of dispersed and innovative new entrants with a downward price influence would be encouraged into a marketplace that is currently a closed shop. This would all amount to a revolution in the relationships we have built between people and a commodity central to their everyday lives. And it would do so in a way which is truly liberal.

The size of the opportunity

What contribution could community-owned renewables realistically make to our energy needs if the appropriate incentives were provided? A comparison with market-leading Germany provides perspective. By 2010 Germany was generating 20 per cent of its total energy requirements through renewable sources, 51 per cent of which (25.5 GW) was in the ownership of individuals, communities and landowners. For wind and solar installations alone, the figure was 65 per cent. In total, over US$100 billion has been invested by German citizens in their country's renewable energy infrastructure, and with nuclear power being phased out by 2020 that figure continues to rise. In contrast, by 2012 only 3 per cent of the UK's energy was being generated from renewable sources (against a 2010 target of 10 per cent). Of that, 90 per cent is in corporate hands. On current rates we are unlikely to reach the EU 2020 target of 15 per cent of all UK energy coming from renewable sources.

The economic opportunity offered by micro-generated renewable energy should also be remembered. Birmingham City Council has estimated that £1.6 billion leak from its local economy every year via individual, public and business energy bills. For towns across Britain to retain even a fraction of the revenue and profit they lose in that way would provide a significant boost to local economies.

We need to acknowledge that our current approach to renewables is not maximising the potential investment, and is instead increasing our reliance on gas to plug the shortfall. There is no reason why a shift in government policy could not see the UK emulate the type of figures that Germany has achieved. It is time that we genuinely empowered ordinary people and communities to take a stake in a key requirement of modern-day existence, helping the UK to reach its national renewable targets as a result.

Conclusions

As a nation we have a responsibility to ensure that our energy infrastructure is as low-carbon as possible. And as liberals we have an additional duty to ensure that it not only builds the truly devolved and empowered society that our political DNA compels us to strive for, but that we also avoid decisions which would erode and destroy agency for a generation to come. Community-owned renewable energy offers the opportunity to achieve both those objectives at once.

A truly liberal response to the energy transition challenge should be to crack open our structurally uncompetitive energy sector. This would provide genuine choice, agency and competition, and help drive down prices and improve service for consumers. Instead the government's current proposed solution seeks to opt largely for new nuclear and gas-fired electricity infrastructure, combined with a push for collective switching as a meek endeavour to create consumer power. This is essentially a declaration of business as usual, as collective switching will fail to deliver any genuine consumer empowerment, instead representing little more than a change in slave-owner.

Rather than destroy agency with this approach for another few decades, as liberals we should strive to do all we can to truly democratise our energy sector. This will require a completely new outlook, one which encourages and facilitates a shift away from centralised corporate production towards decentralised civic and community provision. It may prove unrealistic to provide *all* of our current energy needs solely through decentralised renewables. But it is not unrealistic to expect liberals in government to do all they can to encourage and enable individuals and communities to build agency. And by so doing, our reliance as a nation upon the Big Six oligarchy would be greatly reduced. Decisions on energy must not just be sound economically and environmentally, but must also deliver the core liberal benefit of enhanced agency for future generations.

Chapter 27

Councils, Cities and Energy Transition

Christian Vassie

While national governments, and the European Parliament, decide the legislative, urban planning, and regulatory frameworks that shape how countries move towards a low carbon future, it is at municipal level that change is and will be delivered.

The proof of this is not hard to find. Nations with more decentralised governmental structures are way in front of the UK on delivering the energy transition, and key to this difference is the power and engagement of their municipalities. In most European countries the word municipality refers not only to the local authority but also to the territory it encompasses, its resources and all the actors within it, its citizens, community groups, and businesses.

While local authorities in other nations are busy working together on exchanging best practice, too many UK local authorities are working alone and in ignorance. There are many sources of information on best practice, including Energy-Cities, which has over 1,000 member cities; and the Covenant of Mayors, which counts over 4,600 member cities. Dozens of UK local authorities are members of these organisations, including Bristol, Milton Keynes, Glasgow, Northumberland and Manchester.

The Covenant of Mayors requires its signatories to produce a Sustainable Energy Action Plan. Within these plans, published on their website, are many different and illuminating local authority approaches to reducing carbon emissions.

Energy Cities has thirty proposals for the energy transition of cities and towns, summed up in five themes: empowering local actors, knowing our territories' resources and flows, rethinking finance in general, inventing a new local governance, and urban planning as a way of reducing energy use.

The diversity of legislative, regulatory and cultural experiences of European nations, and the many different local authority structures ensure that we have access to a wide range of different models as to how the energy transition and low carbon future can be delivered.

Owning your own power station

National government must legislate to make municipalities responsible for their territories' energy supply and for knowing their territories' total energy resources and flows.

Pretending that there can exist a model of energy consumption where private power companies will work actively and independently to reduce the sales of the commodity they produce is a sham; it ignores the fact that companies exist to maximise sales and make profits. If we are serious, therefore, in stating a desire to use and produce less energy, we must radically transform the structures that own the production of energy.

In Scandinavian countries and in countries with federal systems of government, municipalities are responsible for their territories' energy supply. This contributes to developing a sense of responsibility among local authorities and provides a source of income, which is powering the transition to a low-carbon future. Munich in Germany, Växjö in Sweden, and Güssing in Austria, to give just three examples, all own the power stations that provide the cities with their heat and electricity.

Why is this important? It is straightforward: if you own your own power station then you benefit directly from each and every saving that you make. When new housing developments are constructed in a city that owns its own power stations it is a given that district heating will be the primary source of heating, because to do otherwise would be to waste energy and increase the city's overall energy bills. Money not wasted on energy can be spent on public transport, health, culture, etc.

Large private companies are largely not interested in heating networks, because these are local, by definition. This fundamental structural flaw, the disconnect between consumer and producer, is the reason why the United Kingdom is engaged in constructing energy-from-waste plants that are throwing billions of pounds of heat into the skies instead of providing district heating to homes, while also spending a fortune on winter fuel payments to vulnerable groups. This is barking mad.

In contrast, in Munich, municipal ownership of power stations is enabling the city of 1.4 million inhabitants to innovate. Munich is committed to switching to 100 per cent renewable energy. They are currently drilling down 5 km beneath the city to source geothermal energy, and creating new ways of harnessing summer solar heat to heat homes in winter. District heating networks transform the energy efficiency of their power stations.

Växjö, a city of 85,000 inhabitants, decided in 1996 to become fossil-fuel-free. A power company was set up bringing together the municipality and local private companies. Växjö's carbon reduction target is 65 per cent by 2020, compared with 1993 levels, and it is committed to becoming carbon-neutral by 2030. Back in 2005, 87 per cent of its heating came from renewable energy sources. And by 2012, 51 per cent of its total energy use derived from sources such as biomass, hydro power and geothermal and solar energy. In little over a decade, emissions have been reduced by 24 per cent per person.

Güssing is the first energy self-sufficient town in Austria. Back in 1992 this small town of 4,000 inhabitants was spending nearly €6 million a year on importing energy, a price it could barely afford. By 2007 Güssing was generating 22 MWh of power a year, including an 8 MWh surplus that it sold to the grid, and had reduced carbon dioxide emissions by 93 per cent from 1995 levels.

The key driver for Güssing was the desire to keep money spent on energy closer to home. While its energy transition was initially based on wood-burning, the town has invested the revenues from its energy surplus to expand the range of renewable energy sources it uses, creating hundreds of local jobs and protecting their biomass resource, their forests.

Once a municipality is responsible for providing the heat and power consumed within its borders it will, of necessity, develop an understanding of its local renewable energy resources, consumption and energy flows – for example, identifying which companies or council operations produce waste heat and where are the potential users of that waste heat.

Identifying the local energy potential enables municipalities to quantify the difference between the resource they have and the energy they use. For example, for Litoměřice, in the Czech Republic, a spatial energy strategy identified the geothermal energy potential in their territory and it is now constructing an 18.4 GWh geothermal combined heat and power (CHP) plant that will feed a district heating network.

In 2008, the old mining town of Heerlen in the Netherlands flooded an old mine over 800m deep to heat water to 35°C. The water is used for heating purposes, and then after the heat has been extracted and the water has cooled to 17°C it is stored in other mine shafts and used as a coolant. The system provides heating and cooling to 400 new homes, 55,000m² of new tertiary buildings and 84,000 m² of existing office space, generating CO_2 emissions savings of 55 per cent.

How can the UK shift to a less centralised system? Is it possible? The great news is that we are not alone in needing to make this shift. Set against the belt of nations stretching from Scandinavia in the north, through Germany and on to Switzerland and Austria, where they have decentralised or federal systems and where municipal power stations are the way things are done, is a second belt of nations that includes the UK, France, Spain, Portugal, Italy, and Greece, where everything is centralised.

In November 2012 France started a consultation on how to move to a more locally based approach finishing in May 2013, the consultation involves local authorities, energy supply companies, universities, trades unions, NGOs, and ESCOs (energy service companies). They are considering setting up Energy Organisation Authorities at municipal level to enable them to move towards the federal countries' model. They are also considering passing legislation so that large power companies that refuse to participate in the creation of a more local system can be excluded from the list of energy suppliers by local authorities.

Experience in Scandinavia, Germany and Austria has shown that SMEs, and larger companies with information and communications technology expertise or engineering competencies, such as Siemens, or companies involved in renewables technologies, are far more interested to expand into this field than are the old monolithic power companies. In Germany there is a growing business of companies which work with local authorities, joining with them to form arms-length local energy companies. They create a vision for energy transition, with 35 per cent of the funding coming from the private specialist company, 35 per cent coming from the local authority, and the rest coming from outside investment or long-term borrowing. These smaller companies are by their nature more flexible and perfectly happy to accept that the local authority is responsible for the strategic vision; as long as everyone is earning a return, then everything works.

The UK is not totally out in the cold either. Leicester has formed a partnership with GDF Suez to provide district heating on a twenty-five-year contract, serving 3,000 dwellings.[1] So we are already on our way.

Tackling fuel poverty

All local authorities should be responsible for ending fuel poverty in their territory.

Experience across Europe shows that entrusting municipalities with the responsibility for their energy supply is a strong lever to energy transition as it increases popular acceptance of the necessary new infrastructures, fosters creativity and innovation, and creates added economic value that remains within the territory.

Once the town of Güssing had made the decision to become energy producers in 1992, the first thing they did was to insulate all the town's buildings.

The result of the energy optimisation of all buildings in the town centre alone brought a reduction of expenditure on energy by almost 50 per cent. Only when this task was complete did they turn to producing their own power because any other approach would have required power plants twice the size they needed to be, at huge extra cost, both during construction and operation.

In Munich and Växjö, and all the other cities that own their own power stations, installing the best levels of insulation is no more than common sense. Every euro invested in insulation is recouped many times over in reduced heating bills. This directly benefits those in fuel poverty. This could happen in the UK. Many councils have run projects to provide free insulation. The benefits accrue to the householder – including those in fuel poverty – and the environment, but not to the local authority – but if the council owned its own power station, energy savings would also have been direct financial savings, making similar projects far more viable on a larger scale.

One company's waste ...

Local authorities should be made responsible for promoting the circular economy within their territories and for creating a territorial bio-waste management plan.

It is not just energy flows that municipalities need to understand and manage. One company's waste is another company's raw material. Huge quantities of materials flow through municipalities: building materials, food products, fuels, waste, manufactured goods, and so on. Understanding and optimising the management of these resource flows is called industrial ecology or the circular economy. Local authorities have a key role in developing synergies between players.

In Kotka, Finland, a public-private partnership runs the energy-from-waste plant, which provides district heating and steam to a local cardboard mill. In Lemvig, Denmark, a town of 21,800 inhabitants, an anaerobic digestion biogas plant takes waste from a variety of sources to provide heat to 1,000 homes. In Barcelona, Spain (3.2 million inhabitants), a metropolitan urban waste management programme processes organic waste to produce biogas and power a CHP plant providing district heating and cooling.[2]

Smart cities and communication

Government must ensure that communication on energy transition is not left to engineers and technical experts, but also involve cultural players and the public itself. Government must require local authorities to give easy public access to real-time data on energy production.

Cities must make more use of smart metering to change energy consumption patterns, as is being done in various countries, but it is a mistake to allow only engineers and energy managers to determine the way in which energy consumption information is communicated, because experts talk effectively only to each other. The public has limited interest in kilowatt hours, volts and the like. Creative and cultural players must be involved to encourage creative and innovative ways of presenting this information, so that it is intelligible by the population.

Local authorities must be required to use smart technology to make all data on renewable energy generation, city-wide consumption, energy saving, etc. readily available and accessible to the public. There exist many models for this in cities across Europe. For example, in Heidelberg, Germany, an electronic public display board outside the city's energy department buildings, which incorporate solar PV arrays and an incinerator that provides district heating, shows the energy produced by the city's various renewable energy resources. Outside the Spittelau incinerator in Vienna, Austria, an electronic public display board not only gives information on energy production but also provides real-time data on emissions.

The public must have access to real-time information to prove that energy plants are performing as designed, to quantify energy savings and emissions and move away from a culture of secrecy and commercial confidentiality towards a culture of openness, so that people can see for themselves the cost of the decisions they make, both in financial terms and in terms of emissions.

A key obstacle to energy saving by individual consumers or businesses is the belief that their actions are irrelevant, that any good deed by them is nullified by the selfishness, laziness or ignorance of others. This state of affairs exists because any collective call to action to reduce consumption and emissions proceeds in the absence of real information.

Local authorities must make creative use of the data collected by smart meters to motivate the entire community. A campaign to require all shops to close their doors in winter, for example, could be accompanied by figures on a display screen in the city showing how much energy was being saved – not a fictional or notional computation but real data charting the impact behavioural change is having on the community's energy consumption.

Regulation

National government must deliver better regulation on emissions and be seen to be enforcing those regulations effectively. The 'polluter pays' principle must be applied across the board.

The UK sees campaigns against each and every plan for an incinerator – but elsewhere in Europe, where the technology has been completely transformed over the past twenty years, public confidence is not an issue.[3] In 2005, for example, the German environment ministry estimated that in 2000 incinerators (of which there were sixty-six at the time) were responsible for 1 per cent of dioxin emissions in Germany, down from 33 per cent just one decade earlier. The Danish Environmental Research Institute concluded in 2006 that incinerators in Denmark were responsible for approximately 0.3 per cent of total domestic emissions of PM2.5 particulates to the atmosphere.[4] In Sweden the figures are even more dramatic; it is estimated that dioxin emissions fell by almost 99 per cent between 1985 and 2004.[5]

The European Commission's standard for the best available technology for emissions of particulates (PM1s and PM2.5s) is 1–5 mg/m^3. UK legislation authorises 10mg/m^3 (of PM10s) with peaks or continuous levels of 30mg/m^3. So incinerators in the UK are authorised to operate at 120 times the levels of emissions achieved elsewhere in the EU. This is unacceptable, rightly agitates the public, and hinders the UK's energy transition.

The UK must enact stricter and more effective regulation to ensure that only incinerators built and operated to the same standards as the best in other EU member states are allowed on UK soil.

Re-regulation of public transport

National government must give municipalities more control over public transport provision.

Another example of the need for new regulation is in the area of public transport. In Malmö, Sweden, over 42 per cent of the city's buses run on biogas. It is tempting to see this as a technological issue but, as usual, the challenges are anything but technical.

Biogas in Malmö is produced from organic waste collected from residents. By 2015 40 per cent of all household food waste will be collected by the local authority. Household sinks in Malmö have garbage disposal units built in to transform food waste into sludge which is then collected in central collection tanks before being taken by the local authority to generate biogas. New luxury apartment blocks and housing association flats alike are included in this programme. Key to ensuring the city's buses run on this biogas, however, is the fact that the city owns and controls its own bus fleet; it knows that if it creates a plant to produce biogas then that biogas will be used to power buses.

When cities across the rest of Europe invest in new tram systems it is in the context of owning the networks they are installing.

It is hard to see how a public transport system like that in the UK, where local authorities cannot even control the existence or frequency of a bus service to any given place, could ever make effective use of biogas produced from food waste collected from the inhabitants. Commercial confidentiality clauses that prevent local authorities from even knowing the passenger numbers on routes they are subsidising are counter-productive and must be changed if public transport is to grow. The deregulation of the buses was a mistake back when it happened in the 1980s. Now, as we try to create a zero-carbon future, a deregulated bus service is an anachronism that needs to be consigned to history.

Rethinking finance

All municipalities should be required to integrate future energy prices, whole-life costings and the 'polluter pays' principle into their budget calculations and into the investment and development decisions that they make. They should be required to dedicate resources and staff to preparing this work.

A budgeting regime that takes no account of anticipated costs five or twenty years ahead cannot properly evaluate the benefits of investment in such large infrastructure projects. Constructing a tram network, for example, requires major financial investment spread over several decades. An over-powerful financial directorate that can veto spending in other council departments without itself having any expertise in the area of energy efficiency, for example, is not well placed to deliver value for money. Whole-life costings must be integrated into financial planning and council budgets.

When looking from a UK perspective at how Heidelberg, in Germany, is able to create Bahnstadt, the largest development built to passivhaus standards in Europe, the first thing to hit you is not the technical mastery of its engineers, architects, and planners, but the way in which Heidelberg solved the problem of how to redevelop the 106 hectare ex-shunting yard. A consortium including the local authority, a regional bank, and a property development company bought half the site and was able to impose a development brief rather than hope it might be adopted by someone else. Without new financial and legislative structures to enable such action to take place, many inner-city sites remain empty or fail to deliver developments that contribute to the energy transition.

In Dijon and Brest, France, a joint procurement order enabled the two cities to save €32 million, a 20 per cent saving, on their purchase of fifty-two trams. When they laid the tram rails they also installed beneath them district heating pipes. Working together and avoiding silo-thinking not only saved the cities huge sums of money, it enabled an exchange of ideas and expertise, and reduced carbon emissions.

To undertake large projects local authorities need to know that they will get a long-term return on their investment in order to repay the loans they take out. Loan streams already exist – the European Investment Bank provided the majority of the funding for the new tram networks in Dijon and Brest, for example. The government's role is to incentivise local authorities in the UK to show the same enterprise as local authorities elsewhere by giving them control over the infrastructure that they create.

Urban planning
The creation of a sustainable low–carbon future needs to be integrated more completely into urban planning. Railway stations as city hubs. Goods delivery networks. Designing around walking and cycling.

Key drivers for change in cities should include the creation of an energy retrofitting plan for the entire building stock, having a network heating plan to inform all development within the city, ensuring that railway stations and not car parks are the hubs around which development takes place, reallocating the road network to ensure that a cycle journey is more direct than a car journey, and developing goods delivery networks within cities to reduce lorry miles.

Co-ordination between different areas of a city's master plan is vital as a way of saving money and making infrastructure improvement possible. For example, in Dijon co-ordination between departments has enabled the city's bicycle hire initiative to be relocated to the new tram stops. Data collected from the ticketing systems for both cycle hire and tram travel enables the local authority to understand how both services impact on each other, with a view to further reducing car traffic through the city.

In Barcelona, the new city planning approach identifies underground, ground level, and above ground as categories that must be considered, to improve the interconnectedness of functions and services in the city.

Local authorities should be required to ensure their strategic plans make railway stations the hubs around which shopping, buses and trams, cycle networks and cycle parking, education, and cultural and recreational facilities are designed. For several decades car parks have become the key hubs around which development is focused while development around stations has ignored their broader value to the structure of the city they serve. It is not a given that private motor cars will exist in 2050.

Designing around cycling involves more than painting dotted lines on roads. The separation of bicycle and motor traffic has been instrumental in achieving a modal shift toward cycling in the Netherlands, Denmark, and Germany. Sometimes this is through the creation of cycle tracks, sometimes it is simply a question of reallocating street use. In Malmö, traffic lights prioritise cyclists over motorists.

Planning frameworks could require the developers of out-of-town shopping centres to contribute to the financing of tram or railway links. In-town shopping centres have problems associated with carbon emissions, noise, and pollution generated by freight deliveries. In La Rochelle, in France (population 200,000), 58 per cent of city-centre businesses use an urban distribution network based around an electric vehicle fleet.

Councils must produce a costed plan to retrofit all buildings. London is currently retrofitting 400 public buildings. In Brussels, all new construction has to be to passivhaus standard since 2010, and all renovation and refurbishment work will be by 2018. Across Europe buildings dating back to the thirteenth century and earlier are being retrofitted to reduce energy waste. If we continue, through our planning regulations, to permit a thousand different grounds for exempting buildings from the requirement to be energy efficient we are, in truth, saying that we do not care about creating a low-carbon future.

Conclusion

The suggestions in this chapter seek to put into practice principles that have been at the heart of Liberal and Liberal Democrat philosophy for decades. Giving local authorities the power and the responsibility to deliver the energy transition goes to the heart of our belief in localism. Until we face up to the massive centralisation of power under successive governments, or the culture of secrecy and commercial confidentiality that hides information from consumers and public alike, or the fundamental contradiction of expecting large businesses to be actively engaged in helping to reduce sales of the commodities they sell, we cannot begin to assemble a low-carbon future because progress is dependent on building trust, empowering all the participants, putting responsibility where it belongs, putting people and the environment above profit, and fostering a culture of innovation and openness.

The proposals in this chapter should not be read as anti-business. Those nations in which municipalities operate their own power stations, for example, work with business to deliver energy to their customers. They are free to sell power to the grid, like any other power company. This approach makes money as well as reducing energy waste, making better use of local resources and cutting carbon emissions, so fears about the cost of such a shift are totally unfounded. The issue is rather one of who should be in ultimate control if we are to succeed in our ambition to create a low-carbon future for our nation – bodies ultimately answerable to shareholders and the generation of profit, or bodies ultimately answerable to the common good? The answer, surely, is obvious.

Notes

1   Leicester District Energy, *Delivering Low-Carbon Energy* (November 2012).
2   See http://ecoparcbcn.com/
3   Dr Dick van Steenis, Waste and incineration, Oral evidence to the Welsh Assembly, 2 July 2012; http://www.senedd.assemblywales.org/documents/ s8650/Dr per cent20van per cent20Steenis per cent20to per cent20Committee. html?CT=2
4   Malene Nielsen, Jytte Boll Hillerup, Christian Lange Fogh and Lars Peter Hansen, *PM Emission from CHP Plants < 25 MW$_e$* (National Environmental Research Institute of Denmark).
5   Swedish Environmental Protection Agency, *A Strategy for Sustainable Waste Management, Sweden's Waste Plan* (2005).

Chapter 28

Community Policies for a Low-Carbon Future

Louise Bloom

Local councils and local communities are well placed to help build a low-carbon future. Councils, whatever their size, are able to use their influence and budgets to create low-carbon economies in their own areas. Local communities are similarly placed to examine local solutions to a global problem. But there are barriers that need to be overcome in order to do this, both real and perceived; the latter are sometimes hardest to deal with. National government at times seems to set out to stifle local councils and communities of their desire to provide local solutions. The media can also be an enemy of innovation, as can those only too willing to play unnecessary party politics.

I want to illustrate what local communities can do and are doing to take action to create low-carbon economies, examine the barriers that are put in their way, discuss how to overcome those barriers and suggest further opportunities that can be explored to further expand those local low-carbon economies. The maxim 'think globally, act locally' has never been more relevant.

Community projects can be both large and small. To take two examples, the villagers of Woolsery in Devon decided to rebuild their village hall and make it a truly sustainable building generating its own energy and selling surplus energy to the national grid; while the Westmill Wind Farm Co-operative in Oxfordshire now generates enough energy to power over 3,600 homes a year and raise over £1 million in income.

Woolsery, with a population of 1,200, decided it wanted to update its village hall to create a warm, inviting and sustainable building that would be an asset for years to come. A charity was set up to oversee the project with a committee of twenty volunteers. The village was fortunate enough to secure funding to completely rebuild the village hall, so started off by fully insulating the new building, installing underfloor heating, rainwater harvesting to flush the toilets and south-facing windows to maximise sunlight.

As the building was in a windy location they next explored installing a wind turbine, then considered using the area's high level of sunshine and, finally, a ground-source heat pump. The volunteers were assisted by Devon County Council's renewable energy advisers who were a great source of advice, assistance and technical information in planning the project. By utilising various grants available, the villagers were able to complete the 'virtuous circle' of wind, sun and earth and generate electricity for the hall from a 6 kW wind turbine, 9 kW of solar photovoltaic (PV) panels and an 8 kW ground-source heat pump.

So now the village hall generates its own electricity and also sells the surplus back to the grid; the balance varies according to the energy needs of the hall at any one time and the amount of energy being generated. Nearly 13 tonnes of carbon are saved each year. After offsetting costs against income and bill savings, the running costs of the hall have come down by ninety per cent. This in turn means that village groups can be charged a low rent for hiring the building so the community really does benefit in every way. It also has many bookings now from people who want to use it as a learning resource, an 'eco hall'. Many people stop to look at the information panel that shows the energy being generated at any time.

Although the costs of £82,000 were covered by grants, if they had not been, and had the project only benefited from the feed-in tariffs scheme, the payback on the original investment would still only be around ten years. Even without the FiTs, the original estimate of twenty-two years would still make it a good deal.

For a scheme like this to work, a pool of volunteers with the time and commitment to see it through is vital, as is technical advice and support; councils can be a good source of such advice and support, as can local energy advice centres. Engagement with the local community is also vital to ensure support and make sure that any concerns can be dealt with and not get tangled up in the planning system. The Woolsery Village Hall committee was successfully able to do this, which meant there were no unnecessary delays to the project. Many local halls are run by groups of volunteers so this example of a really local low-carbon economy could be easily replicated elsewhere, even without the Devon sunshine.

It was the open, flat and windy landscape of Oxfordshire that caused farmer Dan Twine to think that he had a good location for a wind farm similar to those he had seen in Denmark, where 20 per cent of the country's renewable generators are owned by communities. He created the Westmill Wind Farm Co-operative, the first wind farm in the UK to be community-owned from commissioning. Nearly 2,500 people signed up to the original proposition of buying shares in five large wind turbines. After ten years of planning and other battles, the co-operative now generates an annual income of around £1 million and 12 million kWh of energy, enough to power 3,500 homes a year, with an annual carbon saving of 6,500 tonnes.

Funding for this substantial project came from the shareholders, who are a mixture of local people and other investors, and a bank loan from the Co-Op Bank, who also managed the share issue. When the share issue was oversubscribed, priority was given to people who lived within a fifty-mile radius of the site; they received all the shares they requested, while those who lived further away had their allocation reduced.

The co-operative that now runs Westmill, largely on a voluntary basis, set up a charity, the Westmill Sustainable Energy Trust, to further support the local community and economy with energy-saving projects, such as paying for insulation for local community buildings. The fund, with the help of the wind, generates £5,000 – £6,000 a year. A new addition to the site is 82 ha of solar PV, generating around 4.4 GWh of energy per year. This time there were no planning battles, perhaps showing how much public perception of such projects has moved on.

This may sound like a massive project, but it was inspired by one man, who admittedly happened to own a farm, and was carried forward by local people committed to the scheme, both in terms of funding and time dedicated to it, including overcoming opposition.

Local councils have a key role to play as community leaders and funders of the local low-carbon economy. With imagination and political will, councils of any size can tackle climate change and reduce their own carbon emissions, as well as taking action to reduce emissions among the wider community.

Spreading best practice and sharing expertise is vital, as encouraged by the Local Government Association and the now-abolished Beacon Council scheme. Unfortunately councils' approach to this can be patchy, but in the current economic climate it also makes good financial sense for councils to talk to each other about carbon savings.

Eastleigh Borough Council in Hampshire (winner of Beacon Council for Tackling Climate Change in 2008–09) is a medium-sized district council with a population of 125,000. Sustainability and tackling climate change has been a long-term commitment of the governing Liberal Democrat group, and it has embraced the use of renewable technologies as a way of taking this forward. Over the last year or so the council has installed nearly 700 PV panels on ten buildings it owns, including 288 on a leisure centre, one of the largest schemes in the south of England. The total energy generated so far is around 170,000 kWh, enough to power fifty-one family homes for a year. The annual carbon savings over twelve months are around 90 tonnes, far exceeding expectations. The council has invested £650,000, for which it expects an income of £2 million over the lifetime of all the schemes. The council can use this income for the benefit of the local community to keep the council tax low and invest further in the low-carbon economy for, by example, supporting public transport and providing funding for its home insulation programme.

'At the other end of the scale, Bristol City Council with a population of 430,000, has invested £6 million, some of it European Union funding, in solar panels, biomass boilers and wind turbines. Three 6 MW turbines at the port of Avonmouth now generate 15 GWh of energy a year, enough to power nearly 5,000 family homes and saving nearly 15,500 tonnes of carbon.

Bristol has also received £2.25 million of European funding towards the costs involved in setting up an Energy Service Company, or ESCO, and a huge investment programme. An ESCO can be a good way for councils to trade, enabling them to invest in energy-saving projects and infrastructure at arms length from other council business. They can sell energy generated through the ESCO, again keeping it separate from the usual local authority income and expenditure balance sheets. The ESCO set up by Bristol City Council will fund projects worth up to £140 million and create at least 1,000 jobs. It will also lead to increased energy efficiency and lower fuel bills for thousands of residents.

Many of the schemes proposed by Liberal Democrat-run Bristol City Council were opposed by both the Conservative and Labour groups on the council. It took strong political leadership and commitment to the principle of establishing a low-carbon economy that led to Bristol now having the lowest carbon emissions of any major UK city. A 'green thread' has run through Liberal Democrat councils, and party policy, for many years in a way that is not true of the Conservative and Labour parties.

Councils can also work together to create low-carbon economies across larger areas than individual council areas. With political will, they do not have to be of the same parties. Home insulation has to be a national priority; 13 per cent of the UK's CO_2 emissions are derived from the energy used to heat homes, much of which is wasted. Department of Energy and Climate Change (DECC) figures show that up to 12 million homes could benefit from better insulation, which would in turn create up to 225,000 new jobs.

The Insulate Hampshire project, which lasted eighteen months and has recently concluded, was supported by all eleven of Hampshire's district councils and Hampshire County Council, comprising both Liberal Democrat and Conservative authorities. Government money for household energy efficiency programmes, and Scottish Power, under the CERT (Carbon Emissions Reduction Target) programme, provided funding for the scheme. It offered professionally installed cavity wall and loft insulation free of charge to Hampshire home-owners and privately renting tenants (with the landlord's permission), where the property qualified (i.e. two-thirds or more of the loft and/or cavity had to be available and suitable for insulation) and where there was less than 60 mm of loft insulation. All applications were subject to a free no-obligation technical survey. Savings for residents can be up to £300 a year if both cavity wall and loft insulation are carried out.

The County Council, in conjunction with the district councils, organised community DIY insulation events across the county, where residents could collect rolls of loft insulation to top up their own existing insulation. Information on energy saving and other council services on offer were also available at these events. Many of these were organised successfully by local community groups. All the councils involved ran their own publicity and information campaigns for the scheme to try to reach as many people as possible, targeting those households most likely to benefit. Town and parish council offices and notice boards worked particularly well in the more rural areas of Hampshire. In Eastleigh the scheme was supported and promoted by the Mayor of Eastleigh on leaflets and posters to help provide reassurance and credibility to residents. The Mayor's picture, in full robes and regalia, gave an added dimension to the promotion! Monthly reports with league tables were produced to try to encourage competition between councils to spur on their efforts in the publicity campaigns.

By the end of September 2012, over 15,000 insulation measures had been installed across the county, resulting in over £1.8 million of fuel bill savings for residents in the first year. A total of 210 information and advice events had been held, and more than twenty community DIY events where nearly 800 householders took away nearly 100,000 m^2 of insulation. Now that the project has finished, the partners are discussing if it would be possible to continue with the Insulate Hampshire brand and processes for other energy-saving initiatives across the county, possibly utilising the Green Deal. The project showed that districts and the county would work well together; sharing publicity saved costs and created the brand image; the website proved a popular way of accessing information; using town and parish councils to publicise the scheme helped reach a wider range of people; the league table encouraged competition between councils; and the community events were very successful.

The coalition government's major initiative in this area, started by the Liberal Democrat former Secretary of State for Energy and Climate Change Chris Huhne, and now being driven ahead by his successor Edward Davey, is the Green Deal, the proposed solution to the problem of a lack of investment in energy-saving measures in homes and non-domestic buildings. The Green Deal will provide finance to fund improvements to the energy efficiency of properties, with no upfront charge to the home-owner; the costs of the installation will be paid back through the lower bills that will result. The Green Deal is available to owner-occupiers, the private and social rented sectors and the commercial sector funded by local authorities, housing associations or ESCOs or any combination. Additional financial support will be available, through the new Energy Company Obligation (ECO), for low-income households with the lowest incomes and hard-to-treat properties, for example those with solid rather than cavity walls.

Local councils, groups of town and parish councils and other very locally based community organisations have the potential to play a major role in delivering the Green Deal, working with other partners such as housing associations. As well as the direct benefits to residents in terms of lower energy bills and carbon emissions, and less fuel poverty, jobs will also be created locally. Councils will be able to encourage the use of local businesses as suppliers, provide advice and signpost residents to bona fide companies.

Some councils are looking at working together to provide a single offer for the Green Deal, benefiting from economies of scale. Both Green Deal providers (the installation companies) and the potential providers of private finance are more likely to be interested in larger population areas. For example, the councils in the Partnership for Urban South Hampshire (PUSH) are currently considering working together in delivering the Green Deal; as well as its target of reducing carbon emissions, the Green Deal will enable PUSH to further its economic ambitions for the sub-region, generating jobs and economic activity, a true model for the local low-carbon economy. Housing associations in the PUSH area are also being encouraged and supported by councils to get involved. Measures taken to improve energy efficiency in poorly performing blocks of flats could include changing heating systems as well as improving internal and external insulation and fitting solar PV panels. Partnership support to provide advice and information is also being accessed through community-based groups such as GroundWorks and voluntary sector energy advice centres.

The Green Deal will not be straightforward to implement. Not only is the process complicated, energy efficiency can be a difficult message to promote.

The experience with Insulate Hampshire was that many people simply did not believe that they were being offered something for free that would save them money, even when badged as being on offer from their local council. When the offer was explained to people face to face, such as at the community events, however, it was easier to convince people that it was a genuinely good deal.

Thinking more widely, the way communities are built and the way we all live needs to change to ensure a low-carbon future. Most of us travel to work, to the shops and to leisure facilities, and our children are driven to school. Local communities are not truly local, as the facilities and services we need are so spread out. Public transport is not good in many areas of the country, particularly outside major urban areas, so most of us use cars as our primary means of transport.

Eco Towns were briefly seen as a way to solve the issue of how and where we live, but none of the proposed sites have yet been built. Some, for example Borden in Hampshire and North West Bicester in Oxfordshire, still exist in their local authorities' housing allocation numbers and it is hoped they will be built to the original sustainable and low-carbon ideals, but this is by no means certain following a 50 per cent cut in the government budget to support local infrastructure. The concept was never popular, partly because some of the sites were those already rejected through local planning processes, but also as they were seen to be a solution imposed by central government. Even many green campaign groups, such as the Campaign for the Protection of Rural England, did not support them, arguing that many of the sites chosen were unsuitable and that all towns need to be sustainable, not just certain exemplar towns.

There is always a tension between what different groups of people want, what the government wants and what the country really needs to achieve a low-carbon future. In the cases I have illustrated where individuals, communities and councils have taken action to tackle climate change, it has generally been due to the personal or collective commitment and drive of those involved. Where groups of councils have come together it is not necessarily because all members believe in the environmental ideal; the motivation could be a desire to create local jobs, to be seen to 'do the right thing' or purely because everyone else is doing it. Local people buying into community-based renewable energy schemes again sometimes have little interest in the principle, but simply see it as a good investment. I have long believed that it is not necessary to convince everyone of the fact that climate change is man-made to persuade people of the need to work towards a low-carbon economy; for many people the economic argument is enough.

The Climate Change Act 2008 commits the UK to reduce its greenhouse gas emissions, but the requirements apply to central government only. Some people argue that legislation is needed to force local councils to take action on waste and recycling, planning, transport, housing, employment policies and open-space policies to achieve the cuts in carbon emissions we need. Others see this as a move towards yet more centralisation, the kind of society that many of us would not want to live in. Ideally, local decisions need to be taken locally, with local politicians being answerable to their residents. I suggest that a refocusing is needed, in discussion with local authorities and communities, with a combination of carrots and sticks to achieve the carbon reduction targets already legislated for.

Ultimately, however, climate change is too big an issue to leave for politicians to argue about who is responsible for what. So I would like to see a future Liberal Democrat government willing to legislate where necessary; for example, introducing binding local targets to ensure that all local councils, not just those strongly committed to reducing carbon, took their responsibilities seriously. Rewards could come in the form of extra funding, similar to the New Homes Bonus that councils receive based on levels of housing development.

Another barrier to overcome is that many people only take a short-term view of solutions when a long-term look is needed. For example, when building new housing developments, transport infrastructure needs to be built first, not last. This may mean that a transport system runs half-empty in its early years, while the housing is constructed, but it will also mean that as people move in they will see that the need for a car is drastically reduced or even removed.

This does not seem to be so much of a problem elsewhere in Europe. For example, when the German town of Freiburg was rebuilt as an exemplar of an eco-town, all the infrastructure went in first. It was acknowledged that it could take up to twenty-five years for the town to fully develop and for all the cost savings to be achieved, but carbon savings would be realised very early on.

A low-carbon future where we all live sustainable lives is perfectly possible, looking at the many examples of good practice that already exist, but they are not widespread. Local councils and communities need to buy into the ideals and practicalities of what can be achieved and how to achieve it, and, yes, costs and lifestyle choices do need to be made. A very simple example of this is car clubs. Instead of everyone owning their own car, vehicles of varying size are communially owned, costs shared and cars are offered as a bookable service to all members of the club. Booking can be made by the hour, half-day or day. This can also work for commercial organisations in the form of pool cars. IKEA have a pool car scheme as does Eastleigh Borough Council; indeed the Eastleigh scheme was so successsful that a third car was recently bought to add to the original two. Some compromise and forward planning is needed to make the schemes successful, but both carbon and cash can be saved by members.

A future Liberal Democrat government needs to make a real commitment to properly funding the measures that are necessary to achieve carbon reduction targets, recognise how important the green economy is and provide leadership in the way that some councils already do. It is no good sending out the mixed messages we get from the current government, who claim to want to be the 'greenest government ever', but then refuse to provide the funds, legislation and leadership needed to make this a reality. The local successes I have discussed here need to be the rule, not the exception, if we are to achieve the low-carbon future that climate change demands.

Chapter 29

Adapting to Climate Change

Paul Burall

Our climate is destined to change significantly even if substantial mitigation measures are put in place soon. The *UK Climate Projections* published by Defra in 2009 suggest that even if the global temperature increase is constrained to 2°C, temperatures in the south of England could see a rise of 3°C by the 2080s, and an average summer temperature rise of 5°C in the south west of England is possible.[1] Even moderate temperature rises will have significant effects on health, infrastructure, food and water supply and biodiversity, as well as introducing new risks for businesses and the economy.

The UK recognised these facts when, by passing the Climate Change Act in 2008, it became the first country in the world to have a legally binding long-term framework to deal both with mitigating climate change and adapting to the inevitable consequences. The preparation of the climate change risk assessment required by the Act was fulfilled at the beginning of 2012, and will be followed by a national adaptation programme in 2013. This chapter looks at some of the adaptation measures that may be required.

Of course, the UK cannot ignore the effects of climate change on other parts of the world: the repercussions will be felt everywhere. All coastal countries will be more vulnerable to flooding due to sea level rise, with around 50 million additional people placed at risk. The production of staple food crops is likely to decline in countries as far apart as India, Brazil, the US and Russia. Water resources in particular will be stretched, with parts of Italy, France and the US especially vulnerable. It is no wonder that John Beddington, the Government Chief Scientist, has forecast a 'perfect storm' of food shortages, scarce water and insufficient energy resources that threatens to unleash public unrest, cross-border conflicts and mass migration as people flee from the worst-affected regions.[2]

Food and agriculture

The food issue well illustrates the challenges and international ramifications for policy-makers in the United Kingdom. Professor Tim Benton, the Global

Food Security Programme's 'champion', in 2011 pointed out the vast scale of the challenge: the global population is expected to increase by 35 per cent by 2050 with the demand for food rising by 70 per cent.[3] Yet there is no more unused land available for cultivation, climate change threatens to reduce crop yields, and there will be increased competition both for land and water for uses other than food production.

Benton believes that the 'admirable ideals' of self-sufficiency and organic growing would only reduce yields from productive land: 'We are not self-sufficient in Europe, so if we increase organic production our yields will go down and we will need to import more food and will be asking someone else to produce our food for us ... We would be exporting the environmental cost and someone else will be paying for it.' Instead, he suggests that the UK needs to maximise its food production and that managing intensively farmed land alongside non-cropped plots would allow maximum production while maintaining the environment for wildlife and biodiversity. He sees a role for genetically modified (GM) food technologies and for chemical innovations but also wants action to reduce food wastage, stop over-consumption, manage soil better, and farm more efficiently in a system that he describes as 'sustainable intensification'.

Soil management is particularly important, both to prevent loss and retain fertility; more than two million tonnes of topsoil is lost every year in the UK due to erosion by wind and rain, and agricultural land has been consistently degraded over the years by poor land management. These losses can be reduced by measures such as changes to agricultural practices and the planting of hedges and trees to minimise wind and water erosion.

Soil is also a major carbon sink and the evidence is that in recent years it has had a substantial impact on climate change-inducing carbon emissions, not least from the exploitation of peatlands. So, for the benefit both of plant fertility and carbon retention, soil management needs to become a priority, both in terms of preventing activities that emit carbon and by enhancing agricultural practices to increase the organic content of soil.

Lester Brown, President of the Earth Policy Institute in Washington and author of *Full Planet, Empty Plates*, also predicts a food crisis.[4] He is particularly concerned about water and climate change: 'We live in a world where more than half the people live in countries with food bubbles based on farmers' over-pumping and draining aquifers. The question is not whether these bubbles will burst, but when ... Why can't politicians understand that every 1°C above the optimum in the growing season equates to roughly a 10 per cent decline in grain yields?' He believes that the crisis can only be averted by saving water, eating less meat, stopping soil erosion, controlling populations and changing the energy economy.

The UN Food and Agriculture Organisation (FAO) is no less alarmed, warning of 'potentially catastrophic' impacts on food production from climate change and demanding that 'Within the global adaptation architecture greater space be given to the risks linked to slow-onset impacts of climate change, particularly food security risks'.[5] The FAO wants plant genetic material stored in gene banks to be screened with future requirements in mind; additional plant genetic resources – including those from wild relatives of food crops – to be collected to avoid their disappearance; and the breeding of climate-adapted crops such as varieties of major cereals that are resistant to heat, drought, submergence and salty water.

The Climate Change Risk Assessment (CCRA) published by Defra at the beginning of 2012 highlights how UK agriculture may be significantly affected by climate change.[6] Rising temperatures and changing rainfall patterns, changes in sunshine levels and in concentrations of atmospheric carbon dioxide and increasing frequency of weather events currently considered extreme would all have an impact on the sector. The CCRA suggests that mitigation responses should include water harvesting and on-farm storage, combined with irrigation techniques that improve water efficiency; using deep-rooting or drought-tolerant grassland species; changes in livestock production cycles such as autumn lambing and calving; and the planting of trees to provide shade for livestock and windbreaks for crops.

Taking food production off the land also has potential. One example is a three-storey fish and vegetable farm housed in a converted meat packing factory in Chicago, where the plants are grown hydroponically in water fertilised by the fish waste, thus cleaning it in the process so that it can be returned to the fish. Organic waste is used to produce methane for the factory's combined heat and power plant. The magazine *Businessweek* has forecast that such highrise horticulture will be one of the top twenty businesses of the future.[7]

Meat production accounts for at least 15 per cent of all global warming emissions and is also a prime driver of deforestation. One extreme way of tackling this has been demonstrated by researchers at Maastricht University who have already produced muscle-like strips grown from real animal cells that have the same constitution as real muscle,[8] Factory-produced cultured meat would have major environmental benefits. Hanna Tuomisto of the University of Oxford has calculated that cultured meat would require just 1 per cent of the land needed to produce the equivalent amount of conventional beef and that greenhouse gas emissions would fall to around 4 per cent of global emissions.[9]

Globally, climate change may have little effect on total food production, as some parts of the world are likely to become more productive, counterbalancing losses elsewhere. But the challenge of feeding billions more people requires urgent action.

Rising temperatures

While UK food security depends as much on actions elsewhere in the world as here, the same is not true for many of the other challenges of adapting to climate change. One example is the need to adapt British cities to rising temperatures. The CCRA suggests that, even if greenhouse gas emissions are stabilised to constrain the average temperature rise to 2°C, by 2050 the number of days a year when the temperature exceeds 26°C in London will increase from the current 27 to more than 120.

Rising temperatures in urban areas are exacerbated by the heat island effect, which has been found to increase night-time temperatures in London by up to 9°C, in Manchester by between 5°C and 10°C and in Birmingham by between 5°C and 7°C. So mitigation policies are essential to minimise health problems, heat-related deaths and demand for air conditioning, this last leading to an increase in energy consumption and carbon emissions that will outweigh reduced demand due to less cold winters; air conditioning also adds to the heat island effect as it simply moves heat from buildings to the air outside.

The CCRA identifies the need for green space and 'blue' space (ponds and rivers) in towns and cities as a key mitigating factor to provide cooling and to counter the heat island effect, as well as providing a refuge where people can find respite from the heat. The effectiveness of greenery in moderating the heat island effect has been demonstrated by two projects funded by the Engineering and Physical Sciences Research Council. The SCORCHIO project showed that maximum surface temperatures in woodland areas within Manchester were 12.8°C cooler than town centre areas, and the night-time differential was up to 10°C. Adding 10 per cent green cover to the town centre or to high-density residential areas could result in a cooling impact of around 2.5°C; conversely, removing 10 per cent of green cover would result in a temperature rise of up to 8°C.[10] The LUCID project developed a city-scale urban climate model based on the urban heat island effect in London and confirmed that, in cities in general, the urban heat island effect requires extensive greening to achieve a significant reduction in temperature.[11]

Trees – in particular, large trees – are the key to reducing urban temperatures through shading and by cooling through evapotranspiration; grassed areas lose their evaporative cooling function fairly quickly in a drought. The CCRA calls for planners to pay particular attention to vulnerable locations, such as hospitals and care homes and socially disadvantaged areas, which typically having the least urban green space.

Mitigating the effects of climate change demands a new approach to building design, with as much emphasis on keeping them cool in summer as on keeping them warm in winter. The first objective should be to maximise passive cooling and minimise air conditioning; the CCRA suggests that, otherwise, cooling demand in, for example, London, could increase by 50 per cent by 2030 compared with 2004. Measures to be considered should include reflective external surfaces, including white roofs to minimise heat absorption and the heat island effect; external blinds and shutters; and the use of green roofs and other planting to reduce temperatures through transpiration.

Water, droughts and floods

The expected increase in the frequency and severity of droughts and rainfall also require mitigation. Water conservation and on-site water recycling will be essential, as will be the avoidance of impervious hard surfaces that increase the risk of flooding during periods of high rainfall.

Nationally, water is one of the most critical climate change issues; the CCRA forecasts a fall in the public water supply of up to 35 per cent by the 2080s, with the number of people living in areas with a likely water deficit being between 27 million and 59 million by the 2050s. The temptation is to deal with this with grandiose projects such as desalination or a national water grid. But these kind of solutions will dramatically increase the cost of water and require substantial energy to power them, simply adding to climate change. So priority should be given to water conservation, including universal metering so that everyone pays for what they use; an increase in local and sub-regional storage capacity; and moves towards closed-loop water systems for industry.

There is also a need to ensure the resilience of sewerage plants, both to protect their power supplies during severe weather and to ensure that rainfall run-off is not added to polluted water that requires treatment.

The CCRA forecasts that up to 5 million people could be exposed to a significant likelihood of flooding by the 2080s, compared with fewer than a million now. The Environment Agency has warned that much more needs to be done to ensure that farmland drainage schemes and the poor design of new-build developments do not exacerbate flood risk, which is becoming as frequent in summer as in winter. The design of sustainable drainage schemes needs further study to ensure that they can cope with the extreme conditions that climate change is making more likely.

The House of Commons Public Accounts Committee has estimated that 5 million homes are already in danger of flooding, at a cost of £1.1 billion a year; Defra has forecast that flooding caused by climate change could eventually cost up to £12 billion a year. In 2009, the Environment Agency warned that its flood budget needed to be increased by 9 per cent to maintain levels of protection. So it is surprising that the government has cut the flood defence budget by 10 per cent. It is clear that investment in flood defences must be increased if major financial losses and much human misery is to be avoided in the future. There is also a need to ensure that developments in areas at any risk of flooding are designed to minimise damage by, for example, routing ground floor electricity cabling down from the ceiling rather than up from the floor.

Infrastructure at risk

Water supply and flood prevention are not the only infrastructure requiring rethinking in the light of climate change; transport networks are also vulnerable to high temperatures and heavy rainfall. There is a need to review the rail infrastructure to reduce the risk of rails buckling due to high temperatures and to design out the risk of rain-induced mudslides, landslips and erosion damaging tracks. The road infrastructure is similarly at risk.

The energy infrastructure can also be vulnerable: the CCRA suggests that up to 25 GW of generating capacity (30 per cent of the current total) will be vulnerable to significant flooding by 2080. Substations and other components of the electricity distribution system are also vulnerable.

With increasing interdependency between countries, it is also worth noting some other risks. For example, most French nuclear power stations are cooled with water that is extracted from and returned to rivers; there have already been cases where power stations have been shut because the return temperature of the water exceeded 24°C, the limit beyond which river ecology would be damaged. So there is a strong case for developing energy storage systems to counter such interruptions, as well as balance out intermittent renewable sources.

The future of coastal nuclear power stations in particular needs rethinking; as the 2012 PwC Low Carbon Economy Index warned: 'Any investments in long-term assets or infrastructure, particularly in coastal or low-lying regions, need to address far more pessimistic scenarios'.[12] The PwC report warns that 'Businesses, governments and communities across the world need to plan for a warming world – not just 2°C, but 4°C, or even 6°C'.

Economic impacts

Another leading company warning of the economic dangers of climate change is Munich Re, the world's largest reinsurance company. It has pointed out that, already, the number of weather-related loss events in North America have nearly quintupled in the past three decades. In Asia, the increase has been fourfold, with significant increases everywhere else too. This is already raising insurance premiums significantly. Munich Re has called for investment in better risk modelling capabilities as well as such adaptation measures as tighter building regulations and better flood management.[13] But the insurance industry should go further and research how it can pump some of its investment funds into adaptation measures; this could benefit the industry both by direct financial returns in, for example, improving water resources, and by reducing some of the risks exacerbated by climate change.

In November 2012, an alliance of 200 investment institutions controlling US$21 trillion of assets worldwide warned of the damage that climate change could inflict on the global economy. Spokesman Chris Davis pointed to superstorm Sandy, which had devastated parts of New York the previous month, as being: 'Typical of what we can expect if no action is taken and warming trends continue. Investors are rightly concerned about the short- and long-term economic risks of climate change and understand that ambitious climate and clean energy policies are urgently needed to avoid catastrophic impact.'[14]

Without mitigation, the costs of climate change to the world economy are likely to be immense: in 2006, the World Bank put the cost at between US$9 billion and US$41 billion a year, not very different to the estimate in the Stern Review (*The Economics of Climate Change*) published the same year. Early adaptation action can significantly reduce the economic risks, especially by ensuring that new infrastructure spending takes account of future climate change and that sufficient is spent where necessary on adapting existing infrastructure. In 2011, the Royal Academy of Engineering pointed out that such investment 'Will reduce the risk of economic disruption to the country and enable the opportunities from well-adapted infrastructure to be maximised'.[15] And in 2012 Defra pointed out that the annual demand for economic infrastructure investment in the UK is expected to be in the range of £40 billion –£50 billion until at least 2030, going on to say that: 'We need to ensure that large investments take account of future risks from climate change'.[16]

Biodiversity

Biodiversity is also at risk from climate change and it is clear that current policies are inadequate to minimise losses. Natural adaptation – allowing plants and species to migrate to more suitable areas as conditions change – is hindered both by inadequate and somewhat haphazard protected wildlife networks that inhibit migration and by many designated protected sites being too small to be effective. There is also a need to plan for the creation of suitable replacement habitats for those lost either to development or to the consequences of climate change. Planning authorities should have a duty to ensure that these requirements are met, that plans are coordinated with neighbouring authorities, and that new sites are independently evaluated to ensure that they will be effective.

Conclusions

Finally, the CCRA has pointed out that there are many areas where gaps in knowledge currently limit our understanding of potential climate change impacts and adaptation actions; there is a lack of clear evidence about everything from the environmental impacts of drought to the potential impacts of ocean acidification. So there is an urgent need for more research to ensure that we really do understand the potential impacts of climate change so that evidenced adaptation measures can be put in place in time to protect us from what otherwise are likely to be very unpleasant consequences.

Significant changes to the global climate are inevitable, irrespective of what mitigation measures are taken in the future. And the longer we wait for effective mitigation, the more severe the effects of climate change will be. So planning to adapt to climate change is now critical – both to ensure that what we are building now can cope with a changing climate and to minimise the economic risks. The longer we put off the necessary action and investment, the greater the risks to human welfare and the higher the long-term cost to the economy.

Notes

1. See ukclimateprojections.defra.gov.uk
2. Speech by John Beddington at the Sustainable Development UK conference, 19 March 2009.
3. Speech by Professor Tim Benton to the East of England Co-operative Society, October 2012.
4. Lester Brown, *Full Planet, Empty Plates* (Earth Policy Institute, 2012).
5. FAO, 'Climate Change and Food Security', submission to the UN Framework Convention on Climate Change, 2009.

6 Available at http://www.defra.gov.uk/environment/climate/government/ risk-assessment/

7 *Businessweek* 4 November, 2010.

8 Andy Coghlan, 'Meat without slaughter', *New Scientist*, 31 August 2011.

9 'Meat without slaughter', *New Scientist*, 31 August 2011.

10 See http://www.sed.manchester.ac.uk/research/cure/research/scorchio/

11 See http://www.arcc-cn.org.uk/project-summaries/completed-projects/lucid/ lucid-outputs/

12 Available at http://www.pwc.co.uk/sustainability-climate-change/publications/ low-carbon-economy-index.jhtml

13 http://www.munichre.com/en/media_relations/press_releases/2012/2012_10_17_ press_release.aspx

14 Open letter to world government leaders from Ceres (US-based coalition of investors and green groups), 20 November 2012.

15 Royal Academy of Engineering, *Engineering the Future* (2011).

16 See http://www.defra.gov.uk/environment/climate/adapting/

Chapter 30

The Crisis of Environmental Multilateralism: A Liberal Response

Robert Falkner

Introduction: the liberal tradition and global environmentalism

It is now widely recognised that environmental destruction does not stop at national borders. To be successful, environmental protection needs a strong international dimension. Like many other environmentalists, liberals have therefore advocated the creation of international environmental institutions, the negotiation of multilateral environmental agreements, the strengthening of international environmental law and the greening of other international policy areas such as international trade and finance. Environmental multilateralism has become a hallmark of liberal foreign policy around the world.

Despite the dramatic rise of international environmental policy-making, recent developments suggest that environmental multilateralism is entering a period of crisis. As the latest *Global Environment Outlook* report of the UN Environment Programme (UNEP) reveals, multilateral environmental policy has failed to reverse, or even slow down, some of the most threatening environmental trends, such as global warming and biodiversity loss.

Environmental campaigners and diplomats may have succeeded in establishing the environment on the international agenda and negotiating a plethora of environmental treaties, but whether international instruments make a difference on the ground remains far from clear. Moreover, the process of international environmental policy-making has slowed down in recent years. Environmental multilateralism itself is being held back by global power struggles and a general sense of treaty fatigue. A loss of political momentum has been evident for some time in the climate change negotiations, which have failed to deliver a new treaty that could succeed the Kyoto Protocol. This was again noticeable at the 'Rio+20' UN summit of 2012, which fell well below the aspirations and achievements of the original Rio 'Earth Summit' of 1992.

How should liberals respond to the looming crisis in environmental multilateralism, and is there a distinctive liberal approach to alleviating the political gridlock in international environmental politics?

Internationalism plays an important role in liberal thinking and foreign policy, and the crisis in environmental multilateralism therefore poses a particular challenge for liberal environmentalism. The same cannot necessarily be said about other strands of environmentalism. Conservative environmentalists, on the whole, tend to prioritise local and national approaches over international ones. In *Green Philosophy: How to Think Seriously about the Planet* (2012), for example, the conservative thinker Roger Scruton downplays the cosmopolitan environmental responsibility espoused by the modern environmental movement ('think globally, act locally') in favour of a national sense of belonging and stewardship ('feel locally, think nationally'), which he sees as the true source of conservative environmentalism. Global solutions to environmental problems are most likely to arise from decentralised, bottom-up, efforts of local and national communities, while international treaty-based approaches such as the Kyoto Protocol are dismissed as unenforceable and ineffective distractions. In this perspective, the crisis of environmental multilateralism only serves to confirm the conservative predilection for a localist and nationalist agenda.

Socialist and radical environmentalists, too, may see their core beliefs vindicated by the crisis of environmental multilateralism. Although sharing an internationalist outlook with liberals, socialists and radical greens tend to harbour greater scepticism towards the established international processes of environmental negotiation and governance. In their view, global environmental problems are a manifestation of a deeper crisis in global capitalism, and international diplomacy is severely limited in its ability to correct the underlying causes of global environmental destruction. As George Monbiot argued in a critique of the 'Rio+20' summit, the ecological crisis cannot be addressed by governments that represent the interests of the rich: 'It is the system that needs to be challenged, not the individual decisions it makes' (*The Guardian*, 19 June 2012).

How can liberals respond to this crisis in international policy-making? Before I outline an answer to this question, we need briefly to take stock of recent international environmental politics and identify the main shortcomings of global green diplomacy.

Challenges to environmental multilateralism

That environmental multilateralism is said to be in crisis may seem surprising to some. After all, the rise of global green diplomacy in the last four decades has been a resounding success. Several international institutions dedicated to environmental protection have been created – from UNEP to the Global Environment Facility and the Green Climate Fund – and hundreds of environmental treaties have been negotiated on a wide range of transboundary or global environmental threats, from species extinction to air pollution, ozone layer depletion, biodiversity loss and climate change. Today, the vast majority of global environmental concerns are being addressed through one form of international instrument or the other, and there is hardly a day that passes in the diplomatic calendar without some gathering of environmental experts and negotiators on the international stage.

Yet, the latest surveys of the state of the global environment offer a more sobering account of environmental diplomacy. Global warming continues unabated, more than two million people die prematurely every year due to outdoor and indoor air pollution, the per capita availability of freshwater is declining, and rampant species extinction is undermining global biodiversity. There are also notable gaps in the international environmental agenda. The international community has failed to agree any meaningful international action against the loss of tropical forests, for example, and international organisations are slow to deal with emerging environmental and health risks arising from new technologies such as nanotechnology and synthetic biology.

There has also been a notable decline in the pace and ambition of international treaty-making. During the heyday of environmental diplomacy in the 1980s and 1990s, a series of international negotiation rounds produced important environmental treaties, from the 1985 Vienna Convention on ozone layer depletion to its 1987 Montreal Protocol, from the 1992 UN Framework Convention on Climate Change (UNFCCC) to its 1997 Kyoto Protocol, and from the 1992 Convention on Biological Diversity to its 2000 Cartagena Protocol on Biosafety. Since the late 1990s, however, a growing sense of treaty fatigue has set in. The failure to negotiate a successor agreement to the Kyoto Protocol is but the most high-profile example of the growing institutional sclerosis in international environmental politics. At the World Summit on Sustainable Development in Johannesburg in 2002 and again at the 'Rio+20' summit in 2012, the international community was unable to agree specific and ambitious commitments. Instead, world leaders chose lofty promises and flowery rhetoric to cover up the crisis that has afflicted environmental multilateralism.

One of the key stumbling blocks in environmental diplomacy is the reluctance of some global powers to sign on to new international environmental commitments. This has been the case with the United States at least since the early 1990s, when it abandoned its erstwhile environmental leadership role. It has failed to ratify most recently agreed international environmental treaties, from the Basel Convention on Hazardous Waste to the Convention on Biological Diversity and its Cartagena Protocol, the Kyoto Protocol and the Stockholm Convention on Persistent Organic Pollutants. The global power shift to the emerging economies has further complicated the search for international diplomatic solutions. Countries such as China and India, but also Brazil and South Africa, are now playing a more assertive role in international negotiations and are equally reluctant to sign on to binding international commitments, whether on climate change mitigation or in other areas. The emergence of a more diverse set of national interests has increased the number of veto players in international negotiations. It has challenged traditional notions of what environmental leadership by the EU and other progressive countries can achieve.

The search for global environmental solutions is also hampered by the inadequacy of the international institutional architecture. UNEP, which was founded four decades ago as the core environmental institution, has remained the poor cousin in the family of UN institutions. Unlike the World Health Organisation (WHO) and the Food and Agriculture Organisation (FAO), it does not have the status nor the resources of a UN specialised agency. Its funding base has fluctuated in the past and remains relatively modest, amounting to not more than US$220 million per year, and its location in Nairobi has meant that it operates far away from the main UN centres in New York and Geneva.

Moreover, the international treaty system for environmental protection has come under attack from other institutions of global governance. As more and more environmental treaties have begun to regulate environmentally damaging forms of international trade, the World Trade Organisation (WTO) has sought to rein in regulatory interference with the trading system. On a number of occasions, the WTO dispute settlement mechanism has ruled against environmentally motivated trade measures, and many environmentalists now fear that the liberal principles of the international trading order threaten the implementation of existing environmental agreements. Even if the WTO has come to accept the legitimacy of some forms of international environmental regulation, particularly if they are non-discriminatory and based on multilateral consensus, some fear a chilling effect for future international policy-making from the threat of legal challenges at the WTO. The hostile international response to the planned inclusion of all domestic and foreign airlines in the EU's emissions trading system is but the last in a long string of such high-profile trade-and-environment conflicts that may have a dampening effect on future environmental accords.

It is no wonder, then, that business self-regulation and multi-stakeholder initiatives have gained in popularity in recent years. One of the rare achievements of the 2002 World Summit on Sustainable Development was the launch of over 130 public-private partnerships, which are meant to provide policy direction, financing, information services and even regulatory standards in areas from sustainable forestry to fishing, clean water provision and food security. Environmental campaigners and governments have encouraged such private governance initiatives, as a way both to engage those actors that possess problem-solving capacity and to fill regulatory gaps left by the gridlocked multilateral system. Such activities may not amount to a full-scale privatisation of global environmental governance, as some critics claim, but they underline the growing difficulty of advancing the global environmental agenda through traditional multilateral means.

A liberal response: renewing, reforming and expanding environmental multilateralism

How should liberals deal with these challenges? A liberal response needs to identify opportunities for a renewal of global environmental policy while being realistic about the constraints that the international system imposes. The response should include three elements: renewing global environmental leadership; reforming the processes and institutions of environmental multilateralism; and engaging a wider range of actors in global environmental governance.

Renewing global environmental leadership

Retreating from international politics cannot be the answer to the complexities and frustrations of environmental multilateralism. Undoubtedly, global environmental leadership needs to have roots in domestic politics, but local and national efforts risk being environmentally ineffective and deepening political fragmentation if they are not embedded in a framework for global cooperation. The crisis of environmental multilateralism calls for a renewal of environmental leadership and a reassertion of liberal internationalism. On climate change as much as on other environmental threats, international diplomacy needs to continue to seek internationally negotiated solutions.

Keeping multilateral processes on track requires political leadership but will not be easy. If there is going to be any progress, it is bound to be slow

351

– frustratingly slow. The structural barriers to ambitious environmental policies are too entrenched, and the mechanisms of diplomacy too cumbersome, to achieve decisive international breakthroughs. Liberal internationalism thus needs to combine persistence with patience. Even more so than at the national level, politics at the international level is, in Max Weber's words, 'a strong and slow boring of hard boards, requiring passion and perspective'. But without some nations willing to show global leadership, international processes end up lowering rather than raising levels of ambition.

For the last two decades, the European Union has provided such leadership on a number of fronts. Without the EU's commitment to ambitious international agreements, the Kyoto Protocol and its instruments such as emissions trading and the Clean Development Mechanism would not have come into force. And European persistence played a critical role in securing international agreement on other environmental treaties, despite America's retreat from environmental multilateralism.

Whether European leadership will suffice to bring the newly emerging powers of the developing world into the multilateral fold is another question. Recent experiences in the climate negotiations have brought to light some of Europe's limitations in this regard. But the EU continues to command respect for its domestic environmental policies and serves as a model for innovative regulatory approaches. Its economic might as the world's largest market gives it added clout in environmental politics, and the EU's trading partners often find it difficult to ignore Europe's regulatory standards. This alone will ensure that the EU will be in a privileged position to shape the international environmental agenda and set high levels of ambition. Other established or emerging powers may not always wish to follow European leadership, but without the EU setting the pace in international environmental regulation, even less would be achieved multilaterally.

To succeed internationally, European environmental leadership requires a strong domestic basis. The UK has been an important driving force behind the EU's green diplomacy for some time now and must continue to be so. On its own, the UK's voice would carry far less weight internationally. When it comes to environmental multilateralism, the EU is undoubtedly more than the sum of its parts. Working with EU institutions and other European countries is an essential component of Britain's green diplomacy. But to be respected and influential in Europe, the UK must not fall behind its current environmental achievements. It has played a pioneering role in developing new mechanisms for climate mitigation and adaptation, from carbon trading to corporate carbon disclosure and greening international development aid, and the Stern Review of climate change economics has changed the way the world thinks about the costs and benefits of climate action. These achievements have boosted the UK's position within the EU and internationally. Britain needs to continue to drive European environment policy in this way if it is to lead the renewal of environmental multilateralism.

Reforming international processes and institutions

At the same time, the established processes and institutions of environmental multilateralism need to be reformed if they are to remain relevant to the search for global environmental solutions. As regards the international process, UN-style negotiations have been the norm since the 1970s and remain an important route to inclusive, consensus-based, environmental agreements. They command a high degree of legitimacy, particularly in the developing world, and have helped to create a gradually expanding system of legal commitments and governance mechanisms. But the principle of consensus-based agreement strengthens the veto power of environmental laggards and often results in long-drawn-out bargaining. All too often, it produces outcomes that reflect the lowest common denominator. New thinking is, therefore, needed on how to improve the current model of environmental multilateralism where it ends up blocking, rather than promoting, progressive international solutions.

As we have witnessed in the area of climate change, the UNFCCC-based negotiations have not produced the level of ambition and speed that are needed to prevent global warming from exceeding 2 degrees by the end of this century. Even though all major powers have recently expressed their commitment to negotiating a comprehensive climate mitigation treaty by 2015, continued wrangling over the legal status of such an agreement and the specific commitments to be included suggest that a Kyoto Protocol-style agreement by all major emitters is out of reach. We are rapidly moving into a different scenario for building global climate governance, one that is based on partial agreements and varying levels of commitment by different emitter nations.

This 'building blocks' scenario departs from the traditional model of environmental multilateralism as it accepts that a comprehensive, universal and legally binding treaty on climate change is unlikely to be agreed. Instead, it suggests a second-best strategy for building climate governance out of smaller and less ambitious agreements, with countries moving at different speeds and creating governance mechanisms in areas where agreement is feasible. In this alternative scenario, mini-lateral deals may be agreed as stepping-stones towards a broader multilateral agreement. It will remain important, however, to base such action on the existing UNFCCC framework, so as to preserve what has been achieved already and ensure that the different mechanisms and commitments are compatible and comparable.

Reform is also needed for the institutions of global environmental protection. The current institutional architecture delivers important services, from the facilitation of information exchange and negotiation (e.g. UNEP), disbursement of environmental aid (e.g. Global Environment Facility) and administration of environmental agreements (e.g. UNFCCC Secretariat). But the increasingly diverse set of international environmental bodies can often seem confusing and inefficient. The failure at 'Rio+20' to tackle the weakness of UN environmental institutions seems to confirm the view that powerful interests stand in the way of deeper reform efforts. But even if the creation of a centralised UN Environment Organisation remains out of reach for now, the push for a strengthening of the powers and resources of the existing institutions needs to continue. Providing UNEP with an enhanced and more secure funding basis would be an important first step. Strengthening environmental objectives within multilateral development agencies and other international organisations should be pursued whatever happens with UNEP reform. And promoting greater coordination between various environmental treaty bodies would go some way towards a more effective global governance system.

The need for institutional reform also extends to the global economy. The current international rulebook for trade and investment does not fully take into account the environmental costs of global economic exchange. Liberals generally believe in the power of markets to achieve an optimal allocation of capital and to stimulate innovation and growth. But markets produce suboptimal outcomes when they allow individuals and companies to consume natural resources or use the environment as a pollution sink without paying an appropriate price for the environmental damage they cause. If free trade should not cost us the earth, then market failure needs to be corrected through regulatory intervention.

In an era of globalisation, such interventions ought to take place at the international level. International cooperation is needed to put a price on pollution, e.g. on the use of fossil fuel energy in international production and transport. Removing subsidies on fossil fuel consumption would be a first step towards levelling the playing field with renewable energy sources.

Where international cooperation proves too difficult to achieve, leading economic powers such as the EU can still make a difference by setting higher domestic standards and requiring importers to comply with them. Again, multilateral solutions are desirable but mini-lateral steps in that direction may be needed to drive up levels of ambition. The absence of multilateral agreement should not be used as an excuse for inaction, and the international rules on trade and investment must not be allowed to force a lowering of such ambition.

Engaging a wider range of actors

Just as multilateralism needs to be reformed, so we need to engage a wider range of actors in global environmental protection. Political and institutional inertia in international politics make it essential to mobilise pro-environmental forces at all levels of global society, from the international level down to the local, and up again. Where international treaties cannot be agreed, other options need to be explored. The urgency of the climate challenge does not allow us simply to wait for diplomats to resolve their countries' differences. While international climate negotiations carry on, climate action needs to be initiated wherever possible, in municipalities and cities below the national level, in regional networks across national boundaries, in corporate organisations as much as in global civil society. Liberals should encourage the growing diversity of global climate action. We need to harness all forms of political energy to produce the kind of change that will facilitate the transition towards a low-carbon economy. Rather than arguing over whether climate policy needs to be either top-down or bottom-up – a debate that has pitted proponents and critics of the Kyoto Protocol against each other – we should recognise that effective climate action needs to operate at multiple levels and involve different types of actors.

In this context, the growth in private environmental initiatives that have sprung up outside the UN system can be seen as an encouraging development, provided the relationship between private and public environmental governance is managed well. Environmental NGOs have long pushed for international environmental policies by lobbying states and international organisations. They have increasingly targeted multinational corporations and other actors with the capacity to produce environmental change, which has opened up new avenues for promoting environmental sustainability. Eco-labelling initiatives by manufacturers and retailers, for example, allow consumers to make an informed green choice. Collaboration between environmental groups and timber-trading companies has led to certification schemes that promote sustainable forestry practices around the world. And initiatives such as the Carbon Disclosure Project ensure that a growing number of global companies reveal their carbon footprint, which in turn provides investors with critical information on how to reduce their exposure to climate-related risks. Liberals believe in the power of individuals and civil society. Where states fail to lead, citizens need to take the initiative and open up new opportunities for advancing global sustainability.

However, private initiative in global environmental affairs is no panacea for the ills of international governance, nor can it replace a strong role for states and international organisations. Parallel efforts by private and public actors should not be allowed to run in competition but need to be brought together. In fact, states and international organisations can do a lot to promote and direct private environmental initiatives. They can encourage corporations to set their own environmental standards and incorporate sustainability objectives into their operations. The UK's plan for a mandatory requirement for large listed companies to disclose their carbon emissions is an important step in this direction. Public authorities can also provide financial and administrative support to multi-stakeholder initiatives, promote broad and democratic participation in such initiatives, and improve the links between them and established intergovernmental processes. The UN Global Compact, for example, is an innovative initiative that invites global companies to adopt and follow ten principles of social and ecological responsibility. Its global corporate network now includes over 5,000 firms and has become the source of a number of international voluntary standards for environmental investment and production.

Thus, states and international organisations can play an important role in initiating and steering private environmental governance efforts. Leading green states and UN environmental bodies can thus become 'orchestrators' of a new and enlarged form of private sustainability governance.

Conclusion: towards renewed environmental multilateralism

There can be little doubt that environmental multilateralism has entered a period of crisis and is producing diminishing returns. The process of environmental treaty-making is slowing down as major powers are reluctant to agree to new and legally binding international commitments. International environmental institutions suffer from a lack of funding and authority, and efforts to reform the international environmental architecture have made no significant progress. Meanwhile, global indicators suggest a worsening of several major environmental trends.

Whether any political creed can find a solution to this global challenge is unclear. Liberalism, for its part, should face up to the crisis in environmental multilateralism and suggest ways towards its renewal. Inevitably, the liberal response will be gradualist and reformist in nature, based on an acceptance of our inability to plan and execute large-scale political change, particularly at the international level. It will seek to mobilise political and social support at all levels, from the international to the national and local. And it will attempt to accelerate existing efforts to reform global capitalism without abandoning its underlying promise of individual liberty and economic betterment. Above all, liberals need to re-think – but also restate – the case for environmental internationalism.

For as long as the states system plays a critical role in defining the global environmental agenda, environmentally progressive states are needed to set a high level of international ambition. In this regard, Britain and the EU have much to offer. Britain will need to continue to work through European institutions to exercise leadership internationally, and it will need to set an example domestically if its international leadership ambition is to be credible and effective. The current deadlock in many multilateral forums will be difficult to overcome, but a strong and united European stance will be essential if we are to convince other, more reluctant, powers to raise their level of environmental ambition. Domestic political blockage in the United States and diverging interests of emerging powers will make it difficult to create strong environmental treaties in key areas such as climate change. But this should not distract us from the need to work towards a global consensus and establish commitments for environmental protection, whether or not they can be cast in legally binding form.

As suggested above, a number of small steps can be undertaken to renew environmental multilateralism and strengthen the existing international institutional architecture. Reforming and strengthening UNEP, rebalancing the relationship between the WTO and environmental agreements, and promoting measures to make polluters pay and put a price on the ecological costs of economic activities, are all worth pursuing in an international context. States and international organisations should also encourage more private and mixed private-public governance initiatives, in the areas where companies and NGOs have problem-solving capacity and where international cooperation proves elusive. Such private sustainability governance requires careful steering, however, and it is the responsibility of public authorities to provide this role.

In sum, a renewal of environmental multilateralism requires passion and patience. Liberals need to make the case for the continued relevance of international environmental policy amidst profound and often disheartening changes in the international system. Above all, the challenges outlined above call for more, not less, British and European leadership in international environmental affairs.

Chapter 31

Green Policies for Global Economic Justice

Myles Wickstead

O n 20 August 1977 the *Voyager One* spacecraft took off from Planet Earth. On Valentine's Day 1990 it was speeding towards the edge of our solar system, its cameras pointing forwards into uncharted space. At the insistence of cosmologist and philosopher Carl Sagan, who had been present at the launch twenty-three years earlier, the cameras were reversed. What they picked up, just visible against the vastness of space, was what Sagan describes as 'a pale blue dot' – a dot on which everyone who had ever lived, every king and queen, every pauper and peasant, had been born and had died, on which every act of war and peace, of cruelty and compassion, had been played out. Sagan comes to the end of his description thus:

> To my mind, there is perhaps no better demonstration of the folly of human conceits than this distant image of our tiny world. To me, it underscores our responsibility to deal more kindly and compassionately with one another and to preserve and cherish that pale blue dot, the only home we've ever known.[1]

There, in a nutshell, we have it. The need to look after our planet, and to use our resources in a responsible and sustainable way, both for us and for succeeding generations; and at the same time to ensure that the benefits of those resources can be shared in a more equitable way. The need for green policies for global economic justice.

When Sagan asked that the cameras be reversed, some of the more tangible threats to the pale blue dot had receded. The Berlin Wall had fallen, the Cold War had come to an end, and the likelihood of a full-scale nuclear confrontation had decreased significantly. But other threats were beginning to become more apparent. The 1987 Brundtland Report, *Our Common Future*, highlighted a number of environmental issues which were of increasing concern. Scientists were becoming worried about the emergence of holes in the ozone layer, allowing harmful rays to pass through the atmosphere. People generally were becoming increasingly conscious of the impact of a rapidly increasing world population – a population which then stood somewhere between 5 and 6 billion people; which has already, only twenty-five years later, exceeded 7 billion; and which is expected to reach 9 billion by the middle of this century.

In the same year as the Brundtland Report, the Montreal Protocol started the process of banning chlorofluorocarbons (CFCs) because of their damaging effect on the ozone layer. Many of the other key themes emerging from the report were picked up at the Rio 'Earth Summit' in 1992. That conference had some important formal outcomes, including the creation of the UN Framework Convention on Climate Change, the Convention on Biological Diversity and the Convention to Combat Desertification.

This was undoubtedly a decisive moment in the development of international green policies – or at least a clear recognition that they were required. But there was no strong link to issues of global economic justice, and one unintended consequence of the conference was to set 'environmental issues' and 'international development issues' careering down largely parallel tracks, with different international bodies, governments and 'experts' pursuing separate agendas.

Mrs Brundtland had herself recognised the dangers of this happening, and had been very clear that the two sets of issues must be addressed together. In her Foreword to *Our Common Future*, she has this to say:

> The environment does not exist as a sphere separate from human actions, ambitions, and needs, and attempts to defend it in isolation from human concerns have given the very word 'environment' a connotation of naivety in some political circles. The word 'development' has also been narrowed by some into a very limited focus, along the lines of 'what poor nations should do to become richer', and thus again is automatically dismissed by many in the international arena as being a concern of specialists, of those involved in questions of 'development assistance'.[2]

'But', she continues, 'the "environment" is where we all live; and "development" is what we all do in attempting to improve our lot within that abode. The two are inseparable.' She is, of course, right. And the next two or three years provide an important, perhaps unique, opportunity to bring those strands back together and to link green policies and global economic justice.

The international context has changed significantly since Mrs Brundtland's report. In the years immediately following *Our Common*

Future, political systems which had been hardwired by the clash of eastern and western ideologies were in flux – nowhere more so than in the countries of Eastern and Central Europe, demanding the economic and political freedoms so long denied them. The prospect of membership of the European Community became a focus and driver for those aspirations; for example, free and fair elections and respect for human rights were among the conditions for entry.

The international community began increasingly to see the importance of giving voice to similar aspirations in the developing world, both by making aid increasingly conditional on improved governance, but also in trying to articulate those aspirations in a series of potential outcomes which would benefit the poorest and most vulnerable. These eventually found expression in the 'Millennium Development Goals' (MDGs), which emerged from a UN-led process following the Millennium Declaration, which was a powerful statement agreed and signed by all members of the United Nations, enshrining important concepts and aspirations like universal human rights, justice and equity. But some felt that the Declaration was insufficiently specific about what implementing its provisions was designed to achieve by way of concrete outcomes – hence the MDGs, agreed (but not signed up to by everyone) in early 2001.

The overarching goal of the MDGs is about reducing poverty – specifically, reducing by half the proportion of people in the world living in absolute poverty – with a number of other goals around basic health (such as maternal mortality and child survival rates) and primary education. There is nothing in them about the conditions required to bring those things about (such as better governance, economic growth, etc.), though in practice the international community has recognised that the achievement of specific education and health outcomes cannot be achieved without a holistic mix of inputs.

So in one sense the MDGs are a proxy for all the things that need to happen to improve the lives of the poorest people on the planet. The MDGs come to an end in 2015. Even if the world is fully successful in achieving them – and there has been good progress in a number of countries, largely as a result of strong economic growth – that will still leave hundreds of millions of people in poverty, millions of children not reaching their fifth birthday, and millions of mothers dying needlessly in childbirth. So the question is not whether or not there should be a successor to the MDGs, but what that successor should look like.

The discussion has already begun, and will be informed by the recommendations of a High Level Panel – co-chaired by the British Prime Minister

– which will report to the UN Secretary-General at the end of May 2013. Even at this early consultative stage of the post-MDG process, the discussion is beginning to define 'progress' as being not just about increased prosperity, but also about social inclusion, equity and justice, fundamental values enshrined in the Millennium Declaration but which are missing (at least in any explicit way) from the current set of MDGs. This should ensure that there is a stronger emphasis on the most marginalised groups – the disadvantaged, the disabled, and the displaced – going at least some way to ensuring the objective of global economic justice.

There is another major gap – a large, green hole – in any successor to the MDGs which needs to be filled. The only specific mention of the environment currently is in MDG 7, which refers to the importance of ensuring environmental sustainability, yet of course its potential impact on making progress against the MDGs is enormous. It is already evident that the impact of environmental factors on natural resources and ecosystems, and thereby on the livelihoods and food security of poor people, has in some cases been a barrier to attaining and maintaining the education and health MDGs.

This takes us to the heart of why we need green policies for global economic justice. No common challenge is more obvious than that of climate change. There is now almost universal recognition – not common ground until recently – that human agency is largely responsible for this, and has clear implications for sustainable economic development and the need to move away from fossil fuels to renewable, cleaner forms of energy. Unchecked rises in temperature will have profound consequences for food security and agriculture, for the higher prevalence of vector- and water-borne diseases, for the availability of potable water, for biodiversity, for the very ability to feed and support the 9 billion people likely to inhabit this pale blue dot by 2050, a huge increase from the current 7 billion.

So the challenge which now urgently faces us is to bring together the issues around poverty, economic growth and social inclusion which have traditionally been the purview of the international development community, viewed through the prism of the MDGs, and those which are about the survival of the planet which have traditionally been the purview of the environment community.

The challenge is actually more about institutional structures rather than intellectual coherence, as Mrs Brundtland recognised. The period between now and 2015 provides both a threat and an opportunity. As the debate about a successor to the MDGs gets under way, and the High-Level Panel moves towards publishing its Framework Report, an Inter-Governmental Panel is being established as a result of the mid-2012 Conference in Rio de Janeiro (following on from the original Rio Conference twenty years earlier) to look at the creation of a set of 'Sustainable Development Goals' (SDGs).

The threat is that these processes will take on a life of their own, and simply entrench the existing chasm between the environment and development lobbies. Both groups are concerned, with some justification, that there are trade-offs between financial pledges in support of developmental and climate change objectives, given overall constraints on resources. But this is a false dichotomy, because the two sets of objectives are so intertwined – and the opportunity is that in the period ahead the two sets of goals can be integrated, recognising not only that they are compatible but that they are necessarily mutually coherent and reinforcing.

Some people now talk of 'resilience' as the term of art which brings together these twin challenges; others talk of 'human security'. A recent Oxfam discussion paper helpfully conceptualises this as 'the creation of a safe and just space for humanity', which can only exist by taking into account simultaneously 'planetary boundaries' and 'social boundaries'.[3] So there is a set of challenges around environmental degradation, such as climate change, loss of biodiversity, and the acidification of the oceans, and another set of challenges around rights-based issues like social equity and gender equality. Each set of challenges impacts on the other, and they must be addressed together – as Mrs Brundtland insisted a quarter of a century ago.

For example, and looking first at how environmental degradation can impact on poverty, the current and potential impacts of climate change (rising temperatures, rising sea-levels, increased incidence of droughts and floods) are global threats in the medium term but in the short term are already seriously undermining the ability of poor people in poor countries to ensure their food security, health and access to safe water and sanitation. And it works the other way round, too. Simply by meeting the unmet demand for girls' education and family planning, population growth will slow and global carbon emissions will reduce significantly from current projections. Perhaps in no other area of policy is there such a potentially clear benefit both to the environment and to poverty reduction efforts as slowing the rate of population growth – essentially by giving women choices.

And now let's take a look through the other end of the telescope. The main stress on the environment is caused by the wealthiest 10 per cent of the world's population. They hold 57 per cent of the world's global income, and they generate nearly 50 per cent of global carbon emissions. Historically, the main creators of environmental damage have been the better-off, developed, countries, and those who will bear the brunt of a failure to address the issues will be the developing countries. A very modest shift in policy and resources can bring about a good deal of progress on global economic justice. Bringing electricity to the 1.3 billion people in the world who do not have it could be achieved with less than a 1 per cent increase in global carbon emissions. Providing the additional calories needed by the 850 million people who face hunger would require just 1 per cent of the global food supply. Ending income poverty for the 1.4 billion people living on less than us$1.25 per day would require just 0.2 per cent of global income.[4]

We are now on a path on which it is possible to bring together these environmental and developmental priorities. They have been separated for too long; they belong to each other and they must be addressed as one. There is a real – perhaps unique – opportunity to integrate them over the coming three years, which should be reflected in Liberal Democrat policies. What might those policies look like? Here are some ideas.

It is crucial that the proposal to develop a set of SDGs, agreed at the Rio + 20 Conference in June 2012, be integrated into the discussion about what happens after the expiry of the MDGs in 2015. The risk is that the two processes will continue along parallel tracks, one taken forward by an inter-governmental group involving thirty countries from five different regions, the other kick-started by a High-Level Panel with co-chairs from three different countries and regions, with little or no read-across between the two processes or potential new goals. The opportunity is that those involved recognise that issues like food, water, energy, population pressures, jobs, gender and equity are common to both and that the period between now and 2015 be used for real debate and discussion. That must not just be between leaders from three or even thirty countries, but between representative groups across the world; a truly international process, a fundamental tenet of liberal philosophy.

The consultative process, at least for the post-MDG debate, has got off to a promising start. Both processes will report to the UN Secretary-General. So we should provide whatever support we can to his efforts to integrate the two strands, continuing the strong line which Nick Clegg took at the Rio + 20 Conference where he insisted that the SDGs and whatever comes after the MDGs must be thought about in an integrated way.

'Growth' has been seen historically as a necessary precondition for 'development', but an altogether riskier proposition for 'the environment'. We need to re-examine what we mean by 'growth', and specifically 'GDP growth'. Gross domestic product (GDP) measures the value of goods and services in the monetised economy, and has been the traditional way of measuring relative wealth and comparative progress. Increased levels of income for poor people and poor communities in developing countries are clearly necessary, but GDP by itself does not tell the whole story. It tells us a lot about economic growth, little about the distribution of the benefits of that growth, and nothing about the depletion and degradation of natural resources which are ultimately the basis of human prosperity.

So again we should welcome the recognition at the Rio + 20 Conference that we need to develop broader measures of progress to complement GDP (or 'GDP+') in order to allow countries to make informed decisions on the basis of more complete information about natural wealth and social well-being. So a new way of looking at the way growth and those broader measures of progress are integrated is required – known as Natural Capital Accounting – so that the value of natural resources is properly reflected in decision-making. We should applaud the fact that the UK is leading by example in this area, hold the government to its commitment that the UK will measure its prosperity by Natural Capital Accounting from 2020, and encourage the UK to press for its use in measuring progress globally against future goals.

There are other areas too where the UK needs to continue to lead by example. The Rio Conference also recognised the role of business sustainability reporting, and Nick Clegg was able to announce in Rio that the UK would be the first country in the world to oblige large companies to report on their greenhouse gas emissions – a development which the companies themselves have welcomed, and which could lead eventually to a global framework. We should encourage this.

We need also to do at home what we want others to do abroad; we have common but differentiated responsibilities. If we insist on Latin America preserving the Amazon rainforest and on Africa preserving the forests crossing the centre of the continent, then surely the least we should do is preserve our ancient woodlands. They may not be the lungs of the world, but they are the heart – and some would argue the soul – of the UK. We must do our share of adapting to climate change, but must also support less well-off countries as they seek to mitigate the harmful effects of past policies for which they have been least responsible but from which they will suffer the most. This means addressing directly issues such as ocean and atmospheric pollution, over-fishing, deforestation etc., but also providing financial and other support to developing countries as they seek to develop responsible and sustainable growth policies.

This reinforces the need for the UK to build a 'whole-of-government' approach to international development. The fact that the UK will be the first G8 country to reach the UN target of spending 0.7 per cent of its gross national income on official development assistance, in 2013, demonstrates real political commitment, and this, combined with the high quality of its international development programmes, gives it significant moral authority in this area. It should use that position to look carefully at the full range of policies which impact on developing countries – including environment, trade and agriculture policies – to ensure the maximum consistency within and between those policies. That includes the impact on developing countries of tax avoidance and evasion, where a lack of transparency can have particularly detrimental effects on the environment. The Liberal Democrats should in any case develop a set of international development policies along these lines in advance of the next election in 2015.

These policies should recognise explicitly that the challenges of economic growth, equity, transparency and sustainability are issues of common interest for developed and developing countries alike, and require a coordinated approach. They should set out clearly how the UK might support developing countries to address issues such as climate change adaptation and the development of renewable energy sources. Only thus will it be possible to avoid the risk of the discussion degenerating into an 'us' versus 'them' debate, with the developing countries feeling that the mantra of 'green policies' is simply a way of preventing them achieving economic growth as fast and as comprehensively as the developed world. We need to be clear that green growth is good – indeed, essential – for everyone living on the planet, a positive-sum game. This is a discussion not just for and about political leaders – crucial though they will be for any agreement – but must reflect widespread consultation. It is about finding the middle ground between economic growth (as measured purely by GDP) at all costs, and no growth at all and a focus entirely on redistribution. Liberal thinking is perfectly placed to fill that middle ground.

Political will goes so far, but political support is also required, both in the UK and across the globe. Only if people – global citizens, and not just global leaders – really believe that the development of the green economy is in their interests and will bring them benefits will they support it. Securing that support is not straightforward against a background of a continuing economic downturn in the developed world, slowing growth worldwide and very high levels of unemployment in many countries. And yet that support is required now, against a backdrop of looming scarcities in food and water, rapidly increasing population and increasing energy demand, and before those trends become irreversible.